Aesthetics of Music

Volume 4

Books by David Whitwell

Philosophic Foundations of Education
Foundations of Music Education
Music Education of the Future
The Sousa Oral History Project
The Art of Musical Conducting
The Longy Club: 1900–1917
A Concise History of the Wind Band
Wagner on Bands
Berlioz on Bands
Chopin: A Self-Portrait
Liszt: A Self-Portrait
Schumann: A Self-Portrait In His Own Words
Mendelssohn: A Self-Portrait In His Own Words
La Téléphonie and the Universal Musical Language
Extraordinary Women

Aesthetics of Music Series

Aesthetics of Music in Ancient Civilizations
Aesthetics of Music in the Middle Ages
Aesthetics of Music in the Early Renaissance

The History and Literature of the Wind Band and Wind Ensemble Series

Volume 1 The Wind Band and Wind Ensemble Before 1500
Volume 2 The Renaissance Wind Band and Wind Ensemble
Volume 3 The Baroque Wind Band and Wind Ensemble
Volume 4 The Classical Period Wind Band and Wind Ensemble
Volume 5 The Nineteenth-Century Wind Band and Wind Ensemble
Volume 6 A Catalog of Multi-Part Repertoire for Wind Instruments or for Undesignated Instrumentation before 1600
Volume 7 Baroque Wind Band and Wind Ensemble Repertoire
Volume 8 Classic Period Wind Band and Wind Ensemble Repertoire
Volume 9 Nineteenth-Century Wind Band and Wind Ensemble Repertoire
Volume 10 A Supplementary Catalog of Wind Band and Wind Ensemble Repertoire
Volume 11 A Catalog of Wind Repertoire before the Twentieth Century for One to Five Players
Volume 12 A Second Supplementary Catalog of Early Wind Band and Wind Ensemble Repertoire
Volume 13 Name Index, Volumes 1–12, The History and Literature of the Wind Band and Wind Ensemble

www.whitwellbooks.com

David Whitwell

Aesthetics of Music

VOLUME 4
AESTHETICS OF MUSIC IN
SIXTEENTH-CENTURY ITALY, FRANCE AND SPAIN

Edited by Craig Dabelstein

Whitwell Publishing • Austin, Texas, USA

Whitwell Publishing, Austin 78701
www.whitwellbooks.com

© 1996, 2012 by David Whitwell
All rights reserved. First edition 1996.
Second edition 2012

Printed in the United States of America

Paperback
ISBN-13: 978-1-936512-61-4
ISBN-10: 1936512610

Composed in Minion Pro

CONTENTS

	Foreword	vii
	Acknowledgements	xi
1	*Sixteenth-Century Italian Philosophers*	1
2	*Sixteenth-Century Italian Music in Theory*	43
3	*Sixteenth-Century Italian Music in Practice*	65
4	*Sixteenth-Century Italian Poets*	91
5	*Sixteenth-Century Italian Dramatists*	121
6	*Baldassare Castiglione*	135
7	*Cardano*	159
8	*Michelangelo*	177
9	*Sixteenth-Century France*	193
10	*Sixteenth-Century French Poetry*	215
11	*Sixteenth-Century French Prose*	229
12	*Michel De Montaigne*	243
13	*Sixteenth-Century Spain*	273
14	*Sixteenth-Century Spanish Prose*	293
15	*Sixteenth-Century Spanish Poetry*	311
16	*Sixteenth-Century Spanish Drama*	325
	Bibliography	345
	Index	351
	About the Author	355

FOREWORD

WE DEFINE MUSIC to be that form of music performed live before listeners. We define Aesthetics in Music to be a study of the nature of the perception of music by the listener.

We believe the performance of music in actual practice falls naturally into four classes. These are Art Music, Educational Music, Functional Music and Entertainment Music.

I. Art Music

Art Music we believe is defined by four conditions, *all* of which *must always be present*. These are:

1. *Art music is inspired.* Art music is music in which it seems evident that the composer has made an honest attempt to communicate genuine feelings. Feelings, which may range from lofty and noble to superficial and vulgar, must be presumed to be generally recognizable in music, as they are in any other art form, including painting, sculpture, dance, and architecture. In Art Music, lofty and noble feelings are paramount.

    Due to the common genetically understood nature of emotions, it must also be understood that in music emotions or feelings cannot be 'faked.' They will always be recognized as such by any contemplative listener.

2. *Art Music has no purpose other than the communication of its own aesthetic content.* Art Music is free of any purpose or function, save the spiritual communication of pure beauty.

3. *Art Music is that which enjoys a performance faithful to the intent of the composer.*

4. *Art Music must have a listener capable of contemplation.*

If any of these conditions are missing, the performance must result in a lesser aesthetic experience. For example, the *Ninth Symphony* of Beethoven played in a stadium, during the half-time of a professional football game, would fail for the lack of the presence of Condition Number Four. The same Symphony heard in a concert hall, but in a poor performance, not faithful to the intent of the composer, would fail for the lack of the presence of Condition Number Three.

II. Educational Music

Educational Music may or may not have the same conditions as Art Music, excepting Condition Number Two; it may or may not occur within an educational institution. Educational Music is didactic music, music which has the specific and *additional* aim to educate. In the strictest sense, if the *primary purpose* of Music is to educate, it cannot be Art Music—for Art Music has no purpose.

III. Functional Music

Functional Music is music put at the service of something else. We include here, for example, all kinds of religious music, music for weddings, music for the military, and occupational music. Functional Music may share the same conditions as Art Music, excepting Condition Number Two.

One may ask, How can a Mozart Mass be called Functional Music, and not Art Music? If the observer were not contemplatively listening to the music, but were rather contemplating religious thoughts, then the Mozart Mass becomes merely a very high level of Functional Music. If, on the other hand, the observer is a contemplative listener of music, forgetting about religion, then the Mozart Mass is Art Music, but has failed in its purpose as church music.

Military and wedding music are examples of music in which the contemplative listener is missing entirely. How about airport, supermarket and elevator music where there is no listener at all? According to the definition we have given above, recorded music without listeners is not to be considered music at all.

IV. Entertainment Music

Entertainment Music is music with no object other than to please. It will always be missing Condition Four, the contemplative listener. For this reason, Entertainment Music may be inspired music, but the composer is unlikely to be inspired by lofty and noble emotions, knowing there will be no contemplative listener. Entertainment Music and Art Music can never be the same thing because of Condition Number Two: Art Music has no purpose other than the communication of its own aesthetic content. It is inconsistent with the nature of great art to have any extrinsic purpose, including the purpose to entertain.

The first philosopher to address the impact which Art has on an observer was Aristotle, in his *Poetics*, as part of a discussion of Tragedy, which like music has both a material, written form and a live performance form. In this treatise, Aristotle first considers the nature and contribution of each of the specific components of the written form of the Tragedy in his typically methodical style. His great contribution, however, comes when he has completed this discussion, for he then goes beyond the material form of the play itself to discuss the observer. He makes it clear that not only is the end purpose of the elements of the play to produce a specific experience in the observer, but that the nature of this experience is what distinguishes Tragedy from other dramatic forms, such as Spectacle. It was in this moment that he created a new branch of Philosophy which we call 'Aesthetics.'

Our purpose is to provide a source book of representative descriptions of actual performances, observations by philosophers, poets and other commentators which contribute insights to our understanding of what music meant to listeners during the early Renaissance. It is for this reason that when discussing contemporary treatises on music that we concentrate on those passages which offer insights relative to the aesthetics of music and musical performance rather than the usual technical subjects such as scales, modes and counterpoint which fill most books on Renaissance music.

Since traditional musicology has focused almost exclusively on sacred and secular vocal music of the Renaissance, we have also included numerous references which we hope will reveal a much wider world of music during this period.

We are also interested in contemporary views on the physiology of knowing, especially with regard to the relationship of the senses and Reason, and related psychological ideas, such as Pleasure and Pain and the Emotions, which might offer a frame of reference for their perspective on the perception of music.

This is the fourth volume in a series of eight, ranging from the music of the ancient civilizations through the Baroque Period.

David Whitwell
Austin, Texas

ACKNOWLEDGMENTS

This new edition would not have been possible without the encouragement and help of Craig Dabelstein of Brisbane, Australia. His experience as a musician and educator himself has contributed greatly to his expertise as editor of this volume.

David Whitwell
Austin, 2013

1 SIXTEENTH-CENTURY ITALIAN PHILOSOPHERS

A NATURAL RESULT of the intellectual excitement and sense of cultural rediscovery during the earlier years of the Renaissance in Italy is the courtier of the sixteenth century. The courtier, as he is described in one of the most famous books of the Renaissance, *Il Cortigiano* (The Courtier), by Baldassare Castiglione (1478–1529), attempts to become the perfect gentleman or lady not only through deportment but by the acquisition of education and a wide variety of skills. He is, to most of us today, what is meant by a 'Renaissance man.'

Torquato Tasso also wrote of the breadth of knowledge needed by the courtier. Conspicuously missing in his list is music, which he may have regarded as requiring too much work, as indeed was the view of Castiglione.

> He ought to learn mathematics and moral philosophy as well as natural science and theology, and he ought to be well acquainted with the historians,[1] the poets, the orators, and with the noble arts, such as sculpture, painting and architecture. He ought to know enough about all of these subjects so that no one can accuse him of ignorance. Such knowledge will win high honor from his prince, and goodwill will follow honor.[2]

Other writers, such as Guicciardini, saw a clear value in obtaining some musical skills.

> When I was young, I used to scoff at knowing how to play [an instrument], dance, and sing, and other such frivolities. I even made light of good penmanship, knowing how to ride, to dress well, and all those things that seem more decorative than substantial in a man. But later, I wished I had not done so. For although it is not wise to spend too much time cultivating the young toward the perfection of these arts, I have nevertheless seen from experience that these ornaments and accomplishments lend dignity and reputation even to men of good rank. It may even be said that whoever lacks them lacks something important. Moreover skill in this sort of entertainment opens the way to the favor of princes, and sometimes becomes the beginning or

---

1 Pietro Aretino, in a letter to Charles V, made the memorable remark, 'falsehood is the mother of history' [Letter of June, 1536, quoted in Samuel Putnam, *The Works of Aretino* (New York: Covici, 1926), II, 85]. Aretino (1492–1556) was one of the first authors whose books were placed on the Index of Prohibited Books, a development of the Council of Trent.
2 Torquato Tasso, 'Malpiglio, or On the Court,' in *Tasso's Dialogues*, trans. Carnes Lord (Berkeley: University of California Press, 1982), 161.

the reason for great profit and high honors. For the world and princes are no longer made as they should be, but as they are.³

Machiavelli, in turn, recommends in his 'The Prince,' that the wise prince will also show himself to be a lover of the arts by rewarding accomplished men.⁴

For Tasso, the musician was one of several professions which was welcome in court, but again requiring too much effort and specialization to be acquired by the regular courtier.

> Poets, orators, musicians, and the professors of mathematics and natural philosophy can be courtiers just as they can be citizens …
>
> Properly speaking, however, the courtier is the active and prudent man who rules the arts and sciences in a court just as the prudent citizen does in a city.⁵

Too much specialization, even in general knowledge, seems to have been a sensitive characteristic in the presence of rulers who had gained their position by birth or battle, as Tasso warns.

> But since the intellect is meant by nature to rule, it seems that the man who possesses superior prudence ought not to be considered inferior for any reason. And this is why princes usually hate any greatness of mind. When a courtier has great intelligence, which sometimes happens, he ought to cover it up modestly, not show it off with pride. Concealment becomes the courtier more than showing off.⁶

However much the courtier may have appreciated the arts, the genuine artists themselves often lived on the edge of poverty. It was the beginning of the aristocratic patronage system which would remain in place well into the nineteenth century. On advising a correspondent on the life led by poets, Pietro Aretino notes that they are all so poor that a nobleman of Milan once saw a fellow in a ragged cloak and said, 'The man must be a poet.'⁷ He continues,

---

3   Francesco Guicciardini, *Maxims and Reflections*, trans. Mario Domandi (New York: Harper Torchbooks, 1965), C, 179. Guicciardini (1483–1540) as a young man served as an ambassador of Florence to the court of the king of Aragon. Later he served under two papal administrations which led to his appointment as governor of Modena, in 1516, and of Reggio, in 1517. His most important literary effort was a *History of Italy*. Aretino, in one of his letters, mentions overhearing a young man state that he has the necessary qualities to be a courtier: 'I am a good musician, have some learning, and I love the chase.' Letter to Ambrogio degli Eusebii, in Thomas Chubb, *The Letters of Pietro Aretino* (New Haven: Shoe String Press [Archon Books], 1967), 103.

4   Niccolò Machiavelli, *Machiavelli, the Chief Works*, trans. Allan Gilbert (Durham: Duke University Press, 1965), I, 84.

5   Tasso, 'Malpiglio, or on the Court,' 187. Aretino, in a letter to Francesco Salviati, in Chubb, *The Letters of Pietro Aretino*, 210, observes that the courtier, Lorenzetto, had to give up his study of poetry for lack of time.

6   Tasso, ibid., 175.

7   Letter to Giovan Gragoncino, in Chubb, *The Letters of Pietro Aretino*, 95. According to Aretino, in Pietro Aretino, *Dialogues*, trans., Raymond Rosenthal (New York: Marsilio, 1971), 255, scholars had the same reputation. He mentions that a scholar flung his purse at someone and it 'hardly made a sound when it hit the floor.'

> But we live in this world, praise God, nor must we despair because our lot is cruel. After all, it is a fine thing to have our name hawked at every fair, and to hear what we have written sung by the mountebanks. It makes us lose our fear of Death, for poets, he admits, are not food for his teeth. Long before he gets them they will have been devoured by cold and heat …
>
> So if you want to go barefoot and naked, turn yourself into an air-eating chameleon and become a singer of rhymes.

For a writer, Aretino points out, one means for survival was to attempt to publish one's own works for profit, although he personally found this offensive.

> As for having printed at one's own expense and one's own urging the books that a man has drawn forth from his imagination, that seems to me to be like feasting on one's own limbs, and he who every evening visits the bookstore to pick up the money earned by the day's sales, to be like a pimp who empties the purse of his woman before he retires to bed.
>
> For that reason, I hope God will grant that the courtesy of princes rewards me for the labor of writing, and not the small change of book buyers; for I would rather endure every hardship than to prostitute my genius by making it a day laborer of the liberal arts.
>
> It is obvious that those who write for money become hosts to, and even porters of their own infamy, and so if you want the advantage of profit, become a merchant. Frankly call yourself a book peddler, and lay the name of poet aside.[8]

While Aretino, above, prays for a generous prince, his descriptions of such service are not flattering. In a letter of October 1545, to an ambassador, he writes,

> Tell your master that as far as barking goes, poets are like dogs. Unbearable hunger is the evil friend which makes the latter bare their teeth and the former wag their tongues. But the pleasant after-effects of bread set before them at the right hour and time, will quiet the rabies of one and smother the anger of the other. So if His Excellency would only have as much liberality as he has gold, it would be very little trouble for him so to act that the howling of wolves was changed into the sweet singing of swans.[9]

Another letter complains of unfilled promises.

> The lies of those princes who promise to help men of talent are even more dangerous than those of physicians who assure their patients that they will escape death. For the latter species of men learned in presumption, play false only with the purses and the lives of those who are groaning on their sickbeds, but the former rabble of magnificos in appearance only, bring despair to the soul and body of all who have grown lean in praising them. Therefore, he who puts no faith in them is rich, and he who trusts them is a beggar.[10]

---

8 Letter to Francesco Marcolini, in Chubb, *The Letters of Pietro Aretino*, 66.
9 Quoted in ibid., 215
10 Letter to Mutio, January, 1548, in ibid., 245ff.

As Aretino's fame grew he began to take revenge in his writings and he liked to think that in so doing he had improved the lot of artists at court.

> But I for my part have written what I have written for the sake of sacred Genius. Up to now she had been hidden in a dark corner by the avarice of the great lords. Indeed, before I began to lash out and to paint these fellows in their true colors, men of ability had to become beggars for the ordinary needs of life. If any one of them was able to stave off want and misery, he did so by being a clown and not because he was a man of talents. By my pen, armed with its terrors, wrought in such a manner that these mighty folk, aware of its powers, were obliged to receive men of intellect and enforced courtesy even though they hated this worse than some deadly disease.[11]

The sense of intellectual expansion seen in the life of the ordinary courtier can also be seen to some degree in the dogma of the Church. While it had strictly held to the concept of only one path to truth during the Middle Ages, now a writer such as Maffei, in his 'De Institutione Christiana,' could argue for varied paths.

> Just as in the Catholic faith, in which all the equally good and faithful meet together in the same spirit to embrace the one God and Father of all, truth is often thought out by different people in different ways and means so that each one lives more or less according to his own nature, humors, fortune, and grace.[12]

Such liberal thinking soon came under attack by the Counter-Reformation, which might as well be called 'Counter-Renaissance,' in so far as Humanism was concerned. The Church, faced with the challenge of Luther, retreated to its strong point—medieval dogma. Some of these retrenchments, such as abolishing the right of the individual to act on his own conscience or judgment,[13] are with us still today. We can see the impact of this primarily in Rome, where the Humanist School of painting begins to disappear, to be replaced by a style called Mannerist.[14]

In addition, the Renaissance itself suffered a significant setback in Italy due to invasions. Between 1512 and 1530, Brescia, Genoa, Pavia, Naples and Florence were sacked. In the famous 'Sack of Rome,' in 1527, looters even entered the Sancta Sanctorum of the Lateran and played ball with the relic heads of St. Peter and St. Paul![15] Rome did not become a center of the arts again until 1600. Stinger finds in Michelangelo's *Last Judgment* an expression of the somber mood in Rome following the sack and believes it was ordered to reflect 'a forceful reassertion of theology over philosophy, of faith over reason, of divine grace over human free will.'[16]

---

11 Letter to Giantonio da Foligno, in Ibid., 52.

12 Quoted in John D'Amico, *Renaissance Humanism in Papal Rome* (Baltimore: Johns Hopkins University Press, 1983), 196.

13 Anthony Blunt, *Artistic Theory in Italy, 1450–1600* (Oxford: Clarendon Press, 1959), 105.

14 Ibid., 106.

15 Charles Stinger, *The Renaissance in Rome* (Bloomington: Indiana University Press, 1985), 322.

16 Ibid., 325.

ON THE PHYSIOLOGY OF AESTHETICS

One of the curiosities of this period, in which we are sometimes given the impression that most courtiers were striving to ever extend their skills and knowledge, is that some writers found, on the balance, that knowledge traveled in the company of unhappiness. Consider, for example, these reflections by Guicciardini:

> A superior intellect is bestowed upon men only to make them unhappy and tormented. For it does nothing but produce in them greater turmoil and anxiety than there is in more limited men.[17]
>
> ......
>
> In this world it is undoubtedly true that men of mediocre mind have a better time, a longer life, and are in some respects happier than men of high intellect; for a noble mind is apt to be the cause of trouble and worry. But mediocre men participate more in brute animality than in humanity, whereas the others transcend the human condition and approach the celestial natures.[18]
>
> ......
>
> It sometimes happens that fools do greater things than wise men. The reason is that the wise man, unless forced to do otherwise, will rely a great deal on reason and little on fortune; whereas the fool does just the opposite.[19]

Most writers, however, probably would have agreed with Machiavelli:

> For brains are of three types: the first comprehends for itself; the second comprehends when another explains; the third does not comprehend either for itself or by means of another's explanation. The first is exceedingly good, the second good, the third useless.[20]

There were two philosophers in the older tradition who wrote at some length on the nature of the mind and its relationship to the senses. The first, Gianfrancesco Pico della Mirandola (1470–1533), was one of several important philosophers who, as a response to the Reformation, attempted to reconcile the ideas of the humanists with the Church. He was a late medieval Scholastic, but in the dress of the new 'Parisian style,' the Aristotelian School of the University of Paris.

In his treatise, *On the Imagination* (1500), dedicated to Maximilian I, we can see such an effort to combine the Church's 'soul' with the man and his intellect. Pico agrees with most earlier philosophers that all information comes to the mind through the senses, through

---

17　Guicciardini, *Maxims and Reflections*, C, 60.
18　Ibid., B, 115.
19　Ibid., C, 136.
20　Machiavelli, *The Chief Works*, I, 85.

images, from which comes the word 'imagination.'²¹ The soul then conceives a likeness of the objects the senses have experienced (imagination) and 'places them before the intellect.' The soul employs intellect for contemplating abstract ideas, but Reason for contemplating the information of the senses and for things outside the body.²²

Imagination also plays a similar communications role with regard to rational and irrational concepts, preparing Reason for the 'inferior nature' of the irrational.²³ Today we know the left hemisphere's presumption that the right hemisphere of the brain is inferior or even non-existent is a fact. Here, according to Pico, imagination plays a vital role, for if it fails to 'apply itself to the business of virtue' and instead follows 'the pleasures which allure the senses,' it robs man 'of humanity, and takes on bestiality.' In such a case, Reason must come to the rescue, enabling us to 'suppress [imagination] if it errs, and not urge it on, if it is hasty.'²⁴

In Pico's *Commentary on a Canzone of Benivieni* (1519), he is somewhat more specific in his view of the nature of the intellect. In his general map of the mind, Pico finds:

1. Three types of cognitive faculties: sensation, reason and intellect.
2. Three levels of desiring: appetite, choice and will.
    a. Appetite (irrational animals) follows sensation.
    b. Choice (man) follows Reason.
    c. Will (angels) follows intellect.

> The rational faculty, located between sensation and intellect, as a mean between extremes, can address itself to the desires of either one, according to its own choice, now inclining to one, that is downward toward sensation, now rising to the other, that is upward toward intellect.²⁵

The organizational agent for all these faculties Pico assigns to the soul. The ranking he gives them is both a reflection of medieval Church dogma and a value system which remains firmly in place today.

> This same hierarchy of authority can be seen in the microcosm, that is, in the human soul, where lower faculties are corrected and instructed by higher, and as long as each heeds its superior, each faculty carries out all of its functions without any mistakes. Thus the imagination often corrects the mistakes of the external senses; Reason instructs the imagination, and Reason is illuminated by the intellect. The cognitive part of the soul never falls into error except when the imagination is too arrogant and does not trust Reason, or Reason is alienated from the intellect and relies

---

21 Gianfrancesco Pico della Mirandola, *On the Imagination*, trans. Harry Caplan, (Westport: Greenwood Press, 1957), I, 25. Pico was murdered by his nephew, Galeotto.

22 Ibid., II, 29.

23 Ibid., VI, 41ff.

24 Ibid., VII, 45. Pico continues the discussion with some 'weird science,' in which he says the functioning of one's imagination is determined by the relative amounts of blood, phlegm, red bile and black bile in the body. [Ibid., VIII, 51ff.]

25 Giovanni Pico della Mirandola, *Commentary on a Canzone of Benivieni*, trans. Sears Jayne, (New York: Peter Lang, 1984), 101. In view of this organization, it is interesting that Pico spoke of this book in a letter to Benivieni's brother, saying, 'I wrote it when I was bored and had nothing else to do, as a way of relaxing my mind, not of exciting it.'

too much on its own powers. Similarly, among the appetitive powers the sensitive appetite is governed by the rational appetite, and the rational appetite by the intellect.

This hierarchy, which he has constructed, helps explain Pico's objection to music, that it weakens man and makes him effeminate. He points, by way of example, to the failure of Orpheus to rescue Euridice, 'because he had been made soft and weak by his own music.' Pico then leaves us this enigma, with no further explanation.

> I want to leave the reader this knot to untie: the same serpent which deprived Orpheus of Euridice taught him (that is, Orpheus) music, and prevented him from recovering his beloved Euridice through his own death. I do not want to disclose this secret any further. 'Let him who has ears for hearing, listen.'[26]

One often finds in ancient literature, as well as in the entire Christian era through the nineteenth century, philosophers who seems to understand through deduction alone the basic organization of the separate, but equal, twin hemispheres of our brain. Pico was startlingly correct in some of his descriptions.

> Thus our souls, too, before they fall into this earthly body, have two faces; that is, they can at the same time look at the intelligibles and look after the sensibles. But when they descend into the body, it is as if they were divided in half; only one of their two faces is left to them, so that whenever they turn the one face which remains to them toward sensible beauty, they are deprived of the sight of the other [intellectual] beauty.[27]

Later, he correctly deduces that the left hemisphere does not recognize the existence of the right hemisphere. This is the primary reason why we feel the need to conceptualize things which are of the domain of the right hemisphere, such as music. Pico describes this taking over, this conceptualization, as follows:

> The intellect does not permit any lower faculty to function in collaboration with it. Rather, whenever anything comes near the intellect and arouses it, the intellect, like a roaring fire, burns it up, and converts it into itself.[28]

In another place, he writes 'as long as our soul is turned toward sensible things, it cannot enjoy the sight of intellectual beauty.' For this Church-oriented philosopher, this meant, of course, that the priorities are wrong.

---

26 Ibid., 149.

27 Ibid., 127.

28 Ibid., 148.

> But those whose intellect, purified and illuminated by philosophical study, recognizes that sensible beauty is the image of another more perfect beauty, abandon the love of sensible beauty and begin to wish to see heavenly beauty.[29]

Another philosopher whom we associate with the spirit of the Counter-Revolution is Giordano Bruno. Born in Nola, near Naples, in 1548, he entered the Order of Dominic at age fifteen, became a priest at age twenty-four and traveled in university circles in a number of countries, including England and Germany. From our perspective, his philosophic views were very conservative, indeed some call him the last medieval philosopher, but ironically the Church considered him a free-thinker and the Inquisition had him put in prison and then burned.

Bruno was often critical of traditional philosophy, once observing that to call someone a philosopher 'is tantamount to insulting him as a quack, a good-for-nothing, a howling pedant, a charlatan, a mountebank.'[30]

> To tell you the truth, the race of philosophers is rated by the general run of men as more despicable than [the clergy]. The latter, raised up out of every sort of riffraff, have brought the priesthood into contempt; the former, designated out of all sorts of brutes, have dragged philosophy down into disrepute.[31]

He is remembered today as perhaps the most important philosopher of his time to be opposed to the writings of Aristotle, whom he accused of 'impurities, blots, with certain empty conclusions and theories'[32] and 'uncultured ... offensive and pretentious.'[33]

As the reader might guess from this, much of his writings have a certain negative quality. Speaking of philosophers, monks and courtiers, he says that each appears a fool to someone else,[34] and like many Church writers, he was not kind in his writings about women.

> Women are a chaos of irrationality, a wood [hyle] of wickedness, a forest of ribaldry, a mass of uncleanliness, an aptitude for every perdition ...
> [Quoting Secundus], Woman is an obstacle to quiet, a continual damage, a daily war, a life-prison, a storm in the house, the shipwreck of man.[35]

Bruno finds three kinds of intellect: the divine, the mundane and the 'particular ones which become all things.' His concept of divine intellect he formulates as 'world-soul,' which

---

29 Ibid., 128ff.
30 Giordano Bruno, *Cause, Principle and Unity*, trans. Jack Lindsay (New York: International Publishers, 1962), 63.
31 Ibid., 64.
32 Ibid., 69.
33 Ibid., 110.
34 Ibid., 73.
35 Ibid., 118, 120.

encompasses all of Nature. All of Nature, therefore, must be thought of as an act of cogitation. Here, Bruno mentions the musician, in a rare paraphrase of Aristotle which is not critical.

> Aristotle demonstrates this by the example of a perfect writer or lutanist. Here, while nature does not reason and reflect, he doesn't wish the conclusion to be drawn that she works without intellect and final intention, because profound writers and musicians pay less attention to what they create, and yet do not go astray like the more inexpert and clumsy, who, though giving more thought and attention, produce a less perfect result and show no lack of faults.[36]

Bruno shares with earlier Church philosophers a certain distrust of the senses and he points out, in particular, that each of the different senses can deliver a different judgment of the same object. But, on the other hand, he stated that from 'experimental knowledge,' gained from the senses, one 'can proceed on to the discovery of nature's mysteries as effectively as those who begin with rational theory.'[37] In another place, Bruno suggests that since knowledge is dependent to some degree on the senses, if a man lacks a sense he is therefore lacking in some part of knowledge, 'especially that knowledge which is dependent upon that sense.' However, Bruno departs from earlier philosophers in his view of the importance of sight.

> There are those who say that sight is most to be desired for acquiring knowledge; but never did I know a man so foolish who asserted that it is chiefly sight that enables us to understand.[38]

It is no surprise to find Bruno arguing for the existence of a soul, which he describes as follows,

> The soul is in the body like the pilot in the ship, and the pilot, insofar as he shares the ship's motion, is part of it; yet, insofar as he is understood as the ship's guide and mover, he is seen, not as a part, but as a distinct efficient cause.[39]

The Counter-Reformation represented by these two philosophers also resulted in an attempt to insert Puritanism into art. In a famous letter to Michelangelo on the subject of the artist's 'Last Judgment,' Pietro Aretino wrote,

> As a baptized Christian, I am ashamed of the license so flagrant, which you have taken ... Even the Gentiles, depicting the naked Venus, caused her to cover with her hands those parts that should be covered.[40]

---

36 Ibid., 85.
37 Ibid., 110.
38 Giordano Bruno, *The Expulsion of the Triumphant Beast*, trans. Arthur Imerti (New Brunswick: Rutgers University Press, 1964), 170ff [II, ii].
39 Ibid., 84.
40 Quoted in Frank Chambers, *The History of Taste* (New York: Columbia University Press, 1932), 48.

The more conservative philosophers also had, at best, a very cautious attitude toward traditional education. Bruno, for example, wrote,

> Let the Scales [of Justice] roam through the academies and universities where they may examine whether those who teach are of correct weight, whether they are too light or tip the scales, and whether they who presume to teach from their chair and writings need to listen and study. And by balancing their intellect, let [the Scales] see whether that intellect gives those who teach wings or weighs them down. Let them see whether it has the nature of the sheep or rather of the shepherd, and whether it is fit for the feeding of pigs and asses, or rather of creatures capable of reason.[41]

Several reflections of Francesco Guicciardini are equally cautious,

> Learning imposed on weak minds does not improve them, and it may ruin them. But when it is added to natural talent, it makes men perfect and almost divine.[42]
>
> ......
>
> It is a mistake to say that learning spoils the minds of men. Perhaps it is true in the case of weak minds. But learning imposed on a good mind makes it perfect. For a good natural endowment joined with good learning forms a most noble combination.[43]
>
> ......
>
> How different theory is from practice! So many people understand things well but either do not remember or do not know how to put them into practice! The knowledge of such men is useless. It is like having a treasure stored in a chest without ever being able to take it out.[44]

ON THE PSYCHOLOGY OF AESTHETICS

Tasso, reflecting as he often did the Church dogma, found a general distrust on any topic dealing with the emotions.

> Women are related to men as desire is to the intellect, and just as desire, which is in itself irrational, is informed by many beautiful and comely virtues when it subjects itself to the intellect, so a woman who obeys her husband adorns herself with virtues that she would not possess if she were rebellious.[45]
>
> ......

---

41 Bruno, *The Expulsion of the Triumphant Beast*, 232 [III, ii].
42 Guicciardini, *Maxims and Reflections*, C, 47.
43 Ibid., B, 91.
44 Ibid., C, 35.
45 Torquato Tasso, 'The Father of the Family,' in *Tasso's Dialogues*, trans. Carnes Lord (Berkeley: University of California Press, 1982), 85.

Love for what is not esteemed never seems to result from judgment but always from passion.[46]

The more secular Aretino, however, advises a young writer to express feelings, not words.

I urge you to strive to be a sculptor of the things you feel and not to paint miniatures with words.[47]

The emotion most discussed in sixteenth-century Italian literature was, of course, Love. Machiavelli contended that the actions of men are driven primarily by two things: love and fear. For the leader, he observes, it is more effective to be feared than loved.[48]

Aretino, in a rare optimistic mood, once defined Love as 'the desire for the beautiful and longing for the good.'[49] Often, however, one finds him offering warnings to other young men, as in a letter to Ambrogio degli Eusebii.

I warned you to resist the first assaults of love. It is a frenzy that begins by making you satisfy your lustful desires and ends with your repenting the pleasures you had.[50]

When this same correspondent was thinking of marriage, Aretino became more concerned.

Leave the heavy burden of a wife to those who have the shoulders of an Atlas. Leave her nagging to the ears of tradesmen. Leave her notions to someone who knows how to beat her or can put up with them ... And if you must have a son and heir, beget him on some other man's wife ...

But when the day comes when continence has mastered all your lusts, then I will really praise your sense and urge you to take comfort in Poetry.[51]

As for himself, Aretino had earlier claimed disinterest in Love, crediting his old age, 'Love, which should awake me, puts me to sleep.'[52] But then he falls in love and cries out in his torment,

That devil, Love, now bestrides me ... Oh what cruel nights, what disdainful days do we endure because of his rogue doings! ...

I have cut my diet in half so as to grow thin ... I have become like one of those who, wasted by pestilence or famine, are about to depart from this life. They are now but the shadows of themselves.

But to tell you the truth, I feel more sorry for those who are tormented by love, than I do for those who die of hunger or who go unjustly to the gallows. For if you die of hunger, it is through

---

46   Tasso, 'Malpiglio, or on the Court,' 161.
47   Letter to Niccolo Franco, in Chubb, *The Letters of Pietro Aretino*, 71.
48   Machiavelli, *The Chief Works*, I, 477.
49   Letter to Madonna Basciadonna, in Chubb, *The Letters of Pietro Aretino*, 234.
50   Quoted in Ibid., 58.
51   Ibid., 59.
52   Ibid., 54.

your own shiftless ways, and if you are wrongly executed it is the work of unkind fate, but the cruelty which assails a lover comes from his own soft-hearted gullibility, and from his willful submission unto slavery …

Your dinner is poison to you; your banqueting wormwood; your bed a rocky ledge. Even friendship turns into hate as your fancy is fixed upon only one person until I am astonished that a mind can possibly be in such an unending tempest—until I am surprised that you do not even forget who you are in the continuous tempest of your thoughts which makes you tag on behind your beloved one even though she drags your heart in the dirt.

Yet even this might bring you joy if you had any reason to believe that there was any good in any woman. But women never change. To them their love affairs are like a card game—and in their hand they hold the aces and the kings.[53]

Regarding the nature of Pleasure and Pain, Pico concludes, in his 'On the Imagination,' that our displeasure with most pain is due to the imagination, and not to Reason. Thus we can bare even torture if we reflect that it is only a pain inflicted by our opinion regarding the body part.[54]

Most early philosophers had commented on the fact that Pleasure results in Pain and that Pain often leads to Pleasure. Pico enlarges the argument in his attempt to bring the ideas of ancient philosophy and the Church into a sense of agreement. Every pleasure is short and petty, he says, and often,

> is accompanied by disgust and anxiety; that from it follows the loss of a greater good—of inward peace of conscience.[55]

This seems to be the viewpoint expressed in the Florentine intermedi of 1567–1568, performed to celebrate the christening of Francesco's first child, when the allegorical character Pleasure tries to tempt the character Hercules. She promises him 'Pleasure, exceeding all other good things in life,' but he responds, 'No longer impede my path, O temptress; for I shall never change my course for you, but only follow virtue's just advice.'[56]

Similarly, Bruno uses Pleasure and Pain as an illustration of one of his basic tenets, the 'coincidence of contraries.' Thus,

> Just as troublesome and sad is the state of hunger; so, displeasing and grave is the state of satiety; but that which does delight us is the motion from the one to the other …
>
> So mutation from one extreme to the other through its participants, and motion from one contrary to the other through its intermediate points, come to satisfy us; and, finally, we see

---

53　Ibid., 67ff.

54　Pico, *On the Imagination*, X, 73ff.

55　Ibid., X, 75.

56　Quoted in Nino Pirrotta and Elena Povoledo, *Music and Theatre from Poliziano to Monteverdi* (Cambridge: Cambridge University Press, 1982), 184.

such familiarity between one contrary and the other that the one agrees more with the other than like with like.[57]

More traditional reflections are given by Guicciardini,

It is a great misfortune not to be able to have the good without first having to take the bad,[58]

and Machiavelli:

In connection with good there seems always to be something bad, which so easily grows up along with the good that to avoid the bad while striving for good seems impossible. This is apparent in everything men do.[59]

A general warning is found in one of Bandello's Tales, 'Livio and Camilla,' where we read,

Which argueth sufficiently the folly of them that in any degree bestow either joy or sorrow so near their heart, that, besides the destruction of the body, they become the unnatural murderers of their own souls.[60]

ON THE PHILOSOPHY OF AESTHETICS

In this literature one finds many passages which reflect on the general perception of society regarding Art and artists, and it is generally discouraging. Machiavelli, in wondering why the lessons of history are not valued as past works of art are, indirectly offers a perspective on the value given Art in sixteenth-century Italy.

When I consider, then, how much respect is given to antiquity and how … a fragment of an antique statue has been bought at a high price in order that the buyer may have it near him, to bring reputation to his house with it, and to have it imitated by those who take pleasure in that art, and when I know that the latter then with their utmost skill attempt in all their works to imitate it …[61]

---

57 Bruno, *The Expulsion of the Triumphant Beast*, 89ff [I, i].
58 Guicciardini, *Maxims and Reflections*, C, 146.
59 Machiavelli, *The Chief Works*, I, 512.
60 Matteo Bandello, *Tragical Tales*, trans. Geoffrey Fenton (1567) (London: Routledge), 120. Bandello (1480–1562), though trained and active as a member of the clergy, is best remembered for his prose tales of life in Milan.
61 'Discourses on Livius,' in Machiavelli, *The Chief Works*, I, 190.

Later in this same study, Machiavelli concludes that the men and their accomplishments of his time were superior to the ancients, 'if you are not considering the matter of the arts.'[62]

Benvenuto Cellini, in his autobiography, mentions an attempt of his to point out the necessity of supporting artists. In a comment to the pope, he made an analogy by pointing out that cats do better mousing when they are well fed and not starved.[63] For this he received a rebuke for inappropriate address to a pope.

The often negative philosopher, Bruno, had a very dim view of Art. In the following dialogue, in fact, he argues that man will someday be called on the justify his vain worship of artists and objects of art!

> I yearn to understand what that Lyre, made of ox horns in the form of a tortoise, is doing between the remains of Leo and the head of that sweet white Swan. I should like to know whether that region is inhabited in honor of the tortoise, the horns, or the lyre. Or is it that everyone should be aware of the skill of Mercury, who made it, as a testimony of his dissolute and vain boasting?
>
> Here, oh gods, are our works, here our remarkable handiworks, by which we honored ourselves in the eyes of heaven! What beautiful creations, not too unlike those that children are wont to create when they work with clay, paste, small branches, and straw as they attempt to imitate the works of their elders! Do you think that we shall not have to justify these things and account for them? Can you be convinced that we will be summoned, interrogated, judged, and condemned less frequently for our idle works than for our idle words?[64]

One traditional question, regarding the aesthetics of Art in general, was whether Art exists in the finished art object or in the mind of the artist. Vasari, representing a more enlightened view, in his discussion of painting in the second edition of his *Lives*, offers this analysis.

> Proceeding from the intellect it extracts from many things a universal judgment, like a form or idea of all the things in nature ... From this knowledge there proceeds a certain idea or judgment, which is formed in the mind, and this idea to which expression is given by the hands is called drawing. It can therefore be concluded, that this drawing is simply a visible expression and manifestation of the idea which exists in our mind, and which others have formed in their mind and created in their imagination.[65]

Bruno offered a rare opposing (and incorrect) view of the relationship of the form of art in the mind of the artist and the art object.

> Because from the cognition of all dependent things we cannot infer other notions of the first principle and cause than by the rather inadequate method of vestiges: all things being derived from the will or goodness [of the first cause], which is the principle of its operation and from

---

62 Ibid., 321.

63 Benvenuto Cellini, *The Life of Benvenuto Cellini*, trans. John Addington Symonds (New York: Scribner's, 1914), I, lvi.

64 Bruno, *The Expulsion of the Triumphant Beast*, 110 [I, ii].

65 Quoted in Blunt, *Artistic Theory in Italy*, 100.

which proceeds the universal effect. The same situation can be made out in our relation to works of art, insomuch as the man who sees the statue does not see the sculptor. He who sees Helen's portrait doesn't see Helen.[66]

Bruno's idea, which forms the basis for this view, was that the glory and credit for Art belongs to Nature, and not to the artist. His most concise expression of this concept is found in the following dialogue.

> TEOFILO. This natural matter is therefore not as perceptible as artificial matter, because the matter of nature has absolutely no form, but the matter of art is something already formed by nature. For art cannot operate except on the surface of things formed by nature, such as wood, iron, stone, wool, or the like …
> GERVASE. So the things formed by nature are the matter of art and a single formless thing is the matter of nature.
> TEOFILO. That's so.
> GERVASE. Is it then possible for us to know the substratum of nature, just as we can see and know clearly the substrata of the arts?
> TEOFILO. Assuredly, but with different principles of cognition. In the same way as we don't know colors and sounds by the same sense, so we cannot see the substratum of the arts and that of nature with the same eye.
> GERVASE. You mean that we see first with the eyes of sense and the second with the eye of reason?
> TEOFILO. Exactly … The relation and reference that the form of art has to its matter is the same as that which the form of nature has to its matter, allowing for the due differences. In art the forms vary to infinity, but the same matter always persists under them. Thus, the form of the tree becomes the form of a trunk, then of a beam, then of a table, a stool, a chest, a comb, and so on; but the wood remains all the while identical in its being.[67]

The most important discussion of Beauty in sixteenth-century Italy is found in Pico's *Commentary on a Canzone of Benivieni*. He first offers the familiar broad definition, that Beauty is the appropriate harmonization of the individual components.

> Whenever several different things combine to form a new entity, which arises from the appropriate mixing or harmonizing of those disparate components, the attractiveness which results from that proportionate combining is called beauty. Since every created thing is a composite, and since it is composed with as much due measure and proportion as is possible to the nature of that thing, every created thing can be called 'beautiful' in the broad sense of the term. For beauty in this sense consists of nothing more than the harmonizing which caused those elements, in spite of their multiplicity and diversity, to agree and consent among themselves to form a single entity. According to this interpretation, no simple thing can be beautiful.[68]

---

66 Bruno, *Cause, Principle and Unity*, 78.

67 Ibid., 101ff.

68 Pico, *Commentary on a Canzone of Benivieni*, 102.

Pico follows this with what he calls a definition of Beauty in a strict sense.

> In this meaning it is related to the word harmony. Thus God is said to have created the whole world by a musical or harmonic ordering. Although the word harmony in its general sense can mean the normal state of order in any composite thing, strictly speaking it means only the arranging of several notes which fit together to make a pleasant sound. In the same way, although the word beauty can be used for anything which is nicely put together, nevertheless it properly refers only to audible things; and it is this visual beauty the desire for which is called love. Love therefore, arises from one cognitive power only, namely sight, as has always been asserted not only by Mesaeus and Propertius, but universally by all the poets, both Greek and Latin. Plotinus is persuaded by this to believe that the name Eros, which in Greek means love, is derived from the word orasis, which means vision.[69]

Pico realized at this point that by associating beauty with sight he was eliminating any possible concept of intellectual beauty. Therefore he argues for two kinds of vision, corporeal and incorporeal.[70] In view of all these ideas, Pico is now ready to attempt to define Love, a topic he found inseparable from Beauty.

> Earthly love, then, is simply a desire to possess earthly beauty. When intelligible beauty (which consists of the Ideas) first descended into the Angelic Mind, there was born in the will of the Angelic Mind a desire to enjoy that beauty fully; in order to satisfy this desire, it had to turn back toward the source from which that beauty had come to it. In the same way, when the appearance or image of sensible beauty first reaches the human eye, there is immediately born in the sensitive appetite … a desire to enjoy that beauty fully. From this desire there can be born two loves, of which one is bestial and the other is human or rational. But in either case, if one wishes to enjoy this beauty fully, one must achieve union with whatever is the cause or source from which that beauty issued. If we follow the judgment of the senses, which the irrational animals or beasts follow, we shall suppose that the source of this beauty is in the material body in which we see it located, and hence there will arise in us a desire for coitus, which is simply joining oneself with that body in the most intimate way possible. But to dwell on this subject at greater length would be a profanation of the chaste mysteries of Platonic love.
>
> But let us return to our subject. I say that the senses judge that beauty has its origin in the body, and therefore the object of love in all irrational animals is coitus. But the reason judges very differently. The reason knows that the material body is not only not the source or cause of beauty, but is by nature entirely averse to and destructive of that beauty. Moreover the reason knows that the more one separates beauty from the body and considers it in itself, the more beauty has the proper dignity and excellence of its own nature. Therefore the reason does not try to proceed beyond the image received in the eyes to the body itself; on the contrary, if the reason sees any trace of anything corporeal or material remaining in that image, the reason tries to purge the image of it as much as it can.[71]

---

69 Ibid., 104.

70 Ibid., 104ff.

71 Ibid., 123ff.

Tasso discussed Beauty with respect to its moral value, suggesting that it is not true to say 'the beautiful is the good and the good the beautiful,' but rather 'the beautiful will be pleasing, and conversely, the pleasing will be beautiful.'[72] But, is the beautiful that which is pleasing to all the senses, or just some of the senses? Does something have to be useful to be beautiful? Tasso eventually concludes that 'the beautiful' is that to which only the 'nobler' senses (sight and hearing) are attracted.

> The beautiful will then be a part of the pleasing, for as that which gives delight is the object of all the senses, only that small part of it deserved to be called beautiful which is judged to be so by the nobler senses. Not only, therefore, will colors and lights and the various images of things be beautiful, but also songs and the music of instruments, which provide a most beautiful harmony for ears that are suitably refined.[73]

The most debated topic relative to aesthetics in the arts was the general subject of imitation. Beginning in 1512 a debate of sorts, through letters, ensued on the topic of the virtue of imitation in art, between Gianfrancesco Pico della Mirandola and Pietro Bembo. Pico considered imitation to be a danger to man's natural instincts, since every man is by nature unique. Further, since no man is perfect, no man should be imitated. It might also be noted that, unlike Machiavelli, he believed the man of his era far superior to the artist of antiquity.[74]

Bembo, in return, supported the concept of imitation in so far as it meant 'borrowing' the best from a fine model. His procedure was to find the best example of an art and to imitate the best techniques of it with the purpose of surpassing the original.

Pietro Aretino mentions in a letter to the writer, Niccolo Franco, that 'there is a great difference between being "influenced by," and plagiarizing.' He offered a musical analogy as a standard,

> He should take from them spiritual inspiration only, but the music that he plays should have the sound of his own instruments.[75]

Agnolo Segni, in 1573, made the very interesting contention that language, harmony and dance are all imitations of each other.

> All these things—language, harmony, dance and ornament—are imitations one of another, and each accommodates and resembles each other, but all are made similar to a prime [exemplar] and are imitations of it: the life of men, happy or wretched, their actions and morals, and thoughts of the mind.[76]

---

72 Torquato Tasso, 'Minturno, or On Beauty,' in *Tasso's Dialogues,* trans. Carnes Lord (Berkeley: University of California Press, 1982), 223.
73 Ibid., 227.
74 This is discussed in D'Amico, *Renaissance Humanism in Papal Rome,* 131ff.
75 Letter to Niccolo Franco, in Chubb, *The Letters of Pietro Aretino,* 68ff.
76 'Lezioni intorno alla poesia,' quoted in Claude V. Palisca, *Humanism in Italian Renaissance Musical Thought* (New Haven: Yale University Press, 1985), 401.

Vasari, whose *Lives* of 1550 was reissued in an enlarged form in 1568, also devotes much thought to the problem of imitation. In the preface to this work, he advises the painter to imitate both Nature and artists better than himself.

> Our art is all imitation, of nature for the most part, and then, because a man cannot by himself rise so high, of those works that are executed by those whom he judges to be better than himself.[77]

The ideal of Vasari was not to merely imitate Nature, indeed he criticized Titian for not giving his works 'the grace and perfection in which art goes beyond the score of nature.'[78] Nevertheless, in the course of his discussion of the artist Domenico Puligo, Vasari seems to recognize a difference of opinion current at this time, whether one should paint naturalistically or idealistically.

> I have seen some heads portrayed from life by his hand, which, although they have, for example, the nose crooked, one lip small and the other large, and other such like deformities, nevertheless resemble the life, through his having well caught the expression of the subject; whereas, on the other hand, many excellent masters have made pictures and portraits of absolute perfection with regard to art, but with no resemblance whatever to those that they are supposed to represent.[79]

One of the virtues for the study of Nature, according to Vasari, is that it enables the artist, in time, to paint from memory.

In the sixteenth century it became the mark of a fine painter when it was said he had actually surpassed nature, as is suggested in Bembo's lines inscribed on Raphel's tomb,

> Here lies Raphael.
> Nature feared to be conquered when he lived,
> And to die when he died.[80]

Vasari, a contemporary of Raphael, wrote,

> It may indeed be said with truth that the paintings of other masters are properly to be called paintings, but those of Raphael may be called Life itself; for the flesh quivers, the breathing is seen, the pulses beat, and life vibrated in all his figures.[81]

Aretino addressed the question of Art imitating Nature in a letter to the writer, Niccolo Franco. He first observed that in the works of Michelangelo Art and Nature are 'put to such

---

77 Quoted in Blunt, *Artistic Theory in Italy*, 88.
78 Quoted in Ibid., 89.
79 Quoted in Ibid., 89.
80 Quoted in Chambers, *The History of Taste*, 59.
81 Quoted in Ibid., 61.

excellent use that it would be hard to say which was master and which disciple.' He then offers what he calls a parable,

> The alchemists have employed every device that was thought up by their patience and their avarice, but they have never made gold. They have made only what seems like gold. Yet without having the least trouble in the world, Nature makes it fair and virgin …
> Certainly I imitate myself. I do so because Nature is a boon companion who makes us put forth our best efforts, and artifice is a crablouse which needs must fasten on someone else.[82]

This last thought he mentions again, in a different analogy regarding writing, in a letter to Doni.

> Now as to the difference between Art and Nature, every pedant discusses it, but not even those who agree that there is one, understand it. I assert this because true Art comes from a natural vivacity of the pen and is not obtained from the study of books. There is no perhaps about this: Nature is like a vine laden with grapes, and Art, her by-product, is the trellis which supports it.[83]

In a letter to another correspondent, however, Aretino seems to acknowledge some imperfections in Nature.

> For if we laugh at Nature who does her work haphazardly when we see among us a man with an enormous torso set upon weak and spindly legs, what shall we do at Art, which always observes law and order in anything it begins, and yet comes up with a painted picture that lacks all the proportion which is befitting?[84]

Tasso, writing on the nature of imitation in the literary form known as the 'dialogue,' observed,

> Imitation represents either the actions of men or their discussions, and although few deeds are performed without words and few discourses without activity, at least of the intellect, nevertheless I judge deeds to be very different from discourses. Discourses are proper to speculative men and deeds to active men, and there are, therefore, two chief kinds of imitation: one of action and active men and the other of speeches and men who reason. The first of these kinds, moreover, can be further divided into tragedy and comedy with their subdivisions, and the second kind admits similar categories … Dialogues are called tragic and comic only by analogy; tragedies and comedies, properly understood, imitate actions, but dialogues imitate discussions and participate in the tragic and comic only insofar as they deal with actions.[85]

---

82 Letter to Niccolo Franco, in Chubb, *The Letters of Pietro Aretino*, 70ff.
83 Letter to Doni, in Ibid., 297ff.
84 Letter to the sculptor, Danese, in Ibid., 214.
85 Torquato Tasso, 'Discourse on the Art of the Dialogue,' in *Tasso's Dialogues*, trans. Carnes Lord (Berkeley: University of California Press, 1982), 19ff.

Later he notes that the object of imitation in the dialogue is a discussion. From this he now defines the dialogue.

> The dialogue is an imitation of a discussion, written in prose, not intended for performance, and designed for the benefit of civil and speculative men.[86]

He also adds a note on the Liberal Arts,

> Dialogues can be written about arithmetic, geometry, music, and astronomy, as well as about moral, natural and divine philosophy …

Of these various writers, Pietro Aretino exhibited the most concern for the question of the nature of Art with respect to the character of the artist. In considering the nature of Art and the artist, he concluded that the essential gift is one of genetics and not instruction.

> The truth is that art is an innate gift for considering the excellencies of nature that comes to us when we are babes in swaddling clothes. That which is learned later may be called art, but it is not legitimate, whereas you could not call that art bastard which the spider uses in weaving his web.[87]

To another correspondent he states that neither the gift nor the skill is of any importance without heart.[88]

Aretino complains of a 'miraculous' painter, Sebastiano, who has not produced a promised painting, 'when he will do it is the secret of his temperamental nature which rivals that of any of his peers.'[89] He fails to see that this is part of the genetic 'gift' which separates the artist from ordinary men. We see the comment as an indication that painting, which for so many centuries was regarded as a craft, is now becoming an art.

Aretino makes a number of observations on the definition of great art in his letters. To a correspondent whom he is advising to edit his poetry more thoroughly, he observes, 'it is from being good and not merely just good enough that our compositions win their glory.'[90]

To another artist, Jacopo Tintore, he speaks of the importance of the talent given by God and of the goodness needed in the artist.

> It would not be fitting for you to forget to give thanks to God, Whose mercy and loving-kindness have given you a soul no less made for the pursuit of goodness than of art. You well know that the first can exist without the second but that the second cannot exist without the first …

---

86 Ibid., 25.
87 Letter to Coccio, in Chubb, *The Letters of Pietro Aretino*, 236.
88 Letter to Massiminiano Stampa, in Ibid., 39.
89 Letter to the marquis of Mantua, in Ibid., 33.
90 Letter to Giovanni Cazza, in Ibid., 145.

> But being good is not inconsistent with having either a genius or industrious hands, for goodness is not a quality of wit or skill, but of the soul and spirit. It is not an inherent part of our nature, but was breathed into us by Christ.[91]

In several letters to Michelangelo, Aretino mentions those supreme gifts which he recognized in this the greatest artist of his time. In a letter of 1537, in speaking of Michelangelo's ability in drawing human figures, he writes,

> For hidden in your hands lies the secret of a new technique, using which, the difficulties of broad concept (highest knowledge in the mystery of painting) is so easy to you that as you draw in human bodies, you reach the ultimate goal of art: you attain something that Art herself admits it is impossible to attain, for the concept, as you know, must circumscribe the whole and then complete it in such a way that in showing what it does not show, it is able to imply things.[92]

In this same letter, Aretino observes, 'the world has many kings and only one Michelangelo.'

In 1545, Aretino wrote another letter to Michelangelo, one in which he presumes to instruct the great artist on how to better paint his famous 'Last Judgment.' In one of the most famous misjudgments in Art history, Aretino writes,

> Yes, it is in a brothel rather than this holy chapel that your work belongs, and it would be better if you had denied Christ Himself than that you believed in Him and destroy the faith of others. Yet, at that, do not believe that your excellent and audacious masterpiece will go unpunished. Its very marvel makes it certain that your good name will be destroyed.[93]

In a letter to a musician and playwright, Aretino mentions Michelangelo again in a charming anecdote on the subject of modesty.

> It is certain, Parabosco, that you and [Michelangelo] have the same way of praising yourself for what you have accomplished in your arts, but you do so in so novel and ingenious a manner that your boastfulness must be renamed modesty.
>
> For, look, when people say to you that your tragedy, 'Progne' is beautiful, you answer: 'I am a musician, but not a poet,' but then when they praise the songs which you compose for certain well known motets, you shrug your shoulders in a very human fashion and reply: 'I am a poet, but not a musician.'
>
> That is exactly what Michelangelo does.
>
> He apologizes for the ceiling which he painted in the chapel by asserting that he is a sculptor, and not a painter, but when he hears people speak well of his statues of Giuliano and Lorenzo de' Medici, he shakes his head and cries: 'I paint; I don't crave stone.'[94]

---

91 Letter to Jacopo Tintore, February, 1545, in Ibid., 201.
92 Letter to Michelangelo, in Ibid., 79.
93 Letter to Michelangelo, November, 1545, in Ibid., 224.
94 Letter to M. Girolamo, in Ibid., 285.

Aretino also addressed the subject of skill in Art. In sending a painting by Titian to a nobleman, he wrote 'you must not value the gift itself but the skill which makes it valuable.'[95] To another correspondent, he writes,

> To speak plain to you, the best way to imitate Petrarch or Boccaccio is to express your own ideas with the same beauty and skill with which they beautifully and skillfully expressed theirs.[96]

Vasari, in his revised *Lives* of 1568, considers the question of natural skill as opposed to mere hard work, priding himself on his ability to work 'not only with the greatest possible rapidity, but also with incredible facility and without effort.' His chief concern seems to have been that extended work has the potential to dull the effect of the original burst of inspiration.

> Many painters ... achieve in the first sketch of their work, as though guided by a sort of fire of inspiration, something of the good and a certain measure of boldness; but afterwards, in finishing it, the boldness vanishes.[97]

In this regard he particularly criticizes the labor of the painter Uccello, adding,

> for the spirit of genius must be driven into action only when the intellect wishes to work and when the fire of inspiration is kindled, since it is then that excellent and divine qualities and marvelous conceptions are seen to issue forth.[98]

Vasari summarizes his views on this subject by declaring,

> Very great is the obligation that is owed to Heaven and to Nature by those who bring their works to birth without effort and with a certain grace which others cannot give to their creations either by study or by imitation.[99]

Vasari was also concerned with the question of judging Art. In his revised *Lives* of 1568, he introduced a new value of art, grace [*la grazia*], to replace both mere emotional communication and naturalism. He speaks of the importance of 'delicacy, refinement and supreme grace,' and not merely the object of correct proportions,[100] for in the end it is the eye which must appreciate.

---

95 Letter to count Massiminiano Stampa, in Ibid., 38.
96 Letter to Niccolo Franco, in Ibid., 70.
97 Quoted in Blunt, *Artistic Theory in Italy*, 95ff.
98 Quoted in Ibid., 95ff.
99 Quoted in Ibid., 96.
100 Quoted in Ibid., 93.

But no better standard can be applied than the judgment of the eye; for even though a thing is perfectly measured, if the eye is still offended, it will not cease to censure it.[101]

Regarding the purpose of Art, Pietro Aretino, who coined the nice phrase, 'Art is the richness of poverty,'[102] mentioned a utilitarian purpose of Art in the case of a statue of Venus, commissioned for the bedroom and intended to fill one 'with lustful thoughts.'[103]

The Council of Trent, and the Counter-Reformation in general, changed the purpose of painting in particular. An example can be seen in Comanini's dialogue, *Il Figino*, published in 1591. In this work an artistic patron, Guazzo, argues that the purpose of painting is pleasure, or as we would say today, 'Art for Art's sake.' A priest, however, answers him by stating that while it is true painting does give pleasure, its real subject is moral philosophy and therefore its purpose must be utility, not pleasure.[104]

The late sixteenth-century school of painting known as the Classicism attempted to respond to these views by the philosophers of the Counter-Reformation. Giovanni Lomazzo of Milan published in 1584 a treatise, *Trattato dell' Arte pittura, scultura ed architettura*, in which he attempted to define the academic principles of this movement. His basic contentions were,

1. Man invented painting, as writing, to aid the memory and incite the mind to religion.
2. The aim of both painting and sculpture is to resemble things as near to life as possible.
3. An emotion represented in a picture should arouse the same emotion in the viewer.
4. Without geometry and arithmetic, no man could hope to be a painter.[105]

As all of these writers were associated with the higher levels of society, it is no surprise to find a rather condescending attitude toward the general public. Aretino was often contemptuous of the public, whom he mentions would actually hiss a work in public,[106] calling them 'unnumbered hired hacks of ignorance'[107] and 'those who don't know anything.'[108] He apparently included the popes in the latter category, for in one letter he quotes the painter, Giovanni da Udine, saying of his grotesques painted for Leo and Clement, 'I did them to please fools.'[109]

---

101 Quoted in Ibid., 91,

102 Letter to Carolino, in Chubb, *The Letters of Pietro Aretino*, 298.

103 Letter to the marquis of Mantua, in Ibid., 33.

104 Blunt, *Artistic Theory in Italy*, 131ff.

105 Chambers, *The History of Taste*, 76ff.

106 Letter to Galeazzo Gonzaga, in Chubb, *The Letters of Pietro Aretino*, 173.

107 Letter to Giantonio da Foligno, in Ibid., 52.

108 Letter to Danese, in Ibid., 214.

109 Letter to Niccolo Franco, in Ibid., 70.

Equally strong views were expressed by Guicciardini,

> To speak of the people is really to speak of a mad animal gorged with a thousand and one errors and confusions, devoid of taste, of pleasure, of stability.[110]
>
> ......
>
> To speak of the people is to speak of a madman, a monster full of confusion and errors, whose vain opinions are as far from the truth as Spain, according to Ptolemy, is from India.[111]

Bruno, worrying about the reception of his *The Expulsion of the Triumphant Beast*, noted that 'the number of fools and the perverse is incomparably larger than that of the wise and the just.'[112]

ON THE AESTHETICS OF MUSIC

With respect from moving from views of the past toward ideas more familiar to us today, no field of Art was changing as rapidly as Music. First, the Greek myths were no longer a motivating factor. Bruno, in the introduction to his *The Expulsion of the Triumphant Beast*, reviews the long list of Greek myths and their supposed influence on the character of man. We see his often negative perspective in the following reference to Music and the Liberal Arts.

> There, where one sees the nine-stringed Lyre, ascends the Mother Muse with her nine daughters, Arithmetic, Geometry, Music, Logic, Poetry, Astrology, Physics, Metaphysics, and Ethics; whence, as a consequence, fall Ignorance, Inertia, and Bestiality.[113]

Perhaps the most important achievement in music by the humanists, which is not to suggest it is widely recognized today, was to move musical thinking away from the old Scholastic mathematics-based definition of music toward a more valid understanding of an art based on the communication of feelings. In the following passage by Girolamo Mei, we can see this change of philosophy beginning to take shape as he attempts to separate art from science—a distinctly Renaissance attitude.

> The true end of science is altogether different from that of art, since the end and proper aim of science is to consider every contingency of its subject and the causes and qualities of these purely for the sake of knowing truth from falsehood, without caring further how the arts will use this knowledge as an instrument or material or for otherwise gaining their ends ... The science of music goes about diligently investigating and considering all the qualities and properties of the

---

110 Guicciardini, *Maxims and Reflections*, C, 140.
111 Ibid., B, 123.
112 Bruno, *The Expulsion of the Triumphant Beast*, Explanatory Epistle, 70.
113 Ibid., 81.

existing constitution and ordering of musical tones, whether these are simple qualities or comparative, like the consonances, and this for no other aim than to come to know the truth itself, the perfect goal of all speculation, and as a by-product the false. It then lets art exploit as it sees fit without any limitation those tones about which science has learned the truth.[114]

Mei amplifies this in a letter to Galilei, after the latter had raised the question of practice following theory. We see here as well the prejudice toward the practical musician, as compared with the theorist, which was characteristic of one point of view in the Renaissance and remains with us today in some academic circles. The origin of this prejudice, of course, was in medieval Church dogma. Modern clinical research regarding the separate, but equal, natures of the twin hemispheres of the brain completely debunk this entire line of thought.

> You ask me in yours of 17 August how it happens that the practitioner does not follow at all the designs of the theorist, as he should, since the theorist gives the reason why. My answer to you is that considering and understanding are one thing and putting into operation another. The former belongs to the intellect and the latter to the sense. However, the sense of hearing is not as perfect as the judgment of the intellect because of the material and other circumstances that always necessarily accompany the former. Thus the practitioner, having simply to satisfy the sense, does not need as much refinement and punctiliousness, so to speak, as the theorist requires. He does not esteem reason as much as the theorist and is content whenever his art succeeds in satisfying the sense without going any further, his end being none other than this.[115]

With regard to the movement toward a modern understanding of aesthetics in music, the most important aspect of the abandonment of mathematics was the simultaneous rejection of the old artificial polyphonic systems. For the modern musicologists, who have greatly limited our understanding of Renaissance music by pretending that Church music is the sum and content of Renaissance music, to read the suggestions of these humanists that polyphony be abandoned is a very difficult pill to swallow. It is from this perspective that Claude Palisca, in his study of the letters of Mei to Galilei and Bardi, writes,

> It would be too easy to point out Mei's errors of … judgment. For example, his wholesale condemnation of the polyphonic music of his contemporaries, which hardly inspires confidence in either his musical experience or sensitivity, invites refutation.[116]

Curiously, a few pages later Palisca stresses that Mei was not a musician, adding,

---

114 Quoted in Girolamo Mei, *Letters on Ancient and Modern Music*, trans. Claude Palisca (American Institute of Musicology, 1960), 65.
115 Quoted in Ibid., 66.
116 Ibid., x.

> That he was not a musician and did not share the prejudices of the musical theorists of his time was probably one of his greatest advantages, for it saved him from falling into the errors of his contemporaries.[117]

Palisca does not explain, here, what errors of the contemporaries he had in mind, but we must point out that it was primarily the music theorists who were still holding on to polyphony and its old Scholastic, mathematics heritage.

Mei's study of ancient Greek music had convinced him that the purpose of music should not be pleasant entertainment. In his first letter to Galilei he criticized him for suggesting that the purpose of music was for the 'delectation of the ear with harmony.' Likewise he disapproved of Zarlino's definition of the purpose of music being 'edifying entertainment.'

> To Mei such a mean goal was unworthy of an art extolled by the ancient philosophers. Music should not be content with delighting the ear; it should stir men's emotions.[118]

In Mei's view, music should aspire to the same aesthetic end as that expressed in Aristotle's *Poetics*: music should purge men of their passions not by soothing them but by arousing in them those very passions.[119] He, as others,[120] felt sixteenth-century music failed to do this, that polyphony, in particular, all sounded the same. Polyphony reminded him of men pulling with all their forces on ropes from opposite directions. With its separate parts, polyphony,

> conveys to the soul of the listener at the same time diverse and contrary affections as it mixes indistinctly together melodies and Tones that are completely dissimilar and of natures contrary to each other.[121]

This last observation is particularly relevant in view of modern clinical research which proves both that the direction and contour of melody alone carries meaning for most listeners and that the brain has genetic difficulty in understanding such variations as melodies played in retrograde.

These views, together with the fact that Mei was convinced that the ancient Greeks knew no harmony, contributed to his principal objection that polyphony rendered the words unintelligible. This view was an important step on the way to monody and Baroque opera.

> Almost in despite of nature, God's minister, which perfected man by giving him speech so that he could understand the thoughts of others and could make his own understood, they prefer to strive to imitate the warbling and lowing of beasts.[122]

---

[117] Ibid., 2.

[118] Ibid., 11.

[119] Ibid., 70.

[120] Ibid., 72, mentions similar views by Cirillo Franco (1549) and Don Nicola Vincentino (1551).

[121] Quoted in Ibid., 73.

[122] Quoted in Ibid., 74.

Bruno, in a discussion of whether Pleasure is found in goods or wealth, mentions in passing his view of Beauty in music.

> The beauty of the music and the excellence of someone's harmony should not be attributed more to the lyre and to the instrument than to the art and to the artist who produces them.[123]

A report by Gabriele Bombasi of the 1568 performance in Reggio Emilia of the tragedy *L'Alidoro*, speaks of the feelings of the (now lost) music as being so direct in their communication as to be as effective as speech itself.

> Much thought had been given to these by most excellent musicians, who, having looked deeply into their meaning, wrote the songs for them, imitating the words so felicitously, that one would sooner call them speeches than songs ... In the perorations, in the prayers to the gods, in the exclamations, complaints, questions, weeping and sighing [the songs] expressed the affections of the soul as if, far from being fictitious, they came from real feelings of the heart.[124]

Carlo Valgulio, a secretary to the papal treasurer (1481–1485) and later to cardinal Cesare Borgia, translator of Plutarch's 'De musica,' wrote eloquently on the fundamental importance of music. He published in 1509 an answer to some unknown opponent of music,[125] in which he begins by expressing his shock that there could be anyone who did not appreciate music.

> I believe that nothing can be conceived so opposed to reason, so very abhorrent to the senses, and so inimical to common nature and ominous, that it could not be found in the mind of some man. Who would have ever thought that he could discover a man who is so boorish, savage, and grim or so stupid, dull and vile that he hates musical songs, whether issuing from the human voice or instruments, who not only carries this hate around in silence but boasts of it and considers it redounds to his praise. Nothing in the human species exists that is more joyful and sweet, nothing that is more blessed.

He next discusses the relationship of celestial harmony to the parts of the human soul. In the soul he found, unfortunately, that the creator failed to achieve the 'kind of symphony' found in the sky. Accordingly, in man's soul there is a certain amount of internal conflict, which can be brought into harmony by music.

> Yet if that musical moderation and the harmonic temperament were not implanted in our souls by nature, which would have made the diverse appetitive parts of the soul concordant and consonant, nevertheless divine goodness and providence, coming to our aid, granted us by a certain special gift the power and potential for finding and comparing.
> If we call forth the resource of this faculty and summon our effort and careful diligence and study, and if we bring in music, with its most sweet connections and its very suave intervals, we

---

123 Bruno, *The Expulsion of the Triumphant Beast*, 167ff [II, ii].
124 Quoted in Pirrotta, *Music and Theatre*, 202.
125 Quoted in Palisca, *Humanism in Italian Renaissance Musical Thought*, 100ff.

shall be able to tune,[126] almost like strings, the contrary and diverse motions of our souls, and we shall always be able to make them consonant among themselves so that those who are lacking in reason by nature always would obey reason ... If, with the help and resources of music, we attain a motion of our souls similar to the celestial revolutions, we shall maintain constancy and we shall enjoy happiness and an almost heavenly grace ... Therefore anyone who loves peace, tranquility, harmony, and happiness in himself and within the household walls and in the city must have, cultivate, venerate, and embrace music with all effort and zeal and with it musicians too.

We have a particularly interesting personal view of music in the famous *Autobiography* of Benvenuto Cellini. Early in his book he mentions that his father was a proficient musician and was, in fact, a member of the civic wind band of Florence.[127] Cellini speaks often of his father's fervent desire that his son devote himself to music, and just as often of his own preference not to do so. In a typical passage, Cellini clearly suggests that the career of musician was somewhat less than honorable.

> I used to play treble in concert with the musicians of the palace before the Signory, following my notes ... The Gonfalonier, that is, Soderini, ... was wont to say to my father: 'Maestro Giovanni, beside music, teach the boy those other arts which do you so much honor.' To which my father answered: 'I do not wish him to practice any art but playing and composing; for in this profession I hope to make him the greatest man of the world, if God prolongs his life.' To these words one of the old counselors made answer: 'Ah! Maestro Giovanni, do what the Gonfalonier tells you! for why should he never become anything more than a good musician?'[128]

Despite his claim that he found no satisfaction in music, which he concentrated on until age fifteen, he often reveals how much his playing meant to his father.

> I did not, however, neglect to gratify my good father from time to time by playing on the [shawm] or cornett. Each time he heard me, I used to make his tears fall accompanied with deep-drawn sighs of satisfaction. My filial piety often made me give him that contentment, and induced me to pretend that I enjoyed the music too.[129]

In another place, his father pleas,

> My dear son, I too in my time was a good draughtsman; but for recreation, after such stupendous labors, and for the love of me who am your father, who begat you and brought you up and implanted so many honorable talents in you, for the sake of recreation, I say, will not you

---

126 Italians of this period used the term 'distemper' to mean one is 'out of tune,' whereas we apply it only to mad dogs!

127 Cellini, *The Life of Benvenuto Cellini*, I, v. He suggests that most of these musicians had other professions, primarily in the silk and wool trades.

128 Ibid., I, vi.

129 Ibid., I, vii. Cellini's description of his performance with the pope's wind band, we have quoted elsewhere.

promise sometimes to take in hand your [shawm] and that seductive cornett, and to play upon them to your heart's content, inviting the delight of music?[130]

Taking his book as a whole, one finds two quite different attitudes toward music by this famous goldsmith. All references to music in his youth, when he was forced to study, are characterized by strong negative adjectives. For example,

> A certain pupil of my father's, moved by his own bad nature, suggested to the Cardinal that he ought to send me to Bologna, in order to learn to play well from a great master there. The name of his master was Antonio, and he was in truth a worthy man in the musician's art. The Cardinal said to my father that, if he sent me there, he would give me letters of recommendation and support. My father, dying with joy at such an opportunity, sent me off; and I being eager to see the world, went with good grace.
>
> When I reached Bologna, I put myself under a certain Maestro Ercole del Piffero, and began to earn something by my trade. In the meantime I used to go every day to take my music-lesson, and in a few weeks made considerable progress in that accursed art.[131]
>
> ……
>
> My father, in the meanwhile, kept writing piteous entreaties that I should return to him; and in every letter bade me not to lose the music he had taught me with such trouble. On this, I suddenly gave up all wish to go back to him; so much did I hate that accursed music; and I felt as though of a truth I were in paradise the whole year I stayed at Pisa, where I never played the [shawm].[132]

On the other hand, when Cellini was older, and removed from his father's demands that he study music, his attitude toward music was quite different. Now he praises its virtues, as we see first in a passage describing his infatuation with a young boy.

> Paulino was the best-mannered, the most honest, and the most beautiful boy I ever saw in my whole life. His modest ways and actions, together with his superlative beauty and his devotion to myself, bred in me as great an affection for him as a man's breast can hold. This passionate love led me oftentimes to delight the lad with music; for I observed that his marvelous features, which by complexion wore a tone of modest melancholy, brightened up, and when I took my cornett, broke into a smile so lovely and so sweet, that I do not marvel at the silly stories which the Greeks have written about the deities of heaven.[133]

Similar comments can be found throughout his discussion of his later life.

> I took much pleasure in music.[134]
>
> ……

---

130 Ibid., I, ix.
131 Ibid., I, ix.
132 Ibid., I, xi.
133 Ibid., I, xxiii.
134 Ibid., I, xxxiv.

> ... my charming art of music ...[135]

And finally, in explaining an art work made for the king of France, in which various allegorical figures represented philosophy and various branches of the arts and sciences, Cellini remarked to the king, as part of his explanation,

> The third is Music, which cannot be omitted from the sphere of intellectual culture.[136]

Regarding the purposes of Music, we first find in Bruno a reference which bears strong similarity with the concept of 'catharsis' argued for by Aristotle. In an imagined discussion of the Greek gods, he has the various muses thank Jove for their domain. Among them, Music gives thanks that 'there are [more] harmonic forms and symphonies that phantasy could combine.' Then,

> Jove ordered his first-born, Minerva, to hand him the box he kept under the pillow on his bed, after which he drew forth nine boxes containing nine collyria, prescribed to purge the human mind in respect both to its knowledge and to its disposition. And to begin with he gave three of them to the first three [Muses, Arithmetic, Geometry, and Music], saying to them: 'Here for you is the best unguent with which you will be able to purge and make clear your perceptive virtue as regards the number, the size and the harmonious proportion of sensible things.'[137]

The most frequent purpose of Music found in early literature is to offer solace to the listener. Pietro Aretino mentions this once in a reference to 'harmonies that sooth my ears all night long'[138] and again in a related reference to 'persons, who, frightened out of their wits by the shadows of the night, start singing at the top of their lungs.'[139]

Machiavelli, in some 'Tercets on Ingratitude or Envy,' addressed to Giovanni Folchi, begins by saying,

> By singing, then, I strive to take from my heart and to bridle that sorrow for my afflictions that madly pursues my soul ...[140]

In the second intermedio for the comedy *La vedova*, by Giovanbattista Cini, given in Florence in 1569, a sorceress calls us the spirits of poets, painters, sculptors and musicians, who respond, 'the great distress is quickly dispelled, and sweet rejoicing returns for ever.'[141]

---

135 Ibid., I, xxxvii.

136 Ibid., II, xxii.

137 Bruno, *The Expulsion of the Triumphant Beast*, 181ff [II, iii].

138 Letter to Domenico Bolani, in Ibid., 87.

139 Letter to Sinistro, in Ibid., 236.

140 Machiavelli, *The Chief Works*, II, 740.

141 Quoted in Pirrotta, *Music and Theatre*, 190.

A somewhat more practical purpose of music is given by Aretino when he advises a correspondent,

> as all women know, music, songs and letters are the key you need to unlock the gates of their chastity.[142]

Another hallmark of humanism and its escape from the influence of the Church can be seen in the appearance of real musical humor in the Renaissance. An attractive example is the *Frottole libro tertio*, in Petrucci's 1505 collection for solo voice and three instrumentals. When the text speaks of a cat meowing, the three instrumentalists stop playing and voice 'Gnao' (Italian for meow) on specified pitches.

As the ancient Greek writings on music became available in the Renaissance they evidently stimulated thought on that topic which the Greeks seemed to take so seriously, the effect of music on man and his behavior. Some of the references to this topic in sixteenth-century Italy read as if their authors were also quite serious about this. A letter from the first half of the century by one, Matteo Nardo, maintains,

> Whenever doctors of music have to compose a song [Canzone] they are accustomed to ask themselves conscientiously to what end they might be starting and composing it, that is what affections of the soul they ought to arouse with the piece.[143]

But there is a point to be made, even if they were wrong in their practical supposition that the text carried the emotions, for the discussion does tell us that they were thinking about music and its relationship with feeling. Like the ancient Greeks themselves, they were trying to find a way to account for what they were seeing in everyday performance—musicians and listeners being moved by music. The discussion itself is a hallmark of the Renaissance.

THE ACADEMIES

The institutions known as Academies in Renaissance Italy and France were not educational institutions in the modern sense of the word, but more like high level gatherings of intellectuals for discussion and debate. They had begun from mostly philological purposes, for the modern languages were still being formed and none yet enjoyed the respect of Latin.

In retrospect the most influential of these activities was centered in Florence and Marsilio Ficino. Because of the family connections between the Medici and the aristocrats in France, the intellectual ties between Florence and Paris were inseparable.

---

142 Letter to Ambrogio degli Eusebii, in Chubb, *The Letters of Pietro Aretino*, 59.
143 Quoted in Palisca, *Humanism in Italian Renaissance Musical Thought*, 342.

The influence of the Church in Italy results in a more noticeable religious association with the fifteenth-century Italian academies. They viewed the poet as a kind of prophet, in so far as he was divinely inspired. Ficino had stated,

> All those who have invented anything great in any of the nobler arts did so especially when they took refuge in the citadel of the Soul.[144]

It was in this frame of understanding that Ficino also spoke of Love, that Love is more effective than the intellect in search of truth and that 'Love is the Teacher and Ruler of the Arts.'[145]

But these academies can also be looked upon as part of the humanist movement and it was from this perspective that they played an influence on developments in the field of music. Ficino himself was a performing musician and classical scholar, thus was a man with a broad view of culture.

> Our century like a golden age restored to light the liberal arts that were nearly extinct: grammar, poetry, rhetoric, painting, sculpture, architecture, music and the ancient performance of songs with the Orphic lyre.[146]

Because both the Italian and French intellectuals had taken from the ancient Greek writers a concept of music being closely related to the unseen organization of the world, it is no surprise that for them music included poetry and vice versa. Ficino, however, was instrumental in establishing the belief, so strongly held by the humanists, that in sung poetry the emphasis must be on the words, and not the music. Ficino subscribed to the ancient Greek belief that music was important for helping the soul to retune itself to the cosmic, or divine, harmony. No doubt it was believed that this could be observed regularly in performance. A later French philosopher, Pontus de Tyard, who was much influenced by Ficino, used to tell of a banquet in Milan when,

> a lute player ravished the guests utterly out of themselves by his divinely languorous playing; and then, by a more vigorous tune, restored to them the souls which he had before stolen.[147]

However, for Ficino himself it was clear that the greater affect on man came from the poetry.

> But poetry is superior to music, since through the words it speaks not only to the ear but also directly to the mind. Therefore its origin is not in the harmony of the spheres, but rather in the

---

144 Quoted in Frances Yates, *The French Academies of the Sixteenth Century* (London: University of London, 1947; Nendeln: Kraus Reprint, 1968), 4.

145 Ibid., 5.

146 Ibid., 4.

147 Ibid., 41.

music of the divine mind itself, and through its effect it can lead the listener directly to God Himself.[148]

From the perspective of the humanists, who understood the proper relationship between music and the communication of feelings, one can see that the growing dissatisfaction, apparent already in the fifteenth century, with the polyphonic style was a contributing factor in the development of monody in the following century. Consequently, the Camerata considered the madrigal, which expressed feelings in direct, and often somewhat homophonic passages, the highest form of expression in music.[149] The monody style, which is generally credited to the Camerata, also had roots in the villanelle, villotte and canzonette, which were melody oriented styles and were subject to improvisation, as monody would also be.[150]

ART MUSIC

In these books, we have often suggested that brief performances held when banquets were concluded, after the eating was finished, were the earliest representatives of concerts in the modern meaning of the word, that is where persons were contemplative listeners. Cellini, in his autobiography, describes precisely such a concert.

> The supper was followed by a short concert of delightful music, voices joining in harmony with instruments; and forasmuch as they were singing and playing from the book …[151]

Two listeners in particular, Cellini reports, 'dropped their earlier tone of banter, exchanging it for well-weighed terms of sober heartfelt admiration.'

The literature of sixteenth-century Italy contains some touching descriptions of Art Song. In Bandello's Tale, 'Genivera La Blonde,' for example, a gentleman has the dance musicians stop playing so that a lady can sing a song of love. We are told that the emotions of the song could be read in her face and the nobleman declared that 'in his life he had not heard music of more delight.'[152]

Pietro Aretino also left us an interesting description of an Art singer.

> There is no doubt … that our pleasures are the panders of our senses, and that being the case, the things which Franceschina sang yesterday to the tune of her lute, penetrated my heart with so sweet a sort of musical persuasion, that I must needs come to the point of amorous conjunction.

---

148 Ibid., 40.

149 Nino Pirrotta, in *Music and Culture in Italy from the Middle Ages to the Baroque* (Cambridge: Harvard University Press, 1984), 220.

150 Ibid., 221. Pirrotta credits the *Commedia dell'Arte* for laying some of the foundations for improvisation, see Ibid., 343ff.

151 Cellini, *The Life of Benvenuto Cellini*, I, xxx.

152 Bandello, *Tragical Tales*, 509ff.

> Certainly in this lady are found all three kinds of beauty; that of the body, that of the mind, and that of the voice, wherefore those who are wise, note the first with their eyes, the second with their mind, and the third with their ears. Yea, through the means of the above-named senses, she so pleases the spirits of anyone who hears her, understands her, and sees her that he dwells in heaven, not on earth.

In another book, this author describes the performance of a four-part madrigal in a private home.

> While I was being so greatly complimented, the great virtue of music arrived, music which went to the core of my soul. There were four singers, who were looking in a book, and another fellow with a silver lute, which was tuned to their voices. The sang: 'Divine eyes, so calm, so pure …'[153]

In this same work he provides us with some idea of the wide range of songs sung by the solo singer.

> NANNA. Then a skillful rebec player appeared and, having tuned his instrument, sang some strange tales.
> PIPPA. May God save you, what did he sing about?
> NANNA. He sang of the hostility that heat has for cold, and cold for heat. He sang of why the days of summer are long and those of winter short. He sang of the link between lightning and thunder, thunder and the flash, the flash and the cloud, the cloud and the clear sky. He sang about where the rain stays when the weather is good, and where good weather goes when it rains. He sang of hail, hoar frost, snow and mist. He sang, I believe, of the woman who rents out rooms, who refrains from laughter when her lodgers weep, and of another woman who refrains from weeping when they laugh; and at the end he sang about the fire which flickers in the butt-end of a glowworm, and as to whether a grasshopper chirps with its body or its mouth.[154]

And then, there is this curious observation by Bruno.

> In these times the lyre has become the principal instrument for charlatans, by means of which they win over and hold their audience and more easily sell their pills and vials, just as the rebec has now become the instrument of blind mendicants.[155]

The out-door solo singer is most often described singing a serenade, as we read in Bandello's Tale, 'Pandora of Milan.'

> And omitting no means which might move her to take compassion of his pain, he forgot not to pass divers times before her lodging, with a lute or other music of soft melody; whereunto, also,

---

153 Aretino, *Dialogues*, 54ff.
154 Ibid., 242.
155 Bruno, *The Expulsion of the Triumphant Beast*, 181 [II, iii].

he accorded his voice with notes of pleasant tune, and that with such a grace of great delight, that the sweet noise of his harmony seemed a thousand times of more enticing melody than the heavenly [singing] of the nightingale. Wherewith, in short time, he kindled a fire in the heart of this young wanton …[156]

Aretino describes a serenade of a lower order and provides the lyrics.

Barely had Messer Sonnet-Singer received her yes than he gathered together a mob of paper-smudgers and song-screechers and told them: 'I want to give a serenade to a little married whore, a very pretty little piece whom I shall soon muss up a bit. And to show you that this is true, here's a letter in her own hand.' Then he showed them a few lines she had scrawled, and they laughed long and loud over it; then, taking up a lute, he tuned it in a jiffy and struck off a trill in real peasant style. Then, giving a brazen shout, he stationed himself beneath the window of his lady love, which looked out on a lane down which about one person passed each year. Leaning his back against the wall, fitting his instrument to his chest, he lifted his face and, while she glided about above, flashing for moments at the window, he softly chanted this song:
For all the gold in the world, Lady,
In praising you I would not speak a lie,
For then I would shame both myself and you.
No, by God! I will never claim
That your mouth is scented like India or Sabine,
Nor that your hair
Is lovelier than gold.
Nor that love lodges in your eyes,,
Nor that the sun robs its radiance from them …
And have such grace that, to do it
To you a hermit would desert his vows.
Though I will not say you are divine,
And piss orange water instead of urine.[157]

In another place in this work a man remembered 'a lovely morning serenade he gave the widow, for which he gathered together the best musicians in Italy and with and without instruments sang several newly composed verses.'[158]

In terms of larger scale vocal music, we must not forget that the famous Camerata, which we associate with the birth of opera, had its beginnings in the sixteenth century. It seems clear that an important focus of the Camerata's discussions on music, aside from their dreams of a Classic revival, was relative to the communication of feelings. Some of the music of the earliest proto-type operas is lost, making it difficult to appreciate the immediate application of this idea. However, Peri said of Cavalieri's work that its purpose was to use the stage to

---

156 Bandello, *Tragical Tales*, 161ff.
157 Aretino, *Dialogues*, 297ff.
158 Ibid., 356ff. The lyrics for two additional songs are given here.

underline action and emotion and an account of Cavalieri's lost *La Disperazione di Fileno* mentions that the singing of Archilei 'moved the audience to tears.'[159]

This movement can be seen even earlier than the meetings of the Camerata. An anonymous chronicler of a performance of the tragedy *Alidoro*, given in Reggio in 1568, includes the following description.

> An infinite number of singers and instrumentalists started performing together in a truly divine manner; you could hear at once from the gravity of the sound, which was by turns terrible and sad, that the play that was being performed could not be other than tragic ... Not only the music of the opening but all the music heard later [was made] to reflect the terrible and sad qualities of the tragedy and to point to every change of mood.[160]

According to Pirrotta, the whole idea of the *stile recitativo* and *stile rappresentativo* lay not 'so much in the adherence to recitation of the text ... as in the vivid immediacy with which a character's inner affective reactions were to be presented live to the audience.'[161]

Finally, the first generation of original keyboard music is not discussed in this literature with respect to its musical content. Bruno, however, makes a reference to the keyboard style of a young lady as being so light in touch that 'you couldn't make out if she is of corporeal or incorporeal substance.'[162]

EDUCATIONAL MUSIC

Giulio del Bene proposed to the *Accademia degli Alterati* an educational program, inspired by Aristotle's 'Poetics,' which would alter the human personality by imitating nature through the arts. With regard to music, he noted,

> Through music learn to be well ordered and constituted in our minds and to move the affections no less than is done through rhetoric and for delighting and uplifting us in the trials that every day we sustain in human activities.[163]

He also finds that poetry only imitates the emotions, whereas music, presumably, is the real thing. Finally, to this Accademia, Del Bene offers a tpyical prescription for becoming a 'Renaissance man.' He tells them that if they want to 'alter' their minds for the better they should,

---

159 Pirrotta, in *Music and Culture in Italy from the Middle Ages to the Baroque*, 225.

160 Ibid., 230ff.

161 Ibid., 280.

162 Bruno, *Cause, Principle and Unity*, 120.

163 Quoted in Palisca, *Humanism in Italian Renaissance Musical Thought*, 337.

read lectures, compose sonnets, recite orations, write tragedies, canzoni, madrigals, and every other sort of composition, discuss philosophy, and speak extemporaneously on politics, ethics, and poetics.[164]

FUNCTIONAL MUSIC

A passage in Machiavelli's short story, 'Belfagor,' perhaps provides us with a glimpse of the use of ceremonial music in outdoor Church functions.

> So arrange to have set up in the square of Notre Dame a platform big enough to hold all your barons and all the clergy of this city [Florence]; have the platform decorated with cloth of silk and of gold; set up in the middle of it an altar, and Sunday morning I want you and the clergy and all your princes and barons, with regal splendor, with gorgeous and rich costumes, to assemble there; after celebrating a solemn mass ... Besides this, I need to have ready on one side of the square at least twenty persons with drums, horns, kettledrums, bagpipes, shawms, cymbals and noise-makers of every sort; these men, when I lift my hat, will strike up on their instruments and as they play will come toward the platform.[165]

Not everyone enjoyed such displays. Pressure on the Church to take note of the popularity of secular music had been growing since the thirteenth century, as so wonderfully personified in that bishop who asked, 'Why does the devil have all the good tunes?' That there had been some inroads must be assumed by the fact that the practice of music became a topic of the Council of Trent (1545–1563), one of the notable hallmarks of the late sixteenth century conservative movement in Italy. Indeed, the Council of Trent took a very strong and backward looking position in issuing, on 10 September 1562, the following aesthetic goals for Church music.

> All things should indeed be so ordered that the Masses, whether they be celebrated with or without singing, may reach tranquilly into the ears and hearts of those who hear them, when everything is executed clearly and at the right speed. In the case of those Masses which are celebrated with singing and with organ, let nothing profane be intermingled, but only hymns and divine praises. The whole plan of singing in musical modes should be constituted not to give empty pleasure to the ear, but in such a way that the words may be clearly understood by all, and thus the hearts of the listeners be drawn to the desire of heavenly harmonies, in the contemplation of the joys of the blessed ... They shall also banish from church all music that contains, whether in the singing or in the organ playing, things that are lascivious or impure.[166]

---

164 Quoted in Ibid., 338.
165 Machiavelli, *The Chief Works*, II, 876.
166 Quoted in Gustave Reese, *Music in the Renaissance* (New York: Norton, 1959), 449.

On September 17 the Council voted to ban from Church music 'all seductive or impure melodies, whether instrumental or vocal, all vain and worldly texts, all outcries and uproars.'

There was serious discussion aimed at the elimination of polyphony. These views came not only from those conservatives who wanted to return to pure chant, but also from the more humanistic prelates who saw polyphony as making the Sacred words unintelligible. One of the latter, Cardinal Borromeo wrote in January 1565,

> I would like you to speak to the master of the chapel there and tell him to reform the singing so that the words may be as intelligible as possible, as you know is ordered by the Council.[167]

The following March the cardinal commissioned a work to demonstrate the new requirements.

> I desire above all that the matter of the intelligible music succeed according to the hope you have given me. Therefore I would like you to order Ruffo, in my name, to compose a Mass which should be as clear as possible and send it to me here.[168]

By April some works had been composed and the papal singers were ordered to gather in the home of Cardinal Vitellozzi 'to sing some Masses, and test whether the words could be understood, as their Eminences desire.'[169] The result was some compositions in a very simple, even innocuous, homophonic style. Thus, when Ruffo published some of the Masses he had written in the required new style, he dedicated the publication to a politician from Milan, Antonello Arcimboldo, disclaiming to some degree his own work in a clever confession of ignorance.

> When compelled to undertake that task which the Most Illustrious and Most Reverend Cardinal Borromeo formerly laid upon me—that, according to the decree of the sacred Council of Trent, I was to compose some Masses … which should avoid everything of a profane and idle manner in worship, and that the powerful and sweet sound of the voices should soothe and caress the ears of the listeners in a pious, religious, and holy way—I was deeply ignorant which way to turn. You then, however, who were of the same sentiments, came forth to me … and, as it were, showed me the Prototype of this manner of composing music. Accordingly, guided by your help, I composed one Mass in this way: so that the numbers of the syllables and the voices and tones together should be clearly and distinctly understood and perceived by the pious listeners.[170]

We also find in this literature references to changing tastes in music and performance practice. Some passages remind us that, as in any age, not all musicians were good musicians. From the records of the Scuola de San Rocco for 16 July 1531, we reads,

---

167 Quoted in Lewis Lockwood, 'Vincenzo Ruffo and Musical Reform after the Council of Trent,' *The Musical Quarterly* 43, no. 3 (July, 1957): 348, http://www.jstor.org/stable/740279.

168 Quoted in Ibid., 349.

169 Quoted in Ibid., 353.

170 Quoted in Ibid., 354.

> ... to change the players of harp and lute that served us badly to those players who were at the School on Corpus Christi Day ...[171]

An example of the use of music to relieve the boredom of travel is found in the autobiography of Cellini, where he mentions singing 'the whole way to Rome,' with another young artist.[172]

We have an extensive discussion of military music by Machiavelli, in his 'The Art of War.' Particularly interesting is his call for the re-establishment of the practice of marching to music, a military technique which had not been practiced since the time of the Roman army. Machiavelli's argument had considerable influence on Baroque military theorists, who, in fact, reinstituted coordinated marching together with their new standing armies.

> When well handled, this music regulates the army, which by moving in paces that correspond to its beats, easily keeps in rank. Thence it is that the ancients had whistles and fifes [aulos] and musical instruments perfectly modulated; because, just as one who dances moves in time with music and keeping with it does not err, so an army moving in obedience to music does not get disordered. And therefore they varied the music according as they wished to vary the movement and according as they wished to stir up or quiet or to make firm the spirits of the men. As the music was of various kinds, they gave it various names. Doric music produced firmness, Phrygian produced impetuosity. Hence they say that when Alexander was at table and someone played Phrygian music, it excited his spirit so much that he laid his hands on his weapons. It would be necessary to find all these modes again, and if that were difficult, we should at least not omit those that teach the soldiers to obey. Each commander can vary them at will, so long as with practice he accustoms the ears of his soldiers to recognize them. But today military music generally yields no other benefit than the making of a noise.[173]
>
> ......
>
> Because the success of this method of giving orders depends upon the music, I shall tell what music the ancients used. The Lacedaemonians, as Thucydides says, in their armies used flutes [aulos], judging that harmony most apt to make their armies march with firmness and not with excitement. Moved by the same reason, the Carthaginians in their first attack used the lyre. Halyattes king of Lydia used in war the lyre and the flute. But Alexander the Great and the Romans used horns and bugles, thinking that by means of such instruments they enkindled the spirits of their soldiers and made them fight more vigorously. So as in giving weapons to the army we have followed the Greek and Roman manner, in distributing the instruments of music we keep to the habits of the two nations. Therefore near the general I place the trumpets, as better fitted than any other music to be heard in the midst of noise of every kind. All the other instruments near the constables and the officers of battalions I wish to be little drums and flutes, played not as they now are in armies but as they are usually played at banquets. The

---

171 Denis Arnold, 'Music at the Scuola de San Rocco,' *Music and Letters* 40, no. 3 (July, 1959): 232, http://www.jstor.org/stable/729389.
172 Cellini, *The Life of Benvenuto Cellini*, I, xiii.
173 Machiavelli, *The Chief Works*, II, 621.

general, then, indicates with the trumpets when the soldiers are to stop or to go forward or to go backward, when the artillery is to fire, when the irregular velites are to move and, with the variety of such music, he makes plain to the army all the movements that in ordinary course can be made plain. These trumpets then are followed by the drums. In this exercise, because it is very important, the general thoroughly trains his army. The cavalry use trumpets in the same way, but of less power and different tone from those of the general.[174]

......

And if you give orders with music, you must make sure that there be such difference between one kind and the other that one cannot be mistaken for the other ... And everything that can be done with words should be so done; the others should be done with music.[175]

As the trumpet was so associated with battle, it is no surprise that Bruno remarks, 'There is no one among you who is not disturbed by the sound of the trumpet.'[176]

ENTERTAINMENT MUSIC

We find in this literature some views which reflect a general denigration of entertainment. Guicciardini, for example, writes,

> I believe there is nothing worse in this world than levity. For lighthearted men are the ready instruments of any party, no matter how bad, dangerous, or pernicious. Therefore, flee from them as you would from fire.[177]

And Machiavelli observes,

> The friendship of [busybodies] can be gained by pleasing them with banquets and entertainments.[178]

Pietro Aretino makes some interesting observations on the modern jongleur, the street singer, in a letter of 1545. The unknown recipient of this letter had apparently sung some of Aretino's poetry in a piazza in Ferrara. Aretino comments that he is criticized by his 'intellectual snob' friends because he finds pleasure in the fact that he is performed in public in this fashion.

> Poor fellows! They do not know that your profession entertains all the dead-beats of the world ...

---

174 Ibid., II, 646ff.
175 Ibid., II, 669ff.
176 Bruno, *The Expulsion of the Triumphant Beast*, 105 [I, ii].
177 Guicciardini, *Maxims and Reflections*, C, 167.
178 Machiavelli, *The Chief Works*, I, 117.

Street singers, ah? They alone are the ones who, possessing nothing, obtain all, and what is more important, while they posture before the crowd as buffoons, the crowd, making itself the ape of their endeavors, chatters back at them, goes into contortions and splits its jaws laughing …

The street singers I say, set forth with their saddlebags filled with jests, chatter, presumption, persuasive talk, lies, madnesses, intrigues, ballads, and curses. The latter they hurl at themselves when, wounded and slashed, they find the oil that they advertised as the best in the world, absolutely worthless to heal the dagger strokes they get for their jests. They go where their legs take them, and they find money, credit, friendships, harlotries, relatives, offices, together with griefs and woes …

But I don't want to go into the subject any further for then I would have to take up princes, captains, merchants, poets, lawyers, patricians, pedagogues and friars and then they would say I was a whole regiment of Pasquinos.[179]

Finally, aiming for a complete picture and for lack of knowing where else to place this material, we should at least mention Aretino *Dialogues* (1536, 1556), which offer some interesting observations on musical practice. Music is frequently mentioned in this work as an analogy, usually in some pornographic context. A typical example reads,

In the finale the nuns on the bed with the two young men, the General and the sister he was mounted on, together with the fellow at his behind, and, last of all, the nun with her Murano prodder, agreed to do it together as choristers sing in unison, or more to the point, as blacksmiths hammer in time, and so each attentive to his task, all that one heard was: 'Oh my God, oh my Christ!' 'Hug me!' 'Ream me!' 'Push out that sweet tongue!' 'Give it to me!' 'Take it!' 'Push harder!' 'Wait, I'm coming!' 'Oh Christ, drive it into me!' 'Holy God!' 'Hold me!' and 'Help!' Some were whispering, others were moaning loudly—and listening to them you would have though they were running the scales, sol, fa, me, re, do.[180]

Another passage makes the lute an analogy with the woman's body.

And I believe that a different melody entirely is made by a skilled hand which picks lightly at the strings of the lute at the curve of the belly, touching it not too heavily nor too skimmingly. And the sound of this hand when it pats smartly at the sanctum of the buttocks seems to me of a different sweetness from the music made by the [shawm] players in the castle, when the cardinals visit it in those cowls that make them look like owls in a hole.[181]

He describes in some detail one of the lowest types of street singers,[182] the song of a 'street boy who goes past my door every night at ten o'clock'[183] and also suggests that the average

---

179 Quoted in Chubb, *The Letters of Pietro Aretino*, 215ff.
180 Aretino, *Dialogues*, 29.
181 Ibid., 200.
182 Ibid., 178.
183 Ibid., 270.

prostitute herself was capable of singing and playing the guitar and lute.[184] Later he remarks 'a woman who did not know a batch of the newest, most beautiful songs would have been ashamed, and whores as well as bawds enjoyed them.'[185]

In general, he declares 'trumpeters, bell-ringers, street singers, peddlers in the market, lottery sellers, chanters at vespers and ballad-singers' can never keep secrets.[186]

One dialogue is the story of an older prostitute training a young girl on the ins and outs, so to speak, of the profession. In one passage she is discussing the proper social manners for an aristocratic home and instructs the girl on how to pretend she understands music.

> And don't sit there like a ninny or an owl, but do everything graciously; and if they are playing music or singing, listen attentively to the music and the song, and praise the musicians and singers, even if you take no delight in them and do not understand what they are doing.[187]

If this passage reflects a lack of true appreciation for Art Music by the prostitute class, at least they could appreciate the value of the instruments themselves. Instead of money, advises the older prostitute, ask them for musical instruments!

> So ask one man for a lute, another for a harpsichord, this man for a viola, the next for a flute, the third for a little organ, and the fourth for a lyre; it's all to the good. You will then get the *maestri* to come and teach you how to play them, and will try to keep them amused, getting them to play for you for nothing, paying them with hopes and promises and a few pecks at it, but at the gallop.[188]

---

184 Ibid., 233.
185 Ibid., 362.
186 Ibid., 274.
187 Ibid., 181.
188 Ibid., 223.

2 SIXTEENTH-CENTURY ITALIAN MUSIC IN THEORY
[SPECULATIVE MUSIC]

FOR NEARLY 1,000 YEARS philosophers dealing with music followed the medieval separation of music studies into 'Speculative' and 'Practical,' the former being all matters of theory and mathematics and the latter having to do with the actual performance of music. When the modern universities began they said in effect, 'We will teach the speculative and leave the practical to the musicians out in the street.' The fundamental problem with this neat separation is that the 'speculative' branch is not music. Only the 'practical' is real music, since the word 'music' can only refer to the performance of music heard by a listener as even everyone in the sixth century must have understood.

By the sixteenth century, while many universities were still talking about the mathematical definition of music, the very high quality of the actual music now being heard, together with its role in society, resulted in a more extensive discussion of music as it pertains to the performer and listener. In Italy, in particular, the discussions were heated as some philosophers and theorists still argued for the importance of the speculative aspect of music. In order to make these discussions more clear for the reader we have therefore made two chapters representing sixteenth century discussion of music in Italy, one for 'Music in Theory' and one for 'Music in Practice.' In addition, we remind the reader that it is our policy in these books, regarding music treatises, to focus on those portions which might offer insight into aesthetics.

The Italian universities remained bound in the old Scholastic association of music with mathematics. Thus when, for example, Ludovico Ferrari wished to defend Cardano against Niccolò Tartaglia, he offered to debate the latter 'on any mathematical discipline, including music.'[1] These universities, therefore, continued to grind out music treatises in the old Scholastic mathematics-based perspective, a typical example being Stephano Venneo's *Recanetum* (1533).

The second school of thought was that of the humanists, whose great achievement was the restoration of music to its most fundamental purpose, the expression of feelings. They arrived at this purpose from their study of the ancient Greek treatises which discussed music. Vincenzo Galilei (1533–1591) in his 'Dialog on Ancient and Modern Music' recalled the disappearance of the Greek ideals in music during the Dark Ages, a period which he characterizes 'as if all men had been overcome by a heavy lethargy of ignorance, they lived

---

[1] Nan Cooke Carpenter, *Music in the Medieval and Renaissance Universities* (Norman: University of Oklahoma Press, 1958), 129.

without any desire for learning and took as little notice of music as of the western Indies.'[2] Although this treatise is largely an attack on the ideas of Zarlino, Galilei credits him, together with Glarean and Gafurius, as being responsible for the renewal of Greek ideals. He found they did not completely succeed, which 'may have been owing to the rudeness of the times, the difficulty of the subject, and the scarcity of good interpreters.'

Thus, when Galilei speaks of the 'renewal of Greek ideals,' everything he meant by this was related to feelings. Ironically, the humanists set about restoring emotions as the focal point of music by way of a misconception about ancient Greek music. Observing the accounts of the powerful impact on the listeners by the sung poetry of the ancient lyric poets, the humanists mistakenly assumed that, being poetry, it was the *words* which communicated the emotions. They were entirely in error, as we know today from clinical studies of the brain. We know, first, that it is only through the right hemisphere's contribution of emotions that the words of the left hemisphere communicate any feeling at all in oral usage. Second, studies have demonstrated the genetic understanding of melodic materials and they can be associated with the emotions, which are also genetically universal. Man is clearly *born* to understand music, but not language.

The humanists, because of this misconception, constantly write of the importance of expressing the emotions of the *words* in music. It was because of this that they were so critical of polyphonic music, which presents to the listener different words at any given time. One can see that a growing dissatisfaction with the polyphonic style, apparent already in the fifteenth century, was a contributing factor in the development of monody.

Bardi, with whom we associate the famous Camerata, in a letter to Caccini in 1578, begins somewhat sarcastically, observing that the composer of Church polyphony considers it a sin if the various parts play together.

> It would seem, I say, a mortal sin if all the parts were heard to beat at the same time with the same notes, with the same syllables of the verse, and with the same [rhythm]; the more they make the parts move, the more artful they think they are.[3]

This polyphonic style, he says, is more appropriate for instrumental music without words. Then he pleas to the composers of his time,

> to endeavor not to spoil the verse, not imitating the [polyphonic] musicians of today, who think nothing of spoiling it to pursue their ideas or of cutting it to bits to make nonsense of the words.

---

2   Vincenzo Galilei, 'Dialogo della musica antica e della moderna,' in Oliver Strunk, *Source Readings in Music History* (New York: Norton, 1950), 303. His famous son, Galileo Galilei, was the first to point out the mathematical and physical impossibility of the account of Pythagoras' discovery of the overtone series by listening to a blacksmith—a story which had been unchallenged for two thousand years!

3   Giovanni de' Bardi, 'Discourse on Ancient Music and Good Singing,' in Oliver Strunk, *Source Readings in Music History* (New York: Norton, 1950), 294ff. Bardi (b. 1534) was a gentleman vitally interested in the arts. It was in his home, in Florence, where the male 'salon' known as the 'Camerata' met to discuss Greek tragedy. Their discussions were an important step toward opera.

> In composing, then, you will make it your chief aim to arrange the verse well and to declaim the words as intelligibly as you can, not letting yourself be led astray to the counterpoint like a bad swimmer who lets himself be carried out of the course by the current and comes to shore beyond the mark that he had set, for you will consider it self-evident that, just as the soul is nobler than the body, so the words are nobler than the counterpoint. Would it not seem ridiculous if, walking in the public square, you saw a servant followed by his master and commanding him?

Galilei, writing in 1581, concludes that no sacred or secular polyphony of the Renaissance had ever succeeded in achieving the ethical impact of the music of the ancient Greeks.

> For all the height of excellence of the practical music of the moderns, there is not heard or seen today the slightest sign of its accomplishing what ancient music accomplished, nor do we read that it accomplished it fifty or a hundred years ago ... Thus neither its novelty nor its excellence has ever had the power, with our modern musicians, of producing any of the virtuous, infinitely beneficial and comforting effects that ancient music produced.[4]

He finds the reason for this in the elements of music itself, reasons which the polyphonic composers ignore.

> [It is clear] that the rules observed by the modern contrapuntists as inviolable laws, as well as those they often use from choice and to show their learning, [are] directly opposed to the perfection of the true and best harmonies and melodies.

He finds, for example, that high tones have a particular nature, as do low tones, and when they are mixed in multi-part music this automatically causes a conflict in the nature of the music itself. Only by writing simple melodies can the emotions of the words be communicated.

> Using few notes is natural both in speaking and singing, since the purpose of one and the other is solely the expression of the conceits of the soul by means of words, which, when well expressed and understood by the listeners, generate in them whatever affections the musician cares to treat through this medium.[5]

The explanation which Galilei finds for the failure of the sixteenth-century polyphonic composers to understand the importance of the communication of the emotions (through words) is that they simply concentrated on pleasing the ear through sound itself, without consideration of emotion.

> Consider each rule of the modern contrapuntists by itself, or, if you wish, consider them all together. They aim at nothing but the delight of the ear, if it can truly be called delight ... And in truth the last thing the moderns think of is the expression of the words with the passion that

---

4   Galilei, in Strunk, *Source Readings*, 306ff.

5   'Dubbi intorno a quanto io ho detto dell'uso dell'enharmonio,' quoted in Claude V. Palisca, *Humanism in Italian Renaissance Musical Thought* (New Haven: Yale University Press, 1985), 393.

these require ... And if it were permitted me, I should like to show you, with several examples of authority, that among the most famous contrapuntists of this century there are some who do not even know how to read, let alone understand. Their ignorance and lack of consideration is one of the most potent reasons why the music of today does not cause in the listeners any of those virtuous and wonderful effects that ancient music caused.[6]

Failing to recognize that in fact it is the music which communicates emotions of the words, Galilei now sarcastically attacks the inherent virtue of instrumental music. How, he asks, can these humble instruments be capable of anything more important than the delight of the ear.

If the object of the modern practical musicians is, as they say, to delight the sense of hearing with the variety of the consonances, and if this property of tickling (for it cannot with truth be called delight in any other sense) resides in a simple piece of hollow wood over which are stretched four, six, or more strings of the gut of a dumb beast or of some other material ... or in a given number of natural reeds or of artificial ones made of wood, metal, or some other material ... with a little air blowing inside them while they are touched or struck by the clumsy and untutored hand of some base idiot or other, then let this object of delighting with the variety of their harmonies be abandoned to these instruments, for being without sense, movement, intellect, speech, discourse, reason, or soul, they are capable of nothing else.[7]

Galilei now goes into a lengthy discussion by which he hopes to prove that emotions are communicated not by the effects of the music, but by *how* you sing the words. He concludes by mentioning again that polyphonic music has 'for its sole aim to delight the ear, while that of ancient music is to induce in another the same passion that one feels oneself.'[8] Why don't the modern musicians understand this, Galilei wonders?

Every brute beast has the natural faculty of communicating its pleasure and its pain of body and mind, at least to those of its own species, nor was voice given to them by nature for any other purpose. And among rational animals there are some so stupid that, since they do not know, thanks to their worthlessness, how to make practical application of this faculty ... they believe that they are without it naturally ...
    If the musician has not the power to direct the minds of his listeners to their benefit, his science and knowledge are to be reputed null and vain, since the art of music was instituted and numbered among the liberal arts for no other purpose.[9]

In another place, Galilei attacks polyphony with respect to its preference among some singers. In his *Fronimo* (1584), he has a character ask another, surely he does,

---

6   Galilei, in Oliver Strunk, *Source Readings*, 312ff.

7   Ibid., 313.

8   Ibid., 317.

9   Ibid., 318ff. Galilei must have known this last sentence was not true, because it was for its supposed relationship with mathematics that music was accepted among the liberal arts.

not wish to be counted among the majority of modern singers (who call themselves professionals and are taken as such by the common people) who never want to sing or hear anything except new and difficult things composed in many parts—as if beauty and goodness of a composition had as its chosen habitation number of parts, difficulty, and novelty.[10]

Musicians who believe this way, says Galilei, are mistaken.

ON THE PHYSIOLOGY OF AESTHETICS

Earlier philosophers had written extensively on the relative values of Reason and the senses. For those sixteenth-century writers interested in music, this inquiry continued in the form of a debate between the values of knowledge (Reason) and practical understanding, arrived at by the sense of hearing.

Gioseffo Zarlino, in Part Four of his *Le Istitutioni Harmoniche* (1558) follows the old Scholastic dogma that music must be judged by Reason and not merely the senses. In a Chapter entitled, 'What Anyone Must Know Who Desires to Arrive at Some Perfection in Music,' he writes,

> We should not surrender judgment of musical matters to the senses alone, for they are fallible, but rather we should accompany the senses with reason. Whenever these two parts are joined together in concordance, there is no doubt that no error can be committed, and perfect judgment will be made.[11]

This view goes hand in hand with his complete acceptance of the medieval concept of the Liberal Arts, in which music was considered a branch of mathematics. 'It should be known,' says Zarlino, 'that music is a science subordinate to arithmetic.' Curiously, he also makes brief arguments for the importance of the study of geometry, grammar, dialectics, rhetoric, natural science and natural philosophy for the well-educated musician.

He recommends, further, the study of the harpsichord and monochord, primarily as an aid to understanding the mathematical side of music ('investigate the effects of the sonorous numbers'), as well as singing, counterpoint and composition. Only with all this 'speculative' knowledge will the musician be prepared to perform.

> For bringing things of music to life is really nothing other than leading them to their ultimate end, or perfection, as also happens in others arts and sciences (such as medicine) which [also] contain both speculative and practical aspects.

Later he summarized these arguments as follows,

---

10 Vincenzo Galilei, *Fronimo* (1584), trans. Carol MacClintock (Neuhasen-Stuttgart: Hänssler-Verlag, 1985), 82.

11 Gioseffo Zarlino, *On the Modes*, trans. Vered Cohen (New Haven: Yale University Press, 1983), 102ff.

> In order to have perfect knowledge concerning music, it does not suffice to appeal to the sense of hearing, even if it is most keen, but rather one should seek to investigate and know the whole, so that reason is not discordant with sense, nor sense with reason; and then everything will be well.
>
> But just as it is necessary that sense and reason concur in order to make judgment in things of music, so it is necessary that he who wants to judge anything pertaining to art have two capabilities: first, that he be expert in things of science, that is, of speculation; and second, that he be expert in things of art, which consists of practice …
>
> Accordingly, just as it would be insane to rely on a physician who does not have the knowledge of both practice and theory, so it would be really foolish and imprudent to rely on the judgment of [a musician] who was solely practical or had done work only in theory.[12]

In Part Three of this book, Zarlino discusses this question again, now leaning a bit more in the favor of performance.

> Theory without practice is of small value, since music does not consist only of theory and is imperfect without practice. This is obvious enough. Yet some theorists, treating of certain musical matters without having a good command of the actual practice, have spoken much nonsense and committed a thousand errors. On the other hand, some who have relied only on practice without knowing the reasons behind it have unwittingly perpetrated thousands upon thousands of idiocies in their compositions.[13]

Bottrigari also takes the view that practice cannot be respected without theory. After a discussion of the complexities of tuning based on the old tetrachord system, the character Desiderio asks,

> I was thinking about asking you if it is necessary for all musicians, such as those of today who compose madrigals and motets, to know these things, and if they do know them, or if simple practice suffices.[14]

Benelli answers, yes, every musician *should* know these things, but it is also possible to succeed without understanding the theoretical explanations.

> If, then, simple practice is sufficient to such composers to compose madrigals or motets or other kinds of *cantilene*, I will answer 'yes'; since I see and feel that most of them succeed with great applause, and in a short time even youths nowadays do marvelous miracles. But I will add also that it does not seem to me to be a great honor to accomplish things and not to be able to give the reasons for them.[15]

---

12 Ibid., 106.

13 Gioseffo Zarlino, *The Art of Counterpoint*, trans. Guy Marco and Claude Palisca (New Haven: Yale University Press, 1968), 226ff.

14 Hercole Bottrigari, *Il Desiderio*, trans. Carol MacClintock (American Institute of Musicology, 1962), 35.

15 Ibid., 36.

Later he returns to this topic.

> You do not err except that you have always esteemed only those musicians who can string notes together, as they say, and who are entirely practical, about which I do not wish to talk further, having said enough. But if you have any commerce with theoretical musicians you will know what they should be; and the writings of the ancients demonstrate it clearly.[16]

Vincenzo Giustiniani, whose writings reflect the end of the sixteenth century, believed that the reason music was esteemed by intelligent men was to be found in its twin requirements of knowledge and practice. That is, he argued for a balance between knowledge and practice.

> To begin I will tell you that the art of music is placed by liberal men very high, as that art which in order to reach its true perfection should approach, rather than share, the rank held by the sciences. In order that a musical composition succeed in gaining esteem it is necessary that it be composed according to the proper and true rules of this profession and, in addition, with new and difficult restrictions which may not be known to all musicians in general; and not only madrigals and compositions to be sung by several voices, but even in others in counterpoint, and canons, and that which seems more marvelous, the same arias to be sung easily by a single voice. And to succeed in this task the inclination given to many by nature will not be sufficient; there is required also study and application of mind and body. For possessing the rules and the just proportions of numbers, joined with those of the voice or of sound and the knowledge of the effects which are caused by these in the souls of men, not only in general but in particular corresponding to the individual inclinations of everyone and to the taste which prevails in different periods, one may be able to apply skill and experience to his own times, to human inclinations in general, and to the particular tastes of each person. And to attain this ability much application of the intellect is required, and much discussion is necessary to come to some conclusion about the work when the principles have been worked out beforehand.[17]

Later, however, when thinking of music from the perspective of the listener, he places a much greater emphasis on the practical. After a brief reference to the remarkable evidences of the power of music mentioned by the ancient authors, he concludes,

> Notwithstanding the fact that the ancients and moderns tried to attribute them to the proportions of numbers and to the movement of the spheres, this nevertheless does not seem ably fully to satisfy the intellect; therefore one is forced to have recourse to experiment alone, and to a *pratique* based on the hearing, not finding any other reason to explain that the 3rd, 5th, 6th and octave are consonances and the 2nd, 4th, and 7th are dissonances.[18]

---

16 Ibid., 44.

17 Vicenzo Giustiniani, *Discorso sopra la Musica* (ca. 1628), trans. Carol MacClintock (American Institute of Musicology, 1962), 67ff.

18 Ibid., 75.

Finally, Gioseffo Zarlino, in his *Le Istitutioni Harmoniche*, refers to the question of Reason and the senses in a reference to the ancient notion of the 'music of the spheres.' One feels he believed there must be something to this idea, even if we can't actually hear this music.

> Every reason persuades us to believe at least that the world is composed with harmony, both because its soul is a harmony (as Plato believed), and because the heavens are turned around their intelligences with harmony, as may be gathered from their revolutions, which are proportionate to each other in velocity. This harmony is known also from the distances of the celestial spheres, for these distances (as some believe) are related in harmonic proportion, which, although not measured by the sense [of hearing], is measured by the reason.[19]

ON THE PHILOSOPHY OF AESTHETICS

The primary topic which interested the sixteenth century Italian humanists, regarding the philosophy of aesthetics, was the ancient question of whether Art should imitate Nature. We might begin by quoting a lovely tribute to Nature by Galilei. During the sixteenth century one occasionally finds such passages which seem to have a spirit of Romanticism that we ordinarily might not expect to find until Rousseau.

> That man may call himself truly blessed who, fleeing the troubles and fatiguing vanities of the world, the intemperance, pride, adulation, deceptions and pretenses of the courts, brings himself to a solitary and tranquil life; for my part I desire nothing other than to be able to do so without reproof. Truly, each time I steal away from the Palace, and from serious thoughts, and come to this villa on the banks of the river, beneath the shade of tall lime trees and leafy arbors, I seem to be transported from the torments of Hell to the pleasures of Paradise—for what is there here which does not please and give the highest delight? Here the natural colors of the flowers and grass are most beautiful and delightful objects for the eyes, the murmur of the streamlet, the soft movement of the trees, together with the voices of nightingales and other birds, accord so well together that they fill the ear with sweetness; in short, all the sentiments find particular joy and delight.[20]

Most general commentators on aesthetics argued that Art should imitate Nature, but Zarlino states that Art can *never* imitate Nature. He makes this observation in the context of a discussion of the problems resulting from the varying tuning solutions found within the octave at this time among singers, instrumentalists and keyboard players.

> This interval would be very annoying to the listener, more so because such an interval is not heard in voices, which can tune intervals higher or lower as desired and through this bring to

---

19 Quoted in Palisca, *Humanism in Italian Renaissance Musical Thought*, 179.
20 Galilei, *Fronimo*, 31.

perfection any composition. This is not true with artificial [man-made] instruments, because art can never equal nature.[21]

For Galilei this was not an important question. Anyway, he says in his *Discorso intorno*, of 1589, that Art can surpass Nature.

> Art is not necessarily inferior to nature. In those things that art can do and nature cannot, art is superior. In those things that nature can do and art cannot, art is inferior. Art and nature are both efficient causes. In making artificial things nature cannot rival art; nor can art rival nature in making natural things. Art, however, can improve on nature. Painting can represent not only natural and artificial things but also anything that it is possible to imagine. It can surpass nature in providing the eye with everything it can desire in the way of excellence of line and color.[22]

ON THE AESTHETICS OF MUSIC

In sixteenth-century Italy we find much evidence that some humanists were attempting to move away from the old Scholastic theories of music being a branch of mathematics toward a more modern understanding that music is of the province of the expression of feelings. The medieval separation of the study of music into the 'speculative' and the 'practical' was a harbinger of this change. In his book on lute intabulation, Galilei raises the question whether this practice is derived from the ear or from mathematics.

> Tell me, please, if lute intabulation consists solely in the practice of the lute, playing the consonances according to the judgment of the ear, or is it in Art founded on rules, with solid and true principles?[23]

Hedging his bets, Galilei has an answer provided by another character which covers all possibilities.

> The intabulation of music for instruments is understood in different ways by different people. Nevertheless, I hold it to be an art calling for the greatest judgment ... in addition to which one tries not only to be a good singer, and sound contrapuntist, but to be also a sound musician, or theorist, as we like to say.

Later Galilei supplies an answer much more in tune with Humanism. In discussing Pythagoras and his reputed discovery of the mathematical relationships in the lower part of the overtone series while listening to a blacksmith, we find for the very first time, in reference

---

21 Zarlino, *The Art of Counterpoint*, 35.
22 Quoted in Palisca, *Humanism in Italian Renaissance Musical Thought*, 274.
23 Galilei, *Fronimo*, 36.

to this often repeated tale, the thought that perhaps it is the *sound*, and not the mathematics, which we hear.

> FRONIMO. So, because the consonance was contained in certain numbers and not in others, don't you think that in the sound itself was the real reason that one pleased him more than another, because of the proportion and the enjoyment that he perceived more or less by his hearing?
> GALILEI. Truly one should believe thus, since the judgment of sounds was made by the senses long before he was aware of what proportions were and the numbers containing them.[24]

At the end of Part III of his *Le Istitutioni Harmoniche*, Zarlino offers a striking reflection on the aesthetics of music of the future.

> It would have been tragic indeed if the beautiful in music had been set aside and the less beautiful retained. But this would have been incredible, for in the other arts and sciences that are full of grand speculations but are of little utility the good has always survived, while the bad has been abandoned as useless. This, in my opinion, is the way it happened with music.
> I hope some day to see this science [of music] so well established and perfect that no one will desire more than what is actually in use. I say this because I do not see that it is now in such a perfect state as may come. This I cannot describe but can imagine. It may come when music is embraced by some noble spirit whose goal will not be the mechanical one of gain but honor and immortal glory.[25]

ON THE PURPOSE OF MUSIC

For Zarlino, one important purpose of music lay in its ability to aid man in contemplation. In the process, he says, music unites the parts of the body, as well as the soul, and brings them into correspondence with Reason.[26]

It is interesting that the purpose of music to offer solace is not mentioned so much as it was in earlier times. Galilei alone seems to emphasize this, when he speaks of the capacity of 'sweet and harmonious sounds [to] dissipate the melancholy in me, as has happened many times.'[27]

Several writers suggest that the purpose of music is simply to be pleasing to the listener. Zarlino, in Part Four of his *Le Istitutioni Harmoniche* argues that the technical goal of the composer of multi-part vocal music should be to remove the rough places, make the work comfortable to sing and observe the nature of the words. Beyond this, 'he should seek with

---

24 Ibid., 146.
25 Zarlino, *The Art of Counterpoint*, 290.
26 Palisca, *Humanism in Italian Renaissance Musical Thought*, 180ff.
27 Galilei, *Fronimo*, 31.

all diligence to make the tenor ... regulated and beautiful, graceful and full of sweetness.'[28] In another place, however, Zarlino cautions that this quality of 'sweetness' is not universal but may require sophistication in the listener.

> There are different appetites, so that what pleases one does not please another, and while one man is delighted by sweet and smooth harmony, another would like it somewhat harder and harsher. Musicians should not despair when hearing such judgments, even if they hear people condemn their compositions and say everything bad about them. Rather they should take heart and be comforted, for the number of those who have no judgment is almost infinite.[29]

In his *Le Istitutioni Harmoniche* we perhaps see another reference to the sophistication required of the listener in his explanation for the nature of the pleasing quality of consonances.

> Consonances are the more pleasing as they depart from simplicity, which does not delight our senses much, and when they are accompanied by other consonances, because our senses prefer composite to simple things.[30]

Dissonance, he says, is that which 'is disagreeable to the ear and renders a composition harsh and without any sweetness.'[31] Nevertheless, dissonance has an aesthetic purpose.

> Although these dissonances are not pleasing in isolation, when they are properly placed according to the precepts to be given, the ear not only endures them but derives great pleasure and delight from them. They are of double utility to the musician. The first has been mentioned: with their aid we may pass from one consonance to another. The second is that a dissonance causes the consonance which follows it to sound more agreeable. The ear then grasps and appreciates the consonance with greater pleasure, just as light is more delightful to the sight after darkness, and the taste of sweets more delicious after something bitter.[32]

It is significant that Galilei, in speaking of the correct arrangement of notes in two-parts, speaks not of Scholastic mathematics, but 'that the harmony between them is such that the ear derives pleasure from it.'[33]

Giustiniani, reflecting the end of the century, offers three stylistic goals for composition, which he says represents the general opinion of musicians. His conclusion clearly emphasizes that music must be pleasing.

---

28 Zarlino, *On the Modes*, 92.
29 Ibid., 108.
30 Zarlino, *The Art of Counterpoint*, 19.
31 Ibid., 34.
32 Ibid., 53.
33 Galilei, *Fronimo*, 124.

It must be written first of all in good counterpoint founded on the correct rules, with novel and difficult passages to weave together in all the parts without burdening it with superfluous notes ...

Secondly, that the entire composition, and the points of imitation particularly, be easy and flowing in such fashion that the artifices do not make them harsh, else they may not be understood except by persons expert in the profession and who give special attention to such things.

And in the third place, that they be pleasant to hear and have unusual grace. I have learned from experience that many compositions by outstanding composers which meet the first two conditions and lack the third have not been acceptable, and remain in the bottom of a chest or on top of a bookcase covered with dust ... And this third condition is also necessary in the other compositions which are called arias to be sung by one or several voices to instruments; else without it they will be cold and tasteless and, for all their artifice and difficult counterpoint, unknown to others.[34]

Since the musical goals of the humanists were so centered in the ideals which they found in ancient Greek literature, it is no surprise that the purpose of music most discussed was relative to its potential to affect character. Thus, in the *De harmonic* (1518) of Gaffurio, and in an anonymous treatise of 1525, we find lists of very specific emotions which it is contended will be aroused by the various Church modes.[35] Galilei also began his *Fronimo* by reflecting in admiration on the views of the ancient civilizations on the virtues of music with respect to character development.

Music was esteemed to be of such power and virtue by the ancients that it was their opinion that our very souls were harmony, and that sweet and suave harmonies were in this manner inspired to temper uncontrolled emotions so that they should not be discordant with one another. Therefore they took care to introduce good professors of that science, and to honor them with every kind of honor as being useful in their Republics; for the Egyptians never allowed their system of music to be changed by even one note, and just as they had established it, so they continued to accept it for more than ten thousand years, according to their calendar, because they were sure that they could not change the rules and laws of music without serious damage to the body politic.[36]

Galilei was one of the first to come to understand that the Greeks were talking about an entirely different 'Dorian' than the one known to these sixteenth-century writers.[37] Because they were not so confident about the actual fundamentals of Greek music, some were perhaps hesitant to predict precise influences on character for specific types of sixteenth-century music. It was safer to speak more generally and, above all, to emphasize the importance of the character of the performer himself. Thus, for Galilei, character was a necessary element of the definition of the most esteemed musician. After a few observations on deficient

---

34 Giustiniani, *Discorso sopra la Musica*, 73.
35 Quoted in Palisca, *Humanism in Italian Renaissance Musical Thought*, 345.
36 Galilei, *Fronimo*, Preface to the Readers, 27.
37 Palisca, *Humanism in Italian Renaissance Musical Thought*, 345ff.

performers, those with no imagination or poor technique, he says those most esteemed are those who teach us something, meaning affect our character in the manner of the ancient Greeks. It follows, he says, that the character of the musician is an inseparable component.

> For those who teach us a virtue are much more to be esteemed, and the rarer and more excellent they are the more so, than those who merely delight us with their buffooneries; first because it is a greater and a higher thing to know what another does than to do what he does,[38] and then because every purely sensual pleasure ends by satiating us and never makes us thirst for any knowledge. And I say that they are even more deserving when that knowledge of theirs is combined with the highest character, as these are the things chiefly to be desired in the perfect musician and in every follower of the arts, in order that with his learning and his character he may make those who frequent him and listen to him men of learning and good character. In addition I say that it is impossible to find a man who is truly a musician and is vicious, and that if a man has a vicious nature, it will be difficult, or rather impossible for him to be virtuous and to make others virtuous.[39]

Bardi as well found character to be essential to the perfect musician.

> Just as among Moors and Spanish women one may see shameless and wanton customs represented in music and dancing, so the virtuous and perfect musician can represent the contrary, that is, songs and dances filled with majesty and continence.[40]

The writer who was most fascinated with the mystery of the power of music over the character and actions among contemporary men was Giustiniani. He mentions the remarkable anecdotes in ancient literature, but finds many examples in modern life which he cannot explain. Why does music 'move souls to love, particularly in women?'[41] Why does it arouse 'devotion and fervor' in Church Music? Why in fishing for swordfish is it 'reputed necessary to sing, and what is more, to sing with Greek words?' Why does it put human beings to sleep, 'particularly children and the other animals?' Why does song lighten the effort and tiresomeness of the heat for farm workers in the summer, 'even though with singing their thirst increases?' What benefit comes from singing and playing to silk-worms in Lombardy? Why does singing lessen the fear in children when they are walking at night? These questions, he says, must be left to doctors and philosophers who know more about them.

On the other hand, some effects of music seemed more obvious to Giustiniani:

> Songs and appropriate sounds have power to incite the minds of men to various and diverse actions, as I have said, and especially to war; for which purpose are used both the Trumpet and the Drum, at the same time shouting with all the voices together.

---

38 A frequently read prejudice among the Scholastic music theorists of the Middle Ages.
39 Galilei, 'Dialogo della musica antica e della moderna,' in Strunk, *Source Readings*, 320ff.
40 Bardi, 'Discourse on Ancient Music and Good Singing,' in Ibid., 298.
41 Giustiniani, *Discorso sopra la Musica*, 75ff.

> I have found myself in Florence in company with more than a hundred persons who, returning from hunting, sang many crazy songs together in order to relieve the tedium of the journey.
>
> Among the sailors and porters we see it in the custom of accompanying their united efforts with singing in order to lessen fatigue; and so, too, do those who crush drugs and spices on the Rialto Bridge.
>
> Many preachers are heard who in order to move the ignorant and low classes make use more of songs than of ideas, particularly in the sermons for Good Friday.

Even irrational animals are moved by music, as he points out in the case of birds 'who almost seem to compete among themselves to reach a greater perfection and to teach such skill to their young.'

Finally, there are a few references to the power of music going beyond affecting character to what we might think of today as music therapy. Zarlino writes of the power of music to heal the spirit.

> Nature has ordered things well in having joined (as the Platonists believe) our body and soul through the spirit. To each Nature has provided appropriate remedies when they are weak and infirm. When it is listless and infirm, the body is brought back to health with cures wrought by medicine, and the afflicted and weak spirit, by the aerial spirits and by instrumental and vocal music, which are proportionate remedies for it. As for the soul, locked up in this corporeal prison, it is consoled by means of divine mysteries and sacred theology.[42]

Giustiniani mentions the use of music in Puglia and Naples for persons who have been bitten by tarantulas, observing,

> they received great solace and many times total relief from music or the sound of instruments; and what is even more amazing, from one particular kind of music or instrument.[43]

This practice, he says, 'is found to be greater than the remedies the doctors give.'

On the Relationship of Words and Music

As we have mentioned above, the great achievement of the humanists was in arriving at an understanding that the real meaning of music does not lie in mathematics, but rather in the communication of feelings, an awareness they arrived at from their study of Greek treatises which described the singing of poetry. While their end was correct, ironically they arrived there through the misunderstanding that it was the *words*, rather than the music, which had such an impact on the Greek listeners. We can see this clearly in Bottrigari, who, after mentioning several Greek writers, recommends,

---

42 'Le Istitutioni harmoniche,' quoted in Palisca, *Humanism in Italian Renaissance Musical Thought*, 181.
43 Giustiniani, *Discorso sopra la Musica*, 74.

> I think it best to add that no concert of instruments should ever be given without the addition of a human voice—always a voice well suited to the subject of the song. This is to avoid the music and the concert being called 'mute' by connoisseurs and intelligent listeners, or as Aristotle calls it, and Plato calls it more clearly and better in the *Laws*, the 'bare' sound of the Cithara or the Aulos, which they say resembles the sounds made by animals. This is because of the failure to express the *affetti* and because of the poor pronunciation of the words. From the words, especially when they are well mimed by a good musician, truly comes the greater part of the emotions aroused in the minds of the listeners.[44]

Zarlino found that in such solo vocal performances one saw a power over the emotions of the listener which he did not find in performances of polyphonic music. It is clear, however, that he too was thinking primarily about the ability of the listener to hear and understand the *text* of the song.

> Even in our times we see that music induces in us various passions in the way that it did in antiquity. For occasionally, it is observed, when some beautiful, learned, and elegant poem is sung by someone to the sound of some instrument, the listeners are greatly stirred and moved to do different things, such as to laugh, weep, or to similar actions ... If such effects were wrought by music in antiquity, it was sung as described above and not in the way that is used at present, with a multitude of parts and so many singers and instruments that at times nothing is heard but a jumbled din of voices and diverse instrumental sounds, singing without taste or discretion, and an unseemly pronunciation of words, so that he hears only a tumult and uproar. Music practiced in this way cannot have any effect on us worth remembering ... Those songs in which brief matters are related in a few words, as is customary today in certain canzonets called madrigals, truly are able to move the soul but little. Although these delight us greatly, they do not have the force alluded to above. That it is true that music universally pleases more when it is simple than when fashioned with much artifice and sung by many parts may be understood from this: that we listen to a solo singer accompanied by the sound of an organ, lyre, lute, or similar instrument with greater pleasure than to many. Although many singing together stir the soul, there is no doubt that songs in which the singers pronounce the words together are generally heard with greater pleasure than the learned compositions in which the words are interrupted by many voices.[45]

As with most Italian humanists, Zarlino stressed the importance of 'accommodating [music] to the words.' Again like the other humanists, he found his inspiration for this in ancient literature. His argument was as follows.

> If poets are not permitted to write a comedy in tragic verse, it is not permissible for a musician to combine harmony and words in an unsuitable manner. Thus, it will not be appropriate for him to use sad harmony and grave rhythms for cheerful subjects, and he is not permitted to use cheerful harmony and light or fast rhythms, call it what we may, where funereal matters are treated. On

---

44 Bottrigari, *Il Desiderio*, 23.
45 'Istitutioni,' II, 9, p. 75, quoted in Palisca, *Humanism in Italian Renaissance Musical Thought*, 371ff.

the contrary, he should use cheerful harmonies and fast rhythms for cheerful subjects and sad harmonies and grave rhythms for sad subjects, so that everything may be done with proportion.

I think that everyone will know how to accommodate the harmonies to the words in the best way possible when he has studied what I have written in Part III and has considered the nature of the mode in which he wishes to write a composition. He should take care to accompany each word in such a manner that, when the word denotes harshness, hardness, cruelty, bitterness, and other things of this sort, the harmony will be similar to these qualities, namely, somewhat hard and harsh, but not to the degree that it would offend. Similarly, when any of the words express complaint, sorrow, grief, sighs, tears, and other things of this sort, the harmony should be full of sadness.[46]

It is interesting, in this regard, that he still found the major sixth to be 'somewhat harsh.'

In continuing his discussion of how to make the music reflect the words, he distinguishes between 'natural movement' and 'accidental movement' (music with accidentals). Natural movement he finds more virile and sonorous, while accidental movement is 'sweeter and somewhat more languid.'

Rhythm too, he says, must be employed to help express the meaning of the text.

> The primary consideration should be the subject matter contained in the text. If it is cheerful, one should proceed with powerful and fast movements, namely, with note values that convey swiftness of movement ... But when the subject matter is tearful, one should proceed with slow and lingering movements.

The individual rhythms should correspond to the syllables of the text 'so no barbarism is heard ... something heard every day in innumerable compositions and really a shameful thing.' Any use of rests should also follow sentence structure.

In Part III of his book, which Zarlino refers to above, he provides an interesting discussion on the use of rests. Rests, he says, were adopted for the sake of *ornament*, as well as to prevent constant singing, which would be boring.[47] He follows with a wonderful phrase.

> Their function was to indicate an artful inactivity of the voice. 'Artful inactivity' is a good term because it warns us that rests may not be arbitrarily placed in a composition but must arise from art and necessity. Music without properly placed rests is as irritating as a speech without end or aim.[48]

Also in Part III Zarlino also gives more general rules for the composition of music with words. One begins, he says, with a subject, 'without which nothing can be made.' He continues by speaking of the aesthetic significance of the choice of subject.

---

46 Zarlino, *On the Modes*, 94ff. Later, in Ibid., 98, Zarlino gives specific rules for preventing 'barbarism' in assigning note values to words.

47 Zarlino, *The Art of Counterpoint*, 124.

48 Ibid., 124.

Whether the story is of his own invention or borrowed from others, he adorns and polishes it with various embellishments as it pleases him. He omits nothing fit and suitable to delight the minds of his listeners, achieving thus something that is magnificent and marvelous. The musician has the same end, namely to serve and to please the minds of his listeners with harmonic accents, and he also has a subject upon which to construct his composition, which he adorns with various movements and harmonies to bring maximum pleasure to the audience.[49]

Later he summarizes the aesthetic goal of music with words.

The composer will seek, therefore, to make his parts easily singable and formed of beautiful, graceful, and elegant movements. Then his listeners will be delighted with them rather than offended.[50]

On Style and Performance

One of the few specific references to the style of music is given in an often quoted passage by Bottrigari.[51] The word 'concerto,' which had first been used solely to mean an ensemble, such as *Concerti di Milano*, has now taken on a new meaning, a stylistic meaning. He points out that the word now means 'contention or conflict' and does not derive from the verb 'consero,' which means 'to graft, to sow and plant together.' Thus for this period we understand an instrumental composition using dialogue technique to be 'concerto' and one in a motet style to be 'concenti.'

Bottrigari also comments on what he calls two outstanding abuses of present day musicians. The first is that he finds the style of the music he hears too much the same.

The chief [abuse] is the indifference with which they compose the *cantilene*, finding no difference between delightful and lascivious compositions, or between funeral, lugubrious ones and those which ought to serve the divine cult, invoking, thanking and praising the omnipotent majesty of God and His Saints.[52]

The second abuse he found current was the movement toward large ensemble performances, something to which he objected primarily from the problems resulting from the varying tuning systems in use.

---

49 Ibid., 51ff.

50 Ibid., 110.

51 Bottrigari, *Il Desiderio*, 20.

52 Ibid., 44.

Musicians should abstain from *concerti* and not try in the future to make connoisseurs of music laugh at the great confusions of different instruments, by multiplying which they hope to work miracles such as those they have read about as being accomplished by Orpheus and Amphion and all the other ancient musicians. And as long as they so deceive themselves you cannot give them good advice.

By the sixteenth century the problem just mentioned, tuning, had become a central problem in performance practice. It was, for example, the principal reason why the host of new wind instruments were made by the 'case,' that is, a consort made by the same maker at the same time to facilitate playing in tune as an ensemble.[53] Thus we begin to find attacks on the ancient contentions about tuning and the division of the octave. Giovanni Spataro, in his *Errori di Franchino Gafurio da Lodi*, of 1521, says that the old Pythagorean concepts, in so far as modern performance practice is concerned, 'is altogether useless, deceptive, and futile.'

Lodovico Fogliano, in his *Musica theorica*, of 1529, approached his study of music not on the basis of earlier theorists, but on the basis of his own observations. Hence he defines consonance simply as 'that which is pleasing to the ears.' Thus he expanded intervals considered consonant to include the sixths as well as intervals larger than an octave, which he says are delightful and are used by all composers of part music, organists and singers, 'as anyone moderately learned in this discipline knows.' Tuning, for him, should be done by the sense of hearing, not according to mathematics.

Zarlino, too, was aware of the problems with intervalic theory in the ancient treatises, but he did not trust the ear like Fogliano and hence the thrust of his work was to find a rational explanation for that which the ear prefers.

But for some sixteenth-century musicians the ensemble problems in tuning when using the string instruments, which used the old tetrachord system, was more trouble than it was worth. Better, Bardi says, to just leave these instruments out.

> More than once I have felt like laughing when I saw musicians struggling to put a lute or viol into proper tune with a keyboard instrument, for aside from the octave these instruments have few strings in common that are in unison, since until now this highly important matter has gone unnoticed or, if noticed, unremedied. In your consorts, then, you will as far as possible avoid combining lutes or viols with keyboard instruments or harps.[54]

Galilei, in his book on lute intabulation, admits that lutanists had come under criticism because of their old tetrachord system of tuning and that singers, in particular, hesitated to sing with them. But, in his view the old system of tuning gave the lute greater flexibility, with its greater possibilities within the octave, and from this greater sophistication in expressing emotions.

---

53   One who recommended adoption of the consort principle as a solution to tuning was Bottrigari, see Ibid., 21.
54   Bardi, 'Discourse on Ancient Music and Good Singing,' in Strunk, *Source Readings*, 297

I should reply to them thus. Since the most noble and least imperfect instrument in use today must remain excluded, (because of the insolence of some of those for whom it has become such) and therefore become an ignoble and most imperfect instrument, what will it be in the hands of those persons? Since they cannot use it with voices, by what means can they convey the meaning of the affections of the soul with greater efficacy than can be done with the well tempered sound alone? O thought unworthy of a reasonable man![55]

In any case, he says, 'if this defect had been capable of being remedied it would have been foreseen long before this.'

A final interesting observation on performance is found in Giustiniani, who makes 'grace' the most distinguishing quality of a gentleman, much in the spirit of Castiglione's emphasis on nonchalance. Although supposing it to be a gift of God, he finds grace the chief virtue in the beauty of women, in the behavior of the gentleman, in speech and among artists. In the performance of music, he defines grace as follows.

For in the voice as well as for instruments, one will be able to offer the same reasons for grace and melody saying, by way of definition, that singing with grace is nothing other than a close observance of the style and rules of singing and of those rules for using the voice or playing a good instrument so that it shall not be unpleasant or awkward. It is this grace that customarily brings pleasure and delight to the ears of persons of judgment. And so one can say that a person does not have a good voice but sings with grace as, for example, I will mention Cardinal Montalto, who played and sang with much grace and feeling even though his appearance was more martial than Apollonian, and who had a scratchy voice …

And that it is true that grace in singing is a quality provided by nature and not by art … may be seen from the fact that sometimes a singer appears pleasing to one person and tiresome to another; and on the contrary a stupid singer pleases when he ought not to. And the same effect is seen also in other things, especially in the bordellos of Spain and Africa in which there is not a woman that does not find a market, however ugly she may be.[56]

On the Public

Galilei joins nearly all early writers in cautioning the artist against being influenced by the public. We recognize here the influence of Scholasticism, in his repeating the Church's frequent warning against trusting the senses, in his apparent association of 'pleasing the ear alone' with the public and in his suggestion that the word 'Reason' distinguishes the artist.

I exhort you not to allow yourself, as the proverb says, to be deceived by fame, as do many who do not know the truth but only care about the approval of the foolish rabble, nor should you

---

55 Galilei, *Fronimo*, 165ff.
56 Giustiniani, *Discorso sopra la Musica*, 73ff.

wish to be so credulous as to allow some things to please the ear alone without accompanying it by reason, because any one of the senses is fallacious, as you know.[57]

Zarlino, after giving his arguments on the importance of judging music on the basis of both speculative knowledge and practice, notes that he has stressed this because there are some people,

> who, having neither judgment nor knowledge, follow that which pleases the ignorant common people and sometimes want to make judgment of someone's adequacy by virtue of his name, country, native land, those he serves, and his appearance. So if being excellent and outstanding in a profession consisted in one's name, country, native land, service, appearance, and other similar things, I am sure that not many years would pass before no ignorant man would be found ... But in truth the opposite is the case: those who are great and famous in a profession are rare in number, and for each one of them, thousands and thousands of obscure, ignorant, clumsy, and crazy men are born, as one can see from any discussion.[58]

In illustration of the dangers of trusting the 'ignorant common people,' Zarlino quotes an anecdote from Castiglione's *The Courtier* (a story which we also have quoted) which illustrates how the 'common opinion' can completely misjudge a composition. To this he contributes an anecdote of his own regarding a motet by Willaert which had been sung annually, under the name of Josquin, by the papal choir in Rome.

> When Willaert came from Flanders to Rome at the time of Leo X and found himself at the place where this motet was being sung, he saw that it was ascribed to Josquin. When he said that it was his own, as it really was, so great was the malignity or (to put it more mildly) the ignorance of the singers, that they never wanted to sing it again.

ART MUSIC

In *The Courtier* by Castiglione one finds clear evidence that the appreciation of Art Music was considered an indispensable trait of the gentleman. We find this also in Galilei, who has a character say to him 'you know well how much praise the development of his musical talents brings to a gentleman, and particularly to a courtier like you.'[59]

In the *Fronimo* of Galilei, a work on the 'Art of Intabulating for the Lute,' we find a great deal of discussion, particularly that on proportions and counterpoint, which still has strong roots to the old Scholastic mathematics-based perspective of music. While this was a concept of music which the humanists were generally moving away from, we are not surprised to see

---

57 Galilei, *Fronimo*, 72.
58 Zarlino, *On the Modes*, 107.
59 Galilei, *Fronimo*, 36.

these older views appear. Nevertheless, it does seem ridiculous, when Galilei happens upon his friend, Fronimo, a distinguished lutanist, who is sitting outdoors on a stump, playing for himself, that Galilei should describe him absorbed in the mathematics of music.

> He has not yet seen me, so intent is he on considering the proportions of the musical intervals.[60]

Fronimo immediately offers to perform for Galilei, paraphrasing a common objection to singers in early literature—that they never will sing when you want them to, and never stop once they begin.

> I thank you in the highest degree for your praise; and in order not to fall into that common vice of musicians, I will begin without being begged, and will stop when I see that I am beginning to bore you.[61]

EDUCATIONAL MUSIC

In the *Fronimo* of Galilei we find examples of Educational Music in the proper sense of the word. His lutanist friend gives him some music, but stipulates that their purpose is not mere entertainment.

> I don't give them to you to play only to escape boredom, as is done with the Napolitane and other similar trifles, but rather that you may examine them carefully ... for you will learn from them many things.[62]

FUNCTIONAL MUSIC

Regarding occupational music, Zarlino, while discussing the medieval concept of the music of the angels, seems to suggest that some genetic memory of such music impels man to sing as a means of easing labor.

> Many were of the opinion that in this life every soul is won by music, and, although the soul is imprisoned by the body, it still remembers and is conscious of the music of the heavens, forgetting every hard and annoying labor.[63]

---

60 Ibid., 32.

61 Ibid.

62 Ibid., 79.

63 'Le Istitutioni harmoniche,' quoted in Palisca, *Humanism in Italian Renaissance Musical Thought*, 179.

Indeed, Johannes de Colonia's edition of some anonymous three-part compositions includes a woodcut showing three peasants at work and relieving their labor by singing polyphonic music![64]

---

64 Nino Pirrotta, 'Ars Nova and Stil Novo,' in *Music and Culture in Italy from the Middle Ages to the Baroque* (Cambridge: Harvard University Press, 1984), 176.

3 SIXTEENTH-CENTURY ITALIAN MUSIC IN PRACTICE
[PRACTICAL MUSIC]

BY WAY OF INTRODUCTION, we begin with a treatise published in the early years of the seventeenth century which provides an interesting survey of the changing performance styles at the end of the sixteenth century in Italian music. Vincenzo Giustiniani begins with the qualification that he does not intend to speak of the theory of music, nor of the theoretical elements of music, nor of the ancient history of music, but rather he will speak from his personal experience in hearing performances by the aristocrats themselves.

> I will set down familiarly several thoughts that occur to me upon this subject, basing them on the little experience I have acquired while I was conversing in [noble] houses where there was no gambling but rather delightful occupations, particularly music, performed without assistance of paid performers by diverse gentlemen who took pleasure and delight in it through natural inclination.[1]

He begins by telling us that his father sent him to a music school, where he studied the works of Arcadelt, Orlando Lassus, Striggio, Cipriano de Rore and Filippo di Monte, whom he considered the best of their time. There he also studied secular music with 'a certain Pitio, excellent musician and jongleur.'

> In a short space of time the style of music changed and the compositions of Marenzio and Giovanelli appeared with delightful new inventions, either that of singing with several voices or with one voice alone accompanied by some instrument, the excellence of which consisted in a melody new and grateful to the ear, with some easy fugues without extraordinary artifices.

At the same time, he says, Palestrina, Soriano, and Giovanni Maria Nanino 'composed works suitable to be sung with ease in church, of good and solid counterpoint with good melody and decent ornamentation.'

> In the Holy Year of 1575, or shortly thereafter, a style of singing appeared which was very different from that preceding. It continued for some years, chiefly in the manner of one voice singing with accompaniment and was exemplified by Giovanni Andrea, Giulio Cesare Brancaccio and Alessandro Merlo. These all sang bass ... with a variety of [improvisation] new and pleasing to the ear of all.

---

1 Vicenzo Giustiniani, *Discorso sopra la Musica* (ca. 1628), trans. Carol MacClintock (American Institute of Musicology, 1962), 67ff.

This style, he says, soon became popular with the nobles in various courts, where the music masters,

> took the greatest delight in the art, especially in having many noble ladies and gentlemen learn to sing and play superbly, so that they spent entire days in some rooms designed especially for this purpose and beautifully decorated with paintings. The ladies of Mantua and Ferrara were highly competent, and vied with each other not only in regard to the timbre and training of their voices but also in the design of exquisite [improvisation] delivered at opportune points, but not in excess. Furthermore, they moderated or increased their voices, loud or soft, heavy or light, according to the demands of the piece they were singing; now slow, breaking off with sometimes a gentle sigh, now singing long passages legato or detached, now groups, now leaps, now with long trills, now with short, and again with sweet running passages sung softly, to which sometimes one heard an echo answer unexpectedly. They accompanied the music and the sentiment with appropriate facial expressions, glances and gestures, with no awkward movements of the mouth or hands or body which might not express the feeling of the song. They made the words clear in such a way that one could hear even the last syllable of every word, which was never interrupted or suppressed by [improvisation] or other embellishments.

This is a description of a very high level of secular vocal art, all the more extraordinary if one remembers the frequent criticism of Church singers during the sixteenth century.

About this time Giustiniani discovers the music of Gesualdo, which he found exquisite and beautiful. Now he also finds the style of composition changing in Rome, with interest shifting to music for one or two voices with instruments and to improvisation.

> And because this refinement of the rules was wont sometimes to make composition hard and difficult, it was necessary to make every effort to choose the subject carefully, for even though there might be difficulties in its composition, the music should be melodious and emerge so sweet and fluent that when sung it would appear to be easy for anyone to compose.[2]

Regarding Florence he mentions the famous lady musician Vittoria [Archilei] as well as a number of composers writing in the new style.

> And they all sang, whether bass or tenor, with a range consisting of many notes, and with exquisite style and [improvisation] and with extraordinary feeling and a particular talent to make the words clearly heard.[3]

He also mentions the wide support for music among the nobles, in particular Cardinal Montalto who 'played the Cembalo excellently and sang in a sweet and sensitive manner.'

> Even all the Maestri di Cappella undertook to instruct certain castrati and boys to sing in florid style and in the new sentimental style.

---

2 Ibid., 70.

3 Ibid., 70ff.

Since that time there have been many composers such as Claudio Monte Verde, Giovanni Berardino Nanino, Felice Anerio and others who, without abandoning the style of composition of Prince Gesualdo of Venosa, have tried to soften and simplify the style and manner of composing, and in particular they have written many works to be sung in the churches, in various styles and inventions for several choirs, even as many as twelve.[4]

ON THE PHYSIOLOGY OF AESTHETICS

With regard to the ancient debate over Reason versus the senses, even the theorist, Zarlino, in one passage from Part III of his *Le Istitutioni Harmoniche*, seemed to be moving away from the old mathematics-based concept of music in favor of finding aesthetic values in live performance.

> For music, being a science that deals with sounds and tones—particular objects of the sense of hearing—is concerned only with the sonority that springs from pitches and tones, and with nothing else. Therefore it seems to me that all musical speculations not directed toward this end are vain and useless. Since music was really discovered for the purpose of pleasing and edifying, nothing beyond this end is important.[5]

Another who gave considerable thought to the conflict between science and musical practice was Girolamo Mei (1519–1594). It was Mei to whom Vincenzo Galilei wrote in 1572 when he became concerned over contradictions between the ancient Greek treatises and commentators on modern practice. In reply, Mei offered the following attempt to distinguish between science and art.

> The true end of the sciences is altogether different from that of the arts, since the end and proper aim of science is to consider every contingency of its subject and the causes and qualities of these purely for the sake of knowing truth from falsehood, without caring further how the arts will use this knowledge as an instrument or material or for otherwise gaining their ends … The science of music goes about diligently investigating and considering all the qualities and properties of the constitutions, systems, and order of musical tones, whether these are simple qualities or comparative, like the consonances, and this for no other purpose than to come to know the truth itself, the perfect goal of all speculation, and as a by-product the false. It then lets art exploit as it sees fit without any limitation those tones about which science has learned the truth.[6]

---

4 Ibid., 71.

5 Gioseffo Zarlino, *The Art of Counterpoint*, trans. Guy Marco and Claude Palisca (New Haven: Yale University Press, 1968), 264.

6 Quoted in Claude V. Palisca, *Humanism in Italian Renaissance Musical Thought* (New Haven: Yale University Press, 1985), 267. Galilei then adopted this thought in his 'Dialogo della musica antica et della moderna' (1581).

Giovanni Benedetti took a stronger position. In a letter to the composer, de Rore, he maintained that it was wrong to say one could understand the theory of music without experiencing music with the senses, nor can one understand without actually practicing music.[7] Whereas writers such as Zarlino sought scientific reasons to explain the nature of music, Benedetti correctly realized that the actual practice of music is simply not a science.[8]

ON THE AESTHETICS OF MUSIC

The most engaging and vivid discussion of the solutions of the problems faced by musicians in an environment where three different tuning systems were in use is found the *Il Desiderio* (1594) by the nobleman-musician, Hercole Bottrigari. In this dialogue, we meet Gratioso Desiderio, a cultured nobleman, but one with little knowledge of the theory of music, as he admits. It is a very interesting statement because it suggests that society has now moved away from the Scholastic Church dogma.

> I have never done any theoretical study in matters of music, but have only paid attention to the pleasure and delight afforded my sense of hearing by the composition and sound, as is the usual practice in our time.[9]

He has just left an afternoon concert by a large ensemble of some forty instrumentalists and encounters another nobleman, Alemanno Benelli, whose authority on music he respects. The latter has missed the concert because he took a nap, assuming the concert would begin later.

Desiderio explains to Benelli that he has left the concert with 'increased confusion in my mind,' and indeed that he often experiences such disappointment when hearing large ensembles.

> Having gone a number of times to hear various and diverse musical concerts by voices accompanied by different instruments, I have never experienced the great pleasure which I had imagined and supposed, and which, in fact I had hoped to experience. And today particularly, when I attended this one, such was the case; because, having seen a great apparatus of different kinds of instruments—among them a large Clavicembalo and a large Spinet, three Lutes of various forms, a great number of Viols and a similar large group of Trombones, two little Rebecs and as many large Flutes, straight and traverse, a large Double Harp and a Lyre—all for accompanying many good voices—there where I had thought I would hear a celestial harmony I heard confusion rather than the contrary, accompanied by a discordance, which has offended me rather than given me pleasure.[10]

---

7   Quoted in Ibid., 261.

8   Ibid., 265.

9   Hercole Bottrigari, *Il Desiderio*, trans. Carol MacClintock (American Institute of Musicology, 1962), 26.

10   Ibid., 12ff.

Benelli responds that since he knows Desiderio has a good ear, it is possible that in fact he heard discord rather than concord, confusion rather than union and that probably the ensemble was out of tune. Desiderio doubts this,

> since all the musicians who were performing are excellent artists. I know them well, and all are capable of acting as conductors, as sometimes I have seen them do in similar concerts. Therefore there must be some other reason.[11]

Benelli then proceeds to explain the problem which arises from the three different tuning systems in use. First, there are the 'stable' instruments, organs, keyboards and harps, which are tuned to Just Intonation and 'can produce only the pure diatonic scale which pleases most people, or seems to please them.'[12] When what he calls 'stable but alterable instruments' play with the 'stable' instruments, it is therefore necessary for these players to alter their pitches in order to correspond to the keyboard instruments.

> The stable but alterable instruments are all those which, after they have been tuned by the diligent player, can be changed, augmented or diminished in some degree, according to the good judgment of the player as he touches their frets a little higher or a little lower. This occurs with the Lute and Viol, even though they may have the stability of their frets. The same thing happens with the wind instruments, such as the straight and traverse Flutes and straight and curved Cornetts. Even though they may have a certain stability because of their holes, the accomplished player can nonetheless use a little less or a little more breath and can open the vents a little more or a little less, bringing them closer to a good accord. Expert players do this. The instruments which are completely alterable are those which have neither fingerboards nor holes—Trombones, Ribechini, Lire, and the like. These, having ordinarily neither frets nor openings, can wander here and there, according to the will of the player.

Benelli also mentions that he has spoken with the makers of flutes and cornetts and found that they construct these instruments with the holes placed according solely to their ear 'aided by nature,'[13] in other words using the overtone series like singers. Benelli then gets to the real problem, which was that some strings still tuned on the basis of the old tetrachords, which resulted in completely different divisions of the octave, with varying values of steps and half-steps. After illustrating this by a demonstration, Benelli adds an extraordinary observation regarding instances where in some circumstances keyboard players are forced to transpose their music in order to play with one of the strings tuned in the ancient system. He apparently suggests that when a keyboard must transpose a major key to a key impossible in Just Intonation, they played in the parallel minor!

---

11   Ibid., 14.
12   Ibid., 15ff.
13   Ibid., 16.

The players of the entirely stable instruments, as the Clavicembalo, Organ, and others, however excellent they may be, when they wish to transpose a tone lower or higher, or a semitone lower or higher, cannot do so in all places on their instrument. And here is the reason. When it is necessary to play the semitone commonly called major, since they lack it on their instruments they must needs play the one commonly called minor, whence the listeners and they themselves feel that their sense of hearing is offended.[14]

Aesthetics in Singing

There was much discussion in the sixteenth century on the subject of improvisation in singing. Clearly there was a long tradition of improvisation in instrumental music (and probably more than we can document in vocal tradition) and Reese even suggests that the absence of works by many famous sixteenth-century organists may be explained by a practice of improvisation.[15] He also finds this the intent of a Venetian decree of 1546 that no canons or priests should interrupt performing organists, but should remain quiet and patiently await the end of a piece.

Maffei, in 1562, mentions there was much argument on the question of improvisation and recommends it is more suitable for solo than ensemble performance. In the case of the latter, he suggests it should be limited to the penultimate syllable of a word and done by only one voice at a time.[16]

Zarlino, in Part Three of his *Le Istitutioni Harmoniche,* discusses this question in addition to providing an interesting critique of current vocal practice and his aesthetic goals of singing.

> Matters for the singer to observe are these: First of all he must aim diligently to perform what the composer has written. He must not be like those who, wishing to be thought worthier and wiser than their colleagues, indulge in certain improvisation [*diminutioni*] that is so savage and so inappropriate that they not only annoy the listener but are ridden with thousands of errors, such as many dissonances, consecutive unisons, octaves, fifths, and other similar progressions absolutely intolerable in composition. Then there are singers who substitute higher or lower tones for those intended by the composer, singing for instance a whole tone instead of a semitone, or vice versa, leading to countless errors as well as offense to the ear. Singers should aim to render faithfully what is written to express the composer's intent, intoning the correct steps in the right places. They should seek to adjust to the consonances and to sing in accord with the nature of the words of the composition; happy words will be sung happily and at a lively pace whereas sad texts call for the opposite. Above all, in order that the words may be understood, they should take care not to fall into the common error of changing the vowel sounds … It is truly reprehen-

---

14 Ibid., 19.

15 Gustave Reese, *Music in the Renaissance* (New York: Norton, 1959), 544.

16 Quoted in Anthony Newcomb, 'Secular Polyphony in the 16th Century,' in *Performance Practice in Music before 1600*, ed. Howard Brown (New York: Norton, 1989), 235.

sible and shameful for certain oafs in choirs and public chapels as well as in private chambers to corrupt the words when they should be rendering them clearly, easily, and accurately. For example, if we hear singers shrieking certain songs—I cannot call it singing—with such crude tones and grotesque gestures that they appear to be apes ... Who would not become enraged upon hearing such horrible, ugly counterfeits?

A singer should also not force the voice into a raucous, bestial tone. He should strive to moderate his tone and blend it with the other singers so that no voice is heard above the others. Such pushed singing produces more noise than harmony. For harmony results only when many things are tempered so that no one exceeds the other. The singer should know too that in church and in public chapels he should sing with full voice, moderated of course as I have just said, while in private chambers he should use a subdued and sweet voice and avoid clamor. Singers in such places should use good taste, so as not to leave themselves open to rightful censure. Further, they should refrain from bodily movements and gestures that will incite the audience to laughter as some do who move—and this is also true of certain instrumentalists—as if they were dancing.

If the composer and singer observe those things that pertain to their respective offices, there is no doubt that every composition will be sweet, soft, and harmonious, and the listeners will be pleased and grateful.[17]

Later in this book, Zarlino once again condemns improvisation, particularly the practice of adding an entirely new part to the score. Judging by the extraordinary discussion by Praetorius on Church Concerti[18] this was by no means a rare practice. Later Bach would do this by turning his bass/organ part into an entirely new part, making, for example, a trio sonata into a quartet. This improvisation of the bass part must have also been not uncommon for we see Bardi, below, objecting to this very practice.

I have heard at times some presumptuous persons—I will not call them fools—who were arrogant enough to add an extra part not only to a composition of two voices but even of up to twelve, solely to impress the audience with a skill they did not even possess ... They manage to convince those as foolish as themselves that they are performing miracles. The true worth of such performances, however, will be obvious to anyone of good taste. If these improvisations were to be written down, they would be found to contain a thousand errors against common rules and to be full of innumerable dissonances.[19]

Giovanni de' Bardi, in his *Discourse on Ancient Music and Good Singing*, mentions with some displeasure that he had even heard improvisation in the bass part.

When singing alone, whether to the lute or [cembalo] or to some other instrument, the singer may contract or expand the time at will, seeing that it is his privilege to regulate the time as he thinks fit. To [improvise] upon the bass is not natural, for this part is by nature slow, low, and somnolent. Yet it is the custom to do this. I know not what to say of it and am not eager to praise

---

17 Zarlino, *The Art of Counterpoint*, 110ff.
18 *Syntagma Musicum*, III.
19 Ibid., 221.

or to blame it, but I would counsel you to do it as little as possible and, when you do, at least to make it clear that you do it to please someone …

Then you will bear in mind that the noblest function a singer can perform is that of giving proper and exact expression to the canzone as set down by the composer, not imitating those who aim only at being thought clever (a ridiculous pretension) and who so spoil a madrigal with their ill-ordered [improvisation] that even the composer himself would not recognize it as his creation.[20]

Bardi concludes his discussion of singing by giving the aesthetic objective as 'sweetness,' followed by a few comments on the character of the singer.

Finally, the nice singer will endeavor to deliver his song with all the suavity and sweetness in his power, rejecting the notion that music must be sung boldly, for a man of this mind seems among other singers like a plum among oranges or like a man of fierce appearance showing the *giaro* among city dwellers and well-bred people …

One may gather that music is pure sweetness and that he who would sing should sing the sweetest music and the sweetest modes well ordered in the sweetest manner.

Beyond this you will bear in mind that in company a man ought always to be mannerly and courteous, not insisting on his own wishes but yielding to those of others, giving satisfaction to the best of his ability as often as he is called on, not imitating those who always grumble and, if they perform a service, perform it so grudgingly and disagreeably that their compliance becomes a mortification and a burden. Thus your manners will be pleasing and gentle, always at the command of others. When you sing you will take care to stand in a suitable posture … And you will not imitate those who, with much ado, begin tuning their voices and recounting their misfortunes, saying that they have caught cold, that they have not slept the night before, that their stomach is not right, and other things of this sort, so tedious that before they begin to sing they have canceled the pleasure with their exasperating excuses.

Bottrigari also provides an extraordinary account of the improvisation of singers, including during the Church service. His experience also seems to have been that it was not done well.

BENELLI. Because of the presumptuous audacity of performers who try to invent improvisation [*passaggi*], I will not say sometimes, but almost continuously, all trying to move at the same time as if in an [improvisation] contest, and sometimes showing their own virtuosity so far from the counterpoint of the musical composition they have before them that they become entangled in their dissonances—it is inevitable that an insupportable confusion should occur. This increases so greatly as they continue, that even those (and you see clearly how far this caprice and mania has gone) who play the low part, and the Bass, do not remember—not to say are ignorant of the fact—that it is the base and the foundation upon which the *cantilena* was built. And not standing firm beneath it, as the fabric requires, they go on up, they add

---

20 Giovanni de' Bardi, 'Discourse on Ancient Music and Good Singing,' in Oliver Strunk, *Source Readings in Music History* (New York: Norton, 1950), 299ff. Bardi (b. 1534) was a gentleman vitally interested in the arts. It was in his home, in Florence, where the male 'salon' known as the 'Camerata' met to discuss Greek tragedy. Their discussions were an important step toward opera.

nonsensical passages and allow themselves, because they enjoy it, to go so far as not only to pass into the Tenor part but even into that of the Contralto. Even this not sufficing, they go almost to that of the Sopranos, climbing in such a way to the top of the tree that they can't come down without breaking their necks …

Meanwhile the other parts go vacillating, all being in great peril of falling to earth, without hope of having any succor …

DESIDERIO. That explains why I have often heard similar discords and confusions made by the singers in Church when they improvise counterpoint above the *cantus fermus* of the Introit, which because of it often becomes almost odious and ridiculous at the same time.

BENELLI. You may take it for certain that if it is very difficult to do a thing well, even if it is done thoughtfully and carefully, how much easier it is to do it badly if one does it without thought and in haste and, I will add, without any taste, as seems to me to be clearly seen today in all our singers and players. Here is proof of it—they are no sooner in the place where they have to make music than immediately, even if they are late in appearing, they want to rush off to some other place; and while they are singing or playing, they are still able to jabber, laugh, and make jokes with their neighbors. Furthermore, whether the music is sung or played, they have only one kind of expression, so to speak, whether it's a good Madrigal or a Motet; and they are not interested in anything else.[21]

AESTHETICS IN INSTRUMENTAL PERFORMANCE

In his treatise on intabulation for the lute, Galilei frequently gives the purpose for various technical solutions in purely aesthetic terms. He says, for example, that to repeat a note without reason 'would cause the refined ear no little annoyance.'[22] In another place, a lutanist tells him that he chose to repeat a note in a tenor part of a canzone 'for very good reason, because striking it again brought to delicate ears a *je ne sais quoi* of sadness.'[23] Galilei thought that the lutanist might omit repeated notes 'for more grace,' and 'to furnish some novelty of the ear—which, like all the other senses, is fed by it.'[24] Similarly, that the use of rests, depending on their use, can result in 'grace' or 'dullness.'[25]

The art of intabulation, as presented by Galilei, consists frequently in the reduction of a polyphonic vocal work for an instrument. If the player does not, in effect, rewrite the work, leaving out notes which had to be repeated in the original only for the purpose of syllables, the result is a performance with 'little grace [and] often intolerable insipidity.' Galilei makes it clear that the primary aesthetic goal in such transcriptions for instruments is still 'the

---

21   Bottrigari, *Il Desiderio*, 61ff.
22   Vincenzo Galilei, *Fronimo* (1584), trans. Carol MacClintock (Neuhasen-Stuttgart: Hänssler-Verlag, 1985), 54.
23   Ibid., 55.
24   Ibid., 171.
25   Ibid., 54.

conceits of the words,' and not merely 'the pleasure which the variety of sounds brings to the ear.'[26] We should add here that later Galilei makes an extraordinary statement relative to the reduction of larger works for a single lute, a statement which reflects a type of music nowhere mentioned in music history books. In raising the question whether it might be well to add another string to the lute, the answer is, no, good players don't need it. Then he says of Fronimo, his friend the lute player,

> I have often seen him many times intabulate and play music for 40, 50 and 60 parts [!], but never yet ... has he been able to find anything, not the least thing, that might have been necessary to add to the ordinary lute to communicate it perfectly to the ear.[27]

Another aesthetic goal in transcription is that any addition of improvisation [passages and diminutions] must not obscure the original lines. In this regard the lutanist again expresses himself with purely aesthetic goals. Beauty, grace and the delight of the ear is the object, he says, not instilling moral virtues.

> Further, I have never committed [such] errors ... nor have I spoiled or impeded the order of fugues so that they could not be heard entirely. Rather have I proceeded to help them (if I can use that word in such a connotation) by making the voices clear and by augmenting the parts and the whole with sonority, beauty and grace in the best possible way that I knew how and was able to do, in order to completely delight the sense of hearing—which is indeed the proper aim of Music in our time—without any regard to inducing in the souls of the hearers one virtuous habit rather than another, as formerly the ancient Greek writers had it.[28]

A very interesting, and important, observation on performance practice by Galilei is that one should not aspire to simply play what is on the page.

> And let it not come into your mind to try to defend yourself with the silly excuse of some who say they did not feel called upon to do more than that which they found written or printed.[29]

The two reasons he gives for his premise are quite valid, aesthetically. First, written and printed music often has errors, which of course one should not aspire to play, but more important the player's goal toward the composer should be to communicate 'not only what he says but often what he wished to say.'

Finally, a remarkable passage in Galilei's book on lute intabulation gives an almost startling description, even for modern readers, of the emotions capable on the lute. At the same time the passage reads as if such a wide range of emotions was a common occurrence in the sixteenth century. In this passage, Galilei wonders if the lute is not limited, because it

---

26 Ibid., 56.
27 Ibid., 159.
28 Ibid., 61ff.
29 Ibid., 83.

cannot sustain pitches. The lutanist answers that the instrument most capable of this is the organ, but he has found on the contrary that such virtuosi of the organ, such as Claudio di Correggio and Gioseffo Guami,

> not by failure of their art and knowledge but by the nature of the instrument, have not been able, cannot, and never will be able to express the harmonies for *affetti* like *durezza, mollezza, asprezza, dolcezza*—consequently the cries, laments, shrieks, tears, and finally quietude and rage—with so much grace and skill as excellent players do on the lute.[30]

ART MUSIC

ON ARISTOCRATIC MUSIC

Among the popes of the sixteenth century we find several who were unusually interested in music. Leo X, elected pope before he was a priest, as a member of the Medici family received the best possible education, which included musical study with Issac.[31] Leo had a good ear, a fine voice and composed as well. He was active in the development of the papal choir and so it was appropriate that his portrait by Raphael pictures him reading a volume of sacred music.

Leo maintained a wind band which participated in the services of the Sistine Chapel, according to the diary of the papal Master of Ceremonies, Paris de Grassis.[32] Leo's interest in this ensemble is evidenced by his importation of players from Flanders[33] and purchasing trombones from the famous Hans Neuschel of Nürnberg.[34] Leo also had a shawm ensemble from Milan in residence, called the 'quattro sonatori di pifferi milanesi.'[35]

Another pope, Clement VII (1523–1534) was also reared as a son to Lorenzo de' Medici, although he was actually an illegitimate son to Giuliano de' Medici. He was also educated in music and some believe it was to distinguish himself from this pope that Jacobus Clemens took the sobriquet, 'Clemens non Papa.' We have an extraordinary account of an instrumental ensemble performing for Clement, described in the autobiography of Benvenuto Cellini. We assume this was a wind band, because of the mention of a shawm, trombone and a cornett playing the soprano voice. We also assume this to be one of the frequently described brief 'concerts' often heard at the conclusion of banquets, rather than functional music, because

---

30 Ibid., 87. Another advantage he gives for the lute is that you can play it anyplace, 'such as walking, riding horseback, sitting at the window, or in bed.'

31 Issac's *Optime pastor* was composed for Leo's coronation in 1513.

32 Dr. John Shearman, 'Leo X and the Sistine Chapel,' London, BBC Radio 3, August 20, 1971. The Sistine Chapel did not have, and does not have, an organ.

33 Edmond Vander Straeten, *La Musique aux Pays-Bas avant le XIXe Siecle* (1867) (New York, 1969), VI, 432ff.

34 Reese, *Music in the Renaissance*, 656.

35 H. Frey, *Regesten zur päpstlichen Kapelle unter Leo X und zu seiner Privatkapelle*, quoted in Dietrich Kämper, *Studien zur Instrumental Ensemblemusik des 16. Jahrhunderts in Italien* (Köln, 1970), 51.

of the comments by the pope which indicate he was carefully listening. We also notice here that the motets were carefully selected and for this performance the ensemble rehearsed two hours per day for eight days.

> It happened that at that time that one Giagiacomo, wind player [*piffero*] from Cesena, who is now in this capacity with the Pope, a very excellent performer, sent word through Lorenzo, trombonist from Lucca, who is now in the service of our Duke [Cosmo I], to inquire whether I was inclined to help them at the Pope's celebration of the Ferragosto, playing soprano with my cornett in some motets of great beauty selected by them for that occasion. Although I had the greatest desire to finish the vase I had begun, yet, since music has a wondrous charm of its own, and also because I wished to please my old father, I consented to join them. During the eight days before the festival we practiced two hours a day together; then on the first of August we went to the courtyard of the Vatican Palace, and while Pope Clement was at his banquet, we played those carefully rehearsed [*disciplinati*] motets so well that his Holiness protested he had never heard music more sweetly executed or with better ensemble.[36]

For pope Paul III there is extensive documentation for instrumental ensembles, in addition to the papal choir. He maintained a wind band, 'i musici di Castel San'Angelo,'[37] which he took with him when he went to Lucca in 1541 to meet Charles V.[38] When he traveled to visit François I in Paris, in 1538, Paul was accompanied by no fewer than four separate wind ensembles![39]

Many of the lesser Church princes, the cardinals in particular, followed the lead of the popes in supporting music. As an example we might cite a letter by the fifteenth-century German noble, Philip of Hessen, reporting on the music he heard at a banquet in Trent, Italy, given by Cardinal Madruzzo. Philip found the music,

> was quite wonderful and such as never had been heard anywhere ... there were about fifty singers there ... and up to eighty players of all types of instruments.[40]

Perhaps the noble of this period which most musicians associate with the practice of music is Gesualdo. His personal enthusiasm is clearly reflected in a description by Count Fontanelli.

---

36 Benvenuto Cellini, 'La Vita,' in our translation, in *Opere* (Milano, 1968), 94ff.

37 Alessandro Vessella, *La Banda* (Milano, 1935), 103. Vessella also documents papal trumpet ensembles, percussion ensembles and a separate band of the Swiss Guards.

38 E. Rodocanachi, *Château S. Ange* (Paris, 1909) and A. Bertolotti, 'Speserie segrete e pubbliche di Paolo III,' in *Atti e Memorie delle RR. Deputazioni di Storia Patria, per le provincie dell'Emilia*, Nuova serie, III, ia, 181.

39 Henri Prunières, 'La musique de la Chambre et de L'Écurie sous le Regne de François Ier,' in *L'Année Musicale* (Paris, 1911), 238.

40 Quoted in Otto Kade, 'Zwei archivalische Schriftstücke aus dem 16. Jahrhundert,' in *Monatschefte für Musikgeschichte* (1872), IV, 47ff.

> ... about music he spoke at such length that I have not heard so much in a whole year. He makes open profession of it and shows his works in score to everybody in order to induce them to marvel at this art.[41]

Not only did Gesualdo perform,[42] compose and discuss music, but he did not hesitate to make his views known regarding performances he heard, as Fontanelli describes in a letter of 1594.

> On Monday the prince was invited to dine by the patriarch, and there was music. But in Venice they sing badly, and His Excellency has a taste difficult to satisfy, as Your Highness knows. Thus he could not restrain himself from withdrawing from the room, summoning the director and cembalist and reproving them in such a manner that I felt sorry for them.[43]

Some nobles were so protective of their musical possessions that they kept their favorite compositions locked away for their private use. The *Dialogo* (1543) of Antonfrancesco Doni mentions such a policy by the Venetian noble, Neri Capone.

> This Messer Neri spends hundreds of ducats a year on such [divine music], and keeps it all to himself; he wouldn't let a piece of music out of his hands, were it even to his own father.[44]

Gesualdo, in the dedication of his fifth book of madrigals, expressed a similar concern that his compositions might in this fashion disappear and not become known.

> That humble and modest desire, which by nature has been given to Your Excellence to keep your rare musical compositions hidden from public applause as much as possible, has now thankfully been put aside and deemed to be overly contrived. It was with labor that the work was born to light, and its great delight has been enjoyed only domestically, without looking forward to the benefit of the press, which is already declared to be an enemy to the taste of Your Excellence.[45]

Gesualdo goes on to mention that any policy which does not make compositions known to the public results in some persons acquiring copies by illegal means and others attempting to pass off the compositions as their own work.

The court of Ferrara continued its great tradition for the support of music begun during the fifteenth century. For the banquet given on 24 January 1529, as part of the wedding celebrations of Ercole d'Este and Renée of France, we have an eyewitness account of an extraordinary high level of Art Music.[46] During the first course a work by Alphonso dalla

---

41 Quoted in Glenn Watkins, *Gesualdo, The Man and His Music* (Chapel Hill: University of North Carolina Press, 1973), 46.

42 Giustiniani, *Discorso sopra la Musica*, 70, describes him as an excellent player of the lute and Neapolitan chitarrone.

43 Quoted in Watkins, *Gesualdo*, 64.

44 Quoted in Mary Lewis, 'Antonio Gardane's Early Connections with the Willaert Circle,' in *Music in Medieval and Early Modern Europe*, ed. Iain Fenlon (Cambridge: Cambridge University Press, 1981), 210.

45 Quoted in Watkins, *Gesualdo*, 166.

46 Christoforo Messisburgo, *Banchetti, compositioni di vivande, et apparecchio generale* (Ferrara, 1549).

Vivola was performed by singers, five viols, keyboard, lute and flutes in two sizes.[47] During the second course madrigals were performed and for the third course a *Dialoghi* for double choir, with flute, sackbut, lute and viol. During the fourth course another composition by dalla Vivola was performed, with singers, viols, a contrabass viol, a dolzaina, a crumhorn, organ, two recorders and mute cornett. A pure wind ensemble of five sackbuts and cornett accompanied the fifth course, followed by a choral work. The seventh course was given with another choral work, accompanied by two dolzaine, crumhorn, large cornett and sackbut. A large mixed consort played during desert.

Duke Alfonso II of Ferrara was another noble who was a strong supporter of music. Bottrigari writes at length of his musical establishment.

> I am able ... to speak of them as a professional, having been several times to hear and see them in public as well as in private, at which time I heard them *in camera*, I feel that the conclusion that I will make about them is valid for all the other similar concerts, excellent and rare and worthy to be remembered and prized. Now listen. His highness has two large, decorated rooms, called the Musicians' Rooms because there the Musician-servitors ordinarily paid by His Highness go whenever they wish; they (the Musicians) are many—both Italian and Flemish—with good and beautiful voices, and graceful ways of singing, and of the highest excellence in playing as well, some on Cornetti, others on Trombones, Dolzaines, Pipes [shawms]; still others on the Viols, Ribechini, and still others on Lutes, Citharas, Harps, and Clavicembali. The instruments are placed neatly in those rooms near many other different instruments, some used and some not used ...
>
> To these rooms then—which I hope you will not expect me to describe in every particular—the Musicians, all or part of them, as they please, may repair and practice both playing and singing. Therefore there are, in addition to musical compositions in manuscript, many, many printed music books, written by all the talented men in the profession, kept in the greatest order in the places provided for them. The instruments are always in order and tuned so that they can be taken and played at any moment.[48]

Bottrigari explains that on the occasion of the visit of an important prince, the duke would sometimes have organized a *Concerto grande*, in which the entire establishment played together.

> Then they have not one or two, but a number of rehearsals, during which they maintain the highest obedience and attention, and think of nothing except a good ensemble and the greatest possible union without any other consideration; for that reason each performer comes with gracious modesty when he needs to be instructed and corrected by the M. di cappella. And the Sig. Duca also comes in person, with most kind and serene bearing and brotherly majesty, and

---

47 According to Vessella, *La Banda*, 84, the duke himself studied the flute with dalla Vivola.
48 Bottrigari, *Il Desiderio*, 50ff.

when he has heard them often gives them efficacious advice, with his perfect judgment, and admonitions, encouraging them to bear themselves well and to do themselves honor.[49]

Since Bottrigari had earlier discussed at length the inherent problems in tuning in a large ensemble, he points out that in this case they only played two particular compositions, especially written to,

> lessen and minimize the great imperfection of so many kinds of instruments playing at the same time. This is necessary to bring about the sought-after harmony, by which the soul of the listener truly enjoys the hoped-for pleasure and delight.

Desiderio wonders how interest in the court can be maintained when the same two works are performed over and over? Bottrigari advances several answers, including Aristotle's observation in his *Problems* that people enjoy music they already know, in preference to that which they do not know. To this Bottrigari adds the interesting comment,

> And for this reason, even in our corrupt time, after the singing of a new *cantilena* it is repeated again immediately. So it is with this great concert, the accomplished and judicious musicians repeat the music, whence to them and to the hearers the pleasure and delight is increased.[50]

Giustiniani also mentioned these concerts, but recalled somewhat differently that they were 'discontinued because of the difficulty of keeping the instruments in tune.' He also did not prefer the tutti sound.

> Then, too, experience has shown that such diversion, with the uniformity of sound and of the consonances, became tiresome rather quickly and was an incentive to sleep rather than to pass the time on a warm afternoon.[51]

Bottrigari also commented on the decline of music in France and Flanders, which he attributes to both countries having 'departed from the true Christian religion.'[52]

It is also in Bottrigari that we have the most complete description of the famous twenty-three member nun orchestra, the Nuns of S. Vito in Ferrara,[53] whom he introduces as representing 'the highest degree of perfection.'

> How you would melt away when you see them convene and play together with so much beauty and grace, and such quietness! …

---

49 Ibid., 52ff.
50 Ibid., 54.
51 Giustiniani, *Discorso sopra la Musica*, 79.
52 Bottrigari, *Il Desiderio*.
53 He also mentions in passing the three noble ladies in the court of the duchess of Ferrara who performed as part of her private music.

They are indubitably women; and when you watch them come ... to the place where a long table has been prepared, at one end of which is found a large clavicembalo, you would see them enter one by one, quietly bringing their instruments, either stringed or wind. They all enter quietly and approach the table without making the least noise and place themselves in their proper place, and some sit, who must do so in order to use their instruments, and others remain standing. Finally the Maestra of the concert sits down at one end of the table and with a long, slender and well-polished baton, and when all the other sisters clearly are ready, gives them without noise several signs to begin, and then continues by beating the measure of the time which they must obey in singing and playing ... And you would certainly hear such harmony that it would seem to you either that you were carried off to Helicona or that Helicona together with all the chorus of the Muses singing and playing had been transported to that place ...

Neither Fiorino nor Luzzasco, though both are held in great honor by them, nor any other musician or living man, has had any part in their work or in advising them; and so it is all the more marvelous, even stupendous, to everyone who delights in music.[54]

Bottrigari, in speaking further of this female orchestra, reveals two very interesting facts. First, that they ordinarily doubled the voices in church music and, second, that they improvised!

DESIDERIO. But what about the particulars of their learning to sing, and even more, to play instruments, particularly those of wind, which it is almost impossible to learn without maestri. Being women they cannot easily manipulate Cornetti and Trombones, which are the most difficult of musical instruments.

BENELLI. Those instruments are nearly always used doubled in the music which they play ordinarily on all the Feast days of the year. And they play them with such grace, and with such a nice manner, and such sonorous and just intonation of the notes that even people who are esteemed most excellent in the profession confess that it is incredible to anyone who does not actually see and hear it. And their [improvisation] is not of the kind that is chopped up, furious, and continuous, such that it spoils and distorts the principal air, which the skillful composer worked ingeniously to give to the *cantilena*; but a times and in certain places there are such light, vivacious embellishments that they enhance the music and give it the greatest spirit.

DESIDERIO. I am stupefied; I am truly amazed. But, after all, who instructed them in the beginning? It must be necessary if one wishes to maintain, if not to increase the bright splendor of musical concerts, that there be someone who looks after it, and is intelligent and expert enough to instruct, so that it may be done so carefully and dexterously.

BENELLI. That same nun who is the director of the concerto is also Maestra of all the beginners both in singing and in playing; and with such decorum and gravity of bearing has she always proceeded and continued in this office that her equals, as they are, are glad to acknowledge her and esteem her for their superior, loving and obeying her, fearing and honoring her completely.[55]

---

54 Bottrigari, *Il Desiderio*, 58ff.

55 Ibid., 59ff.

The musical activities of the court at Florence have been widely documented and in thinking of this court what we remember most are the extraordinary performances of *intermedi* performed between the acts of comedies.[56] These intermedi, together with the comedies, could last up to four hours, during which time the guests were expected to listen quietly.[57]

While the intermedi themselves were often allegorical, etc., the use of music during the comedies was realistic, the characters using music as they would in real life.[58] Often these theater pieces had a pastoral character, in obvious retrospection of ancient Greece. Indeed Pirrotta finds the pastorale to be 'the fullest attainment of the Italian Renaissance in its attempt to recreate ancient tragedy.'[59]

We might briefly summarize one of these, an Intermedi given on 25 December 1565, between the acts of Francesco d'Ambra's comedy, *La Cofanaria*, as part of the wedding celebrations of Francesco de' Medici and Johanna of Austria. The first intermezzo presented the characters Venus, the three Graces, the Four Seasons, and Cupid and the Four Passions, Hope, Fear, Joy and Pain. The second intermezzo consisted of a serenade of Psyche by Cupid, to two compositions for mixed consort by Alessandro Striggio.

The third intermezzo presented Cupid so taken by love for Psyche that he had neglected mortals, resulting in the appearance of characters representing Frauds and Deceptions. Here a madrigal, 'S'amor vinto, e prigion posto in oblio,' by Corteccia was performed by eight singers, five crumhorns and a mute cornett.

The fourth intermezzo introduced the characters Discord, Ire and Cruelty, reflecting the result of love having died among mankind. This was another madrigal, accompanied by two trombones, dolziana, three cornetts and two tamburi.

The finale is set at the foot of Mount Helicon and one eyewitness reported two cornetts, two trombones, dolzaina, crumhorn, lirone, rebec and two lutes.[60] A noble guest, Duke Ferdinand, gave a different account.

> After the Fifth Act … came twelve naked nymphs and as many satyrs who sang and played on large curved pipes with which harmonized cornetts and trombones.[61]

This same Bavarian duke also reports the music for a breakfast one morning during the celebrations of this same wedding.

---

56 The most important discussion of this music is found in Nino Pirrotta and Elena Povoledo, *Music and Theatre from Poliziano to Monteverdi* (Cambridge: Cambridge University Press, 1982).

57 Ibid., 76.

58 Ibid., 78.

59 Ibid., 268.

60 Domenico Mellini, *Descrizione Dell' Apparato Della Comedia Et Intermedii D'essa Recitata in Firenze il giorno di S. Stefano l'anno 1565 …* (Florence, 1565).

61 Quoted in A. Sandberger, *Beiträge zur Geschichte der bayerischen Hofkapelle unter Orlando di Lasso* (Leipzig, 1895), III, 353.

> At the breakfast ... music was played with cornetts, trombones, also with crumhorns; but they only played [Italian] dances which in my opinion were nothing special.[62]

As time goes on, the accounts of these performances report larger and larger instrumental forces. In the Florentine intermedi of 1567–1568 the fifth intermedio has twelve singers singing a madrigal accompanied by four viols, a cornetto, two trombones, a lyre and a lute, which were answered by another group of four singers, two trombones and three flutes.

The 1586 Florentine intermedi presents shepherds and shepherdesses 'rejoicing and singing to the sound of lutes, harps, dolzaine, bagpipes, bass, tenor and soprano viols, recorders, flutes, transverse flutes and "large flutes," trombones, cornetti, and rebecs.'[63]

An account by Bastiano de Rossi of a 1589 intermezzo for Bargagli's *La Pellegrina* performed in the Uffizi palace mentions a symphony *à 6* which was actually played by

> six lutes, three large and three small, a psaltery, a bass-viol with three tenor viols, four trombones, a *cornetta*, a transverse flute, a zither, a mandola and a *sopranino di viola* played most excellently by Alessandro Striggo.[64]

Another intermezzo for this same comedy, a madrigal *à 6* by Malvezzi, was performed by twenty-four singers, four lutes, four viols, two bass viols, four trombones, two cornetti, a cittern, psaltery, mandola, arcivolata lira and a violin. Later in this production a concluding work was performed by sixty voices together with all available instruments![65]

On Civic Music

By the sixteenth century virtually every Italian town of any size had both a civic trumpet ensemble for ceremonial duties and a wind band of shawms, trombones and cornetts, usually referred to as 'musica di piffari' or simply 'piffari.'[66] A typical description of both ensembles is given by an eyewitness in Bologna, describing a procession of the town council in 1602.

> When they appear in public, these *Signori* are dressed in rich robes of silk, and during the winter they are muffled up with very precious furs as well. They are accompanied by a very respectable household of eight trumpeters, with a drummer or player of the nakers, who with these trumpets play certain Moorish drums. To both the drums and trumpets are attached banners with the

---

62 Ibid., III, 351. For 'Italian' dances, the duke wrote 'Welsche.'

63 Pirrotta, *Music and Theatre*, 210.

64 Ibid., 220.

65 Ibid., 233.

66 Dietrich Kämper, *Studien zur Instrumentalen Ensemblemusik des 16. Jahrhunderts in Italien* (Köln, 1970), 50.

arms of liberty; also eight excellent musicians with trombones and cornettos; a herald; a *spenditore*; nine pages dressed in scarlet cloaks and stockings in the livery of the city—white and red.[67]

The strings were slow in appearing as official members of the civic musical establishments and even in Florence there is not a single reference to a string instrument in the civic archives between 1490 and 1432.[68]

We get some impression of the seriousness of these civic bands in an interesting document relative to the organization and duties of the 'Musica di Palazzo' of Lucca in 1557.

> Nicolao Dorati is to be the director and head of said musicians, and they must obey him in performing whatever music in whatever manner he may choose. When playing at the city hall, before and after the dinner of the *Signoria*, Maestro Bernardino de Padova is to play the first soprano, and Vincenzo di Pasquino Bastini the second soprano; but when playing in the hall or the chambers of the *Signoria*, each one is to play and sing the part assigned to him by said Nicolao, their director. However, outside the city hall, in church, on the public square, at weddings, feasts, serenades, or other events, where they will number at least six, Maestro Giulio is to play the first soprano, Maestro Bernardino, his father, the second, and Maestro Vincenzo the third, that is, contralto. And if by chance, which God forbid, there should arise among them a quarrel, ill-will, or other trouble, Maestro Nicolao is to intervene and restore peace, and if anyone should refuse to listen to reason, he is to be reported to the *Signoria* in office at the time, so that steps can be taken accordingly. And since beautiful music and perfect harmony are the result of constant practice, there should be assigned to them for this purpose a room ... equipped with tables and benches in which they are to meet for practice twice a week for two hours, namely, Wednesdays and Saturdays. From the first of February to the last of September they shall meet in the morning, two hours before dinner, and from the first of October to the last of January, in the afternoon, two hours before supper. In order to enforce these rules, the *maestro di casa* shall take the attendance, and those who are absent, shall be fined one *carlino* for each time, except in case of illness or other legitimate excuse.[69]

The aesthetic purpose assigned in this document, 'beautiful music,' should not be assumed to be rare. Certainly the evidence we have in the extant 'band library' of Girolamo Dalla Casa, the leader of the Venetian Civic Wind Band [*Capo de Concerti delli stromenti di fiato della Illustriss. Signoria di Venetia*] confirms a high level of Art Music. For this purpose we find large instrument collections being assembled in many towns. An inventory of the town's collection in Verona in 1569, for example, lists sixty-six winds, five sets of viols, a lira, a rebechino, seven lutes, two harpsichords and a regal.[70]

---

67 Quoted in Don Smithers, *The Music and History of the Baroque Trumpet* (London: Dent), 78.

68 Keith Polk, 'Civic Patronage and Instrumental Ensembles in Renaissance Florence' (Unpublished).

69 Carl Anthon, 'Some Aspects of the Social Status of Italian Musicians during the Sixteenth Century,' in *Journal of Renaissance and Baroque Music* (New Haven, 1946), II, 225.

70 Quoted in Anthony Baines, *Woodwind Instruments and their History* (New York, 1962), 239.

Bottrigari provides an interesting description of Art Music sung by choruses of common people ('not being of high position'), sung outdoors during the evening.

> Each member, having attended to his own affairs all day, gathered with the others in the evening; and after rehearsing the singing of certain of their *canzoni* went forth together from the house; and for several hours in the evening, sometimes before supper, sometimes after, and even up till the break of day, went wandering through the city greeting with their delightful songs now one, now another, now still another friend, who were most consoled by it. And their desire to perfect this kind of harmony with perfect union was such that besides seeking many times the useful advice of the Maestro di cappella of the cathedral—a musician of great importance at that time—they never ceased to admonish each other most kindly about their own defects; and finally, standing closely together and, wrapped in their mantles, almost hidden in the darkness, they demonstrated that as they were united almost as closely as they could be with their bodies—of which they would indeed have wished to be able to make one body only—likewise they delighted in making as far as they could a true union of their respective voices, from which then came forth, I will say, an almost celestial harmony.[71]

On Soloists

The tradition of sung poetry, which reached such heights in the Greek lyric poets, still existed in Italy throughout the Renaissance. In 1570 the poet Benedetto Varchi recalls being moved by hearing the solo singer, Silvio Antoniano.

> I never heard anything that moved me more inside and seemed more wonderful (and I am old and I have heard a few things) than the singing extemporaneously to the lira of M. Silvio Antoniano, when he came to Florence.[72]

The singer Fomia is described, when she appeared as Cleopatra in an intermedio given in Piccolomini's *Alessandro* in 1558, by one listener as follows:

> [Fomia] when she sings, cannot be compared to any earthly thing, but to the heavenly harmony.[73]

We have mentioned above, Dalla Casa, who was the foremost cornettist of the sixteenth century. Giustiniani mentions another cornett virtuoso, Luigi del Cornetto of Ancona, 'who played marvelously.' We find an insight into the volume of this instrument, when Giustiniani recalls,

---

71 Bottrigari, *Il Desiderio*, 56.

72 Quoted in Palisca, *Humanism in Italian Renaissance Musical Thought*, 375. Palisca gives a lengthy review of this solo singing tradition in pages 369ff.

73 Quoted in Pirrotta, *Music and Theatre*, 198.

he played the Cornett with such moderation and exactitude that it astonished many gentleman present who liked music, because the Cornett did not overshadow the sound of the Cembalo.[74]

He also observed that the art of playing the flute in the German style, 'with grace and nicety,' was not known in Italy, although he singles out the noble, Giulio Cesare of Oriveto, 'who plays upon this instrument, to the amazement of those who hear him.'[75]

Giustiniani was thinking of such soloists when he observed that many had achieved considerable profit.

> At present there are many people who, with the profession of music, have earned more than a thousand *scudi* of income; one cannot begin to name them all.[76]

On the Audience

In these books we have contended that a primary hallmark of art music is the presence of the contemplative listener. During the sixteenth century one can find numerous references which document this prerequisite for art music. For example, Alessandro Striggio, composer of the intermedi of 1567 and 1569, was also a distinguished performer on the viol, who is described as playing 'with such grace and musical knowledge that all listeners marvel.'[77] A first-hand report of a 1589 performance of Caccini's intermedio in *La Pellegrina* by Bargagli, speaks of a performance on the chitarrone by Jacopo Peri which was listened to 'with marvelous attentiveness by the audience.'[78]

No account of sixteenth-century performance so vividly documents the contemplative listener, in a way that seems so modern, as this description of a group of listeners to a performance by the lute virtuoso, Francesco da Milano, in 1555—again performing a concert *after* the banquet was finished.

> The tables cleared, he took up a lute and, as if merely essaying chords, he began, seated near the foot of the table, to strum a fantasy. He had plucked no more than the first three notes of the tune when all the conversation ceased among the festive throng and all were constrained to look there where he was, as he continued with such enchanting skill that little by little, through the divine art in playing that was his alone, he made the very strings to swoon beneath his fingers and transported all who listened into such gentle melancholy that one present buried his head in his hands, another let his entire body slump into an ungainly posture with members all awry,

---

74 Giustiniani, *Discorso sopra la Musica*, 79.
75 Ibid., 80.
76 Ibid.
77 Cosimo Bartoli, 'Ragionamenti accedemici' (1567), quoted in Pirrotta, *Music and Theatre*, 193.
78 Quoted in Ibid., 231, fn. 148.

while another, his mouth sagged open and his eyes more than half shut, seemed, one would judge, as if transfixed upon the strings, and yet another, with chin sunk upon his chest, hiding the most sadly taciturn visage ever seen, remained abstracted in all his senses save his hearing, as if his soul had fled from all the seats of sensibility to take refuge in his ears where more easefully it could rejoice in such enchanting symphony.[79]

FUNCTIONAL MUSIC

For many decades, music history texts and period recordings gave students the impression that sixteenth-century Church music was entirely unaccompanied. Research over the past twenty years, particularly in the area of civic pay documents, has revealed quite a different perspective and today European recordings, in particular, are beginning to use winds to double the voices in polyphonic Church works.

This practice was particularly evident in Germany, where civic records clearly document the regular appearance of the civic wind player in the church on Sundays, both in the Protestant and the Catholic areas.

We find this same kind of evidence in Italy as well, as for example in this civic contract in Bergamo, even though this reference is to festival days. The civic wind players were instructed,

> to serve on festivals in the choir with their instruments, and in the morning and evening; and further to play without extra pay either in part or altogether at all feasts, solemnities and other public occasions on request.[80]

A civic contract of 1556 for Udine seems to refer to their appearances in the regular Sunday Mass.

> To the shawm and crumhorn [?] players in the service of the city, five in number, serving in the choir of the aforementioned church of Udine ...[81]

And of course there is the vast literature of instrumental canzoni, and other forms, which were used as 'occasional' music in the Italian Church services. We can see this practice very clearly in a catalog kept by the organist, Carlo Milanuzzi, of Venezia, which included such items as,

---

79 Pontus de Tyard, *Solitaire second* (1555).

80 Quoted in Denis Arnold, 'Brass Instruments in the Italian Church Music of the Sixteenth and Early Seventeenth Centuries,' *Brass Quarterly* (1957), 84.

81 Quoted in G. Vale, 'La Capella Musicale dl Duomo di udine dal Secolo XIII al XIX,' in *Note d'Archivio* (1930), VII, 106.

> Tibicinibus et aduncorum cornum inflatoribus ...

Canzon à 5 detta la Zorzi per l'Epistola
Concerto à 5 per l'Offertorio
Canzon à 5 detta la Riatelli per li Post Communio[82]

And in this regard, we hardly need mention the extraordinary tradition at St. Mark's in Venice, presided over by Gabrieli. We will let his student, Heinrich Schütz, speak for us as well:

Ye Immortal God! What a man was that![83]

In Venice also, the religious confraternities contributed the resources for making possible larger scale musical performances for special occasions. In 1515, for example, the Scuola di San Marco provided the church of San Zanipolo on the first Sunday of each month twelve singers, in addition to trumpets, shawms, recorders, cornetts, a lute, harp, viol and organ.[84] The purpose of supplying these larger forces is given in a document of 1530: for 'the universal satisfaction of all.'[85] This being the case, the urbane men of the Scuola were quick to criticize their hired performers if they did not meet the artistic expectations, as we can see in a document of 1540.

> There is no money of our Scuola that is spent with less result and more shame and disgrace to the ministers than the payment made to the *cantadori nouvi*, because of their bad manner of singing, without any harmony and sweetness, singing in contempt of all rules, and with great dishonor in general to all; and more so in that they are unprincipled in conduct, behaving as they please and not as they should.[86]

The extraordinary heights reached by performances sponsored by the Scuola di San Rocco can be seen in the 1608 recollection by a visiting Englishman. He found a concert he heard there,

> so good, so delectable, so rare, so admirable, so superexcellent, that it did even ravish and stupifie all those strangers that never heard the like. But how others were affected with it I know not; for mine owne part I can say this, that I was for the time even rapt up with Saint Paul into the third heaven. Sometimes there sung sixteene or twenty men together, having their master or moderator to keepe them in order; and when they sung, the instrumentall musitians played also. Sometimes sixteene played together upon their instruments, ten Sagbuts, foure Cornets, and two Violdegambaes of an extraordinary greatness; sometimes tenne, sixe Sagbuts and foure Cornets.[87]

---

82 Quoted in Arnold, 'Brass Instruments,' 89.

83 Henrich Schütz, in the dedication of his *Sacrae Symphoniae* to the Elector of Saxony.

84 Jonathan Glixon, 'Music at the Venetian Scuole Grandi, 1440–1540,' in *Music in Medieval and Early Modern Europe*, ed. Iain Fenlon (Cambridge: Cambridge University Press, 1981), 193.

85 Ibid., 205.

86 Ibid., 203.

87 Quoted in L. E. Bartholomew, *Alessandro Rauerij's Collection of Canzoni per Sonare (1608)* (Fort Hayes, Kansas, 1965), 36.

Throughout the Renaissance in Italy the Confraternities practiced the singing of Lauds. In the fifteenth century these reflected in style the sophisticated men who made up these organizations. In the sixteenth century, however, following the fervor of Savonarola, this repertoire takes on a religious enthusiasm recalling the first centuries of Christians. An example, from Girolamo Benivienti's first book of Lauds (1524) reads,

> Never was there so sweet a gladness,
> Joy of so pure and strong a fashion
> As with zeal and love and passion
> Thus to embrace Christ's holy madness.
>
> They who are mad in Jesus, slight
> All that the wise man seeks and prizes;
> Wealth and place, pomp, pride, delight,
> Pleasure and fame, their soul despises;
> Sorrow and tears and sacrifices,
> Poverty, pain, and low estate,
> All that the wise men loathe and hate,
> Are sought by the Christian in his madness ...
>
> The Christian listens and smiles for glee
> When he hears the taunt of his foe, for he
> Glories and triumphs in holy madness.[88]

One can find numerous accounts of extravagant aristocratic weddings in which music played a prominent role at this time. One interesting example was the marriage of Lucrezia Borgia (1480–1519), daughter to Pope Alexander VI, to Alfonso d'Este in 1501. The party which left Ferrara to bring her back from Rome included four thousand men, fifty wagons for baggage, thirteen trumpeters and an eight-member wind band.[89] They were met on the steps of St. Peter's by another wind band, probably belonging to the pope.[90] When the party arrived back in Ferrara, bringing eighty-six mules bearing the trousseau and jewels of Lucrezia, they were greeted by floats and eighty trumpeters.[91] The official entertainments included allegorical depictions of The Triumph of Virtue, The Triumph of Agriculture and the Victory of Love and Music over the Rude and Savage Natures—not to mention the banquets which consumed three hundred oxen, fifteen thousand head of poultry.[92]

There are many occasional references to military music in the sixteenth century, but only this passage by Giustiniani offers actual details.

---

88   Quoted in John Addington Symonds, *Renaissance in Italy* (New York: Capricorn Books, 1964), I, 264ff.

89   John Fyvie, *The Story of the Borgias* (New York, 1913), 138, and Ferdinand Gregorovius, *Lucretia Borgia* (New York, 1904), 208.

90   Gregorovius, *Lucretia Borgia*, 216.

91   Ibid., 241.

92   Fyvie, *Story of the Borgias*, 177.

The sound of the Trumpet is suitable for war and to incite and to direct the cavalry in particular actions; however it is not used by noble persons but by mercenaries. In Flanders because of the wars there are many people who play in a better than average way, and the same is true in England. The same may be said also of the Drum and of the Bagpipes of the Comiti di Galere and of the Germans and the Swiss. Pifferi [wind bands] are used in the armed forces and in seagoing vessels; by those that sail the ocean they are played most exquisitely.[93]

The personal trumpets of pope Leo X played a key role in his private hunting, if one can call it hunting. Hunting, for Leo, meant collecting game in an enclosure sealed off by tough sail-cloth. Then, when the trumpets were given the signal from Leo, a gap in the canvas was opened.

Soon a torrent of animals came rushing out into the open, stags and boars, hares and rabbits, wolves, goats and porcupines. The waiting sportsmen would then eagerly fall upon their chosen targets with spear or sword, axe or halbred …[94]

Welcoming music must have been a familiar occurrence during the sixteenth century, but we are attracted in particular to an account of Charles V's arrival on his first visit to Naples in 1536, when he was greeted with villanesca and madrigals, 'very well concerted.'[95]

ENTERTAINMENT MUSIC

Pirrotta points to rather sophisticated entertainment music in the example of the early sixteenth-century repertoire of carnival songs in three or four parts.[96] He also mentions a public entertainment, held outdoors, by the fifteen-year-old Cardinal, Ferdinando dei Medici, in 1567, which included the usual allegorical characters accompanied by two trombones, two lutes, a lira, harpsichord, cornetto and flute.[97]

Finally, a comment by Giustiniani reflects on the use of wind bands for public entertainment.

[The Pifferi] are used … in festivals in small towns and country districts, and also in the great cities at the festivals of the common people.[98]

---

93 Giustiniani, *Discorso sopra la Musica*, 79ff.
94 Christopher Hibbert, *The House of Medici* (New York, 1975), 230ff.
95 Nino Pirrotta, 'Ars Nova and Stil Novo,' in *Music and Culture in Italy from the Middle Ages to the Baroque* (Cambridge: Harvard University Press, 1984), 176.
96 Pirrotta and Povoledo, *Music and Theatre from Poliziano to Monteverdi*, 21.
97 Ibid., 197, fn. 74.
98 Giustiniani, *Discorso sopra la Musica*, 80.

4 SIXTEENTH-CENTURY ITALIAN POETS

THE RAPID EXPANSION OF THE RANGE OF THOUGHT which was unleashed by the Renaissance brought a desire to reconsider the traditional branches of academic study inherited from the Middle Ages, the seven Liberal Arts. In particular those worthy subjects which had been left out of this system, poetry, history, painting and sculplture and philosophy itself, needed to be accounted for. In his study of how poetry differs with music, to which in earlier times it had been united, Girolamo Mei (1519–1594) found poetry had unique characteristics.

> Sculpture and painting imitate bodies directly and only incidentally actions, whereas those arts allied with poetry imitate actions and only incidentally the person acting. A further difference is that the graphic imitations represent things directly to the sense of sight or touch and only secondarily to the intellect through the imagination, whereas the poetic arts are directed to the intellect and only incidentally to the sense of hearing, as when a poem is recited or listened to, and to the sight, when it is read or staged.[1]

The growing status of Art must have been due partly to the growing status of artists, especially following Leonardo and Michelangelo. Tasso, in fact now finds a number of professions more highly regarded than doctors and lawyers.

> It is surely a great misfortune for these times, or rather for our poetic and humane literature, that it is granted no other reward than glory, while lawyers, doctors, architects, sculptors, and painters usually manage to make money and to become rich, as in our own time has happened to Raphael, Michelangelo, and the noble Paciotto …
>
> But I [have] found that musicians and singers were held in higher esteem, and even wrestlers, fencers, and riding masters.[2]

Tasso also mentions the growing involvement of towns in the patronage of the arts,

> Cities there are, most proud of their own worth,
> fervent with deeds and ever lively arts …[3]

---

[1] Paraphrased in Claude V. Palisca, *Humanism in Italian Renaissance Musical Thought* (New Haven: Yale University Press, 1985), 337.

[2] Torquato Tasso, 'Minturno, or On Beauty,' in *Tasso's Dialogues,* trans. Carnes Lord (Berkeley: University of California Press, 1982), 197ff. Francesco Paciotto (1521–1591) was a famous military architect.

[3] Torquato Tasso, *Creation of the World*, trans. Joseph Tusiani (Binghamton: Center for Medieval & Early Renaissance Studies, 1982), III, 1.

although he refers as well to the detrimental effect of the many sixteenth-century battles regarding Art, when he observes 'Reason and art are overcome by wrath.'[4]

Several writers, in fact, complain that poetry, in particular, is becoming *too* popular. Pietro Aretino, who once challenged Tasso to a duel,[5] writes that too many common people are writing poetry.

> The art of making verses is now so widespread among so many people that not only studious and learned souls, but errant and untaught soldiers seem to be Petrarchs and Dantes.[6]

The often negative philosopher, Bruno, agrees, finding 'many vain versifiers who against the wishes of the world want to pass themselves off as poets.'[7]

ON THE PHYSIOLOGY OF AESTHETICS

Tasso, in his *Creation of the World*, repeatedly attacks philosophy. Even in an atmosphere where the rediscovery of the ancient Greek philosophers was creating general excitement, Tasso could write,

> Let Greece refrain from boasting of her old
> philosophers, whose findings are untrue.[8]

A few verses later we find 'as skirmishing philosophers contend, at war with one another.' And '[those] in ancient days, who were unjustly famous as philosophers.'[9] Thus he concludes,

> So let against the truth no false and vain
> experience of erring mortal man
> boast of its conquest for the paltry span
> of a few decades making him so proud.
> For, let me tell you, if you simply think
> of all the countless centuries that sped,
> no human knowledge can avail you now.[10]

---

4 Torquato Tasso, *Jerusalem Delivered*, trans. Ralph Nash (Detroit: Wayne State University Press, 1987), VI, xlviii.

5 Letter to Tasso, October, 1549, in Thomas Chubb, *The Letters of Pietro Aretino* (New Haven: Shoe String Press [Archon Books], 1967), 284.

6 Letter to Faloppia, in Ibid., 175.

7 Giordano Bruno, *The Expulsion of the Triumphant Beast*, trans. Arthur Imerti (New Brunswick: Rutgers University Press, 1964), 213 [III, i].

8 Tasso, *Creation of the World*, II, 75.

9 Ibid., IV, 620.

10 Ibid., III, 420ff.

In this same work, Tasso attacks the integrity of the senses as strongly as the old Church writers. He speaks of 'faulty human senses,'[11] and,

> Nor can man's erring sense show otherwise,
> as is attested by the old mistake
> of those who in this fashion used to deem
> the Red Sea severed from the Indian Sea.
> For neither sense nor true experience
> of skillful men will ever demonstrate
> how all the other seas indeed are one,
> and therefore blended with the Caspian waves.[12]

Even Aristotle, says Tasso, was wrong to trust the senses.

> The mighty teacher of all those who know,
> the one whose many schools still teach mankind,
> is also wrong, though less, in following
> motion and senses, escorts to be shunned.[13]

In only one phrase does Tasso seem to recognize the debt of understanding to the senses.

> Man's intellect has but short wings behind his dying senses.[14]

In early literature we find a frequently expressed prejudice for the right hand, which we understand today as being synonymous with the rational left hemisphere of the brain which, in turn, also tends to ignore the importance of the more subjective right hemisphere (left hand). An example of this prejudice is found in Ariosto, when he writes,

> The man who leaves this path finds on the right only the beautiful and on the left as much ugliness gathered as the world embraces.[15]

---

11   Ibid., II, 101.
12   Ibid., III, 621ff.
13   Ibid., IV, 665ff. Aristotle is criticized again in IV, 1022ff.
14   Ibid., II, 156.
15   Ludovico Ariosto, *The Satires of Ludovico Ariosto*, trans. Peter Wiggins (Athens: Ohio University Press, 1976), 133. Ludovico Ariosto (1474–1533) served the court at Ferrara the greater part of his life and is best known for his masterpiece *Orlando Furioso*.

ON THE PSYCHOLOGY OF AESTHETICS

The one emotion which attracted the attention of these poets was, of course, Love. When it comes to Love, Ariosto recommended following the senses, not Reason.

> I should tell you first of all to follow the lead of your senses if the torch of love makes you take a wife.[16]

A similar thought was given by Ariosto in this passage from his classic *Orlando Furioso*.

> What sweeter, what more blissful state than that of being in love? Whose life could be happier or more blessed than that of Love's servant—were it not for the constant nagging of that dark suspicion, that dread, that torment, frenzy, passion known as jealousy!
>
> Instill any other bitterness into this sweetest of pleasures and it will serve to augment it, to perfect and refine it. Water tastes the better for thirst; hunger adds relish to food; the man who has never known war cares little for peace.
>
> The eye may not see what the heart sees …[17]

ON THE PHILOSOPHY OF AESTHETICS

Regarding the nature of poetry, Aretino offered a definition which centers on the mystery of artistic inspiration.

> O wandering rabble, I tell you, and I tell you again, that poetry is a mere flight of the fancy begotten by Nature in one of her ebullient moods. It needs only its own madness. But if it lacks that it is like a cymbal without any bells on it, it is like a belfry that has no chimes.[18]

Tasso also mentions on the important role of inspiration, when he prays,

> O Lord, you are the hand, I am the harp,
> which plucked by you, with most melodious tunes
> resounds, and softens every hardened heart.
> You are the breath, O Lord, but, being weak,
> I'm nothing but a raucous instrument
> to tell your glory, for my sounding voice,
> if you inspire me not, is quickly stilled.[19]

---

16 Ibid., 129.

17 Ludovico Ariosto, *Orlando Furioso*, prose trans. Guido Waldman (London: Oxford University Press, 1974), the beginning lines of XXXI.

18 Letter to Niccolo Franco, in Chubb, *The Letters of Pietro Aretino*, 70.

19 Tasso, *Creation of the World*, I, 64ff.

Francesco Patrizi discusses the nature of poetry in terms which we believe approach its most important characteristic. Several treatises written at the end of the century attempted to explain that sung poetry is not an *imitation* of the emotions, but is the 'real thing.' Here Patrizi explains that the thought of the poet passes through the ears of the listener to his soul, moving them in the same emotions which arose in the poet.[20]

> The poet singing his poems and his song accompanied by the harmonic sounds of the kithara or lyre or aulos or other such instrument, considered as pure song, realizes an expression of his ideas [*concetti*] but no imitation or resemblance whatever.[21]

Again, he was looking to the emotions of the words for the source of communication, thus he was not so generous toward instrumental music.

> The harmonious sound of any instrument whatever not only is not imitation but it does not even resemble any imitation. Consequently, instrumental sound alone without the company of words and rhythm cannot imitate, nor can it be an imitation.[22]

What Patrizi calls 'pure song,' as opposed to imitation, we would call a form of Truth and we would like to think this is what Tasso had in mind when he wrote,

> Just as a painter, who decides to paint
> the squalid pallor of a dead man's face,
> puts every deadly, bloodless hue on it,
> and in the background adds wild beasts and wraiths
> which he makes very similar to truth—
> a truth that, while it makes all glances fear,
> delights and pleases those who gaze on it
> because of the deception of the scene
> and of the artist's excellent technique.[23]

He makes a similar reference to Truth, with respect to the sculptor.

> And as a sculptor ever takes away
> with his hard chisel the superfluous
> of the white marble till the craven stone
> reveals a breathing, truthful form that lives ...[24]

---

20 'Della poetica, La deca disputata,' quoted in Palisca, *Humanism in Italian Renaissance Musical Thought*, 405.
21 Ibid.
22 Ibid., 404.
23 Tasso, *Creation of the World*, VI, 1197ff.
24 Ibid., VI, 1697ff.

Regarding the purpose of poetry, Girolamo Fracastoro (1483–1553), a poet and doctor of medicine, in his 'Naugerius, sive de poetica dialogus,' criticizes the concept of imitation and contends that 'beauty of expression' is the proper end of poetry.[25]

In a letter of 1548, following the death of Bembo, Aretino recommends that 'the first time you hear a poem you listen to it, the second time you savor it, the third time you judge it.'[26] In a letter to a dissolute young man, he adds the additional purpose of education.

> Read the poems that other men have published, for reading is the nutriment of talent. It restores it if it has gone to rack and ruin.[27]

Tasso offers the following definition of Beauty:

> Beauty, as one of nature's works, consists in a certain proportion of parts, with appropriate size and soft graceful coloring; these qualities having once been beautiful in themselves will forever be beautiful, nor can custom make them seem otherwise.[28]

MARCO GIROLAMO VIDA, *DE ARTE POETICA* (1517)

Vida was born in Cremona some time before the beginning of the sixteenth century, at which time his first poems appear. His poem on chess (*Scacchiae Ludus*) brought him to the attention of Leo X. After the death of Leo X, Vida remained in the papal court of Clement VII, who made him bishop of Alba in 1532. Holding this office, Vida participated in the council of Trent. He died in 1566, respected as much for the conduct of his pastoral duties as for his poetry.

Vida's *De Arte Poetica*, published in 1517, is an extraordinary summary of contemporary understanding of poetry, and is itself set in verse. Joining numerous writers, Vida ignores a thousand years of Church admonition and begins with a plea to the Muses which recognizes the long association of poetry with music.

> Give me, ye sacred Muses, to impart
> The hidden secrets of your tuneful art;
> Give me your awful mysteries to sing …[29]

---

25 Quoted in Palisca, *Humanism in Italian Renaissance Musical Thought*, 255.
26 Letter to Alessandro, in Chubb, *The Letters of Pietro Aretino*, 271.
27 Letter to Pomponio Vecelli, in Ibid., 296.
28 Torquato Tasso, *Discourses on the Heroic Poem*, trans. Mariella Cavalchini (Oxford: Clarendon Press, 1973), 74.
29 Vida, *The Art of Poetry*, trans. Pitt, in Albert Cook, *The Poetical Treatises of Horace, Vida, and Boileau* (Boston: Ginn, 1892), I, 1ff.

The Muses he pictures as forming a choir, singing to Apollo's silver lyre, far above the 'groveling multitude below.'

To begin, Vida notes that poetry is never limited in its subject matter, although he believes it was first associated with religion and to celebrate the deeds of heroes. The additional uses of poetry which he cites are for the theater, for soft elegies to move our pity, to express the flames of love by youth and the lower forms sung by shepherds and 'the low humors of contending swains.'

The best poetry results when you 'let the chief motive be your own delight,' for then 'free and spontaneous the smooth [words] glide.' One should resist writing on demand, for then,

> We toil with fruitless pain,
> And drag the involuntary load in vain.[30]

Before beginning his recommendations to young poets Vida makes some very interesting remarks. First, we wonder if we find another example, among many in early literature, of deduction of the separate natures of the twin hemispheres of our brain, when Vida writes,

> But now, young bard, with strict attention hear,
> And drink my precepts in at either ear …[31]

Equally interesting is a reference to Universality, here in the form of knowledge genetically supplied before birth.

> New wonders the succeeding bards explore,
> Which slept concealed in Nature's womb before:
> Her awful secrets the bold poet sings,
> And sets to view the principles of things.[32]

But Vida warns the young poet that it is not enough to write from his own instinct, ignoring traditional rules.

> One to his genius trusts in every part,
> And scorns the rules and discipline of art,
> While this an empty tide of sound affords,
> And roars and thunders in a storm of words.
> Some, musically dull, all methods try
> To win the ear with sweet stupidity,
> Unruffled strains for solid wit dispense,
> And give us [rhyme] when we call for sense.[33]

---

30 Ibid., I, 55.
31 Ibid., I, 130.
32 Ibid., I, 153.
33 Ibid., I, 180ff.

And Vida also warns that once the young poet is caught up in 'the divine rage' he must keep his purpose and not 'the sense of glory and the love of fame.'

A particularly interesting passage is one which is identical with a warning given young conductors by Bruno Walter four centuries later: early success comes easily, followed by a period of doubt through which one works toward a mature perfection of his craft. Vida puts it this way:

> The hopeful youth, determined by his choice,
> Works without precept, and prevents advice,
> Consults his teacher, plies his task with joy,
> And a quick sense of glory fires the boy.
> He challenges the crowd; the conquest o'er,
> He struts away the victor of an hour.
> Then, vanquished in his turn, o'erwhelmed with care,
> He weeps, he pines, he sickens with despair;
> Nor looks his little rivals in the face,
> But flies for shelter to some lonely place,
> To mourn his shame, and cover his disgrace.
> His master's frowns impatient to sustain,
> Straight he returns, and wins the day again.
> This is the boy his better fates design
> To rise the future darling of the Nine;
> For him the Muses weave the sacred crown.[34]

Similarly, Vida worries 'for him who ripens before his prime; For all productions there's a proper time.' Also, he warns the teacher,

> Nor should the youth too strictly be confined;
> 'Tis sometimes proper to unbend his mind.

But there is also such a thing as talent and Vida has observed that there are some who fervently desire to be poets, yet, in spite of all, are not successful. These, he recommends, might find a suitable career as lawyers!

> How oft the youth, who wants the sacred fire,
> Fondly mistakes for genius his desire,
> Courts the coy Muses, though rejected still,
> Nor Nature seconds his misguided will!
> He strives, he toils with unavailing care,
> Nor Heaven relents, nor Phoebus hears his prayer.
> He with success, perhaps, may plead a cause,

---

34 Ibid., I, 315ff.

Shine at the bar, and flourish by the laws.[35]

Now Vida paints a picture of the young poet in his efforts to turn inspiration into verse.

> Tossed by a different gust of hopes and fears,
> He begs of Heaven an hundred eyes and ears,
> Now here, now there, coy Nature he pursues,
> And takes one image in a thousand views.
> He waits the happy moment that affords
> The noblest thoughts and most expressive words;
> He brooks no dull delay, admits no rest;
> A tide of passion struggles in his breast;
> Round his dark soul no clear ideas play,
> The most familiar objects glide away.
> All fixed in thought, astonished he appears,
> His soul examines and consults his ears
> And racks his faithless memory, to find
> Some traces faintly sketched upon his mind.[36]

It is at this moment, Vida has found, that the patient help of the teacher is most needed. Here he describes a great teacher of any age.

> And here embrace, ye teachers, this advice:
> Not to be too inquisitively nice,
> But, till the soul enlarged in strength appears,
> Indulge the boy, and spare his tender years;
> Till, to ripe judgment and experience brought,
> Himself discerns and blushes at a fault.
> For if the critic's eyes too strictly pierce,
> To point each blemish out in every verse,
> Void of all hope the stripling may depart,
> And turn his studies to another art.
> But if, resolved his darling faults to see,
> A youth of genius should apply to me,
> And court my elder judgment to peruse
> The imperfect labors of his infant Muse,
> I should not scruple, with a candid eye,
> To read and praise his poem to the sky,
> With seeming rapture on each line to pause,
> And dwell on each expression with applause.
> But when my praises had inflamed his mind,

---

35 Ibid., I, 354ff.

36 Ibid., I, 424ff.

> If some lame verse limped slowly up behind,
> One, that himself, unconscious, had not found,
> By [rhyme] charmed and led away by sound;
> I should not fear to minister a prop,
> And give him stronger feet to keep it up,
> Teach it to run along more firm and sure;
> Nor would I show the wound before the cure.[37]

Vida's final advice to the young poet is to follow the example of the ancient Greek poets in fleeing the cares of the city for the tranquility of Nature.

> For what remains: the poet I enjoin
> To form no glorious scheme, no great design,
> Till, free from business, he retires alone,
> And flies the giddy tumult of the town,
> Seeks rural pleasures and enjoys the glades,
> And courts the thoughtful silence of the shades
> Where the fair Dryads haunt their native woods,
> With all the orders of the Sylvan gods.
> Here in their soft retreats the poets lie,
> Serene, and blest with cheerful poverty;
> No guilty schemes of wealth their souls molest,
> No cares, no prospects, discompose their rest,
> No scenes of grandeur glitter in their view;
> Here they the joys of innocence pursue,
> And taste the pleasures of the happy few.[38]

With Book Two, Vida begins his more specific advice on the rules of poetry. He begins by observing that the noblest poetry begins gently and subtly draws the reader in.

> This as a rule the noblest bards esteem,
> To touch at first in general on the theme,
> To hint at all the subject in a line,
> And draw in miniature the whole design …
> Shock not your reader, nor begin too fierce,
> Nor swell and bluster in a pomp of verse;
> At first all needless ornament remove,
> To shun his prejudice and win his love;
> At first you find most favor and success
> In plain expression and a modest dress …[39]

---

37 Ibid., I, 466ff.
38 Ibid., I, 486ff.
39 Ibid., II, 17, 30ff.

Vida stresses the importance of planning the overall form, so 'each part may find its own determined place.' It is here that Reason must aid the poet, 'never,' warns Vida, 'trust to arbitrary chance.' In designing the form, take care that you do not stay too long with one subject, 'For 'tis variety that gives delight!' Similarly, he advises saying things but once, for 'tedious repetitions tire the ear.' All such plans must not be obvious to the reader, 'For art's chief pride is still to cover art.'

It is allowed in poetry, Vida admits, to invent situations, but they must at least appear to be conceivably true.

> Since fictions are allowed, be sure, ye youths,
> Your fictions wear at least the air of truths.[40]

This leads Vida to the ancient question of whether Art should imitate Nature. In his view, this is the very duty of Art.

> Be sure from Nature never to depart;
> To copy Nature is the task of art.
> The noblest poets own her sovereign sway,
> And ever follow where she leads the way.[41]

Vida now makes an important definition: the poet must aim for the heart of the reader, it is to the emotions that poetry must be addressed.

> To bend the soul, and give with wondrous art
> A thousand different motions to the heart;
> Hence, as his subject gay or sad appears,
> He claims our joy or triumphs in our tears.[42]

In the case of the disappointed lover, it is 'with the soft harp the bard relieves his pain.' And speaking of love poetry, here the poet must take care not to be too descriptive in his language.

> Let them be slightly touched and ne'er expressed,
> Give but a hint and let us guess the rest.[43]

Vida now writes more specifically of choice of language. His first rule is to avoid obscurity. The very great possibilities of language can, itself, cause writer's block, for which Vida offers the following advice.

---

40 Ibid., II, 304.
41 Ibid., II, 455ff.
42 Ibid., II, 510ff.
43 Ibid., II, 527ff.

> Expression, boundless in extent, displays
> A thousand forms, a thousand several ways;
> In different garbs from different quarters brought,
> It makes unnumbered dresses for a thought—
> Such vast varieties of hues we find
> To paint conception, and unfold the mind!
> If e'er you toil, but toil without success,
> To give your images a shining dress,
> Quit your pursuit and choose a different way,
> Till, breaking forth, the voluntary ray
> Cuts the thick darkness and lets dawn the day.[44]

Since, Vida maintains, the goal is to move the soul and create delight, and not to 'cloy the mind,' the young poet must seek his inspiration from the Muses, the 'language of the sky,'

> Which first the Muses brought to these abodes,
> Who taught mankind the secrets of the gods;
> For in the court of Jove their choirs advance,
> And sing alternate, as they lead the dance,
> Mixed with the gods; they hear Apollo's lyre,
> And from high Heaven the panting bard inspire.[45]

Vida permits borrowing from another poet.

> Nor would I scruple, with a due regard,
> To read sometimes a rude unpolished bard,
> Among whose labors I may find a line,
> Which from unsightly rust I may refine,
> And, with a better grace, adopt it into mine.[46]

Especially, in this regard, one must not hesitate to borrow from the ancient poets.

> Hence on the ancients we must rest alone,
> And make their golden sentences our own;
> To cull their best expressions claims our cares,
> To form our notions and our styles on theirs.
> See how we bear away their precious spoils,
> And with the glorious dress enrich our styles,
> Their bright inventions for our use convey,
> Bring all the spirit of their words away,
> And make their words themselves our lawful prey![47]

---

44 Ibid., III, 23ff.
45 Ibid., III, 76ff.
46 Ibid., III, 196ff.
47 Ibid., III, 210ff.

On second thought, Vida qualifies this recommendation.

> Steal with due care, and meditate the prey,
> Invert the order of the words with art,
> And change their former site in every part.
> Thus win your readers, thus deceive with grace,
> And let the expression wear a different face.[48]

Finally, Vida reminds the poet that his is a noble art and, as such, the language must be above that of the vulgar, common man. Hence, he seems to conclude, poetry is not for everyone.

> When first to man the privilege was given
> To hold by verse an intercourse with Heaven,
> Unwilling that the immortal art should lie
> Cheap, and exposed to every vulgar eye,
> Great Jove, to drive away the groveling crowd,
> To narrow bounds confined the glorious road,
> Which more exalted spirits may pursue,
> And left it open to the sacred few.[49]

He concludes by observing that even if 'inspired with divine rage,' the poet, in spite of art and all human efforts, is likely to not succeed unless 'the gods … look with kind indulgence from the sky.'[50]

Torquato Tasso, *Discourses on the Heroic Poem*

Lyric and epic poetry are the oldest forms of Western European literature, dating back to the most ancient extant compositions of the Greeks. Epic poetry was that which sang of the great deeds and virtues of former nobles and for this reason was often used as a tool for the education of the young. During the sixteenth century, with much of the support for the arts coming from the nobles, there was, of course, a continuing need for this kind of poetry. Aretino refers to this when he observes,

> We inkpot users have a terrible lot of work to do to lift up into the sky names which are weighed to earth with the lead of every kind of lack of worth.[51]

---

48 Ibid., III, 216ff.
49 Ibid., III, 355ff.
50 Ibid., III, 527ff.
51 Letter to 'S.G,' April 12, 1542, in Chubb, *The Letters of Pietro Aretino*, 177.

Tasso wrote a treatise on the aesthetics and components of this form, which he called 'heroic' poetry, and in his introduction he provides this same traditional purpose.

> Recognizing the virtues of their fathers and forefathers as made, if not more beautiful, at least more various and illustrious by poetry, they try to raise their own minds to its example; and their intellect itself becomes a painter who, following its pattern, paints in their souls forms of courage, temperance, prudence, justice, faith, piety, religion, and every other virtue that may be acquired by long practice or infused by divine grace.[52]

Regarding the basic nature of poetry in general, Tasso defines it as the imitations of actions. As nearly all earlier poetry was sung, it is no surprise to see Tasso still recognizing this relationship.

> Poetry has many species: one is the epic; the others are tragedy, comedy, and songs accompanied by the cithara, bagpipes, reed-pipes, or other pastoral instruments. They are all alike in that they imitate. We may therefore affirm that poetry is nothing other than imitation ...
> Poetry is an imitation in verse. But imitation of what? Of human and divine actions, the Stoics said. It follows that those who do not sing of human or divine actions are not poets.[53]

By the sixteenth century poetry had begun to separate itself from music and the reason which Tasso gives for this is one of competence rather than one of philosophy.

> Originally musicians and poets were the same ... Later the two arts separated because human imperfection makes us inadequate to several tasks.[54]

Nevertheless, even by this time, Tasso adds, epic poetry still can be sung and can be joined together with music without all the other elements necessary to tragedy.

> And if music is a perfection, it is an extrinsic one. Moreover, the heroic poet can have it without all the trouble of spectacle, theater, and machinery, as we have already said. Indeed, heroic poems can be sung to the most perfect kind of music, as Homer's were; and the heroic poem, especially in our language, has rhyme, which is its own natural harmony.[55]

The purpose of epic poetry, Tasso says, is for instruction, to improve man, and to join pleasure and virtue. Both are more noble than profit motives.

> The purpose is to help men by the example of human deeds, since the example of animals cannot be equally useful and that of divine actions is not suited to us. Poetry, therefore, should be directed to this purpose. Poetry, then, is an imitation of human actions, fashioned to teach us

---

52 Tasso, *Discourses on the Heroic Poem*, 5.
53 Ibid., 7.
54 Ibid., 199.
55 Ibid., 204.

how to live ... And although such imitation affords immense pleasure, one cannot say that the purposes are two, one being pleasure and the other utility ... for one single art cannot have two purposes, one independent of the other ...

We should at least grant that the end of poetry is not just any enjoyment but only that which is coupled with virtue, since it is utterly unworthy of a good poet to give the pleasure of reading about base and dishonest deeds, but proper to give the pleasure of learning together with virtue. Hence perhaps the purpose of pleasure ... is not to be scorned; on the contrary, to aim at pleasure is nobler then to aim at profit, since enjoyment is sought for itself, and other things for its sake.[56]

Having made these points, Tasso now summarizes his definition of poetry to read,

Poetry is an imitation of human actions with the purpose of being useful by pleasing, and the poet is an imitator who could, as many have, use his art to delight without profiting.[57]

Tasso distinguishes poetry from philosophy by saying the former considers the beautiful and the latter the good.[58] He defines the end of tragedy as being 'to purge the soul by terror and compassion' and the end of comedy 'to move us to laughter at base things,' while reminding us that drama was still a form of poetry. The end of epic poetry to 'move the mind to wonder and thus be useful.'[59] Later Tasso makes further distinctions between tragedy and epic poetry. Tragedy represents, but epic poetry narrates and they differ in the 'unlikeness of the things they imitate, which is far more significant.' He also makes reference to the fundamental role which music played in ancient Greek tragedy. 'The tragedian, in addition to verse, uses rhythm and harmony, as it were the seasoning of words.'[60] And in another place,

Furthermore, if tragedy did not require music and spectacle to achieve its end, Aristotle would not have included both elements in his definition.[61]

The components of epic poetry are four, according to Tasso. First is that which he calls fable, meaning the action itself and those who perform the action. The remaining components are the moral habits of the persons introduced in the fable, thought and diction.[62] Regarding the first of these, Tasso finds the range of topics available in poetry to be virtually unlimited.

Of all the activities of human reason ... none are more praiseworthy than intellectual choice ...

---

56   Ibid., 10ff.
57   Ibid., 12.
58   Ibid., 13.
59   Ibid., 15ff.
60   Ibid., 43ff.
61   Ibid., 203.
62   Ibid., 17.

> Poetic matter seems vast beyond all others, since it embraces things lofty and lowly, serious and jocular, sad and happy, public and private, unfamiliar and familiar, new and old, national and foreign, sacred and secular, civilized and natural, human and divine.[63]

Later, however, he makes some stipulations regarding suitable subject matter for epic poetry.

> The poet should not take a fancy to oversubtle matters, more suitable to the schools of theologians and philosophers than to princely palaces and theaters …
> And further, let our poet disdain all such low, common, indecent things … Let him add loftiness to the ordinary, clarity and luster to the obscure, art to the simple, ornament to the actual, authority to the fictitious; and if he does occasionally bring in shepherds, goatherds, swineherds, and other such persons, let him consider decorum not only in the person but in the poem as well, and show them as they appear in royal palaces, solemnities, and ceremonies.[64]

By 'thought' Tasso means 'habits of mind, especially prudence, which is one of the intellectual virtues.' He contrasts this meaning of 'habits of the mind' with moral habits, which are traits of character.[65]

Tasso also discusses what he calls the three requirements for epic poetry. The first is verisimilitude, by which, since epic poetry is the imitation of actions, Tasso is most concerned with the accuracy in the treatment of the character's 'age, fortune, birth, office, and rank.'[66] Second, epic poetry must have a certain magnitude, the limits of which he finds are associated with memory.

> Let it then be of sufficient but not excessive length. And as the eye is the right judge of the size of the body, so the memory has jurisdiction over the length of poems.[67]

The third requirement is unity, one imitation of one subject, a principle which he believed epic poets should share with philosophers, painters, sculptors, and comic and tragic writers.

Giraldi Cinthio, *Discorso intorno al comporre dei romanzi* (1549)

In a letter sent to his publisher, Giraldi indicates that he wrote this treatise to refute attacks on Ariosto's *Orlando Furioso*, which he considered a great heroic poem. Thus, while his treatise is about the sixteenth-century heroic poem in general, which he calls the Romance, Giraldi is equally concerned with establishing poetry as an art. In so doing, he presents one of the most important treatises on Beauty to be found in the sixteenth century.

---

63 Ibid., 21.
64 Ibid., 51, 54.
65 Ibid., 90.
66 Ibid., 101.
67 Ibid., 64ff.

One of the first points Giraldi establishes is the ancient connection between poetry and music.

> Nor did this name canto, given to such poems, originate among us so that through the piazzas and public places these compositions might be sung among the benches in the manner of those nowadays who with lyre on arm sing their idle nonsense to earn their bread; this name had a higher and more honorable origin. Among the Greeks and Latins ... it was the custom to sing at banquets and dinner tables, accompanied by the lyre, of the glorious deeds of the great masters and of the mighty exploits of virtuous and brave men. So the Italians, following this ancient custom (I speak of the better poets), have ever feigned to sing their poems before princes and noble company.[68]

And again, 'not from the singing of those plebeians who with their nonsense spread their nets for the purses of whoever would listen to them.'

Later Giraldi returns to this relationship with music and makes an interesting observation on the practice of contemporary Art Music.

> The reason why [the poets] promise at the end of their cantos that they will return to sing and why they feign at the beginning of the cantos that they have returned to sing where they had left off was their need, before resuming the primary material, to get the attention of their hearers. They do this as would a good performer on the lyre or lute or any other similar instrument, who, before he starts to play, takes his instrument in hand and seeks with a few sweeps over the strings to catch the ears of those before whom he is to play.[69]

In turning to the 'first consideration,' the subject of epic poetry, Giraldi adds an educational purpose.

> In the composition of Romances the fable should be founded upon one or more illustrious actions, which the poet may imitate suitably with pleasant language, to teach men honest life and good customs, which should be the foremost end of composing for any good poet.[70]

Later Giraldi speaks of this educational purpose in more specific terms.

> The function, then, of our poet, as regards the inducing of mores, is to praise virtuous actions and censure the vicious; and by means of the terrible and the miserable to make the vicious actions odious to him who reads.[71]

---

68 Giraldi Cinthio, *Discorso intorno al comporre dei romanzi*, trans. Henry Snuggs as *Giraldi Cinthio On Romances* (Lexington: University of Kentucky Press, 1968), 7.

69 Ibid., 36.

70 Ibid., 9.

71 Ibid., 52.

It is in this regard also that Giraldi is concerned with the power which the poet has over the emotions of the audience.

> As [doleful emotions and weeping] are created almost instantaneously, so in a moment they cease; to prolong them would not only be faulty but fruitless. It would be better to dry the tears under the eyes than to start them afresh.[72]

Giraldi specifies that heroic poetry must treat only noble and excellent men, although he adds that while Virgil and Homer wrote of only one man, modern epics include a larger number of characters. Having said this, he makes a rare reference to true Universality in contending that the work should be written in such a way that it pleases not only the learned men, but all men. The poets goal should be to create something like a living person, 'pleasing, graceful, and beautiful.'

In the same way the Romance should contain not one, but many actions, for 'diversity of actions carries with it the variety that is the spice of delight.' The poet must only take care that digressions are related both to the 'continuous thread' and 'convey verisimilitude so far as it belongs to poetic fictions.' This leads him to stress the importance of the overall form and the relationship of all its parts.

> The poet ought to consider not only the whole body but each particular part, so that each may be set with beautiful order in its place, with admirable grace, and with the proper proportion and so that the whole, with that beauty and grace, will be to each of them proper and fitting.[73]

Giraldi now interrupts his discussion of the Romance, as it apparently occurred to him that he should address the question of how one learns the things he is speaking of. His first advice is to talk with the expert who has practical experience.

> To a man not of dull or of weak intellectual capacity, one day's conversation with a man who is learned, prudent, and expert in composing and who will talk of things related to it will do more than a year's study.[74]

But, the attitude of the student is critical!

> It should be pointed out that it is not enough that he who speaks explain and teach faithfully but it is necessary also that he who listens be able to adapt himself to learning, to set aside an arrogant manner and the belief (which is the mortal poison of him who thinks he knows a great deal) that he needs no teacher. Such individuals frequently remain in an elementary state or are enveloped in a thousand errors which fill them with distorted and perplexed conceits,

---

72 Ibid., 54.
73 Ibid., 24ff.
74 Ibid., 25ff.

afterward expressed so tortuously that they seem as drunkards talking in the madness of wine that takes away their sense.[75]

Giraldi also presents a wonderful explanation why the student should also read great works.

Often the same spirit that inspired the poet whom he reads will work also in him and will kindle in him flames which will little by little set his spirit afire and fill it with the same frenzy the Greeks called enthusiasm, by which he, as though touched by a stinging inspiration, will be as though he were driven to set forth on paper those things born in his mind through the reading of his author.[76]

His more precise explanation of how this occurs is a remarkable recognition of the genetic universality of emotions.

This I believe comes about through what our minds naturally have in common to receive that inspiration of which we spoke.[77]

Giraldi gives the overall parts of the form as the argument, the invocation [to the gods] and the narration. All subordinate parts of the narration must be logically connected.

The parts and the episodes should, then, have either a necessary or a probable dependence one upon the other. If the work should not be so made, it could little delight or please.[78]

He gives considerable emphasis to 'decorum,' which he defines as 'that which is fitting to places, times, and persons.' It is essential to observe this, he says, if the poet hopes to gain praise. His emphasis on making speech match the character is one of the hallmarks of sixteenth-century drama.

For one would speak with a king in a different way than he would speak with a gentleman, and a king will answer another king as he would not answer one of his subjects or another lesser prince.[79]

In speaking of language, Giraldi again returns to the idea of that which has been implanted by genetics, which he refers to as Nature.

Good writing is not an involved mystery; nature has planted the seeds of it in our minds and these spring up of themselves not indeed in composition, which is done with great diligence,

---

75 Ibid., 26.
76 Ibid., 27.
77 Ibid.
78 Ibid., 49.
79 Ibid., 56.

but in acts of reasoning, which arise every day not only in men of noble birth but in men of humbler origin.[80]

When he writes 'Nature produces the poets, but art makes the orators,'[81] he is attempting to make a distinction between genius and skill. By 'elocution,' Giraldi means the manner of expressing with fitting words the thought which the poet has in mind. Here he presents a unique and interesting analogy.

> Since elocution has the same place in composition as the skin does in the human body, the poet ought to put his effort on this part, under which stand all the others, as nature does on the skin of the body. Just as nature, a judicious creatress (by virtue of the intelligence which rules her) of that which she produces, took great care to make the skin soft, pliable, and delicate, and to give it the grace of proper colors so that it appears pleasing to our eyes and makes delightful all that is under it, so the poet should put much talent and study on everything pertaining to words. Since they clothe our ideas and carry them from the intellect to the eyes, they ought to be adorned with all the beauty that the industry of the writer can give them. Although in this, no less than in other particulars, one ought to shun such superfluous diligence, lest what one would make good becomes bad, and lest excessive desire to embellish results in fastidiousness. Negligence neatly practiced is sometimes better than too much diligence.[82]

Giraldi contends that epic poetry must be in rhyme. This is only fitting for heroic matter and 'it carries in itself the sweetness of sound and gravity with measure and with the other qualities that belong to the sublime.'[83] Later he adds that words must not only convey thoughts, but in themselves, 'pleasurable beauty.' On the other hand, he warns, the poet must remember his goal is to find words for the thoughts, and not thoughts for the words.

He pauses to comment on the ancient question of the relationship of Art and Nature.

> Of these two, however, the one so needs the other that each is of little value alone. Indeed, art without nature produces such impoverished verses that they seem to have suffered for ten years from the hectic fever. Nature without art makes them like fat peasants who are of good color and health but withal have no gentility.[84]

Therefore, he concludes, that poet who has as his guide both Nature and Art cannot help but succeed. He follows this with a remarkable definition of Art.

> By art I mean here not the intricacies and the entanglements of which I spoke above, which with metaphors, enigmas, and monstrosities would turn authors into alchemists; which precepts can

---

80 Ibid., 64ff.
81 Ibid., 66.
82 Ibid., 72ff.
83 Ibid., 78.
84 Ibid., 93.

make it appear that a man has seen and read much, but are not likely to teach; but that which gives us light, not shadow; makes our way pleasant, not painful; easy, not intricate; level, not steep; that which leads us not through briars but through flowering meadows; that which teaches us without so much tortuousness and such monstrosities of words and images. Like arranged flowers, after we have chosen them from the green fields of poesy, our compositions ought to be set in order with marvelous beauty.[85]

In this regard, Giraldi mentions one of the great themes of the sixteenth-century Italian courtier, that everything done through effort must appear as it had required no effort.

Though one cannot write well without the most intense diligence and great labor (nature has not arranged for excellence to issue from us without labor), nonetheless the writer ought to strive with the utmost effort, not so that the hard work on the composition will be visible, but so that the work will appear to be done naturally.[86]

In writing poetry that also has philosophic pretension, Giraldi finds particular dangers.

It is even more indecorous for the one writing to show himself a philosopher, to neglect poetic grace and beauty, and, concentrating on words and recondite—often ill-fitting mysteries—to write so as to produce something hardly understood by himself and not at all by others, not remembering that clarity, ease, and directness of thought are the glory of good poets' writings. Whereas the good poets are delightful and profitable to those who devote themselves to reading them, the others remain so odious that it could be said they do not write for others, but for themselves. Great prudence, therefore, should be exercised by those who would blend the philosophic with the poetic.[87]

Giraldi now turns to what he calls the *life-force* of poetry, the expression of emotions. While the soul of oratory is in its utterance and action, he finds the soul of poetry,

in the force and virtue of the writing, whence the emotions enter the heart of the reader as if it were a living voice speaking ...
    It also seems to me that the words can be so significant and so apt in revealing the thoughts as to be impressed on the reader's mind with such efficacy and vehemence that one feels their force and is moved to participate in the emotions under the veil of words in the poet's verses. This is the *Enargeia*.[88]

---

85 Ibid., 94.

86 Ibid., 120.

87 Ibid., 125.

88 Ibid., 134ff.

As examples of this vivid expression of emotions through words, Giraldi offers the following:

> These make [the reader] see a wife's mourning her husband's departure or his death, as if one had seen the hand-to-hand combat and heard the outcry. These show a mother's joy in seeing her little son out of danger, as if one should see her heart laid bare. These make us hear the father's reproofs of his little son, as if we should have before our eyes the severity of that grave face full of tender indignation and have put into our ears those words full of loving threat.[89]

With regard to the search for the perfect expression, at the end of his book, Giraldi quotes a lovely anecdote about Leonardo da Vinci and his painting of the 'Last Supper.' According to Giraldi, he had completed everything but the head of Judas when he apparently stopped. Two friars complained to the duke who was paying for the painting and when the duke inquired, Leonardo answered that it was not true, that in fact he devoted two hours a day to the painting of the head of Judas. When after a year the friars complained again, and the duke revisited the question, Leonardo explained that he had continued to work two hours a day.

> I have gone to the suburbs where live all the vile and ignoble persons, for the most part wicked and criminal, only to see if I could find a face appropriate to complete the portrait of that wicked man. I have not yet been able to find it and if I can't I could use as remarkably suitable that of this father prior who now so molests me.

In recognizing the danger that description can go too far, Giraldi addresses the nature of the impact on the senses by way of an analogy with painting.

> In embellishing his poem, therefore, the poet ought to do as the painter does with figures; as the latter, with varieties of colors and shades blended and distributed artfully, makes the figure beautiful and pleasing to the beholder's eyes, so the poet, with variety of ornaments and the placing of other parts that are not ornaments, ought to give grace, life and spirit to his poem. Poetry is like a picture that has life and speech. If one is to err in one of the two ways of erring, it is better to submit to the too-little … than to the too-much, for if those things which greatly please and delight the senses and convey in themselves in the first impression the greatest force are seen at first too often or in too great abundance, they give us not pleasure but incredible irritation. Whence it can be seen that, as irritation lies close at hand to unmeasured pleasure, so excessive reiteration of these excellencies of the work causes, if not death, at least annoyance and satiety so great that one cannot possess the patience to read them. This indeed happens to those who profess to be erudite, who load everything they compose with proverbs, exempla, fables, stories, jokes, customs, philosophies, and old, difficult, foreign words, so that they make their discourse like the driest sand.[90]

Giraldi also has some interesting recommendations to the poet for when his work is finished. He points out that it is good to have a respected person read it, to find what is

---
89 Ibid., 155.
90 Ibid., 153ff.

'displeasing in beauty.' He has found it is profitable to lay the work aside and come back to it at a later time.

> His original fervor and love for it when it was born—almost as if it were a new child—having cooled off, the author sees it as if it were not his own, so that he finds in it much to correct which his original fervor had not permitted him to see.[91]

But then again, he warns against too much correcting and editing.

> Certainly he should avoid excessive use of the file, so that the good is lost along with the bad; as someone said, he ought to know when to lift his hand from the desk, because, as I have often said, excess is bad in any undertaking.[92]

ON THE AESTHETICS OF MUSIC

Tasso, in discussing poetry, obliquely provides a definition of music as well, providing a particularly clear illustration of why we include discussion of poetry in this book.

> The poem that contains so great a variety of matters none the less should be one, one in form and soul; and of these things should be so combined that each concerns the other, corresponds to the other, and so depends on the other necessarily or verisimilarly that removing any one part or changing its place would destroy the whole. And if that is true, the art of composing a poem resembles the plan of the universe, which is composed of contraries, as that of music is.[93]

Tasso found the most important purpose of music to be to soothe the feelings. In speaking of Italian citizens, he writes,

> Others in the sweet harmony of songs,
> or at the sound of zither or of harp,
> which soothes the soul and fills the heart with bliss,
> keeping them glad or sad in various ways,
> forget their sorrows.[94]

For an explanation of how music achieves its power to soothe, as well as achieve catharsis and serve an educational purpose, he reached back to the arguments of the ancient Greeks.

---

91   Ibid., 159.
92   Ibid., 159.
93   Tasso, *Discourses on the Heroic Poem*, 78.
94   Tasso, *Creation of the World*, III, 18.

> The Phrygian and Lydian modes, and the one formed by combining them [Mixolydian] are much more desirable in tragedy and the canzone as in these they can move the mind and, so to speak, draw it out of itself. But they are not suitable for instruction ...
>
> Since music was invented not merely to entertain idleness or as a medicine and catharsis for the mind but for instruction as well ... A solemn and steady music like the Doric will serve the heroic poem better than any other.[95]

Curiously enough, however, he reveals that he wondered if there were such a thing as the 'Doric' style yet in use. Epic poetry, he says,

> can quite appropriately be sung in the Doric or a similar harmony—if we now have any such thing that does not welcome variations but resembles the harmony that won highest praise not only in Socrates and Plato, but from Aristotle ... and other very serious writers.[96]

ART MUSIC

The one sixteenth-century Italian poet who described musical performance at length was Jacopo Sannazaro. Numerous comments made in passing reveal his familiarity with court performances, as for example his comment in the Prologue to *Arcadia* praising pastoral music.

> The waxbound reeds of shepherds proffer amid the flower-laden valleys perhaps more pleasurable sound than do through proud chambers the polished and costly boxwood instruments of the musicians.[97]

Perhaps thinking of contemporary Art Song, Tasso recalled that the ancient lyric poets who participated in the festivals mention the audiences listening to the 'sweetest song' of the 'most noble intellects.' He mentions the 'loud trumpet's far-resounding blast,' which announced the winners and again the lyric poet, 'the one who sings, accompanied by the sweet sound of his canorous strings.'[98]

Ariosto's classic poem, *Orlando Furioso*, describes Art Music at a banquet, including love songs.

---

95 Tasso, *Discourses on the Heroic Poem*, 199.

96 Ibid.

97 Jacopo Sannazaro, *Jacopo Sannazaro, Arcadia & Piscatorial Eclogues*, trans. Ralph Nash (Detroit: Wayne State University Press, 1966), 29. Sannazaro (1456–1530) was born to a prominent Neapolitan noble family, enabling him to acquire the education of a gentleman.

98 Tasso, *Creation of the World*, VI, 16ff.

> Around the festive board zithers, harps, and lyres set the air vibrating with delightful sounds, with soft harmony and tuneful notes. There was song, too, song of love's joys and ecstasies, and recitals of pleasing fantasies framed in verse of happiest inspiration.[99]

The poetry of Sannazaro often suggests the contemplative listener, a prime requisite for Art Music. Even a poor singer, such as Ergasto in *Arcadia*, could move his listeners,

> though with his weak voice and his wretched tones he many times moved us to sighing.[100]

Later in this work we read,

> Galicio, without being asked by any of us, after a number of most ardent sighs, with his Eugenio playing accompaniment on the pipe, thus softly began to sing, everyone remaining hushed …
> Galicio's song was marvelously pleasing to everyone.[101]

One listener, after experiencing 'a most intense pleasure,' was moved to tears.[102] In another place, even though hearing a song in a language not familiar, the music was heard 'by each man with the closest attention.' One, while the singing lasted, was 'profoundly absorbed, in a motionless and prolonged meditation....[103]

In Tasso's *Jerusalem Delivered*, a singer of Art Music is described in analogy as he prepares his listeners for contemplative listening.

> As gentle musician, before he lifts his clear voice high in song, prepares his listeners' minds for harmony with sweet overtures low-keyed …[104]

An extraordinary illustration of the sung epic poetry is found in Vida, *The Christiad*, in which Simon the apostle, here an avid singer, sings of the Hebrew history of the Old Testament. Among these excerpts, the reader will note a description of the attentive listeners of epic song.

> So he spoke, and sang verses to the accompaniment of the mellifluous strings. Every song seemed like an artful painting or storied tapestry. Thus his song told how the sons of Isaac came away from Egyptian shores, how the leader of the refugees smote the surface of the sea with his rod and divided it, how they passed in safety without ships through the deep waters, and how dryshod

---

99 Ariosto, *Orlando Furioso*, VII, 15–23. Ariosto (1474–1533) worked primarily in the court of Ferrara. Sir John Harington's English translation of 1591 gives the instruments for this passage as 'trumpets, shagbot, cornets, flutes … virginals, vials and lutes.'
100 Sannazaro, *Jacopo Sannazaro*, 35.
101 Ibid., 46ff.
102 Ibid., 117.
103 Ibid., 118ff.
104 Tasso, *Jerusalem Delivered*, XVI, xliii.

they walked the ocean floor ... And then he sang how the faithful, when they had passed through the sea, occupied the high beaches, and hid themselves for fear in the woods along the shore ...

Then he sang how the first builder of the stronghold of Jerusalem brought gifts of cultivated grain and cups full of recently discovered wine to the rustic altars, which he had built of green turf and of trimmed mountain ash.

And while all ears were listening intently to these songs, Christ, who knew what had passed, had left the high hills and had again come to the hostile city.[105]

Another description of this same singer credits him with an even wider variety of poetry.

A grave man, he loved singing to the melodious harp as he sat by the banks of a river or near a lovely spring. Knowing the rhythm, the measurements, and the orbits of the heavens, under divine inspiration he often used to sing songs to his farmhands, forecasting the movements of the sun and the monthly cycles of the moon, teaching them the signs that augured rain or shine. Now he had gone to the city, which was astir with anticipation of the rites, so that he could solemnize the holy days according to age—old tradition. And while in other parts of the house the servants were arranging the tables and gifts, he sang of his forefathers' deeds. Now with nimble fingers, now with an ivory pick, he swept the melodious strings of the *citharae* with a light touch. In particular, he traced from the beginning how the law had instituted this feast and these holy services as a custom for the people of old.[106]

Because these writers were interested in the many pastoral poems found in the repertoire of the ancient Greek lyric poets, it is no surprise to find in this sixteenth-century literature descriptions of pastoral song. Sannazaro, in his *Arcadia*, introduces the shepherd singer, Montano, and gives us two titles of his songs, 'Fierce torment' and 'Beautiful soul of mine', which suggest music of real emotional content, as seems confirmed when he relates,

So sweet my torment and my plaint a game,
I play, I dance, and sing
and at my foolish risk
singing and dancing I go languishing.[107]

Another poem in this work contains a plea to the Muses for help in expressing strong emotions.

Begin again, O Muses, your complaint.
And if you, O stream, have ever given ear
to human affections, I pray thee now accompany
the sorrowful sampogna, turned to weeping ...
Why is it, alas, not granted me to temper
so grieving notes to the sound of the curving wood,

---

105 Marco Vida, *The Christiad*, trans. Gertrude Drake (Carbondale: Southern Illinois University Press, 1978), II, 600ff.
106 Ibid., II, 560ff.
107 Sannazaro, *Jacopo Sannazaro*, 38ff.

> that I might purchase grace for my dear pledge?
> And if my verses are not so far renowned
> as those of Orpheus, yet should pity in heaven
> make them sweet, and filled with devotion.[108]

This work also contains examples of the musical contests which were frequently found in the poems of the ancient Greek lyric poets.[109]

In Tasso's *Jerusalem Delivered*, Erminia comes across rural shepherd music, which she later describes as 'honeyed songs.'

> But, while she is weeping, her lamentations are broken by a clear sound that comes to her, that seems (and is) a mingling of shepherds' voices and of rude woodland pipes. She rises and slowly makes her way there, and sees a grizzled old man weaving baskets in the pleasant shade with his flock at his side, and listening to the song of his three sons.[110]

FUNCTIONAL MUSIC

There is a variety of religious music discussed in this literature. In Tasso's *Jerusalem Delivered*, the Crusaders organize a public mass on Mt. Olivet, for which the poet provides an extensive description of the subsequent vocal music.

> … and the choir follows, with solemn step and slow, divided into two long columns. Alternately they made a double harmony, with supplicant singing and with humble countenance …
>
> Singing thus, the devout populace dispreads itself and extends in widening circles …
>
> Thither proceeds the chanting army, and the deep and low-lying vales resound and the lofty hills and their caves, and from a thousand places Echo makes her answer; and almost it seems that a woodland choir is hidden amid those caves and in that foliage …
>
> Meanwhile upon the walls the pagans stand quiet and astonished to marvel at those slow windings and the humble chant …
>
> Hence they are easily able to carry to their end the sacred hymns begun.[111]

---

108 Ibid., 129. The sampogna was a rural musical instrument. The poet devotes an 'Epilogue' to this instrument [151ff] where he says,
> it is not for you to go seeking the lofty palaces of princes, nor the proud piazzas of the populous cities, in order to have the resounding applause …
> And if ever perchance some shepherd should wish to use you in cheerful matters, make him first understand that you know nothing but weeping and making your lament …

109 Ibid., 51ff and 97ff.

110 Tasso, *Jerusalem Delivered*, VII, vi.

111 Ibid., XI, v-xiii.

In Sannazaro's *Arcadia* we read of a rural religious celebration of the feast of Pales, goddess of shepherds. We find that every cottage was heard 'to ring with divers instruments,' farmers singing love songs and shepherds,

> playing the pipes, and some there were, as it seemed, who were endeavoring to match their singing with the pipers' melody.[112]

Later he describes a group of shepherds holding a memorial service at the tomb of a deceased colleague, Androgeo. Accompanied by 'the sound of the pipe and castanets,' one sings, in part,

> Ay me, who now in our woods will sing for the Nymphs? who will give us trusted counsel in our adversities, and pleasing solace and delight in our times of sorrow, as you did often singing your sweetest songs on the banks of the running streams?[113]

Descriptions of military music in this literature center, of course, on the trumpet. In Torquato Tasso's classic *Jerusalem Delivered*, being the story of a crusade, there are numerous references to military trumpets signals. We find them playing a morning signal called 'To arms,'[114] again 'by which each warrior is roused to the march,'[115] 'joyous and shrill' when preparing for battle,[116] and during battle 'in shrilling tones seditious trumpets are heard to sing the song of war.'[117] The effect of the trumpet on the listener is described when the herald plays to announce the battle.

> A sound comes forth that is horribly heard all round and offends like rattling thunder the ears and hearts of those who hear it.[118]

In another place many trumpets play sounding like a single sound, expressing fear, which is compared to,

> The way the lion roars, the serpent hisses, the way the wolf howls and the wild bear raves ...[119]

In this same poem we have a brief description of the military music of the East, as heard by Western ears.

---

112 Sannazaro, *Jacopo Sannazaro*, 42ff.

113 Ibid., 59.

114 Tasso, *Jerusalem Delivered*, XI, xix.

115 Ibid., I, lxxi. When Satan sends his devils to disturb the Crusaders, they also play the trumpet, with a 'piercing sound.' [Ibid., IV, iii.]

116 Ibid., III, i.

117 Ibid., VIII, lxxv.

118 Ibid., VII, lvii.

119 Ibid., XIII, xxi.

... so many discordant languages and so many drums and horns and barbarous brasses and voices of camels and elephants amid the neighing of the spirited steeds ...[120]

Because the trumpet was so much associated with war or battle, its very mention in all early literature is often accompanied by fear in the listener. A typical example is found in Ariosto's *Orlando Furioso*, where we read,

> She gave him another present, too, of far greater use than any gift ever made: a horn which made such an appalling noise that it put to flight all who heard it.
> The horn, I say, made such an appalling noise that whenever it was heard, it sent everyone fleeing; nowhere in the world was there to be found another horn with so irresistible an effect on its hearers: the sound of wind, earthquake, thunder was as nothing compared to this.[121]

Tournaments were not only a form of entertainment, but a form of practice for battle. Thus, Tasso mentions the 'echoing sound of a loud trumpet' in describing tournaments as 'the travesty of a fierce battle.'[122]

The use of signal trumpets to control the movement of ships is also found in this literature. First, in Tasso:

> What festive blare of trumpets all about
> seashores and waters, arsenals and piers,
> teeming with ships and sails of many a shape![123]

Ariosto, in *Orlando Furioso*, also mentions the trumpets used to provide signals necessary for controlling ship movements.[124]

Finally, in Sannazaro's *Arcadia* we read of music being used to relieve the boredom of travel.

> And that we might notice less the tedium of the rocky road, each of us playing his pipe in his turn exerted himself to sing some new canzone as we went.[125]

---

120 Ibid., XIX, lviii.

121 Ariosto, *Orlando Furioso*, XV, 13–22.

122 Tasso, *Creation of the World*, III, 40.

123 Ibid., V, 653ff.

124 Ariosto, *Orlando Furioso*, X, 45–53.

125 Sannazaro, *Jacopo Sannazaro*, 35.

ENTERTAINMENT MUSIC

A description of genuine Entertainment Music is found in Ariosto's *Orlando Furioso*, where we read,

> Now the hour was approaching when chill night invited every creature to rest. Seeing the sun on the point of setting, he began to quicken his pace, until he came to where he caught the sound of flutes and pipes and saw smoke rising from peasant huts, the abode of shepherds … The shepherd offered a courteous and respectful welcome to the warrior and the damsel, and they accounted themselves pleased with his entertainment; it is not only in cities and baronial halls that you will meet civility, but often also in barns and hovels.[126]

---

126 Ariosto, *Orlando Furioso*, XIV, 57–65.

5 SIXTEENTH-CENTURY ITALIAN DRAMATISTS

For the historian, one of the values of sixteenth-century drama is that of all literature it was becoming more reflective of actual life. In the Elizabethan repertoire especially, drama was expected to be a mirror of life. In Italian and Elizabethan plays rarely does musical performance become part of the dramatic action, although Shakespeare presents a wealth of information in his stage directions. Music cannot really be part of the dramatic action in literature, for how can you have someone play a sonata? Does the reader sit and wait five minutes? Do you print the music for the reader to look silently at? On the stage you can see all the emotions in the face, and both the emotions and the facial expressions are universal. But you cannot *see* the emotions in music. Therefore, in general, these plays do not reveal much about performance practice, although they do contain hints of the social conditions of poets and musicians.

One might be surprised, for example, to find treatises in defense of poetry and wonder why they should be necessary. It is in this dramatic literature that we find hints that the reputation of the poet was not what we might expect. For example, in the prologue of Ariosto's *The Students* [*I Studenti*], written by his son, we read,

> There were still other reasons for him to shy away from the ranks of the poets, for nowadays they seem to be a laughingstock. It isn't enough that their toil and long vigils go unrewarded; but a thousand infamies are ascribed to them: they say that poets don't believe in things divine because they sometimes speak of Jupiter, sometimes of Venus.[1]

In this same play we read of the effects of the many battles in sixteenth-century Italy on the daily lives of poets.

> Claudio. He was not able to continue teaching at Pavia, for they had stopped the salaries of all doctors and had suspended studies because the wars were expanding every day.[2]

---

1 Ludovico Ariosto, *The Comedies of Ariosto*, trans. Edmond Beame (Chicago: The University of Chicago Press, 1975), 270.
2 Ibid., 273.

Guarini, speaking through the character Carino, recalls his own experiences as a court poet, changing the names of places.³ Here we read of the importance of foreign recognition, of the necessity of writing on demand or to suit the fashion, criticism of the courtiers and of the general economic difficulties poets faced.

> A love of poetry, and to the loud
> Music of fame resounding in a crowd.
> For I myself (greedy of foreign praise)
> Disdained Arcadia only should my [songs]
> Hear and applaud, as if my native soil
> Were narrow limits to my growing style.
> I went to Elis and to Pisa then,
> Famous themselves, and giving fame to men;
> There I saw I that loved Egon, first with bays,
> With purple then, with virtue decked always,
> That he on earth Apollo's self did seem.
> Therefore my heart and harp I unto him
> Did consecrate, devoted to his name.
> And in his house, which was the house of fame,
> I should have set up my perpetual rest,
> There to admire and imitate the best,
> If as heaven made me happy here below,
> So it had given me too the grace to know
> And keep my happiness. How I forsook
> Elis and Pisa after, and betook
> Myself to Argos and Mycene, where
> An earthly god I worshiped, with what there
> I suffered in that hard captivity,
> Would be too long for thee to hear, for me
> Too sad to utter. Only this much know:
> I lost my labor, and in sand did sow.
> I wrote, wept, sung, hot and cold fits I had,
> I rode, I stood, I bore, now sad, now glad,
> Now high, now low, now in esteem, now scorned;
> And as the Delphic iron, which is turned
> Now to heroic, now to mechanic use,
> I feared no danger, did not pains refuse,
> Was all things, and was nothing—changed my hair,
> Condition, custom, thoughts, and life, but ne'er
> Could change my fortune. Then I knew at last
> And panted after my sweet freedom past.

---

3   Giambattista Guarini, *The Faithful Shepherd* [*Il Pastor Fido*], in *Five Italian Renaissance Comedies* (New York: Penguin Books, 1978), V, 406ff. Guarini (1538–1612) served the courts of Florence and Urbino both as a courtier and in diplomatic and literary duties.

So, flying smoky Argos and the great
Storms that attend on greatness, my retreat
I made to Pisa, my thought's quiet port,
Where—praise be given to the Eternal for't—
Upon my dear Mirtillo I did light,
Which all past sorrows fully did requite …

Courtiers in name, and courteous in their mien
They are; but in their actions I could spy
Not the least spark or dram of courtesy …
Men in appearance only I did find;
Love in the face, but malice in the mind …
To rise upon the ruins of their brothers,
And seek their own by robbing praise from others,
The virtues are of that perfidious race.
No worth, no valor, no respect of place,
Of age, or law, bridle of modesty,
No tie of love, or blood, nor memory
Of good received; no thing's so venerable,
Sacred or just, that is inviolable
By that vast thirst of riches, and desire
Unquenchable of still ascending higher.
Now I—not fearing since I meant not ill,
Wearing my thoughts charactered in my brow,
And a glass-window in my breast—judge thou
How open and how fair a mark my heart
Lay to their envy's unsuspected dart …

Achilles: and my country (which doth bring
Such hapless poets forth as swan-like sing
Their own sad fates) should by my means have now
A second laurel to impale her brow.
But in this age—inhuman age the while!—
The art of poetry is made too vile.
Swans must have pleasant nests, high feeding, fair
Weather to sing; and with a load of care
Men cannot climb Parnassus' cliff: for he
Who is still wrangling with his destiny
And his malignant fortune, becomes hoarse,
And loses both his singing and discourse.

Aretino, in his *Il Marescalco*, reveals that the scholars also had their uncomfortable days at court.

It's amazing how scholars who are so talented and shrewd that they fool and poke fun at everyone become awkward the moment they mingle with courtiers.[4]

ON THE PHYSIOLOGY OF AESTHETICS

There is virtually no discussion in the dramatic literature of the traditional questions regarding the organization of the mind. We do note, however, one passage which seems to deduce the twin sides of the personality (feelings versus thoughts), if not the hemispheres of the brain. Guarini, in describing one trying to gain a lover, writes,

> My heart and thoughts till now were so much set
> To train that foolish nymph into my net.[5]

We find one clear objection to the old Church dogma that of the various faculties, Reason must rule. To the contrary, says Guarini,

> AMARILLIS. The heart may be seen too with the eyes of the mind.
> NICANDRO. Without the senses' help those eyes are blind.
> AMARILLIS. The senses must submit to reason's sway.
> NICANDRO. Reason in point of fact must sense obey.[6]

ON THE PSYCHOLOGY OF AESTHETICS

EMOTIONS

The one emotion which we might expect to find discussed frequently in the dramatic literature is Love. As in poetry, one finds many testimonials to the power of Love, as for example when Guarini writes,

> Examine the whole universe throughout.
> All that is fair or good, here or above,
> Or is a lover, or the work of love.[7]

---

4   Pietro Aretino, *Il Marescalco*, trans. Leonard Sbrocchi (Ottawa: Dovehouse, 1986), III, vii. Aretino (1492–1556) was one of the first authors whose books were placed on the Index of Prohibited Books, a development of the Council of Trent.

5   Guarini, *The Faithful Shepherd*, IV, 373.

6   Ibid., IV, 386.

7   Ibid., I, 286.

Tasso as well, in the Prologue to his play, *The Aminta* (1573), has Cupid observe that such is the power of Love that it often,

> makes to fall from the hand of Mars his bloody sword, makes Neptune, shaker of the earth, drop his mighty trident, and highest Jove his thunderbolt eternal.[8]

And in a Canzone, sung at the end of Act I of *Mandragola*, Machiavelli concludes,

> He who makes no test, Oh Love,
> of your great power,
> must hope in vain ever to have true faith
> in Heaven's highest worth.
> He does not know how at the same time
> one can live and die,
> how one can search of ill and run away from good,
> how one can love oneself less than some other,
> how often the heart is frozen and melted by fear and hope;
> he does not know how men and gods in equal measure
> dread the weapons with which you're armed.[9]

Guarini speaks of the delightful pain of Love.

> Oh, 'twas a torment no man can express![10]

Several passages in this repertoire make the observation that Love is unaffected by Reason. Guarini, for example, writes,

> No outward object can with reason move
> The heart to love it, 'cause it cannot love:
> Only the soul, 'cause that can love again,
> Deserves a love, deserves a lover's pain.[11]

And in another place,

> Desire and reason; an affection mixed
> Of sense and intellect; with knowing, wild;
> With seeing, blind …[12]

---

8   Torquato Tasso, *The Aminta*, trans. Louis Lord (Oxford: Oxford University Press, 1931), 109.
9   Niccolò Machiavelli, *Machiavelli, the Chief Works*, trans. Allan Gilbert (Durham: Duke University Press, 1965), II, 785.
10 Guarini, *The Faithful Shepherd*, I, 293.
11 Ibid., II, 339.
12 Ibid., III, 371.

In Ariosto's *The Pretenders* [*I Suppositi*] a character is described, as we might say, as turning from the left hemisphere to the right, or from Reason to the emotion of Love.

> He immediately fell in love with me, and his love was so vehement that he suddenly changed his mind and cast aside his books and his long gown and determined that I alone would be the subject of his study.[13]

Guarini would seem to agree with this, contending that we learn Love from experience and not from books.

> [Love] is born with us, and it grows up as fast
> As we do, Amarillis; 'tis not writ,
> Nor taught by masters—nature printed it
> In human hearts with her own powerful hand.[14]

Pleasure and Pain

The two most interesting passages in this literature which deal with Pleasure and Pain are found in Machiavelli's *Mandragola*. A canzone intended to be sung at the beginning includes this observation on the importance of Pleasure.

> Because life is short
> and many are the pains …
> he who deprives himself of pleasure
> only to live with labor and toil
> does not understand the world's deceits,
> and what ills and what strange events
> crush almost all mortals.[15]

In a canzone to be sung at the end of Act II, Machiavelli concludes that the best hope for avoiding pain is to have been born stupid.

> Everybody knows how happy he is
> who is born stupid and believes everything.
> Ambition does not disturb him,
> fear does not upset him—
> those two that ever are the seeds
> of pain and discontent.[16]

---

13 Ariosto, *The Comedies of Arisoto*, 55.
14 Guarini, *The Faithful Shepherd*, III, 354.
15 Machiavelli, *The Chief Works*, II, 776.
16 Ibid., II, 793.

ON THE PHILOSOPHY OF AESTHETICS

Two playwrights speak of the importance of inspiration in composing for the stage. In the prologue to Ariosto's *The Students* [*I Studenti*], we read,

> Whoever intends to write fine verses and adorn the stage with beautiful subjects must have help from above.[17]

Guarini makes a similar observation.

> No mortal work successfully is done
> Which with the immortal gods is not begun.[18]

We know from frequent comments in the prologues to plays that the audience was expected to watch quietly and attentively. In Ludovico Ariosto's *The Coffer* [*La Cassaria*], for example, the audience is begged to watch in silence and at the end to give their applause.[19] Similar requests are found in Giovanni Cecchi's (1518–1587) comedy, *The Horned Owl* [*L'Assiuolo*] and in Machiavelli's *Mandragola*.

From several comments, it appears to have been a familiar circumstance to find a playwright borrowing rather directly from early plays. In the prologue to his *The Pretenders* [*I Suppositi*], Ariosto admits that he has taken his plots in part from Plautus and Terence, but he says he has done this to so little degree, that,

> if either Terence or Plautus knew, they would not be offended and would call it poetic imitation rather than plagiarism.[20]

In the prologue to his *Lena* [*La Lena*], he excuses his imitation for a different reason.

> I know from what my teacher taught me that among all poetic invention there is nothing more difficult [than comedy]. The Latin poets wrote very few new ones; instead they translated those of the Greeks. Of the comedies we read today, none of those of Terence and hardly any of Plautus are original.[21]

The more familiar question regarding imitation, whether Art should imitate Nature, is mentioned only once. Pietro Aretino's, *The Courtesan*, the first Italian comedy to depart from the models of Plautus and Terence, mentions an artist little known today,

---

17 Ariosto, *The Comedies of Arisoto*, 269.
18 Guarini, *The Faithful Shepherd*, III, 366.
19 Ariosto, *The Comedies of Arisoto*, 3, 47.
20 Ibid., 53.
21 Ibid., 161.

> Look at Pordonone, whose works make one doubt whether nature imitates art or whether art imitates nature.[22]

AESTHETICS IN THE WRITINGS BY DRAMA THEORISTS

Bernardino Daniello, *Poetics* (1536)

Little is known of Daniello, other than he was a scholar who died in Padua in 1565. His *La Poetica* was one of the earliest Italian works to discuss modern drama. Tragedy, he contends, should display proud men who are victims of 'terrible and pitiful' events of fortune, and not merely the shocking.[23] Unlike ancient Greek requirements, Daniello permits the playwright to introduce humble speech, in order for the noble person to 'weep and lament.' He forbids on the stage such actions as 'cruel deeds, the impossible, and the unseemly.'

Daniello argues for the continued use of the Chorus in Tragedy, as an independent moral force.

> Let the chorus in tragedy, I say, take the part of the just and the good, wrongfully oppressed, and favor these. Let them advise friends, favor those who hate sin, laud sobriety, justice, law and peace, and pray the gods that ... they descend to console the miserable and the afflicted.

In Comedy, he observes, the Chorus is no longer employed, their place being taken by 'music and songs and *Moresche* and jesters, in order that the stage may not remain empty.'

Julius Caesar Scaliger, *Poetics* (1561)

Scaliger, born in Pauda in 1484, moved to France where he died in 1558 as one of the most celebrated men alive. His best known work, a Latin treatise much inspired by Aristotle, *Poetices Libri Septem*, was first published in Lyons in 1561 and for more than a century was an influential treatise.

In his interpretation of Aristotle's famous work on Tragedy, the *Poetics*, Scaliger mentions that Aristotle had included music as an essential element. This Scaliger objects to, contending that acting is the 'one and only' essential.

Scaliger's own first belief regarding the theater is that both Tragedy and Comedy must be patterned after real life. Beyond this similarity, there are four important differences:

1. Comedy deals with rustic characters, or those from lower civic life, while Tragedy deals with nobles, and never introduces persons of lower classes.

---

22 Pietro Aretino, *The Works of Aretino*, trans. Samuel Putnam (New York: Civici, 1926), 226.
23 Barrett Clark, *European Theories of the Drama* (New York: Crown, 1959), 55.

2. Comedies begins with a confused state of affairs which are cleared up at the end. Tragedy opens more tranquilly, but the outcome is 'horrifying.'
3. In Tragedy the language is grave, polished and removed from the colloquial.
4. In Tragedy, 'all things wear a troubled look,' meaning it deals with serious affairs.

Scaliger adds one significant purpose for Tragedy which was not mentioned by Aristotle and the Greeks, that it serve a distinct educational purpose.

> The play is not acted solely to strike the spectator with admiration or consternation … but should also teach, move, and please.[24]

Finally, Scaliger states that the play should 'approach as near as possible to truth' and, in general, be 'concise as possible, yet also as varied and manifold as possible.'

Antonio Sebastiano, *The Art of Poetry* (1563)

Sebastiano, known as Minturno, was bishop of Ugento, and represented that town in the council of Trent. In 1565 he was transferred to Crotone, where he died in 1574. Author of both an *Arte Poetica* (1563, in Italian) and a *De Poeta* (1559, in Latin), his writing was influential in Spain, France and England.

Like Scaliger, Minturno also argues for an educational purpose in Tragedy, but otherwise he permits a much broader range of theater, which he calls 'dramatic poetry.' First, he observes that imitation is the basis of all poetry, as well as painting and sculpture. He includes music as an important element of Tragedy, giving its purpose as 'affording pleasure.' The purpose of dramatic poetry he gives as 'for the pleasure and profit of the onlooker.'

Minturno writes that the subject of Tragedy is limited to serious and grave events concerning persons of high rank. Comedy deals with common folk of the city or country and petty merchants. A third category, satirical poetry, deals with 'humble persons, mean and ludicrous.'

Next Minturno makes a very interesting observation regarding the larger field of poetry in general. The lyric poet, he says, 'narrates, without laying aside his own personality.' The epic poet sometimes retains his own personality and sometimes abandons it, speaking for others. The dramatic poet, 'from first to last, speaks through the lips of others.'[25] We were struck by the comparison one could draw with the field of music, the three being, respectively, the composer, he who improvises and the interpreter.

Minturno makes some interesting comments on the length of a dramatic performance, relative to the attention of the audience. In general, he states that the performance should be not less than three hours nor more than four,

---

24 Quoted in Ibid., 62.
25 Ibid., 56.

lest neither too great brevity rob the work of its beauty and leave the desire of the hearers unsatisfied, nor excessive length deprive the poem of its proportion, spoil its charm, and render it boresome to the beholders. And indeed the wise poet should so measure the time with the matter to be presented that those who hear the work should rather deplore its brevity than regret having remained too long to listen.[26]

Tragedy, says Minturno, uses suave language and produces both the catharsis first described by Aristotle and the new purpose of education. In Minturno's words, Tragedy arouses,

feelings of pity and terror, tending to purge the mind of the beholder of similar passions, to his delight and profit.[27]

Later he emphasizes the educational purpose, saying that 'the ennobling or purification of manners is the end toward which all effort is directed.' Still later he maintains the purpose of all dramatic poets is to instruct.

Minturno returns to catharsis, giving one of the most extended definitions to be found in early literature and offering an interesting analogy with art of the physician. The terror and pity which the observer experiences in Tragedy, he contends,

frees us most pleasantly from similar passions, for nothing else so curbs the indomitable frenzy of our minds. No one is so completely the victim of unbridled appetites, that, being moved by fear and pity at the unhappiness of others, he is not impelled to throw off the habits that have been the cause of such unhappiness. And the memory of the grave misfortunes of others not only renders us more ready and willing to support our own; it makes us more wary in avoiding like ills. The physician who with a powerful drug extinguishes the poisonous spark of the malady that afflicts the body, is no more powerful than the tragic poet who purges the mind of its troubles through the emotions aroused by his charming verses.[28]

According to Minturno, Comedy is a mirror of manners, the image of Truth, and uses suave and pleasing language and music. It differs with Tragedy primarily in presenting 'persons of humble or mediocre fortune.' One cannot help noticing the difference between this rather elegant concept of comedy and that defined by Machiavelli in the Prologue to his Comedy, *Clizia*.

If comedies are to give pleasure, they must incite the audience to laughter, which cannot be done if they keep their language serious and solemn, for the words that cause laughter are either stupid, or biting, or amorous. It is necessary, therefore, to put on the stage persons who are stupid, or sarcastic, or in love, and for this reason comedies that are full of these three types of speech are full of laughter; those that lack them do not find anybody to laugh as he watches.[29]

---

26 Quoted in Ibid., 57.
27 Ibid., 58.
28 Ibid., 58ff.
29 Machiavelli, *The Chief Works*, II, 824.

Ludovico Castelvetro, *Poetics* (1570)

Castelvetro, born in 1505 to an old noble family in Modena, was educated for the law but soon turned to literary interests. His life became a rather extraordinary adventure after his criticism of a poem by Caro in 1553, when subsequent threats of violence caused him to wander from city to city until he was eventually offered protection by Maximilian II in Vienna. It was to Maximilian that Castelvetro dedicated his *Poetica*. His dramatic theories are heavily dependent on Aristotle, but it is for his formulation of 'the three Unities' (time, place and action) that Castelvetro has remained an important figure in drama criticism.

Several of Castelvetro's definitions of Tragedy correspond with aspects of musical performance. For example, he begins with an emphasis not found before, that 'Tragedy cannot effect its proper function with a reading, without staging and acting.' The very same thing could be said, of course, of a musical score. He says, 'Tragedy is not imitation of men, but of action,' as we might say of a violinist: the point is not the violinist, but his music. And the same analogy could be drawn with his statement, 'In most actions, men do not hide their character, but exhibit them.' When he says that tragic poetry should exist for delight, and not for utility, he is giving one of our primary definitions of Art Music as well. Finally, one of his observations on drama reminds us of a distinction we often make, regarding educational music, between that which is 'inspired music' and that which is 'constructed music.'

> Poets who make tragedies without character and thought, do not really imitate human action; for in the operation of human action, character and thought are always revealed, though sometimes more, sometimes less.[30]

Sometimes Castelvetro seems to contradict himself, as after arguing for the importance of 'one action only,' as one of this three unities, he then seems to argue for more variety.

> There is no doubt that there is more pleasure in listening to a plot containing many and diverse actions than in listening to that which contains but one.[31]

And after observing that 'Tragedy can have either a happy or a sorrowful ending, as can comedy,' he then writes,

> Tragedy without a sad ending cannot excite and does not excite, as experience shows, either pity or fear.[32]

The purpose of Comedy, according to Castelvetro, 'is being moved by pleasing things appealing to the sentiments or the imagination.'

---

30 Clark, *European Theories of Drama*, 65.
31 Ibid., 64.
32 Ibid., 65.

ON THE AESTHETICS OF MUSIC

In general there is little reference to aesthetics in music in these plays. Most often, reference to music is in the form of a metapahor, as in Guarini.

> Would'st thou not say, Nature is out of tune,
> The world is sick, and like to die in June?[33]

The only purpose of music one finds given is to inspire love. In Ariosto's Comedy, *The Necromancer* [*Il Negromante*], in the prologue, he observes,

> Don't you think it strange if you hear that wild animals and trees followed Orpheus from place to place; and that by their singing both Amphion in Greece and Apollo in Phrygia imbued stones with such lust that they began mounting one another—as many of you here would do if given the opportunity.[34]

One finds two interesting references to musicians in general. In Aretino's *Il Marescalco*, there is a passage which reflects the fact that there were distinguished women musicians in sixteenth-century Italy. In this comedy, the point is also made that such talent in wives presents a problem for husbands.

> COUNT. Let's change the subject and get back to the bride: she is talented, you know.
> CAVALIER. It's true. She composed the new madrigal everyone's singing to that tune of Marchetto's.
> JACOPO. That's all I ever sing.
> MARESCALCO. So she is accomplished?
> COUNT. Very accomplished.
> MARESCALCO. And a poet?
> CAVALIER. She is, as you've heard.
> MARESCALCO. It's all clear to me. I can feel them; I can see them coming! She composes? The moment women begin composing songs, husbands begin to feel a weight on their foreheads.[35]

And Machiavelli, in his *Clizia*, observes that it is of no use to confide one's experiences to a singer, for he, being self-absorbed, will not pay attention. The character, Palamed, says,

> I've heard again and again that one ought to run away from three sorts of men: singers, old men, and lovers. For if you're with a singer and tell him some affair of yours, when you think he's listening to you, he lets out *ut, re, mi, fa, sol, la*, and gurgles a ballad in his throat.[36]

---

33 Guarini, *The Faithful Shepherd*, I, 286.
34 Ariosto, *The Comedies of Ariosto*, 101.
35 Aretino, *Il Marescalco*, V, ii.
36 Machiavelli, *The Chief Works*, II, 825.

ART MUSIC

In view of the Italian humanists' interest in the use of music in the dramas of ancient Greece, it seems odd that the contemporary plays do not contain more references to music. There is music, however, most often in the form of independent songs sung at the beginning or end of the play. For example, a canzone to be sung at the beginning of Machiavelli's *Clizia* recalls the pastoral world of nymphs and shepherds.

> Fair the days and quiet,
> happy and beautiful the land
> where of our songs the music is heard!
> Hence, light-hearted and joyful,
> these efforts of yours
> we shall accompany with our songs,
> with such sweet harmony
> as never you have heard before.[37]

The only references to performances of Art Music in the actual plays is usually to the singing of love songs. An interesting example is found in Aretino's *Il Marescalco*.

> How well I would act a lover slain by Love! No Spaniard or Neapolitan could surpass the wealth of my sighs, the abundance of my tears, the profusion of my words … I'd have madrigals composed in her praise, and Tromboncino would set them to music.[38]

An humorous description of an older man singing love songs is found in the comedy, *The Deceived*, written as a collaborative effort by a literary society in Siena.

> If there's any sort of festival late at night, he's there, armed with a funny curved dagger; he sings all day in his dirty, cracked old voice, to the music of a lute that's more out of tune than he is himself.[39]

Finally, there is a passing reference to keyboard music, when a character in Ariosto's *Lena* [*La Lena*] says, 'Do you call it a favor to make twenty-five florins tinkle out of your pocket like the notes of a cembalo?'[40]

---

37 Ibid., II, 822.
38 Aretino, *Il Marescalco*.
39 *The Deceived*, in *Five Italian Renaissance Comedies* (New York: Penguin Books, 1978), I, 212.
40 Ariosto, *The Comedies of Ariosto*, 164.

FUNCTIONAL MUSIC

There is likewise little reference in these plays to Functional Music. Guarini, in his *The Faithful Shepherd*, makes one reference to attending the temple,

> But such sweet harmony and redolence
> As heaven affords—if heaven affect the sense.[41]

The same play also mentions hunting music. The play begins with a reference to hunting horns, 'Rouse eyes and hearts with your shrill voice and horn!'[42] A stage note soon describes the huntsmen leaving, 'sounding their horns.' And later, 'Soon as it dawns, I hear his cursed horn.'[43]

---

41 Guarini, *The Faithful Shepherd*, V, 431.
42 Ibid., I, 283.
43 Ibid., III, 357.

6 BALDASSARE CASTIGLIONE

BALDASSARE CASTIGLIONE (1478–1529), as a diplomat for the duke of Urbino and popes Leo X and Clement VII, had the opportunity to observe Italian culture at its highest level. From this experience came one of the most famous books of the Renaissance, *Il Cortigiano* (*The Courtier*), which attempts to describe the attributes of the perfect gentleman[1] and lady from the sixteenth century perspective. In spite of some very modern goals for his perfect gentleman, Castiglione remained in some ways an old-fashioned Church philosopher, as is especially reflected in his views on women and on the relationship of Reason and the emotions.

Castiglione's ideal man, the *l'uomo universale*, must be noble born, skilled and learned in virtually all fields, gentle, sensitive and tactful. In the spirit of the latter, Castiglione says he has tried to use language which is graceful, euphonious, valid and expressive.[2] He also promises us the truth, for as a 'worthless painter,' Castiglione says he lacks the skill to 'adorn the truth with pretty colors or use perspective to deceive the eye.'

His book, which presents a discussion on the definition of the perfect gentleman by a group of nobles, is dedicated to a young courtier 'of perfect behavior and proficient in everything,' Alfonso Ariosto, who died at a young age. 'Fortune,' says Castiglione, 'hasn't changed her ways: she still hates virtue as much as she ever did.'[3]

ON THE PHYSIOLOGY OF AESTHETICS

In spite of the broad and diverse range of skills which Castiglione recognizes as needed by the gentleman, in the end he holds to the old Church view that Reason must govern over all other aspects of man. He discusses this at length in an attempt to bring together the concepts of the senses, the emotions, and Pleasure and Pain all under the control of Reason.

---

1 Baldassare castiglione, *The Courtier*, II, 145ff., trans. George Bull (New York: Penguin Books, 1967). We can see the significance of this purpose, in the eyes of Castiglione, when he describes the following deportment of some courtiers.

> Sometimes they push one another downstairs, belabor each other with sticks and bricks, throw handfuls of dust in each other's eyes, cause their horses to collapse on one another in ditches or downhill; then at table they hurl the soup, or the sauce or jelly, in one another's face, and they burst out laughing.

2 Ibid., Prologue, 34. Citations will give the Book number of the original, in addition to the page number from this edition.

3 Ibid., Prologue, 32.

This discussion begins with Cardinal Bembo,[4] who introduces the sin of incontinence, in response to a suggestion that most men sin out of ignorance.

> 'It is certain that even men who are incontinent form their judgment reasonably and logically, and are fully aware of the evil and sinful nature of what they desire. So they use their reason to oppose and resist their desires, and this causes the battle of pleasure and pain against judgment. Then eventually the desires prove too strong for reason, which abandons the struggle, like a ship which for a time resists the storm but finally, battered by the overwhelming fury of the winds, with anchor and rigging smashed, lets herself be driven by the tempest, unresponsive either to helm or compass. So the incontinent commit their follies with a certain hesitant remorse, as if despite themselves. And this they would not do if they did not know that what they were doing was evil; on the contrary, without any resistance from reason they would abandon themselves utterly to their desires, and in this case would not be incontinent but simply intemperate. And this is far worse, since reason plays a part in incontinence, which is therefore a less serious vice; just as continence is an imperfect virtue, since it is influenced by the emotions.'
>
> 'Well,' answered signor Ottaviano, 'your argument sounds very fine. Nevertheless, I don't think that it is really valid. For although the incontinent sin in that hesitant manner, and their reason does struggle with their desires, and they realize what evil is, yet they lack full knowledge and do not understand evil as well as they need to. Possessing only a vague notion rather than any certain knowledge of evil, they allow their reason to be overcome by emotion. But if they enjoyed true knowledge there is no doubt that they would not fall into error. For reason is always overcome by desire because of ignorance, and true knowledge can never be defeated by the emotions, which originate in the body rather than in the soul. And if the emotions are properly governed and controlled by reason, then they become virtuous, and if otherwise, then vicious. However, reason is so potent that it always makes the senses obey it, insinuating itself by marvelous ways and means, provided what it ought to possess is not seized by ignorance.'[5]

The topic turns to temperance, and Ottaviano continues,

> 'Unruffled temperance is like the commander who conquers and rules without opposition; and when it has not only subdued but totally extinguished the fires of lust in the mind which possesses it, like a good ruler in time of civil war, temperance destroys all seditious enemies within and hands over to reason the scepter of absolute power. Thus this virtue does no violence to the soul, but gently infuses it with a powerful persuasion that turns it to honest ways, renders it calm and full of repose, in all things even and well-tempered, and informed in all respects with a certain harmony that adorns it with serene and unshakeable tranquility; and so in all things it is ready to respond completely to reason and to follow wherever reason may lead with the utmost docility …
>
> I did not say that temperance completely removes and uproots the emotions from a man's soul, nor would it be well for it to do so, since there are good elements even in the emotions.

---

4   Pietro Bembo (1470–1547), after serving in the court of Urbino, became a papal secretary to Leo X. He was an important scholar and poet.

5   Ibid., IV, 292ff.

But what it does do is to make what is perverse and opposed to right conduct in the emotions responsive to reason.

Later, in the voice of Cardinal Bembo, Castiglione speaks more of the relationship of the senses to Reason in a series of definitions which clearly follow Church dogma.

> Now in the human soul there are three faculties by which we understand or perceive things: namely, the senses, rational thought and intellect. Thus the senses desire things through sensual appetite or the kind of appetite which we share with the animals; reason desires things through rational choice, which is, strictly speaking, proper to man; and intellect, which links man to the angels, desires things through pure will. It follows that the sensual appetite desires only those things that are perceptible by the senses, whereas man's will finds its satisfaction in the contemplation of spiritual things that can be apprehended by intellect. And then man, who is rational by his very nature and is placed between the two extremes of brute matter and pure spirit, can choose to follow the senses or to aspire to the intellect, and so can direct his appetites or desires now in the one direction, now in the other.[6]

Interestingly enough, Castiglione does not seem bothered to find, in the daily conduct of life, that things such as style are often governed more by popularity than by Reason.

> Familiarity often causes the same things to be liked and disliked: and thus it sometimes happens that the customs, behavior, ceremonies and ways of life approved of at one period of time grow to be looked down on, and those which were once looked down on come to be approved. So we can see clearly enough that usage is more effective than reason in introducing new things among us and in wiping out the old.[7]

Regarding education, as we shall see, Castiglione expected his perfect gentleman to possess a wide assortment of skills, including music. In addition to these, he observes,

> I should like our courtier to be a more than average scholar, at least in those studies which we call the humanities; and he should have a knowledge of Greek as well as Latin, because of the many different things that are so beautifully written in that language. He should be very well acquainted with the poets, and no less with the orators and historians, and also skilled at writing both poetry and prose, especially in Italian; for in addition to the satisfaction this will give him personally, it will enable him to provide constant entertainment for the ladies, who are usually very fond of such things.[8]

Castiglione adds, regarding one's poetry, that one must be on guard against flattery and praise, for 'there is no sound or song that comes sweeter to our ears.'

---

6   Ibid., IV, 325.

7   Ibid., I, 39.

8   Ibid., I, 90.

He places the burden of education on the teacher, whom he defines as follows:

> It is a convincing proof of whether a man understands something that he has the ability to teach it.⁹

The central purpose of the teacher must be to instill moral values.

> It is necessary to have a master who by his teaching and precepts stirs and awakens the moral virtues whose seed is enclosed and buried in our souls and who, like a good farmer, cultivates and clears the way for them by removing the thorns and tares of our appetites which often so darken and choke our minds as not to let them flower or produce those splendid fruits which alone we should wish to see born in the human heart.¹⁰

In turn, this morality-based education fosters ideal learning attitudes in the student. He follows this thought with an interesting observation on France.

> Socrates was perfectly right in affirming that in his opinion his teaching bore good fruit when it encouraged someone to strive to know and understand virtue; for those who have reached the stage where they desire nothing more eagerly than to be good have no trouble in learning all that is necessary ...
>
> However, in addition to goodness, I believe that for all of us the true and principal adornment of the mind is letters; although the French, I know, recognize only the nobility of arms and think nothing of all the rest; and so they not only do not appreciate learning but detest it, regarding men of letters inferior and thinking it a great insult to call anyone a scholar.¹¹

ON THE PSYCHOLOGY OF AESTHETICS

Emotions

Through our our modern knowledge of the twin hemispheres of the brain, we know that the emotions are better communicated by the expressions of the face than by words. Castiglione accurately reflects this, although, as was the case with many early writers, he incorrectly concluded that it was primarily the eyes, and not the face itself, which reflects emotions.

> In my view when the courtier wishes to declare his love he should do so by his actions rather than by speech, for a man's feelings are sometimes more clearly revealed by a sigh, a gesture of respect or a certain shyness than by volumes of words. And next he should use his eyes to carry

---

9 Ibid., I, 85.
10 Ibid., III, 291.
11 Ibid., I, 88.

faithfully the message written in his heart, because they often communicate hidden feelings more effectively than anything else, including the tongue and the written word.[12]

As was the case with many medieval and Renaissance writers, Castiglione finds Love the most familiar vehicle to discuss the nature of the emotions. He has one character say that he has been accused of never experiencing the passion of love and the reason is that he has observed the general pain and sadness of lovers.

> I have been frightened off by the endless laments of certain lovers, who are pale and sad and taciturn and who always seem to carry their unhappiness in their eyes. And when they do speak they accompany every word with repeated sighs and talk of nothing else save tears, torments, despair and their longing for death.[13]

Pietro Bembo, who in this book speaks for Platonic Love, adds that he also has always found Love to be a bitter experience.

Castiglione has the character Gaspare[14] contend that women find enjoyment in causing this pain, observing that not only can women 'make men miserable as well as happy, and that they can give them life or death as they please.'

> So they feed on this kind of satisfaction, for which they are so greedy that in order not to go without it they neither give their lovers what they want nor make them utterly despair. Rather, in order to keep them in a continual state of anxiety and desire, they adopt a certain haughty and disdainful attitude, and mingle threats with promises, and they like their slightest word or look or gesture to be received with rapture.[15]

One of the best known parts of this book is Cardinal Bembo's argument for Platonic Love being more beautiful than sensual Love. He begins with his definition of Love.

> Love is simply a certain longing to possess beauty; and since this longing can only be for things that are known already, knowledge must always of necessity precede desire, which by its nature wishes for what is good, but of itself is blind and so cannot perceive what is good. So Nature has ruled that every appetitive faculty, or desire, be accompanied by a cognitive faculty or power of understanding.[16]

The problems begin when man desires not the beauty, but the body of his lover. This, concludes Castiglione, is because Love makes the error of following the senses instead of Reason.

---

12 Ibid., III, 268.

13 Ibid., I, 49.

14 Pallavicino Gaspare (1486–1511) was one of the younger members of this cast of characters. A Lombard, he died young after a life of illness.

15 Ibid., III, 274.

16 Ibid., IV, 325.

> Thus the mind is seized by desire for the beauty which it recognizes as good, and, if it allows itself to be guided by what its senses tell it, it falls into the gravest errors and judges that the body is the chief cause of the beauty which it enshrines, and so to enjoy that beauty it must necessarily achieve with it as intimate a union as possible. But this is untrue; and anyone who thinks to enjoy that beauty by possessing the body is deceiving himself and is not moved by true knowledge, arrived at by rational choice, but by a false opinion derived from the desire of the senses ... Lovers of this kind, therefore, are always most unhappy; for either they never attain their desires, and this causes them great misery, or if they do attain them they find themselves in terrible distress, and their wretchedness is even greater. For both at the beginning and during the course of this love of theirs they never know other than anguish, torment, sorrow, exertion and distress; and so lovers, it is supposed, must always be characterized by paleness and dejection, continuous sighings and weepings, mournfulness and lamentations, silences and the desire for death.
>
> We see, therefore, that the senses are the chief cause of this desolation of the spirit ... Because the senses are deceptive they fill the soul with errors and mistaken ideas.[17]

Beauty comes from goodness, contends Cardinal Bembo, and evidence of this goodness can be perceived in the face of man and animals!

> We know this from the way physiognomists often establish a man's character and sometimes even his thoughts from his face. Moreover, even in animals the qualities of the soul as far as possible impress themselves upon the body and be perceived from their physical appearance. Consider how clearly we can perceive anger, ferocity and pride in the face of the lion, the horse and the eagle; and a pure and simple innocence in lambs and doves; evil guile in foxes and wolves, and so with nearly all the animals.[18]

From this he concludes,

> It can be said that in some manner the good and the beautiful are identical, especially in the human body. And the proximate cause of physical beauty is, in my opinion, the beauty of the soul.[19]

Bembo's prescription for avoiding the dangers of desiring the body, instead of the beauty of the soul, is centered in the use of the appropriate senses.

> He must also reflect that just as a man cannot hear with his palate or smell with his ears, beauty can in no way be enjoyed nor can the desire it arouses in our souls be satisfied through the sense of touch but solely through what has beauty for its true object, namely, the faculty of sight. So he should ignore the blind judgment of these senses [touch and taste] and enjoy with his eyes the radiance, the grace, the loving ardor, the smiles, the mannerisms and all the other agreeable adornments of the woman he loves. Similarly, let him use his hearing to enjoy the sweetness of

---

17 Ibid., IV, 326ff.
18 Ibid., IV, 330.
19 Ibid., IV, 332.

her voice, the modulation of her words and, if she is a musician, the music she plays. In this way, through the channels of these two faculties, which have little to do with corporeal things and are servants of reason, he will nourish his soul on the most delightful food and will not allow desire for the body to arouse in him any appetite that is at all impure.[20]

The good cardinal does allow in Platonic Love the possibility of kissing, which, because it is a union of body and soul, allows one 'to be transported by divine love to the contemplation of celestial beauty.'[21] On the subject of this higher divine love, Bembo becomes quite excited and Castiglione tells us that 'having spoken in this way with such vehemence that he seemed transported out of himself, Bembo then remained silent and still, looking towards heaven, as if dazed.'

Pleasure and Pain

Castiglione introduces his discussion of the nature of the perception of Pleasure by an interesting observation that in every generation the older members think that everything is going from bad to worse and that nothing is as good as it once was. His analysis for this predilection in the older man is as follows:

> I think that the reason for this faulty judgment in the old is that the passing years rob them of many of the favorable conditions of life, among other things depriving the blood of a great part of its vitality; and in consequence the physical constitution changes and the organs through which the soul exercises its power grow feeble. Thus in old age the gay flowers of contentment fall from our hearts, just as in autumn the leaves fall from the trees; and in place of bright and clear thoughts the soul is possessed by a dark and confused melancholy attended by endless distress. Thus the mind as well as the body grows weak; it retains only a faint impression of past pleasures, and only the image of those precious hours of youth, when, so long as they last, heaven and earth and the whole of creation seem to be rejoicing and smiling as we look, and a gay of springtime of happiness seems to flower in our thoughts as in a delightful and lovely garden ... It seems to me that the old resemble those who, as they sail from harbor, keep their eyes on the land and imagine that their ship is motionless whereas the shore is receding, though the contrary is true. For, like the harbor, time and the pleasures of life stay the same while we, sailing away in the ship of mortality, cross the stormy sea which engulfs and swallows us up one by one.[22]

Later he adds, 'for in truth our minds detest all the things that have accompanied our sorrows and love all those that have accompanied our joys.'

In another place, Castiglione reflects on a theme often mentioned in early literature, that Pleasure and Pain seem inexorably linked.

---

20 Ibid., IV, 334ff.
21 Ibid., IV, 336ff.
22 Ibid., II, 107ff.

> Thus Socrates is very right when he wonders, as Plato describes, why Aesop did not write a fable pretending that, since He had never been able to unite them, God had joined pain and pleasure end to end, so that the beginning of one should be the end of the other. For we find that we are never allowed pleasure without pain beforehand. And who can enjoy his rest unless he has felt the burden of fatigue? Who enjoys eating, drinking and sleeping unless he has first known hunger, thirst and sleeplessness?[23]

In the end, for Castiglione, Pleasure and Pain were inevitably tied to Good and Evil, again reflecting the medieval Church viewpoint.

> True pleasure is always good, and true suffering always evil; therefore these men deceive themselves when they take false pleasures for true and true suffering for false. And so their false pleasures often earn them genuine pain. It follows that the art that teaches us to distinguish the true form of the false can certainly be learned; and the virtue which enables us to choose what is genuinely good and not what wrongly appears to be so may be called true knowledge, which is more advantageous in life than any other kind, because it rids us of the ignorance which ... is the cause of all the evils there are.[24]

In another place, Castiglione comments on the danger of Pleasure, 'since it only too easily persuades and corrupts our judgment.'[25]

ON THE PHILOSOPHY OF AESTHETICS

Castiglione begins his discussion on the general principles of aesthetics by pointing to the importance of the individuality in the artist. One of the nobles present, Federico,[26] suggests that Petrarch and Boccaccio copied earlier models. The Count[27] responds that this is impossible, for those who are copied must be superior to the imitators, in which case we would know the names of the original writers and not Petrarch and Boccaccio. He continues,

> For myself, I believe that their true teacher was their own instinctive judgment and genius; and no one should be surprised by this, since in every sphere one can almost always reach the height of perfection in various ways.[28]

---

23 Ibid., II, 110.

24 Ibid., III, 292.

25 Ibid., IV, 314.

26 Federico Fregoso, a friend of Castiglione and Bembo, was a scholar of philology and linguistics. He was made a cardinal in 1539.

27 Cesare Gonzaga (1475–1512).

28 Ibid., I, 81.

In another place, Castiglione contends, through the character Federico, that the artist should correlate his work with his own nature.

> I certainly don't deny that men possess varying opinions and talents; nor do I believe that a man who has an emotional and assertive nature should set himself to write about restful subjects or still less a serious and grave man write in a frivolous way. For as far as this is concerned it seems to me reasonable that everyone should follow his own inclination. And this, I think, was what Cicero meant when he said that teachers should pay regard to the nature of their pupils and not act like stupid farmers who would sometimes sow grain in ground fit only for vines.[29]

The essential role played by the individual artist is one of judgment, according to Castiglione.

> But surely however brilliant he is, a man receives good and bad ideas, of lesser and greater worth; and then these are corrected and refined by judgment and art, which reject the bad and select the good.[30]

However, in spite of his ability to judge regarding his choice of ideas, the artist, Castiglione found, sometimes could not accurately judge the *worth* of his own work.

> Boccaccio was a man of noble discernment by the standards of his time, and although to some extent he wrote with discrimination and ability, nevertheless he wrote far better when he let himself be guided solely by his natural genius and instinct, without care or concern to polish his writings, than when he went to great pains to correct and refine his work. For this reason ... he greatly deceived himself when he judged his work himself, and he put little value on what has done him honor and a great deal on what is worthless.[31]

In another passage related to this topic, Castiglione wonders by what 'perverse instinct or irrational motive,' men strive to do things they cannot understand.

> I know an outstanding musician who has given up music and devotes himself completely to composing poetry, in doing which he imagines he is a great genius, and he makes everyone laugh at him and has now lost even his music. Another, one of the world's finest painters, despises the art for which he has so rare a talent and has set himself to study philosophy; and in this he has strange notions and fanciful revelations that, if he tried to paint them, for all his skill he couldn't.[32]

Castiglione himself trusted the ability of the general public to judge his book as literature, even if they judged on the basis of instinct and not knowledge. It seems clear that he means by this what we call Universality, that quality in an art work or work of literature which speaks to all men. Therefore, he says, he leaves the defense of his book, against all accusations,

---

29 Ibid., I, 83.
30 Ibid., II, 153.
31 Ibid., Prologue, 33.
32 Ibid., II, 149.

> to the tribunal of public opinion, because more often than not, although the many may not understand everything, they can tell by natural instinct what seems good or bad, and, without being able to give any reason for it, they enjoy and love the one and reject and despise the other. Therefore if the book meets with general approval, I shall take it that it is good and believe that it will survive; and if, on the other hand, it fails to please, I shall take it that it is bad and shall at once accept that it must sink into obscurity.[33]

Beyond that, he reflects, Time, the father of truth and a dispassionate judge, will pronounce a sentence of life or death upon his book.

On the other hand, Castiglione observed that in many things everyone judges differently. This was most conspicuous to him in the example of Love.

> Therefore it often happens that what one person finds adorable another finds most detestable. Despite this, we are all alike in cherishing the one we love, and quite often the blind devotion of the lover makes him think the person he loves is the only one in the world possessing every virtue and completely without defect.[34]

He attributes this to Nature, who being fond of variety 'has made one man sensible in regard to one thing and another in regard to something else.' This explains the variety of preferences among individuals.

> One man [is] foolish [for] verse, another in music, another in dancing, another in ballet, another in riding and another in fencing: each according to his own innermost vibrations.

He adds another fascinating illustration of the uniqueness of the individual.

> They say in Apulia when someone is bitten by a tarantula many musical instruments are played and various tunes are tried until the humor which is causing the sickness all of a sudden responds to the sound with which it has a certain affinity and so agitates the sick man that he is shaken back into good health.

In another place, Castiglione observes that the recognition of true perfection is almost impossible, because of the manner in which opinions vary. Still, he says,

> I do think there is a perfection for everything, even though it may be concealed, and I also think that this perfection can be determined through informed and reasoned argument.[35]

Castiglione writes little of the most discussed topic regarding aesthetics in general, the question of whether Art should imitate Nature. Perhaps this was a matter of small concern in his circle, for he notes,

---

33 Ibid., Prologue, 36.
34 Ibid., I, 46ff.
35 Ibid., I, 53.

Nowadays we are so headstrong that we are contemptuous of doing what the best men did in the ancient world, namely, of practicing imitation.[36]

The only other reference to this subject is by the character, Giovanni Cristoforo,[37] who observes,

> I willingly accept that both painting and sculpture are skillful imitations of Nature; yet I still do not understand how you can maintain that what is real and is Nature's own creation cannot be more faithfully copied in a bronze or marble figure, in which all the members are rounded, fashioned and proportioned just as Nature makes them, than in a picture, consisting of a flat surface and colors that deceived the eye.[38]

He is answered by the count, who points out that painting, through color, shading, light and shade can more approximate Nature than sculpture.

Castiglione's discussion of painting is a curious mixture of ancient and modern definitions. The principal virtue he assigns to it suggests the ancient philosophy of painting being primarily a craft, for he says it is valuable for sketching 'towns, rivers, bridges, citadels, fortresses and similar things.'[39] But then he says ancient statues and paintings have come down to us as 'inspired works of art,' reflecting a more modern view.

A passage which speaks of the importance of teaching painting as part of education is also curious, for he asserts that painting was originally a member of the Liberal Arts, which it was not (Leonardo da Vinci made anguished complaints that it *should* be a part of the Liberal Arts). The Count says,

> I should like us to discuss something else again which, since I consider it highly important, I think our courtier should certainly not neglect: and this is the question of drawing and of the art of painting itself. And do not be surprised that I demand this ability, even if nowadays it may appear mechanical and hardly suited to a gentleman. For I recall having read that in the ancient world, and in Greece especially, children of gentle birth were required to learn painting at school, as worthy and necessary accomplishment, and it was ranked among the foremost of the liberal arts; subsequently, a public law was passed forbidding it to be taught to slaves.[40]

Later the count returns to a description of the purpose of painting which again sounds rather utilitarian.

> And even if it had no other useful or pleasurable aspects, painting helps us to judge the merits of ancient and modern statues, of vases, buildings, medallions, cameos, intaglios and similar works, and it reveals the beauty of living bodies, with regard to both the delicacy of the coun-

---

36 Ibid., I, 73.
37 Giovan Cristoforo Romano (ca. 1465–1512), an accomplished musician and sculptor.
38 Ibid., I, 98.
39 Ibid., I, 97ff.
40 Ibid., I, 96.

tenance and the proportion of the other parts, in man as in all other creatures. So you see that a knowledge of painting is the source of very profound pleasure.[41]

With regard to the aesthetic qualities of literature, Castiglione first focuses on the importance of polish and the use of beautiful words. The noble, Count Lodovico Canossa[42] observes,

> For it is my belief that writing is nothing other than a kind of speech which remains in being after it has been uttered, the representation, as it were, or rather the very life of our words. And so in speech, which ceases to exist as soon as it is uttered, some things are perhaps tolerable which are not so in writing; because writing preserves the words and submits them to the judgment of the reader, who has the time to give them his considered attention. Therefore it is right that greater pains should be taken to make what is written more polished and correct; not, however, that the written words should be different from those which are spoken, but they should be chosen from the most beautiful of those employed in speech.[43]

The character, Federico, argues to the contrary.

> I cannot deny, Count, that writing is a kind of speech. I would say, however, that if the spoken word is at all obscure what is said will fail to penetrate the mind of the listener and, since it will not be understood, will be useless. And this is not the case with writing, for if the words used by the writer carry with them a certain, I will not say difficulty but veiled subtlety, and so are not as familiar as those commonly used in speech, they give what is written greater authority and cause the reader to be more attentive and aware, and so reflect more deeply and enjoy the skill and message of the author; and by judiciously exerting himself a little he experiences the pleasure that is to be had from accomplishing difficult tasks. If the reader is so ignorant that he cannot overcome these difficulties, that is not the fault of the writer and his language should not, on this account, be judged to lack beauty.

Castiglione attempts to reconcile these views by discussing language in terms of oratory. It is important to observe here that he values content above delivery.

> What the courtier especially requires in order to speak and write well ... is knowledge, because the man who lacks knowledge has nothing in his mind worth hearing, has nothing worth writing or speaking. Then, it is necessary to arrange what is to be said or written in its logical order, and after that to express it well in words that, if I am not mistaken, should be appropriate, carefully chosen, clear and well formed, but above all that are still in popular use. For it is the words themselves which give an oration its greatness and magnificence, provided the orator employs good judgment and care, knows how to choose those which best express what he means, and how to enhance them, shaping them to his purpose like wax and arranging them in relation to

---

41 Ibid., I, 101.

42 Lodovico Canossa (1476–1532) was a member of a noble Veronese family and a relative of Castiglione. A friend of Erasmus and Raphael, he was a diplomat for the pope as well as king François I.

43 Ibid., I, 71ff.

one another so well that their clarity and worth are immediately evident, as if they were paintings hung in a good and natural light.[44]

To this, he says, the orator must add suitable gestures, which he defines as follows. We note here his emphasis on the facial expression of the emotions of the words.

> These should consist in certain movements of the entire body, not affected or violent but tempered by an agreeable expression of the face and movement of the eyes giving grace and emphasis to what is said, together with gestures to make as plain as possible the meaning and sentiments of the orator.

Finally, the count raises the important subject of the orator engaging the emotions of the listener.

> He should be capable of speaking with dignity and emphasis, and of arousing our deepest emotions, kindling and stirring them as the need arises. And at other times he should know how to speak with such simple candor that it seems like Nature herself softening and, as it were, drugging our emotions with sweetness.[45]

Castiglione's only reference to drama is the passing comment that Comedy, more than any other form, reflects the nature of human life.[46]

ON THE AESTHETICS OF MUSIC

Castiglione presents an extensive argument for the true gentleman being, in addition to everything else, a musician. This remarkable passage speaks of the gentleman not only being expected to read at sight, but play several instruments; the aesthetic quality of music appreciated at court and the virtues of music—especially as reflected in ancient literature; and its purposes and usages, including the occupational music of the lower classes. The count, begins,

> 'Gentlemen, I must tell you that I am not satisfied with our courtier unless he is also a musician and unless as well as understanding and being able to read music he can play several instruments. For, when we think of it, during our leisure time we can find nothing more worthy or commendable to help our bodies relax and our spirits recuperate, especially at Court where, besides the way in which music helps everyone to forget his troubles, many things are done to please the ladies, whose tender and gentle souls are very susceptible to harmony and sweetness. So it is no wonder that both in ancient times and today they have always been extremely fond of musicians and have welcomed music as true refreshment for the spirit.'

---

44   Ibid., I, 76ff. Castiglione says the voice of the orator should neither be thin and soft like a woman's, nor hard and rough as to sound boorish, but sonorous, resonant and well articulated, with distinct enunciation.
45   Ibid., I, 78.
46   Ibid., II, 107.

Signor Gaspare commented: 'I think that music, like so many other vanities, is most certainly very suited to women, and perhaps also to some of those who have the appearance of men, but not to real men who should not indulge in pleasures which render their minds effeminate and so cause them to fear death.'

'Do not say that,' retorted the Count, 'or I shall launch into oceans of praise for music and remind you how greatly it was honored in the ancient world, and held to be sacred, and that the wisest of philosophers held the opinion that the universe was made up of music, that the heavens make harmony as they move, and that as our own souls are formed on the same principle they are awakened and have their faculties, as it were, brought to life thorough music. And because of this it is recorded that Alexander was sometimes so stirred by music that almost against his will under its influence he was constrained to rise from the banquet table and rush to arms; then the musician would play something different, and growing calmer he would return from arms to the banquet. And, let me also tell you, grave Socrates, when he was already very old, learned to play the cithara. Moreover, I remember having heard that Plato and Aristotle insist that a well-educated man should also be a musician; and with innumerable arguments they show that music exerts a powerful influence on us, and, for many reasons that would take too long to explain, they say that it has to be learned in childhood, not so much for the sake of its audible melodies but because of its capacity to breed good new habits and a virtuous disposition and make the soul more receptive to happiness, just as exercise makes the body more robust; and they add that music far from being harmful to the pursuits of peace or war is greatly to their benefit. Then again, in the stern laws which he made, Lycurgus gave his approval to music. And we read that in battle the bellicose Spartans and Cretans used citharas and other sweet-sounding instruments; and that many outstanding commanders of the ancient world, such as Epaminondas, practiced music, and those who were ignorant of music, such as Themistocles, were far less respected. Have you not heard, as well, that among the first subjects which the good Chiron taught to the young Achilles was music, and that this wise and venerable teacher wished the hands that were to shed so much Trojan blood often to be employed in playing the cithara? What kind of warrior, then, would be ashamed to follow the example of Achilles, let alone all the other famous commanders whom I could cite? So you must not wish to deprive our courtier of music, which not only soothes the souls of men but often tames wild beasts. Indeed, the man who does not enjoy music can be sure that there is no harmony in his soul. And remember that it has such powers that once it caused a fish to let itself be ridden by a man over the tempestuous sea. We see it used in sacred places to render praise and thanks to God; and we may well believe that it is agreeable to God, and that He has given it to us as a soothing balm for our toils and tribulations. Thus common laborers in the field working under the burning sun will often relieve their tedium with simple country songs. And the ordinary peasant girl, rising before dawn to spin or weave, uses music to ward off sleep and make her work agreeable; distressed mariners, after the rains and the winds and the storms, love to relax with the help of music; weary pilgrims find solace in music on their long and exhausting journey, as so often do chained and fettered prisoners in their misery. As even stronger evidence that even the most unsophisticated melodies lighten the burden of all our toils and tribulations in this world, we find that Nature herself has taught it to the nurse as the sure way to still the persistent crying of young babies, who are lulled to quiet rest and sleep by the sound of her singing, forgetting the tears which at that age are right and proper as a presage of our later life.'

After the Count had been silent for a moment, the Magnifico Giuliano[47] said:

'I am not at all of the same opinion of signor Gaspare; on the contrary, for the reasons you have given and for many others besides, I believe that music is not only an ornament but a necessity for the courtier. However, I should like you to explain how he is to practice this and the other accomplishments that you assign to him, and on what occasions and in what manner; for there are many things which in themselves are commendable but which are most unseemly when practiced at the wrong time; and on the other hand, there are many things that seem inconsequential but which are greatly esteemed when performed on the appropriate occasion.'[48]

Castiglione does not immediately supply answers to these questions, but in his account of the following day he has Federico observe,

I think the courtier should possess good judgment, the need for which was rightly mentioned by the Count yesterday evening. If he does have it, then he needs no other instructions about how to practice what he knows at the right time and in the proper manner. To attempt to provide him with more precise rules would be too difficult and surely superfluous. For I do not know who would be so inept as to want to take up arms when others are attending to music; or to do a Morris dance in the streets,[49] no matter how good he is at it; or comfort a mother for the loss of her son by laughing and joking. I'm sure no gentleman would do such things, unless he were completely out of his wits.[50]

In addition to the purposes of music given in the above, in another place we find one not previously mentioned in early literature.

… like children in the dark singing to themselves to pluck up courage, as if they were driving away their fears with song.[51]

In the lengthy discussion of music above, we have seen the count argue that every gentleman must be a performing musician, and the Magnifico Giuliano call music 'a necessity for the courtier.' These views, however, may have been included by Castiglione for the purpose of representing another point of view, for they are somewhat in conflict with his fundamental attitude toward a gentleman's activities. While Castiglione gives abundant evidence that the gentleman should appreciate listening to music, being a skilled performer was quite another matter. Basically, Castiglione believed the gentleman should display a certain nonchalance

---

47 Giuliano de Medici (1479–1516), brother to pope Leo X, led a dissolute life. Nevertheless, his portrait was painted by Raphael and he was the subject of a sculpture by Michelangelo.

48 Ibid., I, 94ff.

49 In another place, Ibid., II, 117, Castiglione says, 'a gentleman should never honor by his personal appearance a country show, where the spectators and participants are common people.'

50 Ibid., II, 112ff.

51 Ibid., II, 124.

about all skills and should not be expected to apply himself in any form of hard labor which might result in excellence in any skill. For example, he calls chess a refined recreation, but for the defect that it demands so much knowledge. Since this requires much time and study, he concludes that, with regard to being a chess player, 'mediocrity is more to be praised than excellence.'[52] Likewise, he recommends tennis as a game worthy of the courtier, but he cautions,

> Even though his performance is outstanding, he should not let it be thought that he has spent on it much time and trouble. Neither should he behave like those people who are fond of music and, whenever they are speaking with someone, if there is a lull in the conversation always start to sing *sotto voce*.[53]

His basic contention seems to be that 'affectation,' being an enthusiast of, or expert in, any activity deprives one's performance of grace, and that the highest form of grace is simplicity and nonchalance.

> Leaving aside those who are endowed with [grace] by their stars, I have discovered a universal rule which seems to apply more than any other in all human actions or words: namely, to steer away from affectation at all costs, as if it were a rough and dangerous reef and to practice in all things a certain nonchalance which conceals all artistry and makes whatever one says or does seem uncontrived and effortless. I am sure that grace springs especially from this, since everyone knows how difficult it is to accomplish some unusual feat perfectly, and so facility in such things excites the greatest wonder; whereas, in contrast, to labor at what one is doing and, as we say, to make bones over it, shows an extreme lack of grace and causes everything, whatever its worth, to be discounted. So we can truthfully say that true art is what does not seem to be art; and the most important thing is to conceal it, because if it is revealed this discredits a man completely and ruins his reputation.[54]

He cites here ancient orators who purposely tried to hide their skills, for if the populace perceived their true skills they would be frightened of being deceived.

In another place he claims that it was believed among great painters of the ancient world that excessive diligence is harmful. He mentions in particular an ancient painter, Protogenes, who did not know when to stop and was blamed for finishing his work too thoroughly. Castiglione then continues,

> So this quality which is the opposite of affectation, and which we are now calling nonchalance, apart from being the real source of grace, brings with it another advantage; for whatever action it accompanies, no matter how trivial it is, it not only reveals the skill of the person doing it but also very often causes it to be considered far greater than it really is. This is because it makes the

---

52   Ibid., II, 140.
53   Ibid., II, 118.
54   Ibid., I, 67.

onlookers believe that a man who performs well with so much facility must possess even greater skill than he does, and that if he took great pains and effort he would perform even better.[55]

In this regard he gives the example of a musician.

> When a musician is singing and utters a single word ending in a group of notes with a sweet cadence, and with such ease that it seems effortless, that touch alone proves that he is capable of far more than he is doing.

Later, Castiglione returns to the attitude of nonchalance which the gentleman must exhibit relative to his own performance as a musician. The subject is introduced by Federico.

> 'For there is nothing so perfect in the world that the ignorant do not tire of it and despise it when they see it often. My judgment is the same with regard to music. Thus I should not like our courtier to behave as do so many others as soon as they put in an appearance, even in the presence of gentlemen who are strangers to them, immediately, hardly waiting to be asked, start showing off what they know, and often what they don't know, in such a way that it seems that they have come along just for this purpose and that it is their main pursuit in life. So the courtier should turn to music as if it were merely a pastime of his and he is yielding to persuasion, and not in the presence of common people or a large crowd. And although he may know and understand what he is doing, in this also I wish him to dissimulate the care and effort that are necessary for any competent performance; and he should let it seem as if he himself thinks nothing of his accomplishment which, because of its excellence, he makes others think very highly of.'[56]

Castiglione in numerous places treats the gentlewoman as distinctly disadvantaged as compared to the gentleman.[57] From this it followed that she should not engage in the activities of the gentleman, such as playing tennis for example. She was for this reason more limited in her opportunities as a musician.

> For example, when she is dancing I should not wish to see her use movements that are too forceful and energetic, nor, when she is singing or playing a musical instrument, to use those abrupt and frequent *diminuendos* that are ingenious but not beautiful. And I suggest that she should choose instruments suited to her purpose. Imagine what an ungainly sight it would be to have a woman playing drums, fifes, trumpets or other instruments of that sort; and this is simply because their stridency buries and destroys the sweet gentleness which embellished everything a woman does.[58]

---

55 Ibid., I, 69ff.

56 Ibid., II, 120.

57 On the inferiority of women, see Ibid., II, 201. He does acknowledge that in earlier times there had been women who were 'very talented in music, painting and sculpture.' [Ibid., III, 240] An even more interesting observation is made by Giuliano de Medici, that 'there can be no doubt that being weaker in body women are abler in mind and more capable of speculative thought than men.' [Ibid., III, 218] Somewhat more patronizing is Castiglione's observation, 'think of the noble poems we would not have if the poets thought little of women.' [Ibid., III, 256]

58 Ibid., III, 215.

In only one place does Castiglione offer details of actual musical materials, but it is an interesting passage, used for the purpose of illustrating the principle that nonchalance carried to an extreme is a fault.

> It certainly holds true in music, in which it is very wrong to have two perfect consonances one after the other; for our sense of hearing abhors this, whereas it often likes a second or a seventh, which in itself is a harsh and unbearable discord. This is because to continue in perfect consonances produces satiety and offers a harmony which is too affected; but this disappears when imperfect consonances are introduced to establish the contrast which keeps the listener in a state of expectancy, waiting for and enjoying the perfect consonances more eagerly and delighting in the discord of the second or seventh, as in a display of nonchalance.[59]

ART MUSIC

Castiglione provides lengthy descriptions of an environment of Art Music among the aristocracy of sixteenth-century Italy. He sets the stage for these comments by describing an ideal palace, that of Duke Federico of Urbino, which is adorned 'with the usual objects, such as silver vases, wall-hangings of the richest cloth of gold, silk and other similar material,' but also countless antique statues of marble and bronze, valuable paintings and 'every kind of musical instrument.'[60] He also mentions 'musical performances' in a list of activities appropriate to the well-born gentlemen of this court.[61] In the rooms of the duchess as well, the activities include 'constant music and dancing.' Therefore, he concludes, in this court were to be found 'poets, musicians, buffoons of all kinds, and the finest talent of every description anywhere in Italy.'

Castiglione displays his disdain for the man who will not listen to music, and thus has no place in court, in the following anecdote about a courtier whom a lady had asked to dance,

> and who not only refused but would not listen to music or take part in the many other entertainments offered, protesting all the while that such frivolities were not his business. And when at length the lady asked what his business was, he answered with a scowl: 'Fighting ...'
> 'Well then,' the lady retorted, 'I should think that since you aren't at war at the moment and you are not engaged in fighting, it would be a good thing if you were to have yourself well greased and stowed away in a cupboard with all your fighting equipment, so that you avoid getting rustier than you are already.'
> And of course everyone burst out laughing at the way she showed her contempt for his stupid presumption.[62]

---

59 Ibid., I, 69.
60 Ibid., I, 41.
61 Ibid., I, 42, 44.
62 Ibid., I, 58.

Castiglione, in making the point that each artist has his own personal style and therefore dissimilar styles can merit equal praise, provides us with a valuable portrait of the sixteenth-century Italian singer of Art Song. That this is art music is clearly evidenced by the impact on the contemplative listeners.

> In music, for example, the strains are now solemn and slow, now very fast and different in mood and manner. Yet the performance is always agreeable, though for varying reasons. For example, Bidon's style of singing is so skillful, quick, vehement and passionate, and of such melodious variety, that the spirits of those listening are excited and aroused, and feel so exalted that they seem to be drawn up to heaven. Then the singing of our own Marchetto Cara is just as moving, but its harmonies are softer; his voice is serene and so full of plaintive sweetness that he gently touches and penetrates our souls, and they respond with great delight and emotion.[63]

Later we find an extraordinary and extensive discussion of aesthetics in Art Music, introduced by Gaspare.

> 'There exist many different kinds of music, both vocal and instrumental. So I would be gratified to hear which is the best of all and on what occasion the courtier should perform.'
> 'Truly beautiful music,' answered Federico, 'consists, in my opinion, in fine singing, in reading accurately from the score and in an attractive personal style, and still more in singing to the accompaniment of the viol. I say this because the solo voice contains all the purity of music, and style and melody are studied and appreciated more carefully when our ears are not distracted by more than one voice, and every little fault, too, is more clearly apparent, something which does not happen when a group is singing, because then one singer covers up for the other. But above all, singing poetry accompanied by the viol seems especially pleasurable, for the instrument gives the words a really marvelous charm and effectiveness. All keyboard instruments, indeed, are harmonious, because their consonances are perfect and they make possible many effects which fill the soul with sweetness and melody. And no less delightful is the playing of a quartet, with the viols producing music of great skill and suavity. The human voice adds ornament and grace to all these instruments, with which I think it is good enough if our courtier has some acquaintance (though the more proficient he is the better) without concerning himself greatly with [the aulos] which both Minerva and Alcibiades rejected, because it seems [to] have something repulsive about [it]. Then as to the occasions when these various kinds of music should be performed, I would instance when a man finds himself in the company of dear and familiar friends, and there is no pressing business on hand. But above all, the time is appropriate when there are ladies present; for the sight of them softens the hearts of those who are listening, makes them more susceptible to the sweetness of the music, and also quickens the spirit of the musicians themselves. As I have already said, one should avoid playing in the presence of a large number, especially of the common people. But in any case, everything should be tempered by discretion; for it is just not possible to imagine all the circumstances possible, and if the courtier is a good judge of himself he will adapt himself to the occasion and will know when his audience is in the mood to listen and when not; and he will act his own age, for it is certainly most

---

63 Ibid., I, 82.

unbecoming and unsightly when an old grey-haired gentleman, who is toothless and wrinkled, takes up the viol and plays and sings in front of a gathering of ladies, even if his performance is quite good. This is because the words of songs are nearly always amorous, and in old men love is altogether ridiculous; although it sometimes seems that Cupid along with the other miracles he works delights in melting even the icy hearts of the old.'

Then the Magnifico replied: 'Do not rob such poor old men of this pleasure, Federico; for I have known men of advanced years who possess the most perfect voices and are accomplished musicians, and far more so than some young men.'

'It is not my wish,' answered Federico, 'to rob them of this pleasure, but it certainly is my wish to rob you and these ladies of the chance to laugh at their absurdity; and if old men have the desire to sing to the viol, then let them do so in private with the object of shedding from their minds the disturbing thoughts and bitter vexations of which life is full, and of tasting the divinity which, I believe, Pythagoras and Socrates attributed to music. And even if they do not practice it themselves, if they have cultivated a taste for music they will enjoy it far more than those who know nothing about it. After all, very often, because he exercises them a great deal, a blacksmith whose body is otherwise puny will have stronger arms than someone who is more robust; likewise, someone whose ears have been trained to listen to harmony will understand it better and more readily and appreciate it more intelligently than others whose hearing may be very sharp and sound but whose ears are untrained in the varieties of musical consonances; for the modulations of music have no significance for ears that are unaccustomed to them, though admittedly music can tame even a wild animal. This, then, is the pleasure that old men may suitably take in music.'[64]

This fascinating passage provides us with a number of specific aesthetic values in music from the perspective of the sixteenth-century Italian noble. First, that the highest aesthetic in art music is fine singing, reading from score and with an attractive personal style.

Performance mediums are clearly ranked with regard to aesthetics, the highest being solo singing, keyboard playing and chamber music. The aulos, the most important instrument of the ancient world, is now looked down upon.

Castiglione makes a passing negative reference to polyphony, representing a characteristic view of Italian humanists and of the sixteenth century in general. He mentions this in another place, where, in speaking of friendship,[65] Castiglione says it is dangerous to have more than two real friends. 'The reason for this is that, as you know, harmony is more difficult to achieve with several instruments than with two.'

We are also given the most aesthetic environment for Art Music: a relaxed atmosphere, when no one has pressing business at hand, when the listeners are in the proper mood, and when ladies are present. These should be private performances, not before large audiences or the common people.

---

64 Ibid., II, 120ff.
65 Ibid., II, 138.

Closely related is his objection to older men being public performers. Castiglione mentions the unsuitability of old men making music in another passage, here recommending they should not actually perform but only give advice and teach.

> Then if the courtier should be so old that it is unbecoming to him to indulge in music, merrymaking, games, arms and similar recreations, even so one cannot say that it is impossible for him to win his prince's favor in this way. For even if he is too old to take part in these things himself, he can still understand them; and, given that he has practiced them when young, seeing that years and experience bring with them so much more knowledge of everything, age does not prevent his having a more perfect judgment, and a more perfect understanding of how to teach them to his prince.[66]

And finally, the misinformed view that one can only appreciate music if one has 'cultivated a taste' for it, or is a trained listener. This is disproved by the simple fact that everyone in the world appreciates music, while few are knowledgeable listeners. We see the other side of this coin, where knowledge can adversely affect the listener, in the following where Castiglione is speaking of the dangers of relying on the opinions of others.

> And to prove this, consider that not so long ago, when certain verses were presented here as being by Sannazaro, everyone thought they were extremely fine and praised them to the skies, then when it was established that they were by someone else their reputation sank immediately and they seemed quite mediocre. Then again, when a motet was sung in the presence of the Duchess, it pleased no one and was considered worthless, until it became known that it had been composed by Josquin des Près.[67]

ENTERTAINMENT MUSIC

Castiglione introduces the topic of entertainment by stipulating that even in these circumstances the proper gentleman must maintain grace and discretion.

> I would like the courtier sometimes to descend to calmer and more restful games, and to escape envy and enter pleasantly into the company of all the others by doing everything they do; although he should never fail to behave in a commendable manner and should rule all his actions with that good judgment which will not allow him to take part in any foolishness. Let him laugh, jest, banter, romp and dance, though in a fashion that always reflects good sense and discretion, and let him say and do everything with grace.[68]

---

66 Ibid., IV, 320.

67 Ibid., II, 144ff.

68 Ibid., I, 64.

Under the general subject of appropriate court entertainment, Castiglione presents a very lengthy discussion of humor. We find particularly interesting the following introduction to the topic of laughter.

> I shall say, as briefly as I can, whatever occurs to me on the subject of the causes of laughter, which is so natural to mankind that to define a man it is customary to say that he is an animal capable of laughing. For laughter is seen only in men, and it is nearly always the sign of a certain inward hilarity of the spirit, which is naturally attracted to pleasure and desirous of rest and recreation. So we see many things devised by men for this purpose, such as festivals and various kinds of spectacle. And because we like those who are responsible for providing us with our recreations, the kings of the ancient world, the Roman, the Athenian and many others, in order to secure the goodwill of the populace and to feed the eyes and mind of the multitude, used to build great theaters and other public edifices, and there they would show new kinds of sport, horse and chariot races, combats, strange beasts, comedies, tragedies and mime. Nor were grave philosophers adverse to such displays, and they would often, both at spectacles of that kind or at banquets, relax their minds which were weary from their exalted discourses and inspired thoughts; and this is something all kinds and conditions of men willingly do, for not only laborers in the fields, sailors and all those who do hard and rough work with their hands but also holy men of religion and prisoners waiting in hourly expectation of death, all seek solace in light recreation. Therefore everything which provokes laughter exalts a man's spirit and gives him pleasure, and for a while enables him to forget the trials and tribulations of which life is full.[69]

On the subject of laughter, Castiglione hastily adds that to *cause* laughter is not appropriate to the gentleman, but rather the fool, drunkard, 'stupid clowns and buffoons.' Neither should the gentleman cause laughter by sarcasm or mockery of the unfortunate. Even in telling jokes, Castiglione warns the courtier to remember 'always our dignity as gentlemen, eschewing vile words and indecorous acts, not contorting the face or person grotesquely.'[70]

Castiglione gives a wide representation of types of jokes and various forms of humorous speech. Two of these illustrations involve music. The first involves a peasant boy who makes his first visit to the large city, to Venice to attend the Feast of the Ascension. When the boy returns he is asked what he found most remarkable and he mentioned, among other things, 'so much music and singing that it seemed just like heaven.' When pressed further what kind of music most pleased him, he follows with this description of one who had seen for the first time the slide trumpet. The instrument was played with one hand holding the mouthpiece on the lips, while the other hand made the entire remaining instrument slide back and forth.

> [The music] was all good. But I especially noticed someone playing on a strange sort of trumpet which with every move he thrust down his throat more than two palms' length, and then straight away would draw it out, only to thrust it down again; and you never saw the like![71]

---

69 Ibid., II, 155.
70 Ibid., II, 160.
71 Ibid., II, 163.

The second illustration involved a play on words. A duke, about to cross a river, gave an order for the appropriate signal to his trumpeter: *Passa* ['Cross now']. The trumpeter turned to the duke and answered very respectfully: *Passi la Signoria Vostra* ['After you!'].[72]

We are given one final view of court entertainment music, when the aristocratic company has tired of their discussions of the desirable qualities of the courtier and are in the mood to dance. At this time, we are told, they call upon Barletta, 'a delightful musician and an excellent dancer, who always kept the Court agreeably entertained.'[73]

---

72   Ibid., II, 170ff.
73   Ibid., I, 104.

7 CARDANO

WE HAVE SET GIROLAMO CARDANO (1501–1576) ASIDE from the others who wrote sixteenth-century treatises on music, as he alone has written much which characterizes music in a negative light. We have seen nothing quite like these views since the earliest years of the Christian era.

Cardano's education began under his father, a lawyer in Milan, who taught him arithmetic, geometry[1] and astrology. Music lessons were made possible, secretly, through the aid of his mother. In later years he would remember this music teacher, Leo Oglonus, for his high moral standards. As for himself, in his autobiography Cardano recalled 'wandering through Milan from dusk until daybreak, dripping with perspiration from the exertion of serenading with his musical instruments.'[2] A friend, who later became the archbishop of Milan, recalled that Cardano performed with grace.[3]

After a violent family argument, the father allowed Cardano to study medicine at the University of Pavia, but after one year the university was closed due to war and he transferred to the University of Padua. Here he proved an outstanding student, was active in debate and obtained the student office of Rector. He received the Doctor of Medicine degree, after three faculty ballots, but was refused permission, due to the suspicion that he was of illegitimate birth, by the College of Physicians in Milan, to practice in the town where his mother now lived.

Cardano settled in the village of Sacco, near Padua, where he experienced little financial success in his medical practice, but otherwise enjoyed his most pleasant years.

> I gambled, played musical instruments, took walks, and was of good cheer and studied only rarely. I had no pains, no fears; I was treated with esteem and respect and I associated with the nobles of Venice. In short, it was the springtime of my life.[4]

After his marriage, Cardano moved to Milan, where his repeated requests for permission to practice medicine were turned down. He was able to gain appointment as a lecturer in

---

1 The father was consulted several times on geometry by Leonardo da Vinci.
2 Girolamo Cardano, *Hieronymi Cardani Mediolensis opera omnia*, I, 1.
3 Alan Wykes, *Doctor Cardano* (London: Muller, 1969), 18.
4 Quoted in Oystein Ore, *Cardano The Gambling Scholar* (New York: Dover, 1953), 10.

mathematics for the Piatti foundation, which was the turning point in his career. He attracted large audiences for his lectures and published his first two books on mathematics in 1539.

With this boost to his self-confidence, Cardano began to fight back against the doctors of Milan. He published a book called *On the Bad Practices of Medicine* which was immediately popular with the public.

> The things which give most reputation to a physician nowadays are his manners, servants, carriage, clothes, smartness, and caginess, all displayed in a sort of artificial and insipid way; learning and experience seem to count for nothing.[5]

Public pressure caused the College of Physicians to relent and within a few years Cardano became one of the most famous physicians in Europe. Receiving offers from nobles everywhere for his services, Cardano traveled widely and was always received with the greatest acclaim.

Cardano took advantage of his fame by beginning to publish an incredible stream of books on nearly every subject, including mathematics, astronomy, physics, morals, dialectics, ethics, philosophy, the immortality of the soul, the mysteries of eternity, works of history, music, games of chance, chess, gems, dreams, and religious studies. His *De Subtilitate Rerum*, a work on science and natural philosophy became one of the best sellers during the second half of the sixteenth century. Another popular book, *Consolation*, was translated into English in 1573, read by Shakespeare and is considered to have influenced Hamlet's famous soliloquy. In all there were 131 published works, 111 in manuscript and another 170 which he burned, considering them worthless. It seems clear that this enormous output was driven by a passion to perpetuate his name, something he became obsessed with during his youth after noticing that a close family friend was never mentioned again after his death.

Cardano's spirit was completely broken in 1560 when his son, Giambatista, was imprisoned for the poisoning of his unfaithful wife. In spite of the efforts of Cardano, Giambatista was hanged at age twenty-six, after having his left hand struck off under torture. Another son, Aldo, saddened his father by being repeatedly jailed for theft. Cardano resigned his professorship in Milan, but after two years, through the intervention of old friends, accepted a professorship in medicine at the University of Bologna.

In October 1570 Cardano was arrested as a heretic and placed in jail. He was removed from his university position and forbidden to have any more books published. He moved to Rome where, in spite of his sentence, he was invited to become a member of the College of Physicians and received a pension from the pope.

It is no longer possible to determine why the charge of heresy was brought against him. The most likely reason was a passage in his *De Subtilitate* in which he describes a religious debate between a Christian, Jew, Mohammedan and a heathen, in which he unfortunately forgot to find in favor of the Christian. Otherwise there was nothing in his personal conduct typical of the heretic. In fact, when the king of Denmark wanted him as his personal physi-

---
5   Ibid., 12.

cian, Cardano answered by writing that it would be repugnant to him to live in a country of heretics (Protestants).

All in all, this was a strange man and before continuing with his writings it might be well to let him describe himself.

> Nature has made me capable, pious, faithful, meditative, inventive, courageous, cunning, crafty, sarcastic, industrious, diligent, ingenious, impertinent, contemptuous of religion, grudging, envious, sad, treacherous, magician and sorcerer, miserable, hateful, lascivious, solitary, disagreeable, rude, divinator, changeable, irresolute, indecent, quarrelsome, and because of the conflicts between my nature and soul I am not understood even by those with whom I associate most frequently.[6]

The last phrase suggests that he might have added 'observant' to this long list. It is true he was not understood, had few friends and history has never known quite what to think about him. It would be easy to discount much of his writings, for some are filled with contradictions and some are on pseudo-science, such as metoposcopy (determining character by the face), chiromancy (palmistry) and geomancy (predicting the future). Yet, he made significant contributions, such as his description of typhus fever and his discoveries in algebra, including his perception that quadratic equations might have negative roots.

Neither do we know what to think about some of his comments on music. After telling us of his love for music in his youth, and that his devotion to music remained one of his recreations throughout life, could he have really have been as negative toward music as he appears in some of his writings?

He was best summarized by the famous German mathematician and philosopher Leibniz, who wrote,

> Cardano was a great man with all his faults; without them he would have been incomparable.

ON THE PHYSIOLOGY OF AESTHETICS

Although Cardano was a published scholar on numerous topics, he seemed to retain a faith in the effectiveness of practical experience over intellectual propositions.

> I have been more aided by experience than by my own wisdom or by the faith in the power of my art.[7]

......

---

6   Ibid., 25ff.

7   Ibid., 47.

> Perhaps someone will quite rightly ask whether the same people who know these rules also play well or not. For it seems to be a different thing to know and to execute … The same question arises in other discussions. Is a learned physician also a skilled one? In those matters which give time for reflection, the same man is both learned and successful, as in mathematics, jurisprudence, and also medicine …
>
> But in those matters in which no time is given and guile prevails, it is one thing to know and another to exercise one's knowledge successfully, as in gambling, war, dueling, and commerce. For although acumen depends on both knowledge and practice, still practice and experience can do more than knowledge.[8]

Cardano discussed the senses with respect to their contribution to pleasure. This is a very rare instance of a philosopher finding the sense of hearing superior to the sense of sight.

> There are three conditions common to all the senses. First, they arise in a proportion, for as such they are known and thus are pleasing. So it happens that an octave in 2:1 relationship is highly pleasant to the ears …
>
> Secondly, all things in moderation are pleasing, but not the kind of low and powerful sound which deafens men, as that in the mountains of the Spanish isle, nor the weak kind of sound which causes fatigue in just trying to hear it. The same is true of fast and slow, high and low, soft and rough.
>
> Thirdly, better things are always pleasing after worse ones, but the reverse is displeasing. So light pleases after darkness, sweetness after bitterness, oil of roses after dill, and consonant tones after dissonances.
>
> Of necessity pleasure and delight exist in every sense. But each sense is subject to change, and the change is to the opposite, as from good to evil, which then result in sadness. Thus pleasure will come from a change of evil into good, yet it is necessary that evil had been present previously. Who takes pleasure in eating without hunger? In drinking without thirst? In loving without desire? In material gain without cupidity? Thus the pleasure of gambling is so strong through the frequent alternation of winning and losing, which also accounts for the constant repetition of this pleasure.
>
> There is also pleasure in learning, for what we do not know we learn. But is there any pleasure in contemplating what we already know? Absolutely none, or at least less than what we experience while learning. Yet we are not pleased by uninterrupted learning, since a lack of knowledge has not preceded it. The first impulse comes from a certain lack of knowledge. In this way the poor, since they are affected more by sadness, seem to enjoy pleasure to a greater degree than the rich and powerful.
>
> In the same way the sound of a fifth above and a fourth below offends the ears, while the opposite is pleasing, for a low tone strikes the ears after a high tone and remains longer; therefore, when the simpler interval is below it will be more pleasing than when it is above …
>
> Just as this occurs in sounds so also it happens in pictures that things which disturb the eyes should be mixed with those that are pleasing. A twofold rule must be observed: [1] let things that disturb the visual sense impress this sense less than things that please it; [2] do not let things be

---

8 Girolamo Cardano, *The Book on Games of Chance*, trans. Sydney Gould (New York: Dover, 1953), 225.

divided so minutely that the sense does not perceive them. Remember, we said a consonance or harmony is the ratio of many tones recognized aurally. If, therefore, they are divided so minutely that they are not perceived by a sense they not only will not please but will even offend.

So a painting of very minute flowers is neither grateful nor pleasing, and the same is true of very small handwriting …

But the sense of hearing recognizes even smaller differences than the visual sense or any other sense. It is so acute that it very beautifully distinguishes the removal of one part from thirty-three or even from eighty, for a ditone without this decrease sounds harsh, but with it the interval sounds smooth. In temporal relationships a beat [*ictus*] is divisible into sixteen parts.

Thus the sense of hearing is more subtle than the sense of sight, either because as I said, it alone is concerned with motion, or because the objects of sight, namely colors, mutually nullify each other through their strong contrast, or because sight relates to many objects and hearing to one very simple object.[9]

ON THE PSYCHOLOGY OF AESTHETICS

Cardano discusses the emotions extensively with respect to his observations on music, as we shall see below. With respect to Pleasure and Pain as an abstract topic, this unhappy man found 'even the notion of happiness is far from our nature.'[10]

> Nor does sorrow serve any other end than to increase our cares and render our minds more inept for counsel.[11]

He joins all philosophers in pointing out that Pleasure and Pain always go hand in hand.

> Many things which appear painful and absurd at first may change and conversely many agreeable and useful things may later take on a painful aspect.[12]
>
> ......
>
> There is nothing that brings greater sorrow with it than joy, for pleasure when gone is succeeded by sadness.[13]

But, for Cardano, to say that they go hand in hand did not mean they have equal impact.

> A little bile in a great deal of honey and a little bit of rottenness in a large mixture of pleasant things can do far more to produce vomiting than all the rest can do to produce delight.[14]

---

9   Quoted in Clement Miller, *Hieronymus Cardanus, Writings on Music* (American Institute of Musicology, 1973), 211.
10 *De Propria Vita*, quoted in Ore, *Cardano the Gambling Scholar*, 9.
11 Ibid., 32.
12 Ibid., 28.
13 Ibid., 33.
14 Cardano, *The Book on Games of Chance*, 231ff.

ON THE AESTHETICS OF MUSIC

Cardano was first and foremost a mathematician and it is in this field that he is most remembered today. It is no surprise, therefore, that in his own catalog of his manuscripts, his music treatise is found listed under the category of mathematics. It was no doubt mathematics he was thinking of when he defined music as 'a discipline which teaches men to recognize the meaning of sounds and to listen to their differences.'[15]

Nevertheless, at times the feeling side of him took precedence over the mathematical side, as, for example, when he asks regarding sixths, 'why should we reject what the ear already approves,' even if the mathematical ratios do not agree. Such things, he concludes, cannot yet be explained.

> So it is necessary to consider why a connection of tones which is pleasing to the ears does not have a rational explanation. Accordingly, the usefulness of the aural sense is clear, but its rationale is found in the discovery of many things which are not yet fully known through experience, or in the need for a proper measure of its use …[16]

It is also interesting that his predilection for mathematics did not lead him to a preference to the polyphonic style, a fact he mentions several times. His preference for the music of his own humanistic generation can be seen in a comment he made after discussing Ockeghem.

> But the music of our day is as much more elegant as it was more elaborate in earlier times.[17]

On the Purpose of Music

In the most general sense, Cardano finds the purpose of music in three broad categories.

> There are three reasons for the invention of music, which are pleasure, grief and divine inspiration.[18]

He begins his treatise, 'On Music,' with his contention that the real purpose of music must be found in the present, and not in the past.

---

15   Quoted in Miller, *Hieronymus Cardanus*, 37.

16   Ibid., 104.

17   Ibid., 153. Cardano refers here to an unknown thirty-six voice canon by Ockeghem.

18   Ibid., 175.

I do not consider that music should be esteemed for its antiquity or its glorious inventors, two reasons commonly given in laudatory introductions to the arts, but for its usefulness, excellence, subtlety, and value among other arts and disciplines.[19]

The specific purpose of music which Cardano mentions most frequently is that it is for the purpose of pleasure. He often mentions this by way of defining something, as for example in discussing complex proportions he dismisses the ones resulting in the fastest notes, saying 'whatever the ear cannot perceive does not produce pleasure.'[20] He discusses pleasure with respect to purpose of the various elements of music, as we can see in these reflections on ancient music.

Harmonic music consisted of words and music and their concord. It was entirely directed towards pleasure. Rhythmic music existed in a similar way in different countries. It is common, popular, and in use now in Africa and Italy, formerly in Judea. It exists to produce a certain pleasure in the minds of the common people. Metric music, which includes artistic poetry, offers much pleasure in epics and fine poetry, and shows the mores of humanity.[21]

In another place, Cardano elaborates on the manner in which emotional content produces pleasure.

The first rule of artistic music: there is nothing more efficacious for pleasure than proper imitation. It has three parts: manner [*modus*], sense [*sensus*], and sound [*sonus*]. These three do not always coincide. For example, if one imitates the song of small birds, it is not necessary to imitate the sense, for their chirping has no meaning, but only their sound and manner …

We imitate by sense when there is great emotion, such as in the four moods of sorrow, joy, tranquility, and excitement …

A mood of commiseration proceeds in music in slow and serious notes by dropping downward suddenly from a high range. This imitates the manner of those who weep, for at first they wail in a very high and clear voice and then they end by dropping into a very low and rather muffled groan.[22]

Cardano's most specific reference to music having the purpose of offering solace, and it is one he qualifies, is found in a discussion of the cithara.

If there is an instrument appropriate to tranquility and also a relation of meter and poetry to it, the instrument will be a cithara and the song will be mournful and almost tragic. In this way

---

19   Ibid., 37.
20   Ibid., 71.
21   Ibid., 96.
22   Ibid., 142ff.

we can lighten the cares that result from the misery of human misfortune, although I do not necessarily recommend this.[23]

As an amateur performer himself, it is no surprise that Cardano recommends music for a profitable use of leisure time. In his *The Book on Games of Chance*, in arguing against gambling as a form of leisure, he includes music as one of several more profitable activities, together with his reasons.

> As for the excuse made by some that [gambling] relieves boredom, this would be better done by pleasant reading, or by narrating tales or stories, or by one of the beautiful but not laborious arts. Among the latter, playing the lute or the cembalo, or singing, or composing poetry will be more useful, and for three reasons. First, because such a change from serious business is more praiseworthy than gambling, either since something is produced, as in the case of painting, or because it is according to nature, as in music, or because the man learns something, as in reading ... Second, it does not rob us, against our will, of more time than it should ... Third, such employment of leisure is more respectable and does not present a bad example, as gambling does, particularly to one's children and servants.[24]

In several places Cardano stresses the utilitarian purposes of music. In the following passage, which again mentions its use for leisure, he is concerned primarily with music's contribution to education. Also interesting here is a reference to Aristotle's concept of catharsis, the 'cleansing of the spirit.' Finally, we find here the negative attitude which often enters Cardano's discussion of music, in this case his suggestion that some believe music adversely affects character and in his expression that music affords an 'innocuous' pleasure.

> [Music's] usefulness is divided into three parts, for it pertains to instruction and study, or to the cleansing of the spirit, or to spending time pleasurably in leisure, tranquility, and freedom from the pressure of more serious matters. It is often said that emotions in music reflect weakened and enervated morals, but I believe such emotions consist of gentle virtues, and correspond to those more appropriate to action and also to those most divine virtues suitable for intellectual endeavor. Accordingly music celebrates those moral virtues which are especially appropriate to that useful quality which pertains to learning. Teachers and disciplinarians have agreed on the expiative and purgative force of strong emotions. When these emotions subside they may become excessively reversed and softened by giving way especially to emotions of misery and pity, causing dejection and depression. Music also proposes to fill such moods with a certain innocuous pleasure.[25]

In a discussion entitled 'On the Value of Music,' Cardano's negative attitudes about music become pronounced. Music may be honorable, but it is not essential or necessary. We see

---

23 Ibid., 204.

24 Cardano, *The Book on Games of Chance*, 186. Cardano also makes the interesting observation that the Christians tolerate gambling, but do not allow cursing.

25 Miller, *Hieronymus Cardanus*, 105.

here one of his more heated attacks on singers and how having them in his home, he claims, corrupted his own children. It is better, he concludes to have the children play instruments that do not require any other musician—although not the wind instruments, for reasons of health.

> It is useful to consider whether the study of music is worthwhile. It appears to have value, for both Plato and Aristotle state that boys should be instructed in it. Reason also recommends this, since one cannot be constantly engaged in laborious pursuits, so that leisure time is a necessity. Yet leisure that is inane and empty cannot create a rewarding life, because a rewarding life consists in work. Thus it is necessary to engage in some sort of activity during leisure hours; even though it is not necessary or essential it should be honest and honorable. Such an activity is the study of music.
>
> Music is also of worth because it is a pleasing pastime and is useful for discipline and as a cultural value of life. Also, since it affords pleasure without detriment it is beneficial to all and especially to children.
>
> Yet if one considers our presently complicated way of singing, which consists of many persons singing together and which cannot take place at one's own leisure, since there is a need for fellow singers and since so many of them have dissolute morals, we conclude that this practice is really of no use to anyone. You find hardly any musician in our time who does not abound in every kind of vice, and thus such a musician is the greatest impediment not only to a poor and busy man but to all men in general. And why don't you find a musician among the distinguished men of our time, men such as Erasmus, Alciatus, Budé, Jason, Vesalius, and Gesner?
>
> But since this kind of music has subverted my own home, so to speak, I will present the facts in my own case. For not only did I sustain a heavy loss of money, but what is worse, I corrupted the morals of my own children. It is hard to assemble four or five persons who can sing readily. Since we want this activity to take place frequently it occurs during leisure time. If we do it at home the singers will be maintained at great expense and they will corrupt the characters of our young boys and adolescents, for most of them are drunkards and gluttons, also wanton, fickle, impatient, coarse, indolent, and tainted with every kind of unlawful desire. The best of them are fools.
>
> Does this mean then that music must be expelled from the home and the education of children? Not at all. Music has three attributes: sound, rhythm, and cognition arising from perception. Cognition is useful in all activities, in recognizing men of talent, in deriving pleasure from listening to singers, and in pursuing music yourself, although I will say later how you do this. It is also worthwhile to grasp the rhythm for the sake of the poetry and for the pleasure, understanding, and practice of the music. But sound must be employed to the degree that it can be applied to musical instruments, not to singing polyphonically. Such instruments are the lute, lira, pipe organ, and other string instruments. These instruments are complete in themselves and need only one person to play them, so that one can practice by himself and receive pleasure. In this kind of music one can satisfy the three conditions that Aristotle proposed, namely, the confirmation or change of morals, moods, or actions. These conditions also apply to the present times, both in the morals of children and adolescents and in the organization of life.

> Yet the rich can learn polyphonic music thoroughly and can form a group of singers from chosen men; although this is difficult it still can be done. But for the poor, or children, or youths, or those who want to teach their children at home, social music is not practical. Understanding it is more beneficial than participation, also having a knowledge of the complete instruments, but not of the kind of instrument in which the cheeks are puffed up; among such instruments I detest mostly the playing of horns, because their use is neither distinguished nor noble nor beneficial to the brain, lungs, or abdomen, for it causes hernias. And when Aristotle did not approve of the use of the same instruments that we have just praised, he was considering their public use, while we were thinking of their appropriateness for individuals.[26]

Later he continues in the same vein, denigrating singers and now even finding complaints with playing a solo instrument.

> In our time a person may seek to study music, and when he has barely mastered it after much effort he finds that there is a lack of fellow singers. And even if he meets with them they often make mistakes, causing laughter among the listeners, so that he gets contempt in place of praise and sorrow in place of pleasure. When they do sing well one wants to be more prominent than another, a circumstance which creates tension.
>
> If the instruction has been satisfactory another concern may come to mind, [should] you learn to play the lute or recorder. How much labor and tedium is there in this effort? After an entire year of work, if the study is as successful as you had wished, you will be pleased with a few things, but not without great effort. Meanwhile one thing or other will be lacking, and even if everything has turned out well you find that your efforts are disdained more than they are praised. Your incentive disappears, and cares of the family and business interfere. One becomes a servant of fellow musicians, and must put up with all their faults and troublesome natures.
>
> So you can see how hostile these things are to tranquility; nor is the source of this impediment to be found anywhere but in ourselves. But you say: 'I enjoy music a great deal and have studied since childhood.' In that case there is no instrument more perfect than a lira, none more unlimited, none more pleasant, none more comfortable. Yet it causes a great deal of inconvenience when strings are tightened, loosened, changed or restrung.
>
> When they are tuned they break from humidity and rain or from dryness and wind.[27]

On the Elements of Music

Cardano calls the first elements of music, tone, pitch and volume. Then in an example of the contradictions which abound in his writings, he says the quality of a tone *differs* with either of these two, although he immediately defines quality in these same terms.

---

26 Ibid., 197ff. Aristotle disapproved of the aulos in education, but only because the tone was too exciting.
27 Ibid., 200.

> There are harsh [*asperae*] tones that may be high, or powerful, or weak, although in a weak tone harshness is less offensive. In the same way there are soft or mild tones that may be high or low or powerful or weak.[28]

It is interesting that Cardano associates time in music with emotions.

> There is nothing that moves the affections more than the division of temporal values.[29]

Regarding consonance and dissonance, Cardano believed that the ear does not recognize either consonance or dissonance in 'intervals that are widely separated.'[30] In several places he suggests that the ear accepts dissonance only when heard in passing.

> Dissonances are not allowed to remain sounding, for just as with men who have become frozen stiff through immoderate cold and remain so even when heat is applied, so also a consonance following a dissonance will greatly please the ears if the dissonance's movement is not delayed, but if the dissonance is retained it will destroy all harmony.[31]

Cardano also becomes contradictory when discussing the ancient modes. In one place he describes Dorian as 'sharp, unpolished, hard,' in another context as 'filled with majesty' and in yet another place that it 'withdrew from passionate emotions and led to moderation.'[32]

On Instruments and Instrumentalists

Cardano also discusses the physical nature of instruments at length, including the materials used in their construction ('The best gut strings come from dogs'). Some of his observations make little sense, as when he distinguishes between a *fistula* in which the 'tone is formed in the throat' and the recorder or *syrinx*, 'which merely uses the breath but forms the tone within itself.'[33]

His most interesting discusson on this topic provides several criteria for judging the excellence of musical instruments,[34] most of which are aesthetic in nature:

1. The range should be ample, at least two octaves.
2. The sound should be pleasing, not harsh or clamorous.

---

28 Ibid., 39.
29 Ibid., 137.
30 Ibid., 40.
31 Ibid., 42.
32 Ibid., 97, 100, 101.
33 Ibid., 51. In Ibid., 60, Cardano discusses the nature of breath used in a wind instrument, but he is generally misinformed.
34 Ibid., 55.

3. The sound should be easy to produce. For these three reasons trumpets are imperfect and inferior: they are far more difficult to blow than recorders, their tone is raucous and clamorous, and they exceed an octave range by only one tone. Horns [*cornua*] are also more inferior because of the last two reasons.
4. They should sound well with the human voice and other instruments. On this account recorders are the least praiseworthy, for hardly any other instrument blends less well with the voice and other instruments.
5. Those with many strings are preferable to those with three or less.
6. They should be able to sustain a tone.
7. They should have a full tone.
8. They should be capable of producing very small and a great number of intervals. In this regard the lute is superior to the organ.

Cardano also ranks the aesthetic order of instruments according to their similarity to the human voice. Thus winds are superior to strings, although he hastens to say that the viol is preferable to the fife.[35] We learn the full extent of his meaning of 'similarity' in this remarkable description of the possibilities of the recorder.

> The things that are true for the recorder are true for all instruments, but they are even more appropriate for this instrument. A particular property is imitation of the human voice, not simple imitation (for this is common to all instruments) but rather exact imitation is proper to the instrument. This happens by using a relaxed tone in laments, a strong tone in excitement, a smooth, connected tone in serious moods, and so forth concerning the other emotions.[36]

Most interesting is this passage which reveals that bagpipe and string players sometimes simultaneously played and sang!

> It is common to all pipers and to string players who sing as they play that they should not move their heads about nor contort their lips nor do anything indecorous. Again, they should always adjust their voices and sound by listening, and should carefully watch others beating time. Thirdly, they should keep the beat, which is far easier to do in singing than in playing, since a constant pulse is less evident. Finally, in instruments which are played by blowing a pleasing quality must be kept in every respect, for although in singing one can pronounce words, in playing tonal sweetness and a suitable imitation of mood reach the highest summit of artistry.[37]

Finally, Cardano mentions the actions of wind players necessary in accommodating the several tuning systems currently in use.

---

35 Ibid.
36 Ibid., 69.
37 Ibid., 189.

Just as musicians of our time have given sufficient attention to the chromatic genus ... so in the enharmonic they have been negligent because they have not understood it up to the present, although many woodwind and horn players apply it by gradually raising and lowering tones, as in dividing the distance between *mi* and *fa* so that the last tone forms a concord.[38]

On the Voice

In the following description of the basic requirements for a good singer, we find the final line most interesting—that a man is called a musician on the basis of his ears, that is, in his success in actual performance. This is a very significant departure from the long tradition of medieval writers, who always made a careful distinction between singers and musicians, by which they meant that the knowledge of the mathematics behind music distinguishes the musician—and therefore singers were not musicians.

> It happens that an innately vocal sound acquires most of its attributes or its impediments from nature. Indeed, if a voice is to be pleasant it should be pure, sonorous, firm, and capable of rising high and descending low. Also, it should have a youthful quality and should be capable of producing natural differences in whole tones and semitones. Finally, the singer should have an adaptable and highly developed sense of hearing, for the ears are more influential than the voice. They direct not only one's own musical sounds but also those of others as well as those of instruments. A man deserves to be called a musician because of his ears, not his voice.[39]

Cardano follows this with curious reflections on vocal technique and its effect on character.

> It is proper to sing motionlessly and with an open mouth, yet not indecorously, so that the sound is not checked by the lips or by the teeth. A low tone arises from the chest and a high tone from the head, that is, it is expelled from the palate, although its origin is the larynx. This is the reason why those who practice music assiduously from childhood on, injure themselves from constant singing and become mentally dull and morally deficient.

In another place, Cardano presents a major discussion of, and a particularly hostile attack on, singers under the title, 'Precepts for Singers.' Perhaps the most interesting subjects which Cardano mentions here are the ill health effects of singing, his belief that it is the words, and not the music itself, which convey emotion and the reference to improvisation in polyphonic music.

The first precept pertains to morals. Singers are accused of three things (and not without cause):

---

38   Ibid., 127.
39   Ibid., 107.

1. Their morals are depraved, they are gluttons and disreputable purveyors of every kind of vice. During their leisure time they constantly associate with those who live in debauchery and themselves acquire depraved morals ...
2. They are accused of acting like fools; also, few have money, for riches follow the prudent. Their foolishness results above all from intemperance, especially drinking wine, and also because their musical tones are carried to the brain with force and weaken it. They associate with the imprudent and occupy themselves with fun and frolics. They also teach, but their pedagogy is senseless ...

The second precept is that:
1. a singer should know how to produce notes very correctly and very swiftly.
2. He should have a steady beat and keep it absolutely even ...
3. His eyes should always look ahead, so that if any difficult place occurs he will be prepared for it.
4. He should examine the music before beginning ...
5. Let him take the greatest care to sing exactly on pitch and not let the note rise or drop ...
6. Let him produce a tone that is clear but not violent, for in this way many singers suffer a ruptured blood vessel or a hernia.
7. A singer produces a pleasant tone gradually, for from a hard and violent breath ... a harsh tone will result.

The third precept states that you must pass from the notes to the words, and this should be observed carefully, for music is ridiculous which is sung only on *ut, re, me, fa, sol, la*. There are four reasons for this:
1. What is heard should always be the same as what you have seen;
2. In this way you can truly convey the music's meaning, which depends mostly on the words, whether grave, doleful, or vivacious;
3. When one person sings *re*, another *sol*, and another *fa*, this ... causes great confusion in the music [a reference to polyphonic music];
4. Thus the music is not complete in your ears, and its consonances are understood only by naming the notes but not by their harmony.

The fourth precept states that after you have learned the words you may relinquish the beat gradually, for in this way you compel your ears to listen to the other parts ... If you lose your place you will immediately find it again as you listen to the other singers ... The beat must be retained privately with the first finger and not by the ear alone ... This is especially helpful in regard to what I said about the lack of time beating in woodwind and lira players, since they cannot perform this hand action and are so busy playing.

The fifth precept ... is that first the songs of others should be studied, not of all composers but of those who are especially known for skill and beauty ...

The sixth precept depends on the preceding one. It is in two parts, as it can be accomplished by the ear and by the voice. For you will learn to sing [improvisation] above another voice-part which moves in breves so as to regulate the second apart ... Next you will sing against two, three, or more parts.

> The seventh precept [is that] you shall train your ears so carefully that you can recognize the movements of individual voices and their harmonic content ... [The singer] should be careful not to correct someone else needlessly, which is a fault of a great many singers as they show off in front of the listeners.[40]

On Music with Words

For Cardano, song meant poetry. It is in this context that he says, 'song is related to music.'

> A song is related to music just as it relates to sound. But since it pertains largely to poetry it reaches the highest perfection in their combination.[41]

Cardano provides a lengthy discussion on the principles of composition for music with words. The focus here again is on his belief that it is the words, and not the music, which conveys meaning. It is for this reason that he stresses the ethical character of the words and the importance of the maintenance of their mood. His statement that the listener cannot recognize a fugual passage unless the same words are maintained, reveals the extent to which the sixteenth-century listener focused on the text in preference to the music.

> Care should be taken that words set to music are serious and honorable. To be avoided are obscene, base, vile, filthy, vulgar, and bacchanalian texts ... From such a song a listener will get not so much pleasure as he will be offended by the subject matter of the poem or the vileness of the text, and a musician who writes notes above such a text is himself made disreputable. The mind is revolted by such a base and uncouth kind of song in which nothing worthy of the art can be created. Artistic forms to be used are heroic, lyric, and decently amatory poems, also elegies, commemorations of saints, laments, prayers and many others which avoid all foulness, wantonness, and turpitude.
>
> Moods should be applied to subject matter and text. There are four simple and rather celebrated groupings: humility and pride, excitement and calm, joy and sorrow, and cruelty and tenderness. From the last two groups comes alacrity, namely, from joy and cruelty, and weeping from tenderness and sadness, for a song that is sad and full of compassion is appropriate to excite weeping. In addition there are other individual types, as prudence and boldness, amorousness and lowliness, virtue and wantonness, seriousness and frivolity, and many others, but these are well known and effective. In each type there are three intermediaries, for either they have no part in either extreme, or they are mixed and participate in both, or they are varied and are not consistent.
>
> A song should always retain its mood, but within a mood's limits it can wander freely; in this way it will not appear disordered nor will its variety bring a satiety of different styles.

---

40 Ibid., 182ff.
41 Ibid., 108.

Care must be taken that a song does not sound too empty because many voices are silent longer than they are heard. The opposite must be avoided, in which the voices are like racers running continually on a track from beginning to end, for the listeners will feel no pleasure and the singers will get no rest.

Care must also be taken that a song is not so very short that the end is reached while the listeners are still hoping to hear the fullness of the harmony, or so long that the song produces weariness for the listeners and labor for the singers.

When a song contains a *fuga* or exact imitation the same words must be repeated, otherwise the artistry of the music will be lost, for the musical imitation will hardly be recognized with a change of words.

All doleful songs and those evoking compassion should be weighty and stable. All lively songs require notes of short time value ... A rousing kind of song is written when syllables are sung very quickly and on the same pitch. We use this type in battle music, for such songs are especially lively.

A song should not begin with dissonant tones, and they also should not strike together, for this is troublesome to singers and detrimental to art.[42]

On Dance

Cardano observes, 'In antiquity dancing was called a sixth part of music.'[43] A more accurate representation of the view of the ancient Greeks would be to say that they believed dance to be the part of music you could see. This viewpoint must be understood in their constant reference to the fact that music is the only art which one cannot see. A more interesting observation on the relationship of ancient dance and music, and one we have not found in extant ancient literature, is that the movements of Greek choral performances were patterned on even earlier statues.

> Dancing and gesticulation express the ample movements that were left from antique statues, and the movements were then transferred from the figures to choral dances, and from choral dances to wrestling schools.[44]

Finally, Cardano presents a section called 'Musical Problems,' in which he poses rhetorical questions, much like the famous *Problems* of Aristotle. In the third question quoted here, we again see Cardano with a negative perspective of music.

---

42 Ibid., 149ff.
43 Ibid., 117.
44 Ibid., 119.

Why does one tone tend to induce sleep while harmony and aural pleasure consist of many concordant tones? Is it because sleep does not overcome us because of pleasure but rather because of weariness?

......

Why does a musical proportion consist of unequal and dissimilar numbers while arithmetic and geometric proportions arise from similar numbers? ... Is it because the highest pleasure in human affairs cannot exist without a corresponding pain?

......

Why do musicians rarely become rich? We exempt those who serve under kings, for 'to have pleased rulers is not the final reward.' It is because the art is esteemed lightly and is not a necessity of life, so that it is considered servile and unworthy of large gifts? Or is it because its practitioners, addicted to sensual pleasure and gluttony, squander money as fast as they make it? Or is it because the art loses favor on account of their youth? Since the age of youth is a little foolish and despised, is every advantage lost for that reason? Or is it because in their capriciousness they cannot keep friends or possessions? Yet all human endeavors, especially those pertaining to wealth, require time for their acquisition. Or is it because music is opposed to prudence, as wealth demands great prudence in its retention and especially in its disposition, or because those who had been poor from the beginning have worked hard to become accomplished, yet only improve their poverty with difficulty? Or does this happen in our territories because of the great number of musicians? For in various ways their practice and employment is hindered, so that they are frequently without work. A musician has so many obstacles, so much time is required for practice that produces weariness rather than pleasure. Something is always lacking, the perfection that is a necessary end, and consequently material gain. Or is it because those who take pleasure in the art are foolish adolescents who have little money and who are not equipped to go into other activities that are more physical in nature?[45]

ENTERTAINMENT MUSIC

Virtually all of Cardano's discussion of music seems to be related to Art Music. Perhaps his failure to give us more observations on Entertainment Music can be found in his admission,

> I was useless in conversation and entertainment and this was also one of the reasons why I avoided large banquets.[46]

There is one reference to popular music which is rather interesting.

---

45 Ibid., 207.
46 Quoted in Ore, *Cardano the Gambling Scholar*, 27.

This was the manner of singing songs in ancient times, also practiced now by strolling players in the market, when with lyre in hand they raise and lower its tones through only three or four intervals.[47]

---

47   Miller, *Hieronymus Cardanus*, 122.

8 MICHELANGELO
[1475–1564]

FEW PERSONS WOULD OBJECT to our calling Michelangelo the greatest sculptor who has yet been born. Fortunately for him, painting and sculpture were becoming recognized as arts, as opposed to the 'crafts' they had been since the ancient world. We can see him arguing for this new definition in a conversation he reportedly had with a contemporary.

> Works ought not to be esteemed because of the amount of time employed and lost in the labor, but because of the merit of the knowledge and of the hand which did them; for if it were not so, they would not pay more to a lawyer for an hour's examination of an important case, than to a weaver for as much cloth as he may weave during the course of his whole life.[1]

But this was a view of society which was only in the process of changing. Michelangelo would live long enough to see his efforts recognized as Art, but he was born too early to enjoy the financial rewards appropriate to his work.

> Painting and sculpture, hard work and fair dealing have been my ruin and things go continually from bad to worse. It would have been better had I been put to making matches in my youth.[2]

Although he rarely praised his own work, some hints of the value he placed on it can be found in comments in his letters. Before beginning the work on the tomb of Julius II, Michelangelo writes a friend that if the pope carries the plan out 'there will be nothing to equal it in the world over.'[3] Another letter to his family is most anxious,

> I wrote and told you that none of my things, either the drawings or anything else, were to be touched by anyone. You have not replied to me about this.[4]

His growth as an artist continued throughout his life so that as an older man, when physical problems made his work difficult, he lamented that he had only just begun to understand his art. One of his poems reads,

---

1 Quoted in Robert J. Clements, *Michelangelo; A Self-Portrait* (New York: New York University Press, 1968), 15ff.
2 Letter to Luigi del Riccio, Fall, 1542, in E. H. Ramsden, *The Letters of Michelangelo* (Stanford: Stanford University Press, 1963), II, 26.
3 Letter to Giuliano da Sangallo, May 2, 1506, in Ibid., I, 15.
4 Letter to Lodovico Buonarrota, October 4, 1511, in Ibid., I, 62.

> No one has mastery
> Before he is at the end
> Of his art and his life.⁵

Indeed, as he lay dying, he confessed to Cardinal Salviati,

> I regret that I have not done enough for the salvation of my soul and that I am dying just as I am beginning to learn the alphabet of my profession.⁶

It is no surprise that his evaluation of his contemporaries was so perceptive that the artists he admired are those still recognized as the best in their fields, including Albrecht Dürer,⁷ Lorenzo Ghiberti, Donatello and, with reservations, Titian.

Michelangelo's comments on his own work focus almost entirely on the sheer difficulty of the labor of the sculptor.

> I'm living here in the greatest discomfort and in a state of extreme fatigue; I do nothing but work day and night and have endured and am enduring such fatigue that if I had to do the work over again I do not believe I should survive.⁸

Two similar complaints date from the period of his work on the Sistine Chapel.

> I am living here in a state of great anxiety and of the greatest physical fatigue; I have no friends of any sort and want none. I haven't even time enough to eat as I should.⁹
>
> ......
>
> I work harder than anyone who has ever lived. I'm not well and worn out with this stupendous labor.¹⁰

In a rare comment on the end of this labor, he is reported to have expressed the same philosophy as Castiglione's definition of the nonchalance which should characterize the work of the gentleman.

---

5 Creighton Gilbert, *Complete Poems of Michelangelo* (Princeton: Princeton University Press, 1963), 173. An unfinished sonnet of 1552 contains these lines,

> The soul gains more the more it's lost the world,
> And death and art do not go well together. [Ibid.,158]

6 Bernini, quoted in M. de Chantelou, *Journal du voyage du Cavalier Bernin* (Paris, 1885), 140.

7 It is reported that when Michelangelo met the emperor Charles V in person and was asked for his evaluation of Dürer, he responded,

> I esteem him so much that if I were not Michelangelo, I should prefer to be Albrecht Dürer than emperor Charles V!

8 Letter to Buonarroto Buonarrota, October 19, 1507, in Ramsden, *The Letters of Michelangelo*, I, 40.

9 Letter to Buonarroto Buonarrota, October 17, 1509, in Ibid., I, 54.

10 Letter to Buonarroto Buonarrota, July 24, 1512, in Ibid., I, 70.

I wish to tell you, Francisco de Hollanda, of an exceedingly great beauty in this science of ours, of which perhaps you are aware, and which I think you consider the highest, namely, that what one has most to strive for in painting is to do the work with a great amount of labor and study in such a way that it may afterward appear, however much it was labored, to have been done almost quickly and almost without any labor, and very easily, although it was not.[11]

ON THE PHYSIOLOGY OF AESTHETICS

While, as we shall see below, Michelangelo clearly understood Art to be in the mind of the artist, and not in his hands, he did not engage in his correspondence or in his poems in the debates enjoyed by philosophers on the roles of Reason and the senses. In his single reference to the contention so often argued by others, that man must be ruled by Reason, we are happy to see him admit the proposition—but as an artist, only reluctantly. In a poem on the death of his father, he observes,

> And even though the soul consents to Reason,
> It does it so stiffly …[12]

ON THE PSYCHOLOGY OF AESTHETICS

Michelangelo's comments on the emotions are confined to Love. In two places he acknowledges the observation made frequently in early literature that Love involves a fundamental conflict with Reason. In a sonnet of 1529 he writes,

> I am complained of and reproached by Reason
> When I, in love, hope to get happiness.[13]

In a madrigal he mentions the interference by Love of the rational processes of speaking and thinking.

> Above myself so high,
> Lady, you make me leap,
> Not only I cannot speak
> But cannot think, being no longer I.[14]

---

11 Quoted in Clements, *Michelangelo; A Self-Portrait*, 18.
12 Gilbert, *Complete Poems*, 62.
13 Ibid., 26.
14 Ibid., 102.

Like a troubadour, his most passionate cries are relative to the pain of Love. In one madrigal he pleas, 'Since, Love, for joy you'd have us weep and suffer …'[15] Another will stand for the many poems of his which focus on this subject.

> How much less pain I'd have from dying quickly,
> Than, one by one, a thousand deaths to suffer
> From her who wills my death because I love her.
> Oh what infinite grief
> My heart feels when it chances to perceive
> That she I love so greatly feels no love.[16]

Michelangelo, in his poems of the 1530s and 1540s, reveals a new appreciation of spiritual Love over the physical. This is clearly seen in his poems to Tommaso de' Cavalieri after 1532, as, for example,

> Had my soul not been created god-like,
> It would still seek no more than outward beauty, the delight of the eyes;
> But since this fades so fast, my soul soars beyond, to the eternal Form …
> Unbridled and sensual desire kills the soul, love does not.
> Such love as ours perfects friendship on earth and,
> In death, makes it yet more perfect in Heaven.[17]

Michelangelo makes little reference to the philosophical natures of Pleasure and Pain, but he touches on Fortune's role in an unfinished sonnet.

> After being happy many years, one short
> Hour may make a man lament and mourn.[18]

ON THE PHILOSOPHY OF AESTHETICS

It is no surprise, of course, that this great artist has left much more comment on the general subject of aesthetics in Art. First, there are several observations relative to how Art was viewed by society. In one interesting example, after a casting has gone badly, Michelangelo

---

15 Ibid., 92.

16 Ibid., 8.

17 Quoted in Anthony Blunt, *Artistic Theory in Italy, 1450–1600* (Oxford: Clarendon Press, 1959), 68. Much of our knowledge of Michelangelo's views on Art comes from three of his contemporaries who knew and worked with him, the Portuguese painter Francisco de Hollanda, principally in *Four Dialogues of Painting*; Vasari, in his *Lives*; and Ascanio Condivi, a student of Michelangelo, who published a biography of his master in 1553.

18 Gilbert, *Complete Poems*, 3.

wrote his brother saying that the craftsman at fault 'has so disgraced himself that he can no longer hold up his head in Bologna.'[19]

In several places he mentions that the climate of war which Italy was experiencing during the sixteenth century made his profession difficult. A letter to his father is typical.

> I have finished the chapel I have been painting; the Pope is very well satisfied. But other things have not turned out for me as I'd hoped. For this I blame the times, which are very unfavorable to our art.[20]

Regarding Beauty, Michelangelo clearly perceived initially at the level of physical beauty, making such observations as 'The heart is slow to love what the eye cannot see.'[21] A sonnet of 1529 wonders if Beauty is in the object or the beholder.

> Love, do my eyes, O tell me as a favor,
> See the actual beauty I desire,
> Or is it in me, so that as I stare
> At every point I see her face in sculpture?[22]

He answers this in an unfinished sonnet. Even if circumstances should destroy his work, the Beauty of it remains forever in the memory of the artist.

> There is much joy for just and perfect taste
> In work of the first art, when it assembles
> From gestures, faces, and the liveliest members,
> A human body in stone or clay or wax.
>
> If time thereafter, hurtful, harsh and base,
> Breaks it, or twists, or thoroughly dismembers,
> The beauty earlier there he still remembers,
> And keeps the vain joy for a better place.[23]

We see in this sonnet one of the core thoughts of Michelangelo, that the Art which must be respected is not found in the art object, or in the hands which created it. Sometimes he spoke of the Art being in the mind of the artist, but often there is a divine connection behind it. This was an idea he chose to express through poetry. In a madrigal, he writes,

> As a sure guide to me in my vocation
> The idea of beauty, which is a mirror and a lamp to both my arts,

---

19 Letter to Buonarroto Buonarrota, July 6, 1507, in Ibid., I, 36.
20 Letter to Lodovico Buonarrota, October, 1512, in Ibid., I, 75.
21 Quoted in Blunt, *Artistic Theory in Italy*, 68.
22 Ibid., 25.
23 Ibid., 132.

> Was bestowed upon me at birth.
> Whosoever conceives otherwise is mistaken.
> This idea alone lifts my eyes to those high visions
> Which I set myself to paint and carve here below.
> If men of rash and foolish judgment drag sense-ward the beauty
> Which moves and transports every right intelligence to Heaven,
> It is because weak and wavering eyes, and even eyes fixed steadily on things above,
> Cannot pass from the mortal to the divine,
> For without grace it is vain thought that one may rise thither.[24]

Similarly, in a sonnet.

> If my rough hammer in hard stones can form
> A human semblance, one and then another,
> Set moving by the agent who is holder,
> Watcher and guide, its course is not its own.
>
> But that divine One, staying in Heaven at home,
> Gives others beauty, more to itself, self-mover;
> If hammers can't be made without a hammer,
> From that one living all the others come.[25]

In the poetry of his later years, an even stronger association with the divine Beauty appears.

> Of Thy mercy, make me see Thee in all places.
> If mortal beauty sets me aflame, my fire shall seem spent when brought near to Thine.
> Yet in Thy flame shall I be once more on fire.[26]

On no aspect of aesthetics does Michelangelo write and speak more frequently than of his conviction that Art is that which is within the mind of the artist, and not in that which he accomplishes with his hands. An early letter in which Michelangelo addresses this distinction between mind and hand is a complaint regarding his treatment at the time he was working on the tomb for Julius II.

> I'll always go on working for Pope Clement with such powers as I have, which are slight, as I'm an old man—with this proviso, that the taunts, to which I see I am being subjected, cease, because they very much upset me and prevented me from doing the work I want to do for several months now. For one cannot work at one thing with the hands and at another with the

---

24 Quoted in Blunt, *Artistic Theory in Italy*, 69.
25 Gilbert, *Complete Poems*, 28.
26 Quoted in Blunt, *Artistic Theory in Italy*, 79.

head, particularly in the case of marble. Here it is said that they are meant to spur me on, but I assure you they are poor spurs which drive one back.²⁷

Michelangelo states this principle very clearly in some of his poems, one of which reads,

> The greatest artist has no conception
> Which a single block of marble does not
> Potentially contain within its mass,
> But only a hand obedient to the mind
> Can penetrate to this image.²⁸

Another, a sonnet for Tommaso Cavalieri, has the same meaning.

> In the same way that pen and ink embrace
> The high and the low style and the middle,
> And rich pictures or crude are in the marble,
> Whichever our wits are able to express …²⁹

Nothing testifies to this more clearly than Michelangelo's unfinished sculptures. Anyone who sees one of these pieces is struck by the illusion of a work already finished within the marble, just waiting for the unneeded stone to be struck away.

Perhaps the fact that there is relatively little commentary on his finished pieces in his letters is due to his awareness that the version in his mind was more beautiful than that which he completed. A contemporary, Condivi, who recalls Michelangelo having discussed this very point with him, described him as having had,

> a most powerful imagination, whence it comes, chiefly, that he is little contented with his works and has always underrated them, his hand not appearing to carry out the ideas he has conceived in his mind.³⁰

Michelangelo found this to be the chief obstacle for the less gifted artist, as another contemporary remembered him saying.

> What is marvelous is that a bad painter neither can nor knows how to imagine, nor does he even desire to do good painting; his work mostly differs but little from his imagination … for if he knew how to imagine well … he could not have a hand so corrupt as not to show some part or indication of his good will. But no one has ever known how to aspire well in this science, except the mind which understands what good work is, and what he can make of it.³¹

---

27 Letter to Giovan Francesco Fattucci, October 24, 1525, in Ramsden, *The Letters of Michelangelo*, I, 162.
28 Quoted in Blunt, *Artistic Theory in Italy*, 73.
29 Gilbert, *Complete Poems*, 58.
30 Quoted in Blunt, *Artistic Theory in Italy*, 72.
31 Quoted in Clements, *Michelangelo; A Self-Portrait*, 17.

In this regard, it is interesting that Michelangelo criticized Raphael for not finding his art within, but 'only acquiring it by long study.'[32]

Other contemporaries report Michelangelo as having observed that the role of the eye is to measure the degree to which the hand reflects the Art within the mind.

> It is necessary to keep one's compass in one's eyes and not in the hand, for the hands execute, but the eye judges.[33]
>
> ......
>
> Among men all the proportions of geometry and arithmetic or examples of perspective are of no avail without the eye, that is, without exercising the eye to learn how to see.[34]

Art being defined as within the artist, it is no surprise to find Michelangelo equating a man's character with his art. In a comment recalled by his contemporary, de Hollanda, he speaks of the painting of religious art, which, of course, he was much involved in his career.

> In order to imitate in some degree the venerable image of Our Lord, it is not enough to be a painter, a great and skillful master; I believe that one must further be of blameless life, even if possible a saint, that the Holy Spirit may inspire one's understanding.[35]

In this regard, Michelangelo praised the artist Fra Angelico, but was very modest regarding his own character.

> This good man painted with his heart, so that he was able with his pencil to give outward expression to his inner devotion and piety, which I can never achieve, since I do not feel myself to have so well disposed a heart.[36]

In view of such statements, it is remarkable that at the end of his life his religious feelings caused him to seemingly doubt, if not renounce, the importance of this inner vision. In a sonnet of 1554 he writes,

> In a frail boat, through stormy seas,
> My life in its course has now reached the harbor,
> The bar of which all men must cross to render account of good and evil done.
> Thus I now know how fraught with error
> Was the fond imagination which made Art my idol and my king,
> And how mistaken that earthy love which all men seek in their own despite.
> What of those thoughts of love, once light and gay,

---

32 Condivi, quoted in Blunt, *Artistic Theory in Italy*, 76.

33 Quoted by Giorgio Vasari, *Le Vite de' piu excellenti pittori, scultori, ed architettori* (Florence, 1878), VII, 270.

34 Quoted by Giovan Paolo Lomazzo, *Trattato della pittura, scultura ed architettura* (Roma, 1844) II, 36.

35 Quoted in Blunt, *Artistic Theory in Italy*, 71.

36 Quoted in Ibid., 78.

> If now I approach a twofold death.
> I have certainty of the one and the other menaces me.
> No brush, no chisel will quieten the soul,
> Once it is turned to the divine love of Him, who,
> Upon the Cross, outstretched His arms to take us to Himself.[37]

Regarding the purpose of Art, in a letter written to Niccolò Franco we find a definition which seems very much in the spirit of Aristotle's famous concept of catharsis.

> And who does not know that a noble and sublime subject gives greatness to our souls and lends wings to the most humble and modest intellect?[38]

A letter to his father reveals an occasion on which Michelangelo's purpose was for his own pleasure.

> I bought a piece of marble for five ducats, but it wasn't a good piece and the money was thrown away; then I bought another piece for another five ducats, and this I'm working for my own pleasure.[39]

Another letter seems to suggest the same purpose, for here he clearly states that he creates under compulsion, not under commission.

> If a Florentine citizen wants to have an altar-piece painted, he must find a painter—and [tell him] that I was never a painter or a sculptor like those who set up shop for that purpose ... Although I have served three Popes it has been under compulsion.[40]

One of the most familiar topics relative to the aesthetics of Art is the question regarding whether Art should imitate Nature. It is a topic Michelangelo addresses several times, for it appears to have been for him most natural to imitate the beauty of Nature. A contemporary has reported him saying,

> The painting which I so much vaunt and praise will be the imitation of some single thing among those which immortal God made with great care and knowledge and which He invented and painted, like a Master: and so downward, whether animals or birds, dispensing perfection according as each merits it. And in my judgment that is the excellent and divine painting which is most like and best imitates any work of immortal God, whether a human figure, or a wild and strange animal, or a simple and easy fish, or a bird in the air, or any other creature.[41]

---

37 Quoted in Ibid., 80.
38 Quoted in Clements, *Michelangelo; A Self-Portrait*, 13.
39 Letter to Lodovico Buonarroti, August 19, 1497, in Ramsden, *The Letters of Michelangelo*, I,5.
40 Letter to Lionardo Buonarroto, May 2, 1548, in Ibid., II, 92.
41 Quoted in Clements, *Michelangelo; A Self-Portrait*, 12.

It follows, that Michelangelo's method, according to Condivi, was first one of observation and choice.

> He loved not only human beauty but universally every beautiful thing ... choosing the beauty in nature, as the bees gather honey from the flowers using it afterwards in their works.[42]

One of Michelangelo's poems, from 1505–1511, suggests that perhaps he felt he was following a divine model by following this method.

> He who made the whole universe made every part
> Then from the whole chose what was most beautiful
> To reveal on earth as He has done here and now
> His own divine art.[43]

Next, he applied his inner imagination to create an image more beautiful than the original.

> As my soul, looking through the eyes
> Draws near to beauty as I first saw it,
> The inner image grows, while the other recedes,
> As though shrinkingly and of no account.[44]

If he were successful in doing this, then the artist might be thought of as conquering Nature.

> Since I've the beautiful art, that those who bear it
> From Heaven use to conquer Nature with ...[45]

Another poems reads,

> If with the chisel or colors
> Thou hast made art equal nature,
> Now thy hand has even surpassed her,
> Rendering us her beauties more beautiful.[46]

One contemporary recalls an amusing reflection on this subject, made when Michelangelo was lecturing his students against haste.

---

42 Quoted in Blunt, *Artistic Theory in Italy*, 62. Raphael, in a letter to Castiglione, suggests a similar method.

> To paint a beauty I need to see many beauties, but since there is a dearth of beautiful women, I use a certain idea which comes into my mind. [Ibid., 64]

43 Quoted in Ibid., 62.
44 Quoted in Ibid., 63.
45 Gilbert, *Complete Poems*, 70.
46 Quoted in Frank Chambers, *The History of Taste* (New York: Columbia University Press, 1932), 59.

Whereas Art, which is imitative of Nature (if it wishes to be praised for its function) should not depart from that very method which Nature uses in the generation of animals: the longer the life that these animals are to have, the more time Nature spends in producing them.[47]

In one poem of 1533, referring to a letter of praise by Francesco Berni, Michelangelo expresses a momentary doubt as to whether the painter can truly imitate Nature.

For love of me let Berni then be thanked,
The truth of me he understands alone
Of many, they who admire me much mistake.

But the full light his teaching surely can
Provide me; it will be miraculous
To make a painted man a genuine man.[48]

But if someone else expressed such a doubt with regard to *his* art, Michelangelo's reaction was quite different! Niccolò Martelli recalled Michelangelo's answer when the complaint was made that his portrait of Lorenzo and Giuliano de' Medici was not 'life-like.' Well, said Michelangelo,

A thousand years from now no one could judge that they looked otherwise![49]

When discussing his own paintings, Michelangelo, clearly aware that he was an even greater sculptor, often denied that he was a painter to begin with. Toward the beginning of his work on the Sistine Chapel, he wrote his father expressing his dissatisfaction with the progress of the work, adding,

This is due to the difficulty of the work and also because it is not my profession.[50]

When the work was completed Michelangelo signed a receipt, on 10 May 1508, in which his careful choice of words speaks for itself.

I, Michelangelo Buonarroti, *sculptor*, have received from his Holiness 500 ducats of the Camara, on account, for the *paintings* of the vault of the Chapel of Pope Sixtus.[51]

At this time he sent a sonnet to John of Pistoia in which he refers to how difficult it is to paint lying on one's back.

---

47 Giraldi Cinzio, *Hecatommithi, overo Cento novelle* (Venice, 1608), II, 218.
48 Gilbert, *Complete Poems*, 50.
49 Quoted in Charles De Tolnay, *The Medici Chapel* (Princeton, 1948), 68.
50 Letter to Lodovico Buonarrota, January 27, 1509, in Ramsden, *The Letters of Michelangelo*, I, 48.
51 Quoted in Clements, *Michelangelo; A Self-Portrait*, 19.

> And judgment, hence, must grow,
> Borne in the mind, peculiar and untrue;
> You cannot shoot well when the gun's askew.
>
> John, come to the rescue
> Of my dead painting now, and of my honor;
> I'm not in a good place, and I'm no painter.[52]

On only one occasion, perhaps in a moment of jealousy, did Michelangelo unhesitatingly call himself a painter.

> Raphael had good reason to be envious, since what he knew of art he learned from me.[53]

Being both a painter and a sculptor, Michelangelo appears to have given considerable thought to the aesthetic differences between these two arts. He once offered to a contemporary this distinction:

> This must be kept in mind, that the closer you see paintings approach good sculpture, the better they will be; and the more sculptures will approach paintings, the worse you will hold them to be.[54]

He elaborated on the meaning of this in a letter to Benedetto Varchi in 1547 and then explains that he had now come to understand painting and sculpture to be two forms of the same purpose in Art.

> I admit that it seems to me that painting may be held to be good in the degree in which it approximates to relief, and relief to be bad in the degree in which it approximates to painting. I used therefore to think that painting derived its light from sculpture and that between the two the difference was as that between the sun and the moon.
>   Now, since I have read the passage in your paper where you say that, philosophically speaking, things which have the same end are one and the same, I have altered my opinion and maintain that, if in face of greater difficulties, impediments and labors, greater judgment does not make for greater nobility, then painting and sculpture are one and the same, and being held to be so, no painter ought to think less of sculpture than of painting, and similarly no sculptor less of painting than of sculpture. By sculpture I mean that which is fashioned by the effort of cutting away, that which is fashioned by the method of building up being like unto painting. It suffices that as both, that is to say sculpture and painting, proceed from one and the same faculty of understanding, we may bring them to amicable terms and desist from such disputes, because they take up more time than the execution of the figures themselves. If he who wrote that paint-

---

52   Gilbert, *Complete Poems*, 6.
53   Letter to Monsignore …, Fall, 1542, in Ramsden, *The Letters of Michelangelo*, II, 31.
54   Giovan Battista Armenini, *De' veri precetti della pittura* (Ravenna, 1586), 226ff.

ing is nobler than sculpture understood as little about the other things of which he writes—my maidservant could have expressed them better.[55]

An occasional remark by Michelangelo, however, reveals that his true love was sculpture. A contemporary reports his having observed,

> There is as much difference between painting and sculpture as between shadow and truth.[56]

And we are especially fond of a remark reported by a French visitor:

> If a room were adorned with tapestries woven with gold, and in another room there were only one beautiful statue, the latter room would appear to be adorned royally and would make the first look like a nun's cell.[57]

Michelangelo made one very interesting observation regarding architecture. It is a reflection we wish he had chosen to discuss at length.

> It is therefore indisputable that the limbs of architecture are derived from the limbs of man. No one who has not been or is not a good master of the human figure, particularly of anatomy, can comprehend this.[58]

Although Michelangelo wrote an extensive amount of poetry, again, as with painting, he pretended to have little ability. In 1547 he received a 'commentary' of praise of one of his sonnets by Luca Martini, a member of the Accademia Fiorentina and a patron of the arts. Michelangelo's answer reads in part,

> I have received a letter of yours, together with a treatise—a commentary on a sonnet by my hand. The sonnet is indeed by me, but the commentary is from Heaven and is really admirable …
> As regards the sonnet, I know it for what it's worth; but be that as it may, I cannot pretend that I do not feel a little vainglorious in being the subject of so fine and learned a commentary.[59]

When he sent a requested sonnet to a correspondent in 1550, Michelangelo instructs him.

> If you like it, give it to him; if not, consign it to the fire, reflecting that I contend with death and that my mind is on other things.[60]

---

55 Letter to Benedetto Varchi, March, 1547, in Ramsden, *The Letters of Michelangelo*, II, 75.
56 Anton Francesco Doni, *Disegno* (Venice, 1549), 44.
57 Quoted in Chantelou, *Journal de voyage du Chavalier Bernin*, 103.
58 Letter to Cardinal …, December, 1550, in Ramsden, *The Letters of Michelangelo*, II, 129.
59 Letter to Luca Martini, March, 1547, in Ibid., II, 72.
60 Letter to Giovan Fattucci, February 16, 1550, in Ibid., II, 118.

Michelangelo seemed to share with a great many early philosophers a general distrust for the broad public and its ability to understand and judge Art. A contemporary reports him having said,

> How wrong are those simpletons of whom the world is full, who look more at a green, a red, or similar high color than at the figures which show spirit and movement.[61]

And in one of Michelangelo's sonnets, we find the lines,

> The evil, foolish and invidious mob
> May point, and charge to others its own taste …[62]

Michelangelo is somewhat more philosophic in one of his madrigals, where he comments on how rare good taste is. He also suggests that the artist might appear to paint for the public, but maintain a separate and private understanding.

> Not all men always give so dear a price
> For what the senses love
> But someone will perceive
> How, though it seems so sweet, it is bitter and base.
> Good taste's a thing so scarce
> He yields to the shifting crowd,
> Seemingly, but his inner joy's his own.[63]

ART MUSIC

It is to be regretted that Michelangelo made no comments on the aesthetics of music. In fact, he rarely mentions music at all. On one occasion, he sent some poetry he had composed to Fra Sebastiano del Piombo in Rome to have them set to music as madrigals. They were set to music by Constanzo Festa and Giacomo Concilion and after they were returned, Michelangelo wrote a note of thanks, pretending not to have even heard the music himself.

> I have received the two madrigals and Ser Giovan Francesco has had them performed several times; according to what he tells me, they are considered wonderful things to sing; the words

---

61 Armenini, *De' veri precetti della pittura*, 72.
62 Gilbert, *Complete Poems*, 57.
63 Ibid., 77.

didn't merit such a setting ... Please will you let me know what I should do for the master who wrote the music, so that I may not appear more ignorant and ungrateful than need be.[64]

However, one passing remark to de Hollanda, in the course of criticizing the painting of Flanders, offers a clue that he may have been a more experienced listener after all.

It will please likewise friars and nuns, and also some noble persons who have no ear for true harmony.[65]

FUNCTIONAL MUSIC

Michelangelo found true peace only in occasional walks into the country. In one poem he describes the music of the goatherd. He may not have found the music sophisticated, but he did notice its communication of feeling as the peasant was 'pouring his soul out.'

It is a novel and superior pleasure
To see the daring goats climbing a rock,
Making one peak and then the next their pasture,
And down below their owner, with harsh music,
Pouring his soul out in a rough-hewn measure,
Playing as he stands, or at a gentle walk ...[66]

---

64 Letter to Fra Sebastiano del Piombo, August, 1533, in Ramsden, *The Letters of Michelangelo*, I, 185. He mentions another madrigal, apparently set to his poetry, in a letter to Luigi del Ricco, in the Summer of 1542 [Ramsden, *The Letters of Michelangelo*, II, 17.]

65 Quoted in Clements, *Michelangelo; A Self-Portrait*, 37.

66 Gilbert, *Complete Poems*, 42.

9 SIXTEENTH-CENTURY FRANCE

As in the rest of Europe, exciting new intellectual and musical ideas were transforming the course of music in France. But these ideas were not coming from the Church or from the universities. The University of Paris, for all its importance, was still locked into the medieval misconception of music being but a branch of mathematics. Carpenter documents this extensively and lists numerous sixteenth-century treatises which link music and mathematics.[1] It seems odd to the modern reader that a professor such as Oronce Finé, professor of mathematics in the Collège de France and himself an outstanding performer on the lute, did not perceive that to speak of mathematics is to miss the point in music. However out of touch the universities were, their influence was still present. Thus, Anthoine de Bertrand (b. 1545), when publishing some of his music in 1587, felt the necessity to add the observation that 'music should appeal to the senses and not be bound by mathematical subtleties.'[2]

With the court of Louis XII (1498–1515) the century began with only the most necessary ceremonial music, the king observing, 'I had rather make courtiers laugh by my stinginess, than make my people weep by my extravagance.'[3] Under François I (1515–1547), however, it was a different story. This king,[4] who devoted so much attention to poetry, language, art and music, established an administrative basis for music which would influence all aristocratic music until the end of the eighteenth century.

One group of ensembles was organized under an administrative wing called the *Chambre*. Here one found a category called *Les officiers domestiques*, which included singers, organists, and lute players. Here also was *Les cornets*, virtuosi who seemed to have always come from Italy, and Verona in particular. Also under this administrative wing were two ensembles of musicians for ceremonial purposes, *Les flutes hautbois et trompettes* and the *Les fifres et les tabourins*.

---

1 Nan Cooke Carpenter, *Music in the Medieval and Renaissance Universities* (Norman: University of Oklahoma Press, 1958), 140ff.

2 Quoted in Gustave Reese, *Music in the Renaissance* (New York: Norton, 1959), 389.

3 Fr. Guizot, *History of France* (London: 1872), II, 627. Louis was discerning enough to hire Josquin, who wrote the well-known 'Vive Le Roy' and the famous vocal work in which the part for Louis to sing has but one pitch throughout.

4 History concentrates mostly on the battles of François against the emperor, Charles V. After his famous meeting in 1520, 'The Field of Cloth of Gold,' with Henry VIII of England, Henry himself described François as,

> stately of countenance, mery of cheer, roune coloured, great iyes, high nosed, bigge lipped, faire brested and shoulders, small legges, and long fete. [Edward Hall, *The Triumphant Reigne of Kyng Henry VIII* (London, 1542), I, 200]

An entirely separate administrative unit which included musicians was called the *Écurie*, which arranged all important musical entertainments. Here one finds the first record of the historic ensemble under Louis XIV known as the *Grand Hautbois*. In 1529 this ensemble is called *Joeurs d'instrumens de haulxbois et sacqueboutes* and consisted of eight Italian musicians.[5] Several sources report this wind band traveling with François I to the Conference of Cambrai in 1529.[6] Under this administrative wing as well was an additional ensemble for ceremonial music, *Les fifres et les trompettes*, which appears to have consisted of five players of the fife and six trumpeters.

Sometime later, in 1543, François I founded his *schola cantorum*, consisting of two undermasters, six children, two cornett players, twenty-six singers, twelve clerics and two grammar teachers for the children.[7]

We might also note that François I was always generous in rewarding visiting musicians. In 1538 alone, he rewarded a visiting band of cornetts belonging to the queen of Hungary, an oboe band of the duke of Mantoue and no fewer than four ensembles (two of trumpets and two of oboes) of Pope Paul III.[8]

During the relatively brief reigns of the following kings, Henry II (1547–1559), François II (1559–1560),[9] Charles IX (1560–1574) and Henry III (1574–1589), one finds few accounts of music which extend beyond the ceremonial necessities. Even in the case of Henry III, who seemed to have an enlightened regard for poetry, we find Arbeau describing the court music as 'lascivious and shameless.' This seems confirmed by another observer.

> The Court of Henry III was a mass of corruption. The King had his pimps and minions, and did not much discriminate between male and female bedfellows, frequently following his orgies of lust with public exhibitions of repentance,[10] when he dressed in sackcloth and scourged himself with whipcord ... When some of his male lovers were murdered by the followers of his brother, he gave them state funerals and raised marble monuments over their graves ... Rings, bracelets and earrings adorned his person; his body was anointed with perfumes, his face painted and powdered; and occasionally he dressed as a woman, with a pearl necklace on his open bosom, being waited on by court ladies attired as men.[11]

Above all, it was the humanists and the 'practical' musicians who were carrying the art of music forward. It was the latter who created the demand leading to important develop-

---

5 Henri Prunières, 'La musique de la Chambre et de L'Écurie sous le regne de François Ier,' in *L'Année Musicale* (Paris, 1911), 241.

6 Edmond Vander Straeten, *La Musique aux Pays-Bas avant le XIXe Siecle*, (New York, 1969), IV, 189; and George Grove, *The New Grove Dictionary of Music and Musicians*, ed. Stanley Sadie (London: macmillan, 1980), XVII, 242.

7 *Recueil des Choses Notables qui ont esté faites à Boyonne ...* (Paris, 1566), 7.

8 Prunières, 'La musique de la Chambre,' 238.

9 Husband to Mary Queen of Scots.

10 In one of these episodes of repentance, in 1583, he dismissed his musicians. See Jean Mariéjol, *A Daughter of the Medicis* (New York, 1929), 146.

11 Hesketh Pearson, *Henry of Navarre* (New York: Harper & Row, 1963), 20.

ments in the publishing of music, and for whom Attaingnant alone published in Paris more than 2,000 chansons and 900 instrumental dances between 1528–1555. And, as Freedman points out, the fact that the publications of Attaingnant were widely exported and reprinted by other French publishers invites the conclusion that they had a strong influence on taste.[12]

In spite of all of this activity, the average working musician had to search in every possible direction to make a living. Cunningham's description of Jean d'Estrée no doubt represents many. She points out that he was not only,

> a member of the king's *musicque de l'écurie* as *joueur de hautbois du roi*, but he could further augment his salary as a royal musician by playing in small dance-bands for non-court functions, and by making perhaps even more money in editing and arranging the *Danseries* for Nicolas du Chemin. Sixteenth century Paris was a small place, and the boundaries between the activities of musician, courtier, printer and composer were evidently not as great as we might think.[13]

Even the outstanding Janequin, the first to hold the title 'composer in ordinary' to the king (1559), speaks in one publication of his poverty.[14]

ON THE PHYSIOLOGY OF AESTHETICS

Among the humanists who were the moving force in rethinking the nature of music, was the group of poets known as the Pléiade. Among these men was one who was an important philosopher as well, Pontus de Tyard. His *Solitaire premier, ou, Prose des Muses & de la fureur Poetique* (1552) contains an interesting discussion of the nature of the intellect, and its relationship with the arts. Medieval philosophers had attempted to explain Reason as part of a hierarchy of faculties which included the senses, intuition, divinely (genetic) supplied understanding, etc. Tyard also creates a hierarchy, but it is one of kinds of knowledge. While he recognizes science as the starting point, he finds there are many paths, including 'doctrines, disciplines and arts,' available in the 'raising of the intellect.'

The Platonic philosophers believed that the soul in descending into the body loses its association with the divine and it is the burden of man to climb back and regain what had been lost. It is in Tyard's exposition of this concept that we find his vision of the role of the arts. First, regarding this descent, he writes,

---

12 Richard Freedman, 'Paris and the French Court under François I,' in *The Renaissance* (Englewood Cliffs: Prentice Hall, 1989), 187. Daniel Heartz, in his study, *Pierre Attaingnant Royal Printer of Music* (Berkeley, 1969), 91, establishes that the dance music had its origin in the court.
13 Caroline Cunningham, *Estienne du Tertre, 'Scavant Musicien,' Jean d'Estrée, 'Joueur de Hautbois du Roy,' and the Mid-Sixteenth Century Franco-Flemish Chanson and Ensemble Dance* (Dissertation, Bryn Mawr, 1969), 191.
14 Reese, *Music in the Renaissance*, 296.

The four stages of the descent are, first and highest, the Angelic understanding, second the intellectual Reason, third Opinion, and fourth Nature.[15]

The ascent is possible through the employment of four kinds of *fureur divine*, the first and third of which include music.

> In four ways ... man may be seized by divine enthusiasm. The first is by poetic enthusiasm, proceeding from the gift of the Muses; the second is by the knowledge of the mysteries and secrets of religions under Bacchus; the third is by the ravishment of prophecy, vaticination, or divination under Apollo; and the fourth is by the violence of amorous affection under Love and Venus.

Tyard discusses the role of music, in particular, in the attempt of the soul to rise from the lowest point from which it has fallen.

> The lowest point which the soul, in falling here below, has reached is the body, to which she is so firmly attached ... that the superior part is stunned and astonished ... by its fall, and the inferior part agitated and full of perturbations, whence arises a horrible discord and disorder ... She seems incapable of any just action unless, by some means, this dreadful discord is transformed into a gentle symphony, and this impertinent disorder reduced to a measured equality, well ordered and ordained. And to do this is the peculiar duty of Poetic enthusiasm, awakening the drowsy part of the soul by the tones of Music, and soothing the perturbed part by the suavity of sweet harmony: then by the well-accorded diversity of musical accords, chasing away the dissonant discords, and ordered in the gracious and grave facility of verses regulated by the careful observance of number and measure.

In Tyard's second book, *Solitaire second*, a character named 'le Curieux,' speaks of the ancient Greek notion of the universe being a kind of harmony, in which all of its parts have some comparable relationship with the harmony found in music. He mentions the 'Music of the Spheres,' offering the explanation for man's inability to hear it, that, taken together, its effect is that of silence. Then he contends that the basic elements of the earth are related as the tones of the tetrachord, earth being as the lowest pitch, then water, air and fire.

Of particular interest is the observation by the character, 'Solitary,' regarding the harmonic proportions of man's body. He finds, for example, that 'the spread of the two arms and the extreme openings of the legs correspond to the height of the man: as does the length of the head multiplied eight or nine or ten times.'[16] But, he is quick to point out, the harmony of the form is not so important as the harmony of a virtuous character. The virtuous character is made possible only by the true harmony of the soul. And music is the 'true portrait of temperance,' the sum of all virtue, so that the man ignorant of music is lame in soul.[17]

---

15 Quoted in Frances Yates, *The French Academies of the Sixteenth Century* (London: University of London, 1947; Nendeln: Kraus Reprint, 1968), 80ff.

16 Ibid., 86, fn. 6.

17 Ibid., 86ff.

ON THE PSYCHOLOGY OF AESTHETICS

Among the documents reflecting the debates of the Palace Academy, discussed below, one finds an interesting use of music as an analogy to explain how man should deal with Pleasure and Pain. The speaker, Fremy, observed,

> We conclude that moral virtue is exercised on the affections and passions, the principal of which are Joy and Sorrow, and that it is most certain that virtue does not lie (as the Stoics falsely assert) in uprooting all affections, such as pleasure and pain, from our soul, but in tempering them well together. And just as health, which is a temperance of the powers of the body, does not consist in taking away heat and cold, moist and dry, but in well proportioning them with one another; and just as in music accordance and harmony do not lie in removing treble and bass but in well according them with one another, in doing which the good consonance of perfect music is produced, and the dissonance and false accords of bad music rejected; so in well tempering together Joy and Sorrow and the other affections and passions which God has implanted in us for good end, we shall remove from ourselves vices and perverse passions and plant good customs and virtues.[18]

In one of Baïf's poems, from *Chansonettes mesurées* (1586), he seems resigned to enjoy his pain.

> You are killing me so gently
> With such benign torments,
> That I know no sweetness
> More sweet than my sweet death.
> If one must die, let's die of love.[19]

Two years later, Arbeau quotes a song which has similar text,

> Angel, my life's eclipse
> In thine embrace I die,
> The honey of thy lips
> Sweetens my parting sigh …[20]

---

18 Ibid., 116.

19 Quoted in Daniel Heartz, 'The Chanson in the Humanist Era,' in *Current Thought in Musicology* (Austin: University of Texas Press, 1976), 229.

20 Thoinot Arbeau, *Orchesography*, trans. Mary Evans (New York: Kamin Dance Publishers, 1948), 66. Another song bears the title, 'The Grief that Tortures Me.' [Ibid., 115.]

ON THE AESTHETICS OF MUSIC

In sixteenth-century French literature one occasionally reads of the importance of inspiration, as opposed to mere technique, as when the poet Marot, in his 'Enfer' of 1526, spoke of Venus coming to Paris in her chariot and speaking to him 'in a voice more sweetly resonant than Orpheus singing to his harp.'[21]

We also find French composers beginning to extend their search for expressivity. According to Lesure, under the influence of Italy, French composers made their music become more and more a literal rendition of the emotions of the texts. Many musicians set Ronsard's poems to music and one notable example was Anthoine de Bertrand, who in his setting of a sonnet set the word 'death' to quarter tones in an attempt to make the music more expressive. However, he hastens to add the note,

> Those who find this singing difficult may sing as though the signs had no meaning.[22]

In the preface to some of his songs published by Le Roy and Ballard in 1576, Bertrand makes reference to an Italian publication by Nicola Vincentino, *L'antica musica ridotta alla moderna prattica*, which was set for a quarter-tone harpsichord.[23]

Certainly one aesthetic objective was the communication of feeling in music and we see this in particular in the art chanson. Jean-Antoine de Baïf, in a sonnet praising Janequin, speaks of the composer,

> For where does one not hear the sound, the plea,
> Of this voice-weaver, this musician, who,
> Drugging his hearer's with a nectar brew,
> Compels their souls the body's cage to flee?[24]

Lesure also comments on this purpose.

> For the subjects of François I, the *chanson* was the vehicle of all feelings. They were rarely impassioned, but in turn pensive, light-minded, obscene, melancholy, although in general more inclined to laughter than to weeping. Were they without depth? The question is ill-posed. We have seen that on occasion certain musicians shied away from just superficial or facile poems, that at any rate they were capable of emotion, even if the stimulus of such emotion was a woman's body rather than a lover's grief or the spectacle of death.[25]

---

21 Clément Marot, 'Le Second Chant d'amour fugtif,' in *Oeuvres satiriques*, ed. Claude Mayer (London: Athlone Press, 1962), 87.

22 Quoted in François Lesure, *Musicians and Poets of the French Renaissance*, trans. Elio Gianturco (New York: Merlin Press, 1955), 71ff.

23 Heartz, 'The Chanson in the Humanist Era,' 212.

24 Quoted in Reese, *Music in the Renaissance*, 296.

25 Lesure, *Musicians and Poets of the French Renaissance*, 40.

The first great period of French chansons coincides with the reign of François I (1515–1547). Reese finds this music much in the tradition of Italian and Netherlands traditions, but with the addition of French grace and wit, 'calculated to delight the courtiers of Fontainebleau and Paris.'[26] He also reminds us that many of the composers of French chansons held church positions.

But for the sixteenth-century composer, the expression of feeling in a song was still understood to be centered in the text more than in the music. Heartz, in this regard, points to a French proverb, 'L'air ne fait pas la chanson,' or, 'The melody does not make a chanson.'[27]

The Academies

The most important commentary on aesthetics in music is found in the discussions of several academies formed in Paris in the second half of the sixteenth century. As with the academies in Italy, those in France were not educational institutions in the modern sense of the word, but more like high level gatherings of intellectuals for discussion and debate. A large part of their purpose was philological, attempting to raise French to a level of literary acceptance formerly enjoyed only by Latin.

It was in their relationship with the humanist movement that these academies played an influence on developments in the field of music. In France the Baïf Academy and the group known as the Pléiade were especially concerned with the liberal arts, and in particular the relationship of poetry and music. Because both the sixteenth-century Italian and French intellectuals had taken from the ancient Greek writers a concept of music being closely related to the unseen organization of the world, it is no surprise that for them music included poetry and vice versa. Thus it was in the discussions of these academies that the Italians, under Bardi, moved toward monody and opera and the French, under Baïf, concentrated in making measured music fit measured poetry.

One of the foremost intellectual influences in Paris was the group of poets known as the Pléiade, led by Pierre de Ronsard.[28] This group seems to have come into formation at the Collège de Coqueret under Jean Dorat. Dorat was a charismatic lecturer on classical literature, who specialized in explaining how important truths were hidden in fables and poetry. The background of this view was the humanist interpretation that the ancient Greek artist was at once, musician, poet and a kind of prophet.

He attracted Ronsard and also Jean-Antoine de Baïf, son of Lazare de Baïf, an important literary advisor to François I, who would create the most famous of the academies. Dorat introduced his students to a wide variety of ancient and modern literature and apparently

---

26 Reese, *Music in the Renaissance*, 290.
27 Heartz, 'The Chanson in the Humanist Era,' 194.
28 The members included Dorat, Ronsard, Du Bellay, Baïf, Belleau, Tyard, and Jodelle.

inspired considerable devotion. A contemporary observed that Ronsard would study until 2:00 AM and then awaken Baïf 'who rose and took the candle from him.'²⁹

The informal meetings of these poets in the home of Baïf to discuss philosophy, rhetoric and poetry were a clear harbinger of the first important French academy, the *Académie de poésie et de musique*, formed by Baïf and Courville in 1570.

The writings of the members of the Pléiade clearly testify to the humanistic aims of the group. Pontus de Tyard wrote a treatise on music in which he testifies on behalf of the ethical impact of music.

> [Among the ancients] music served as an exercise to temper the soul to a perfect condition of goodness and virtue, exciting and appeasing, by its native power and secret energy, the passions and affections, as the sounds were carried from the ear to the spiritual parts.³⁰

Du Bellay, one of the most important poets of the group, wrote of their interest in sung poetry as the primary vehicle for their ethical goals.

> Sing to me those odes, yet unknown to the French muse, on a lute well tuned to the sound of the Greek and Roman lyre … Above all, take care that the type of poetry be far from the vulgar, enriched and made illustrious with proper words and vigorous epithets, adorned with grave sentences, and varied with all manner of colorful and poetic ornaments.³¹

The best known poet today, of those among the original Pléiade, was Pierre de Ronsard (1524–1585). We can see in him the strong humanist interest in ancient Greece.

> And, if I am able, I will reinstitute the use of the lyre, which in our day has been revived in Italy: which lyre alone should, and has the power to infuse soulful expression into verse and can give it the right weight of grave earnestness.³²

Similarly, in his 'Abrégé de l'art poétique françois' he speaks of the perceived Greek ideal of the combination of poetry and music.

> Poetry without instruments, or without the charm of a single or several voices, is just as little delightful as are instruments lacking the expressiveness of melody produced by a pleasant voice.³³

And again, in one of his poems,

---

29   Quoted in Yates, *The French Academies of the Sixteenth Century*, 14. One is reminded of the young Picasso who once shared a room with one bed with a burglar in Paris. Picasso worked during the day while the burglar slept and the burgler worked at night while Picasso slept.

30   Pontus de Tyard, *Solitaire Second ou Discours de la Musique* (Lyons, 1552), quoted in Ibid., 41.

31   Quoted in Reese, *Music in the Renaissance*, 382.

32   Quoted in Lesure, *Musicians and Poets of the French Renaissance*, 56,

33   Quoted in Ibid., 57.

> To wed odes to the lyre,
> To know where the fingers stray on strings,
> Which song may well lie with them,
> And which tune may not be suited.[34]

Another poem refers to an early deafness which hindered his own musicianship.

> I sing at times,
> But that is rare, for my voice is poor.[35]

Ronsard's most important statement on the view of aesthetics in music from the perspective of the Pléiade group is found in his dedication to François II of his *Livre des mélanges* (1560). First, he speaks of the fundamental relationship of man and music.

> He that hearing a sweet accord of instruments or the sweetness of the natural voice feels no joy and no agitation and is not thrilled from head to foot, as being delightfully rapt and somehow carried out of himself—it is the sign of one whose soul is tortuous, vicious, and depraved, and of whom one should beware, as not fortunately born. For how could one be in accord with a man who by nature hates accord? He is unworthy to behold the sweet light of the sun who does not honor music as being a small part of that which, as Plato says, so harmoniously animates the whole great universe. On the contrary, he who does honor and reverence to music is commonly a man of worth, sound of soul, by nature loving things lofty, philosophy, the conduct of affairs of state, the tasks of war, and in brief, in all the honorable offices he ever shows the sparks of his virtue.[36]

Next he cites a number of the familiar myths and stories of music in ancient Greece and promises his royal patron that music will lighten his cares and allow him to return to his royal burden fresher and better disposed. Then Ronsard makes an interesting observation on the difference between the arts and science.

> The divine inspirations of music, poetry, and painting do not arrive at perfection by degrees, like the other sciences, but by starts, and like flashes of lightening, one here, another there, appear in various lands, then suddenly vanish. For that reason, when some excellent worker in this art reveals himself, you should guard him with care, as being something so excellent that it rarely appears.

He then lists a number of composers as examples of 'excellent workers in this art,' including des Prez, Willaert, Jannequin, Arcadelt, and Orlando Lassus, of whom he says 'seems alone to have stolen the harmony of the heavens to delight us with it on earth.'

---

34 Quoted in Ibid., 55.

35 Quoted in Ibid., 54.

36 Quoted in Oliver Strunk, *Source Readings in Music History* (New York: Norton, 1950), 287.

The official beginning of Baïf's Academy is acknowledged by the Letters Patent issued by Charles IX in 1570. The principal objective given in this document is to reestablish 'both the kind of poetry and the measure and rule of music anciently used by the Greeks and Romans.'[37] The document indicates that work and discussion along these lines had been in progress for three years, resulting in some progress in 'attempts at measured verses set to measured music.'

The Academy was to consist of members in two categories: 'composers, singers and players' and listeners. The following statutes are very similar to, and unquestionably derived from, constitutions of the musician guilds of Paris and elsewhere. In particular, the musicians are to meet at specified times to rehearse together and separately, there is provision for sick members, a medallion is to be worn by the members (to be returned by his heirs upon his death) and finally, restrictions against quarrels and fighting amongst members—within one hundred feet of the meeting place.

Some of the language in this document is particularly interesting for its aesthetic insights. When performances are underway, in particular singing, the listeners must not speak, whisper, nor make any noise. No one can enter during a song, but must await its conclusion. Interestingly enough, the listeners were not to approach the musicians in the private place where they prepared before the performances.

In a broader sense, Charles IX notes, in this same document, that his grandfather was a strong supporter of the arts and that in following suit he is acknowledging their importance to society. In particular, he states that in the opinion of the great legislators and philosophers among the ancients,

> it is of great importance for the morals of the citizens of a town that the music current and used in the country should be retained under certain laws, for the minds of most men are formed and their behavior influenced by its character, so that where music is disordered, there morals are also depraved, and where it is well ordered, there men are will disciplined morally.[38]

This is very similar to what we find in Baïf's own statutes for his academy, before he spells out his specific interest in recreating the supposed Greek union of text and music among the lyric poets.

> In order to bring back into use music in its perfection which is to represent words in singing completed by sounds, harmony and melody, consisting in the choice and regulation of voices, sounds and well harmonized accords, so as to produce the effect which the sense of the words requires, either lowering or raising or otherwise influencing the spirits, thus renewing the ancient

---

37 Quoted in Yates, *The French Academies of the Sixteenth Century*, 21.
38 Quoted in Ibid., 23.

fashion of composing measured verses to which are accommodated tunes likewise measured in accordance with the metric art.[39]

We find additional valuable information regarding the aesthetic purpose of Baïf's Academy in the form of a document discovered by Yates, written early in the seventeenth century by the famous Marin Mersenne. It is apparently based on personal information given Mersenne by an older man who had been a member of the Academy. This document is the principal source for our understanding that the Academy studies ranged far beyond music and poetry.

> [The Academicians] did not wish to bring in a new kind of music, unless you call that new when something is restored to wholeness, but wished to recover those effects which, as we read, were once produced by the Greeks, by joining Gallic verses to our carefully cultivated music. For they hoped to exhilarate the depressed spirit, to reduce the over-elated spirit to modesty, and to stir themselves to other feelings by their own music …
>
> When Jean Antoine de Baïf and Joachim Thibault de Courville labored together to drive barbarism from Gaul, they considered that nothing would be of more potency for forming the manners of youth to everything honorable than if they were to recover the effects of ancient music and compose all their songs on the models of the fixed rules of the Greeks.
>
> Wherefore they wished so to provide that nothing should be lacking in the Academy which should make it suitable for the perfecting of a man, both in mind and body. Therefore they appointed to this Academy men most skilled in every kind of natural sciences, and instituted a prefect of it who should be called the Head Teacher. I leave out the other masters, of sciences, of tongues especially, of music, of poetry, of geography, of the various parts of mathematics, and of painting, who promoted the good of the mind, and the military prefects who taught all those things which are useful for military discipline and for the good of the body.[40]

The purpose of the Academy to recreate the aesthetic aim of Greek music was to acquire the direct ethical effects of that music. As Yates observes,

> These artistic labors were undertaken, not for art's sake alone, but for certain effects which are expected of them. These melodies in the antique manner are believed to have the power of refining and purifying the minds of the auditors, and, through this purification, of initiating them into higher states of knowledge.[41]

So sure was Baïf that he had succeeded in this purpose, that six months after the official formation of his Academy he wrote King Charles IX, requesting that he summon all the best

---

39 Quoted in Ibid., 23. It gives one pause that the impact of music on man is so little discussed today, as it was here and had been for two thousand years by the sixteenth century. Yates, the author of this brilliant book, in a comment which seems addressed more to our time, wryly adds here, 'Unless these phrases are meaningless verbiage, it would seem that … poetry and music was valued.'

40 Quoted in Ibid., 24.

41 Ibid., 36.

musicians to a 'public competition' to demonstrate the superiority of the music of the new Academy. He wanted to demonstrate that the purpose of this music was,

> not to leave the minds of the hearers where we find them, as most men of today maintain, but, according to the meaning of the words, to produce the three effects ... namely to restrain, excite and calm the minds of the hearers who are deeply affected by the song, by means of the words, well-composed, well-sung, and carefully listened to.[42]

The goal of Baïf was clear, but a fatal problem remained. Since virtually no complete music exists from the period of the ancient Greek lyric poets, no one can know what this music was like, nor how they combined words and music.[43] In view of this fact, for all their study of the Greek texts, the Renaissance humanists could finally agree on only two conclusions: that the ethical impact must be centered in the words themselves and that the polyphonic Church style was therefore unacceptable, as one heard different words at the same time. This objection to polyphonic music was shared by nearly all humanists in Italy and France. A typical comment, here by Pontus de Tyard, one of the members of the Pléiade, reads,

> Music's purpose seems to be that of setting the word in such a fashion that anyone listening to it will become impassioned and carried away by the mood of the poet. The musician who knows how to deploy the solo voice to this end best attains his goal, in my opinion. Contrapuntal music most often brings to the ears only a lot of noise, from which you feel no vivid effect.[44]

Baïf is of interest as one of few people who went beyond simply pointing to the priority of words over music to actually proposing a specific method. His method, basically, was to attempt to coordinate the rhythm (long and short) of French verse [*vers mesurés*] and the accompanying music [*musique mesurée*]. The text of the poetry therefore determined both the form and the rhythm of the music, resulting in a kind of chordal texture.[45] But while this can result in the emphasis of the words, it does not really have anything to do with enhancing the ethical or emotional impact of the experience. In fact, recent clinical evidence clearly demonstrates that it is melody, and not rhythm, which carries feeling content in music. Needless to say, Baïf soon floundered in difficulties and one has to acknowledge that his theories, taken literally, had no future.[46] We might add, however, that Heartz points to a song by Courville, who was himself a singer, which was composed in the *musique mesurée*

---

42 Quoted in Ibid., 36.

43 It is our belief the when the ancient philosophers speak of the correspondence of words and music they were actually speaking of the correspondence of the emotions of both, and not of a specific technique of melody, rhythm or harmony.

44 *Les Discours philosophiques* (Paris, 1587) quoted by Heartz, 'The Chanson in the Humanist Era,' 227.

45 Reese, *Music in the Renaissance*, 383, identifies the *Le Printemps* of Claude Le Jeune (1525–1600), composed to the poetry of Baïf, as an example of music composed according to these principles. After the academies were closed, Eustache Du Caurroy (1549–1609) was still composing according to the ideals of *musique mesurée*.

46 Yates, *The French Academies of the Sixteenth Century*, 52ff, discusses the inherent difficulties faced by Baïf.

style, but was then highly ornamented, resulting not only in something more musical but in something equivalent to the monody tradition which developed from similar ideals in Italy.[47]

Regardless of the failure of the ideas of the Academy to find much development in future music, a contemporary records that at least the Academy was the source of fine concerts.

> It was in this pleasant residence that he had established an Academy where the best musicians in the world came in troops to accord the melodious sound of their instruments with that new cadence of measured verses which he had invented. The fame of these new and melodious concerts was so widespread that the King himself and all the princes of the court wished to hear them; and they did not disdain to divert themselves by often visiting our Baïf whom they found always in the company of the Muses or amongst the accords of music.[48]

Another contemporary, d'Aubigné, reports of hearing at the Academy a performance which included 'an excellent concert of guitars, twelve viols, four spinets, four lutes, two pandoras and two theorboes.'[49]

One composer influenced by Baïf was Claude Le Jeune, who in the preface to his 'Printemps,' deplored that the ancient art of the Greeks had been lost and that his purpose was to restore music to its rightful place that it might stir 'the soul of man to such passions as [the Greeks] intended.'[50] One of his contemporaries, Odet de la Noue, believed he had been successful, for he writes in a eulogy,

> by the efforts of his melody he flings out soul wherever he pleases;
> He casts it down to grievous death, or stirs it up to joy;
> He instills courage into the most dejected heart;
> And to raving men he restores meekness.[51]

To these lofty ideals there were, as there always are, detractors. Some worried that there might be composed songs against the honor of the king or of France. The faculty of the University of Paris was of course jealous and concerned that their role was being usurped. Growing efforts to eliminate the Academy were eventually silenced by the king himself and interestingly enough his ultimatum was addressed to the Faculty of Medicine.[52]

Under Henry III a similar academy, known as the Palace Academy, came into being and it is not clear if it was entirely separate from Baïf's group or consisted of the same people.[53]

---

47 Heartz, 'The Chanson in the Humanist Era,' 215.
48 Scévole de Sainte Marthe, quoted in Yates, *The French Academies of the Sixteenth Century*, 20.
49 Quoted in Reese, *Music in the Renaissance*, 566.
50 Quoted in Lesure, *Musicians and Poets of the French Renaissance*, 111.
51 Quoted in Ibid., 112.
52 The reader is reminded that Apollo was the god of both music and medicine.
53 The Palace Academy was apparently organized by 1576 and among those attending were three members of the original Pléiade poets, Ronsard, Tyard and Baïf.

Both academies, however, came to an end about 1584, due to the civil wars resulting from the religious turmoil.

It is somewhat of a surprise to find Henry III, whose character is so criticized by some contemporaries, described by one early writer as,

> always in the company of the Muses and amongst the sweet accords of the children of music, for he loved music and had a marvelous understanding of it. This liberal and magnificent prince gave a handsome remuneration and accorded him from time to time newly created offices and certain confiscations which procured for Baïf the means of maintaining in their studies several men of letters, of entertaining in his house all the learned men of the age, and of dispensing much hospitality.[54]

In any case, the Palace Academy seems to have been more centered in philosophy than music. An Englishman who visited on one occasion, described the members as discussing, for as much as four hours at a time, '*de primis causis de sensu et sensibiliti*.'[55] Needless to say, with the affairs of state in growing disarray, Henry III came under considerable criticism for spending his time in such discussion.

Arbeau's *L'Orchésographie* (1588)

Thoinot Arbeau[56] (1519–1595), a canon of Langres, has left the most important sixteenth-century French treatise on dancing, a work which also has interesting comments dealing with the aesthetics of music.

In the beginning pages, which survey the history of dance, we are surprised to read that there was still some remaining dancing associated with the Church, not only in association with weddings, but also 'in the rites of our religious festivals.'[57] Arbeau is quick to point out that these traditions are under attack by the reformers, whom Arbeau suggests 'deserve to be fed upon goat's meat cooked in a pie without bacon'—which we take to be a canon's curse!

Arbeau says that dancing depends on music, which he still identifies as one of the seven liberal arts.[58] He laments that, as with music, knowledge of the ancient Greek dances have been lost with time. It is interesting that whereas the ancient Greeks' described dance as the part of music which could be seen, Arbeau describes it as 'a kind of mute rhetoric.'[59] When mime is added to dance, Arbeau finds it has the power to stir the emotions, 'now to anger,

---

54 Guillaume Colletet, quoted in Yates, *The French Academies of the Sixteenth Century*, 29.

55 Quoted in Ibid., 33.

56 Reese, *Music in the Renaissance*, 564, gives his real name as Jehan Tabourot.

57 Arbeau, *Orchesography*, 13. He mentions the pavan as one which 'our musicians play when a maiden of good family is taken to the Holy Church to be married.' [Ibid., 57]

58 Ibid., 14.

59 Ibid., 16.

now to pity and commiseration, now to hate, now to love.' As the Church had for most of the Middle Ages attempted to ban theater, for its display of dance, our canon points out that Church law was only aimed at dancers who danced for money, not those 'who gave their talent without reward.'[60]

Several times Arbeau indicates that the musicians accompanying dance were free to improvise. The goal of the improvisation was to produce a result which was 'most pleasing and euphonious'[61] and 'to please themselves.'[62] We may assume the musicians were very accustomed to improvisation, for several times Arbeau advises the dancer that if he wants a particular tune he should just tell the musicians how it begins.[63]

In his description of the instruments used to accompany dance, Arbeau describes the shawm as being 'harsh and wailing and blown with force.'[64] While they tend to drown out any accompanying flutes, they sound good with percussion and especially if the treble and tenor are used together.

> There is no workman so humble that he does not wish to have shawms and sackbuts at his wedding.[65]

Regarding specific dances, it is interesting that Arbeau recognizes that the basse danse has been out of date for forty or fifty years. This dance was the most popular among the aristocracy during the fifteenth century, but they immediately stopped dancing it when the common people began to dance it in the sixteenth century. In a reference to the civil wars, Arbeau also observed that when he was young, people talked only of dancing and gaiety, 'but for some time now all I have met with nothing but sorrow and it has made me old and dull.'[66]

One dance which Arbeau still associates with the aristocracy is the pavan.

> On solemn feast days the pavan is employed by kings, princes and great noblemen to display themselves in their fine mantles and ceremonial robes. They are accompanied by queens, princess and great ladies, the long trains of their dresses loosened and sweeping behind them, sometimes borne by damsels. And it is the said pavans, played by shawms and sackbuts, that announce the grand ball.[67]

It is to be hoped, observes Arbeau, that such dances as the pavan and basse danse will be reinstated 'and replace the lascivious, shameless ones introduced in their stead to the regret

---

60   Ibid., 17.
61   Ibid., 34.
62   Ibid., 39.
63   Ibid., 52.
64   Ibid., 50.
65   Ibid., 51.
66   Ibid., 140.
67   Ibid., 59.

of wise lords and ladies and matrons of sound and chase judgment.' He also adds that the pavan can be sung or played in four-part harmony without dancing.

Arbeau finds the galliard is also now danced 'regardless of rules,'[68] whereas in earlier days 'it was danced with much more discernment.'[69] He also identifies this as a dance which admitted unlimited improvisation by the dancer. In the double branles he also observes that 'young men of exceptional agility improvise at their pleasure but I advise you to dance them soberly.'[70]

The branle known as the *haut Barrois*, Arbeau records is 'danced by lackeys and serving wenches' and only by gentlemen if in disguise. In dancing the branles in general, he cautions that in order to perform them well 'you must know the tunes by heart and sing them in your head' while dancing.[71]

Several times Arbeau suggests that court dancing was not merely for personal pleasure but was a form of performance to be viewed by the spectators. In describing the branle, for example, he describes one step as permitting the dancer to 'glance modestly at the spectators.'[72] And even the ladies, in dancing the pavan, appear,

> with demure mien, their eyes lowered save to cast an occasional glance of virginal modesty at the onlookers.[73]

Finally, it is also interesting, in discussing the capriole, that Arbeau mentions,

> You have observed in a musical composition how musicians pause for a moment after the penultimate chord before playing the final chord in order to make an agreeable and harmonious ending.[74]

Praetorius mentions this in the third volume of his *Syntagma musicum* of 1619, although he says the tradition was to place a fermata *on* the penultimate chord for the same purpose. He adds that he hesitates to mention this, since everyone knows it.

---

68 In discussing the galliard, Arbeau observes that one should,
> Spit and blow your nose sparingly, or if needs must turn your head away and use a fair white handkerchief.

69 Ibid., 77.
70 Ibid., 132.
71 Ibid., 137.
72 Ibid., 55.
73 Ibid., 59.
74 Ibid., 92.

ART MUSIC

The Ballet comique, like the English masque of the following century, was one of the many roots of opera. We find a description of one given for the engagement of the Duc de Joyeuse to Marguerite de Vaudemont, in 1581, which mentions that it included 'the most harmonious [music] that had ever been heard.'[75] Another Ballet comique, given a month later for the actual wedding celebrations included numerous musical numbers as part of a great allegorical pageant. One saw eight of the king's musicians, appearing as tritons, singing and playing instruments, ten violins performing for a ballet of the twelve naiads and eventually forty musicians and singers performing 'the most learned and excellent music that had up to then been heard or sung' for the descent of Jupiter from the heavens.[76]

Accounts of similar large-scale productions which were held outdoors do not always provide the necessary information to distinguish between art music and entertainment music. Sometimes, however, the word 'concert' is used for such performances, as in an account of a series of entertainments held at Fontainebleau in 1564, in honor of the visit there by Charles IX. Here we are also provided some interesting descriptions of the actual performances. On the day of his arrival, in addition to the usual formal poems of greeting, he heard a consort of cornetts.

> As the king entered, he heard a concert of very excellent cornett players. And meanwhile from the end of the main canal came three Sirens, who were three young children having excellent voices and looked so natural that they appeared to be nude, their navels lower than their long gilded braids, in silver and azure, decorated like Dolphins, in the way in which Sirens are ordinarily painted, and swam in the middle of the water upright, with admirable guile. As they came in front of the king, the cornetts stopped.[77]

Following this performance, Neptune appeared in a floating chariot, drawn by four marine horses, to the music of another ensemble.

> [When the poems were finished] they discovered at the head of the other canal, a Neptune, holding a Trident in hand, seated on a chariot pulled by four marine horses, swimming with similar guile to the Sirens, and as they came slowly, they heard a concert by two shawms and a sackbut. And as it came in front of the king, the concert stopped.[78]

---

75 Yates, *The French Academies of the Sixteenth Century*, 237.

76 Ibid., 242ff.

77 *Le recueil des Triumphes et Magnificences qui ont estez faictes au Logis de Monseigneur le Duc D'orleans, frere du Roy ...* (Troyes, Trumeau), 1. [The only extant copy of this print is in the Bibliothèque Méjanes, Aix-en-Provence]

78 Ibid., 2. A reader of the accounts of this period is astounded by these mechanical devices which operate in water. We have found only one account in which one of them is described as not operating properly. During the reign of Henry III, the cardinal de Bourbon gave a marriage reception for the Duc de Joyeuse which included mechanical sea-horses—apparently disguised boats which contained trumpet, clarion, violin and shawm players. When the grand moment came, the sea-horses refused to leave their mooring. The king waited more than two hours and finally left weary and angry. See Catherine Charlotte, *The Last of the Valois* (Paris: Grolier Society), II, 155.

That evening we read that when the king was seated at the banquet table, 'as the first service was presented there began a concert of cornetts and a sackbut.'[79]

The consort principle which we observe in these descriptions was an important new development of sixteenth-century music, replacing the medieval 'loud-soft' principle of instrumental ensemble organization. New developments in woodworking crafts after 1500 were directly responsible for the two most significant characteristics of these new consorts: the availability for the first time of true bass instruments and the idea of building and selling a family of instruments by the case.[80] The latter idea was very valuable from the player's perspective, for when an ensemble performed on a family of five instruments made by the same maker, intonation was greatly enhanced. Variety in instrumental color during performance was then achieved by simply changing the consort, the family of instruments, which resulted in the extremely large collections of instruments owned by many nobles and cities.

So enthusiastically was this new consort principle adopted by nobles everywhere for their musical establishments, that one Englishman goes so far as to suggest that the best equipped household will even have the dogs in its kennels organized in a consort!

> If you would have your kennels for sweetness of cry then you must compound it of some large dogs that have deep, solemn mouths ... which must as it were bear the bass in consort, then a double number of roaring and loud-ringing mouths which must bear the counter tenor, then some hollow, plain, sweet mouths which must bear the mean or middle part and so with these three parts of music you shall make your cry perfect.[81]

Can one take this seriously? Shakespeare, in his *A Midsummer Night's Dream*, gave a similar description. 'My hounds,' says Theseus, 'are,'

> Slow in pursuit, but matcht in mouth like bells,
> Each under each. A cry more tuneable
> Was never holla'd to, nor cheer'd with horn.[82]

Although we do not read much of exceptional individual artists in sixteenth century France, there must have been many. The poet Marot praised the playing of the royal lutenist, Albert de Rippe, saying it was even more prized than that of Orpheus.[83]

Finally, we should mention the the civic music guild of Paris, the 'La confrèrie Saint-Julien,' was continuing to prosper during the sixteenth century. It now had some one hundred

---

79 Ibid., 5.

80 Several European museums, as well as the Brussels Conservatory of Music, house extant consorts in their original cases. Numerous works of art produced during the sixteenth century also picture these consorts. A brilliant example is the intarsia (wood inlay), ca. 1510, by Fra Giovanni da Verona, now in the Vatican, which shows five crumhorns in careful detail.

81 Quoted in Elizabeth Burton, *The Pageant of Elisabethan England* (New York: Scribner's), 190.

82 William Shakespeare, *A Midsummer Night's Dream* (IV, 1).

83 Heartz, 'The Chanson in the Humanist Era,' 210.

'masters,' in addition to some lower members known as *Compagnons*. The guild also sold licenses which enabled new players in town to play on a limited basis. One such license was issued to Yves de Brie, 'player of violin and hand-drum,' in 1585, on the understanding that he could play so long as he was without fault and created no scandal.[84] The Paris guild was also making attempts at this time to organize other cities in France under their control.

We also have more information for this period of the apprenticeship requirements. The average apprentice was from ten to sixteen years of age and was expected to sign, with his parents, a legal document regarding the conditions of his service. The duration of the apprenticeship was officially six years, but if one were the son of a 'master' it was usually less. The master was expected to treat the apprentice humanely and to provide for his welfare.

FUNCTIONAL MUSIC

For the coronation of the queen of François I we have an interesting description of the performance of the ceremonial ensemble known as the 'Les flutes hautbois et trompettes.' An eyewitness reports their 'sounding together very melodiously, as a sort of decorous recreation [*récréation honnête*].'[85] The queen of Charles IX, Elizabeth of Austria, was welcomed to Paris in a procession which included a wind band of musicians in the employ of Charles consisting of fifteen 'sacquebutes, hautbois et cornets.'[86]

When Charles V was welcomed in Valenciennes, in 1539, one heard not only the usual trumpets and drums, but also the local civic wind band playing new chansons.

des jouers de hautbois qu'il fait moult bon ouyr pour leurs chansons nouvelles.[87]

Tournaments, of course, always included the fanfares of trumpets and drums to announce the participants. In the extraordinary accident in which Henry II was killed in a tournament, it was noted that, as if by prescience, for once the trumpets did not announce him.[88]

By the sixteenth century it is no longer a surprise to find instruments participating in the Mass, as for example during the meeting of François I and Henry VIII, in 1520, one eyewit-

---

84 François Lesure, *Musique et Musiciens Français du XVIe Siècle* (Genève, 1976), 115ff.
85 Quoted in Catherine Charlotte, *The Court of France* (Boston: Grolier Society), 107.
86 *L'estat de l'Écurie* (1571), quoted in Henri Prunières, 'La musique de la Chambre et de L'Écurie sous le regne de François Ier,' in *L'Année Musicale* (Paris, 1911), 246ff.
87 Jean Jacquot, ed., *Les Fêtes de la Renaissance* (Paris, 1973), 242.
88 E. R. Chamberlin, *Marguerite of Navarre* (New York, 1974), 3.

ness reports a Mass, composed by Perino, performed with organ, sackbutts and cornetts.[89] One observer declared 'it was heavenlie hearing.'[90]

During the visit of Charles IX to Bayonne, a Te Deum was performed in the cathedral by the king's sisters, accompanied by 'excellent cornetts.'[91] Certainly all Church events connected with State policy must have had ceremonial music, as for example when the queen of Charles IX was welcomed to Paris, at Notre Dame Cathedral,

> she was led through a gallery expressly made, to the door of the church up to a great stairway, decorated and ornamented very magnificently, by which she climbed to the great room prepared for this effect, whereupon entering she was greeted by a great number of trumpets, clarions and cornetts, witness to the incredible joy that everyone felt in her presence.[92]

But it is somewhat of a surprise to read an account during the religious strife under Catherine de Medici which indicates that perhaps even the execution of Huguenots were accompanied by music—which in one case is described as 'drums and fifes playing gay airs during the executions.'[93]

Craig Wright has documented continued problems with the singers of the cathedral at Cambrai, suggesting not only insufficient musicianship but also peculiar disciplinary problems—such as one tenor who came to the divine service attired as a woman.[94]

It is especially interesting to find in the records of this cathedral, that when a reference to singing *in musica* is used, it refers to polyphony and not chant.[95] No doubt an exception in this definition was made when singers improvised over chant, a practice which Wright documents at Cambrai over some years.[96]

The great Frenchman of the Reformation was of course Jean Calvin. With regard to church music, Calvin was more conservative than the Catholics. He wanted music which did not attract attention to itself, thus unison singing of Psalms was appropriate but not part-singing. Instrumental music was discouraged since it tended to 'turn the believer's spiritual attention to profane diversions.'[97]

---

89 Joycelyne Russell, *The Field of Cloth of Gold* (New York, 1938), 175. The celebrant on this occasion was cardinal Wolsey, even though he had not personally conducted a Mass in years. But, this *was* a special occasion, with three kings, three queens, twenty-one bishops and three cardinals present.

90 Ibid., 174.

91 *Recueil des Choses Notables qui ont esté faites à Bayonne …* (Paris, 1566), 8.

92 *Bref et sommaire recueil de ce qui a esté faict, et de l'ordre tenüe à la joyeuse et triumphante Entrée de Prince Charles IX de ce nom Roy de France, en sa bonne ville et cité de Paris …* (Paris, 1572), 21.

93 Paul Van Dyke, *Catherine de Medicis* (New York, 1922), II, 14.

94 Craig Wright, 'Performance Practices at the Cathedral of Cambrai 1475–1550,' *The Musical Quarterly* 64, no. 3 (July 1978): 295–328, http://www.jstor.org/stable/741504.

95 Ibid., LXIV, Nr. 3, 298.

96 Ibid., LXIV, Nr. 3, 322.

97 Lesure, *Musicians and Poets of the French Renaissance*, 44ff.

Calvin arrived in Strasbourg in 1538 to begin work on his own Psalter to reflect these views. When published, in 1543, it included a clear exposition of his views of the aesthetics of church music. Because of the power of music, he says, the character of the music used in church becomes an important consideration.

> We know by experience that song has great force and vigor to move and inflame the hearts of men to invoke and praise God with a more vehement and ardent zeal. It must always be looked to that the song be not light and frivolous but have weight and majesty.[98]

He recognizes that music used for entertainment at banquets or in the home was a gift of God for the recreation of man and to give him pleasure. But, once again, because of the power of music to affect character, care must be taken in the choice of the music itself.

> We must be the more careful not to abuse [music], for fear of soiling and contaminating it, converting it to our condemnation when it has been dedicated to our profit and welfare. Were there no other consideration than this alone, it might well move us to moderate the use of music to make it serve all that is of good repute and that it should not be the occasion of our giving free rein to dissoluteness or of our making ourselves effeminate with disordered pleasures and that it should not become the instrument of lasciviousness or of any shamelessness. But there is still more, for there is hardly anything in the world with more power to turn or bend, this way and that, the morals of men, as Plato has prudently considered. And in fact we find by experience that it has a secret and almost incredible power to move our hearts in one way or another.

His final thought, after calling attention to the just concern of the early Church fathers, is quite interesting. While the humanists, who concentrated on sung poetry, always emphasized that it was the words, and not the music, which produced the greater impact on feelings, Calvin found a greater danger in the music than the words.

> For this reason the early doctors of the Church often complain that the people of their times are addicted to dishonest and shameless songs, which not without reason they call mortal and Satanic poison for the corruption of the world. Now in speaking of music I understand two parts, namely, the letter, or subject and matter, and the song, or melody. It is true that, as Saint Paul says, every evil word corrupts good manners, but when it has the melody with it, it pierces the heart much more strongly and enters within; as wine is poured into the cask with a funnel, so venom and corruption are distilled to the very depths of the heart by melody.

---

98 Jean Calvin, *Geneva Psalter*, quoted in Strunk, *Source Readings in Music History*, 346ff.

ENTERTAINMENT MUSIC

When François I met with Henry VIII in 1520 he obviously wanted to represent himself with the most elaborate entertainment music available to him. In their first banquet he had Henry greeted by twenty-four trumpets and one account of the final banquet describes music by numerous rotating consorts.

> During the meal, the royal musicians played in turn; trumpets, cornetts, fifes [shawms?], sackbutts, trombones, sourdines, a tabor, a viol and a *luiſolo*.[99]

During the reign of Henry II (1547–1559) we encounter the first of the elaborate entertainment pageants which included music. When visiting Lyons in 1548, as he sailed up the Saône he saw allegories which included Greek temples and centaurs, obelisks, fountains of wine and a great artificial forest with Diana, her nymphs and trumpets.[100]

Some of the most extraordinary descriptions of royal musical entertainments are relative to the meeting between Charles IX and the queen of Spain organized by Catherine de Medici in Bayonne. We read of a picnic with 'tabourins, trompettes, [and] hault-bois sounding noble melody all around.'[101] Another eyewitness describes this same ensemble as 'trompettes, doulcines, et clairons' sounding 'around the canopy, echoing on the shore their high and gracious fanfares.'[102]

On the second day a great allegorical play was given representing 'The Temporary Victory of War over Peace.' The king found many members of his court captured by a 'giant' and upon their delivery one heard 'the harmonious sound of fanfares and joyous sounds [*allegresses faictes*] of trumpets, clarions, and other 'gracious' instruments.'[103] Two days later, the court journeyed, in an elaborate boat built like a castle, upriver from Bayonne to an 'enchanted island.' They encountered Neptune, riding in a magnificent shell boat drawn by three marine horses, who greeted the company with a poem. This was followed by six 'Tritons' who 'made a consort of their six cornetts, and they were very pleasant to the ear.'[104] On the island itself a performance of six 'excellent musette' players was heard.

Finally, a note regarding the peasant version of the chanson. Pierre Belon, writing about the nightingale in 1555 remarks that peasants are capable of imitating its singing to perfection and that, taking that bird's call as their theme, they compose chansons upon it so obscene that they cannot be published in his book.[105]

---

99 Russell, *The Field of Cloth of Gold*, 177.

100 Edith Sichel, *Women and Men of the French Renaissance* (Port Washington: Kennikat Press), 358.

101 Abel Jouan, *Recueil et Discours de Voyage du Roy Charles IX* (Paris, 1566), 46.

102 *Ample Discours de l'Arrivee de la Royne catholique soeur du Roy à sainct Jehan de Lus: de son entrée à Bayonne …* (Paris: Jean Dallier Labraire, 1565), 4.

103 Ibid., 9.

104 *Recueil des Chose Notables*, 50ff. On this river trip the court also encountered many other aquatic spectacles, among which was a great mechanical whale 'killed' by a group of local whale hunters!

105 Lesure, *Musicians and Poets of the French Renaissance*, 35.

10 SIXTEENTH-CENTURY FRENCH POETRY

IN SIXTEENTH-CENTURY POETRY we find an interest in the development of the French language but little serious discussion of the values of music. Even in the midst of the greatest functional musical establishment in Europe, the court of François I, the young Clément Marot seemed only to notice the girls. Even his 1543 setting of the Psalms in verse, which were set to music by Goudimel and became popular, were dedicated to 'the ladies of France.'

The French poets were still sufficiently in awe of the Italians that many of them made sabbatical trips to Italy, Marot among them. This attraction also explains in part the fact that during the first three decades much of the poetry by French poets was in Latin, which also served as an international language.[1]

Joachim du Bellay found Rome the epitome of all his objections to the life of the courtier. He called Rome the 'public stage of all the world' and noted, 'here courtiers make love and their affairs progress.'[2] And in another sonnet he reflects of Rome,

> Here the endless hatred, envy, avarice—
> Of petty courtiers poisons every hour.[3]

On the trials of working in such an environment, he observed,

> If I were a satirist—I wish I were—
> I'd attack others and not feel a thing,
> My pen would run freely, I'd not be wondering
> What my superiors would have to say.
> I tell you, Vineus, the only true superior
> Is he who is not in duty bound to please
> And can write as he will from day to day.[4]

In another sonnet he elaborates on this problem.

---

1 Marot, a leader of the Neo-Latin poets, is pictured in some contemporary engravings looking more like a Roman emperor than a poet.

2 Joachim du Bellay, *The Regrets*, trans. C. H. Sisson (Manchester: Carcanet Press, 1984), Nr. 82. Bellay (born in 1525), was a friend to most of the sixteenth-century French poets, including Ronsard, with whom he taught at the college of Coqueret in Paris. He traveled to Rome with a relative, cardinal Jean du Bellay, in 1553.

3 Ibid., Nr. 115.

4 Ibid., Nr. 42.

> Speaking ill is a hundred times more delightful
> Than praising people, because it means telling the truth,
> While praising means, often, that one cannot choose
> And has to be servile to say anything at all.[5]

In yet another sonnet, he reflects on his bitter experience with the life of the courtier in Rome.

> To walk solemnly and with a frowning look,
> And greet everyone with a sober smile,
> To weigh all words and answer with a nod,
> With a 'no signor,' or a 'si signor':
> To put in often a little 'just so,'
> And mimic the honest man with a 'your servant, sir,'
> And, as if one had had something to do with the conquest,
> To talk of Florence and of Naples too;
> To show deference to every man by kissing his hand,
> And, following the custom of the Roman courtier,
> To hide one's poverty under a brave appearance;
> There you have the great virtue of this court,
> From which, frequently, ill mounted, in ill health,
> Ill clad, beardless and penniless one returns to France.[6]

ON THE PHYSIOLOGY OF AESTHETICS

The only one of these poets to discuss Reason with any emphasis was Joachim du Bellay and his views are removed from Italy and the long tradition of Italian Church philosophy. Far from the Church dogma that Reason must rule, Bellay also recognizes action and experience.

> Happy the Ulysses who gets back home,
> The Jason who conquers the golden fleece,
> They can be full of reason and experience
> And impress the relative who did not go![7]

In another poem, 'La Lyre chrestienne,' he even suggests that Reason is sometimes pretense.

> My muse, which strolls through
> Anjou and through Maine,

---

5   Ibid., Nr. 76.

6   *Oeuvres poétiques*, II, sonnet lxxxvi, quoted in L. Clark Keating, *Joachim du Bellay* (New York: Twayne, 1971), 81.

7   du Bellay, *The Regrets*, Nr. 31.

> Spoke this pleasant speech,
> Laughing at the errors of the world,
> Whereupon I take my stand on reason,
> Pretending to be wise.[8]

We are confident that du Bellay trusted his feelings more than Reason, for he confides in his 'Les Regrets,'

> I shall content myself with simply writing down
> What my emotions alone make me say,
> Without looking elsewhere
> For more solemn arguments.[9]

In references to education by these poets, in no place do we find Music included among the important topics. Joachim du Bellay, for example, describes philosophy and mathematics as education, but music as only a recreation.

> I will master the secrets of philosophy,
> Of mathematics and of medicine as well,
> Become a legal expert and—who can tell?—
> Perhaps even aspire to theology:
> For recreation painting and playing the lute …[10]

In another sonnet he provides an interesting comment on the nature of teachers.

> A pedant and a king
> Have a lot in common, don't you think?
> Something psychological, I would say.
> The pedant sees his scholars as his subjects,
> His classes are states, his ministers are his prefects,
> His college is the entire works of government.
> That is why the tyrant Dionysius,
> Having been driven from his throne in Syracuse,
> And unable to be a king, set up as a pedant.[11]

Marguerite de Navarre speaks of the difficulty and rewards of the study of the liberal arts, in particular philosophy and mathematics.

> Along one side I set Philosophy
> Where reason challenges dull ignorance
> And makes man prize himself above his worth.

---

8   Quoted in Keating, *Joachim du Bellay*, 47.
9   Ibid., 74.
10 du Bellay, *The Regrets*, Nr. 32.
11 Ibid., Nr. 66.

> Those books are hard to force or break; close sealed,
> They cannot be laid open to the eye
> Without a struggle that no words can tell;
> And when at last the battle has been won
> And something of that hidden lore laid bare,
> A man can never rest, he must press on,
> Intent on knowing all the learned know …
>
> Then next I put together those fine books,
> So full of strange delights, where you can read
> of Mathematics. Study them with zeal
> And you will give up all the body craves,
> For they hold lore so subtle and so rare
> A man's whole self must work to master it;
> The way is barred by thorns, and hard it is
> To bend those briars and make a passage through;
> But he who, once that tedious task is done,
> Can freely roam about the verdant plain,
> The fruitful garden of those liberal arts,
> Would not exchange the joy they give to him
> For all the treasures of the Caesars, nor
> For all their pomp and mad delight in fame.[12]

Her study of religious texts was not so rewarding.

> I spent long hours in going through those books
> But found no satisfaction as I read;
> For differences so great divided them
> That some make hope spring up and grow in me
> While others gave me cause to feel despair.[13]

---

12 Marguerite de Navarre, *The Prisons*, trans. Hilda Dale (Reading: Whiteknight's Press, 1989), III, 37ff., 85ff. This long poem is fiction and does not describe actual prison life. Marguerite (1496–1549) was a sister to king, François I, and mother to an extraordinary woman, Jeanne d'Albret, mother to Henri IV.

13 Ibid., III, 261ff.

ON THE PSYCHOLOGY OF AESTHETICS

Emotions

The emotion most mentioned by these poets was of course Love. As they were court oriented poets, we find sometimes a lament almost in the style of the thirteenth-century troubadour, as for example in the anonymous poem, 'O mal d'aymer qui tous maulx oultrepasse,' set as a chanson as Janequin.

> Oh pain of love, all woes surpassing
> Pain of love who martyrs men and wishes me dead,
> Oh grief that weighs heavy on my tired heart.
> Be gone all ills, source of laments, tears, griefs, groans.
> Oh sickness which surpasses all others
> May you one day be weary of tormenting me.[14]

It is perhaps to avoid such pain that Marguerite de Navarre describes first refusing the pleasures of Love and then abruptly changing her attitude to adopt the prerequisite court habits, including performance ability in music.

> While love endured I lived in chastity,
> Refusing all base pleasures, for I wished
> To look and act as one who, angel-like,
> Kept himself free from every mortal taint …
> I'll try new ways and learn to paint my face,
> Use language that is flowery and refined,
> Invent new fashions for my style of dress;
> I'll learn to dance with ease, play instruments,
> Be skilled in horsemanship and use of arms,
> Or make my eyes seem often full of tears
> And languorously turn them heavenward,
> Showing their whites as stricken lovers do;
> And I will seek to hide my evil thoughts
> Behind a mask of wordless suffering.[15]

A Ronsard poem reminds the listener that Love is of another realm than Reason.

> Then you shall know that Love is reasonless,
> A sweet deceit, a dear imprisonment,

---

14 Quoted in Jane Bernstein, *French Chansons of the Sixteenth Century* (University Park: Pennsylvania State University Press, 1985), 35. This volume also includes several examples of obscene poetry set as chansons.

15 Marguerite de Navarre, *The Prisons*, II, 328ff.

An empty hope that feeds us with the wind.[16]

In fact, Ronsard in another poem speaks of Love making the lover mute—the ultimate denial of Reason. It must instead be the emotions expressed in the face which communicate.

> Mine eyes do fear to meet [thine eyes],
> My soul doth tremble neath those rays divine,
> Nor tongue nor voice can to its function move.
> Only my sighs, only my tear-stained face
> Must do their office, speaking in their place,
> And bear sufficing witness of my love.[17]

Joachim du Bellay finds that the poetry which arose from his youthful passion has become, as literature, the pride of his old age.

> If verses have been the folly of my youth
> In my old age at least they will have some use,
> They were my madness, they will be my reason …[18]

Pleasure and Pain

In one of the odes which accompanied his 'War of the Muses,' Joachim du Bellay mentions the traditional observation that Pleasure and Pain seem to follow one another in cycles. He seems to suggest that one must prepare for this following the example of the musician.

> Up then, and wipe away all tears and care.
> Fine weather and rain thus follow each other.
> He who tunes the sound of his lyre
> Looks to more than one string
> And to more than one song.[19]

Marguerite de Navarre seems to go beyond the usual alternation of Pleasure and Pain to recognition of a synthesis, the delight of suffering.

> 'My friend,' he said, 'since for my fellow men
> I feel compassion and true friendliness,

---

16   Quoted in Curtis Page, *Songs and Sonnets of Pierre de Ronsard* (Westport: Hyperion Press, 1924), 4.
17   Ibid., 7.
18   du Bellay, *The Regrets*, Nr. 14.
19   Quoted in Keating, *Joachim du Bellay*, 35.

> I come to you, drawn by your countenance
> Which clearly shows you in the grip of pain
> Or moved by Pleasure to such ecstasy
> That you delight in cruel suffering …'[20]

In another poem, Joachim du Bellay presents a brief, but rare, discussion of the physical nature of pain itself.

> But in fact crying has no value at all,
> Because whether you don't bother yourself with it
> Or whether you lament day and night,
> The grief whatever it is will run its course.
> The heart sends this vapor to the brain
> And the brain, through the eyes, sends it down again,
> But the evil is not distilled out through the eyes.
> Then what is the use of all this blubbering?
> It is like pouring on oil to stop something burning,
> And you simply lose your sleep and lose your appetite.[21]

Nevertheless, he values Pleasure for its own sake.

> Shall we therefore live the life of beasts?
> No, but with our heads held high, at least
> Sometimes taste all the sweetness of pleasure.
> Only a fool would always give up
> The certainty of pleasure for a doubtful hope,
> And always go against his own desire.[22]

ON AESTHETICS IN POETRY

The sixteenth-century French court poets remind us time and time again that poetry is for the elite, and not for the ordinary citizen. For example, a poem of Ronsard begins,

> Holy Euterpe teaches me to hate
> The common crowd …[23]

---

20 Marguerite de Navarre, *The Prisons*, II, 487ff.
21 du Bellay, *The Regrets*, Nr. 52.
22 Ibid., Nr. 53.
23 Quoted in Page, *Songs and Sonnets of Pierre de Ronsard*, 98.

Marguerite de Navarre also suggests that poetry is not intended to be understood by everyone.

> Pleasure it is to learn such poetry
> For those to whom the meaning shines out clear,
> But understanding is not given to all,
> Only to him who is a poet born.[24]

For her, clearly, the delight in poetry was found in its inner meaning and not in its external sensory pleasure.

> Now more than ever poetry delights;
> I do not stop at words or melody
> But, pressing on, I seek the poem's heart;
> For I am not held back as once I was
> By too much pleasure in the outward form.[25]

Joachim du Bellay finds more practical purposes in poetry.

> If I am worried by my creditors
> Poetry banishes thoughts of them at once:
> And if a job I asked for is badly done
> I put up with it and write some more.
> If anyone loses his temper with me
> I sick my heart out all over my poems:
> And if work makes me too tired to go on
> A few verses soon make the work seem easy.
> Poetry soon drives away idleness,
> Poetry does not make me love liberty less
> But sings for me the things I dare not say.[26]

In his *L'Olive*, du Bellay addressed the question of imitation of earlier poets.

If the reading of good books has impressed on my mind certain features, which, on a subsequent occasion when I come to express my modest ideas, flow more easily from my pen than they return to my memory, should they for this reason be called borrowed materials? I might even add that those who have read Virgil, Ovid, Horace and Petrarch, and many others, whom I have sometimes read rather carelessly, will find in my writings much more of natural invention than of artificial or slavish imitation … In my writings I have not tried to resemble anyone but myself,

---

24 Marguerite de Navarre, *The Prisons*, III, 57ff.
25 Ibid., III, 944ff..
26 du Bellay, *The Regrets*, Nr. 14.

and if in some instances I have taken over certain metaphors and figures of speech in imitation of foreigners, there was really no law or copyright to keep me from doing so.[27]

The growing interest in Paris at this time in Greek literature is reflected in references by these poets to the ancient Greek lyric poets. An Ode by Pierre de Ronsard reflects that in as much as the great Greek lyric poets are now all but forgotten, what hopes can he have for posterity?

> How can a Frenchman,
> A composer of barbaric poetry,
> Be hopeful that his voice
> Will ride the greedy ages?[28]

In another poem, anticipating his own death, he looks forward to hearing these famous poets in heaven.

> Ah, God! to think, mine ear
> Alcaeus' lyre shall hear,
> And Sappho's, over all
> Most musical![29]

A new appreciation for epic poetry can no doubt also be attributed to the Greek models. A poem of Ronsard contends that no monument can preserve a man's fame like the song of the lyric poet.

> Columns uplifted high,
> Or living bronze,
> Or stone carved skillfully,
> Fame's clarions—
>
> Never to men can give
> Their deathless meed
> Like song that makes to live
> Each noble deed.[30]

Joachim du Bellay agrees with this value of epic poetry. It is, he says, more valuable than gold.

> Gold is not so precious, nor the bold metal
> Which devours all its brothers so lasting

---

27 Quoted in Keating, *Joachim du Bellay*, 21.
28 Nicholas Kilmer, *Poems of Pierre de Ronsard* (Berkeley: University of California Press, 1979), 63.
29 Quoted in Page, *Songs and Sonnets of Pierre de Ronsard*, 113.
30 Quoted in Ibid., 97.

> As a verse which honors us.
> Verses are sweeter than honey.[31]

Regarding dramatic poetry, although some treatises of earlier dramatic criticism were published in the fifteenth century, the mature period of French thinking begins with the publication in 1548 of the *Art Poétique* of Thomas Sebillet.[32] This was the first French work which begins to demonstrate the influence of Aristotle's *Poetics* and is interesting to drama critics for its discussion of the older French Morality plays in their relationship with Greek Tragedy. Indeed, he observes that,

> If the earlier French had managed to make the ending of the Morality plays invariably sad and dolorous, the Morality would now be a tragedy.[33]

Sebillet finds the chief virtue of the Morality play 'the expression of the moral sense of the piece.'

He found less to praise in the French Farce. He observes that while Greek and Latin Comedy had 'more morality than laughter,' the Farce 'presents only unrestrained laughter, for every license [is] permitted.'[34]

Jean de la Taille (born 1540) was a noble, soldier and practicing playwright. His views on dramatic poetry, which are important for the first formulation in France of the three unities, are found in the preface to his play, *Saül le furieux* (1572).[35] In an important break with older Church dogma, Taille declares,

> Tragedy is by no means a vulgar kind of poetry; it is rather the most elegant, beautiful, and excellent of all.[36]

The subject of Tragedy must be the 'pitiful ruin of lords,' and similar noble circumstances, and not those things which happen every day 'which do not easily move us and would scarcely bring a tear to the eye.'

For Taille, the purpose of Tragedy 'is to move and arouse keenly the passions of each of us.'[37] This is accomplished by a subject 'pitiful and poignant in itself,' which is able to 'at once arouse in us some passion.'

---

31 Quoted in Keating, *Joachim du Bellay*, 36.

32 Sebillet (1512–1589) was educated in law but his interest soon turned to literature. He traveled in Italy and was a political activist, for which he was once jailed.

33 Quoted in Barrett Clark, *European Theories of the Drama* (New York: Crown, 1959), 75.

34 Ibid.

35 Taille calls his play the first true Tragedy written in French. [Ibid., 78]

36 Ibid., 76.

37 Ibid., 77.

In addition to the unities of day, time and place, Taille adds of the plot that 'there must be nothing in it useless, superfluous, or out of place.' But this is not to say there cannot be variety.

> The principal point in tragedy is to know how to dispose and construct it well, so that the story may change, rise and fall, turning the minds of the spectators hither and thither, allowing them to see joy suddenly turned to sorrow, and sorrow to joy, as happens in actual life.[38]

Taille was particularly contemptuous of the Morality play, in which he found 'neither sense nor reason, but only ridiculous discourses and nonsense.' Such works, as well as farces,

> are not constructed with true art ... and are consequently ignorant, ill-made, and insignificant things, good merely as pastimes for the lower classes, the common people, and frivolous-minded. I wish that all such trivial nonsense which spoils the purity of our language, could be banished from France.[39]

For all this, Taille does find that high tragedy and comedy can be a form of pleasure. Provided they are acted by intelligent actors, speaking with direct and fearless pronunciation in French, and not Latin (not reminiscent of the student or pedant), and with none of the nonsense of farce, such plays would,

> serve as the most pleasant pastime to the great—when they come for rest to the city, after exercising, hunting and hawking.[40]

Taille also makes a few comments on the audience. They must 'not listen coldly, but with attention.' He is evidently thinking here of the nobility and the following no doubt reflects the fact that he found they often looked down on men of letters. But this, he protests, does not bother him!

> I do not care about the bitter malice and brutal contempt of those who, because they are fighters, look down upon men of letters, as if knowledge and virtue, which reside only in the spirit, enfeebled the body, the heart, and the arms; and nobility were dishonored by another sort of nobility, to wit, knowledge.[41]

---

38 Ibid.
39 Ibid., 77ff.
40 Ibid., 78.
41 Ibid.

ON THE AESTHETICS OF MUSIC

Regarding the purpose of music, Ronsard cites the familiar virtue of the ability of music to soothe,

> Then set my lyre, song's handmaid, by my side—
> For if I may, I'll charm away the gloom …[42]

And again,

> The sweet-toned lyre alone
> Can comfort hearts that moan
> And charm away all cares
> Of he who hears.[43]

Joachim du Bellay also reflects on the ability of music to sooth in one of his sonnets.

> They call them songs, Magny, I call them tears,
> Rather I sing all right, but blubbering
> And sing to charm my tears as much as anything:
> Nothing could give me reason to sing oftener.[44]

Another poem speaks of persons in diverse occupations who find solace in music.

> So workmen sing who do not like their job
> Or ploughmen when the furrows are too long
> Or travelers who cannot get back home,
> So young men who have trouble with their girls
> Or sailors when the oars are hard to pull
> Or prisoners desperate to be out of prison.[45]

On the other hand, an anonymous poem, 'Las, voules vous q'une personne chante,' set as a chanson by Lassus, speaks of the inability of music to sooth.

> My heart is sighing;
> Yet alas, you ask for song.
> Let those sing who are happy,
> And leave me to endure my single grief.[46]

---

42 Quoted in Page, *Songs and Sonnets of Pierre de Ronsard*, 77. In the 'Sonnets for Helen,' Book I, lviii, Ronsard also speaks of singing to sooth,

   Taschant à soulager les peines de mon ame.

43 Quoted in Page, *Songs and Sonnets of Pierre de Ronsard*, 113.
44 du Bellay, *The Regrets*, Nr. 12.
45 Ibid., Nr. 12.
46 Quoted in Bernstein, *French Chansons of the Sixteenth Century*, 138.

Another poet who failed to find solace in music was Marguerite de Navarre, who wrote,

> I laughed at those who studied music's art
> And hearing its sweet strains were satisfied;
> Your voice to me was perfect harmony
> And filled my prison with melodious sound—
> Wherein lies all my joy and happiness—
> So that I had no need of instruments,
> Of organ, lute or fife and viol; all
> That I desired I found in your sweet words.[47]

One poem, 'Musiciens qui chantez à plaisir,' set as a chanson by Hubert Waelrant of Antwerp offers some insights into performance practice. He seems most concerned that improvisation stay in character with the emotions of the text.

> Musicians, you who sing at will, who improvise, divide the note;
> Take a tone most sweet and slow signifying what the song means.
> Keep in tune like the linnet who takes pleasure in her graceful song.
> Be alert of ears and eyes or otherwise keep silent;
> And take good care not to sing unless you have had plenty to drink![48]

FUNCTIONAL MUSIC

One reference to Church music by Marguerite de Navarre offers a rare purpose of abstract delight.

> I took delight in hearing those new chants …
> 'This is true paradise,' I told myself,
> 'If what's within resembles the outside;
> Indeed melodious song is all I hear,
> With organ music played to give delight.'[49]

Regarding the functional music of the tournament, Marguerite de Navarre describes trumpets acknowledging the winners, like a modern marching band performing the 'fight song.'

> And soon began the jousts and tournaments,
> With men unhorsed and many a broken lance
> Till, in the end, I saw the champion given

---

47 Marguerite de Navarre, *The Prisons*, I, 71ff.
48 Quoted in Bernstein, *French Chansons of the Sixteenth Century*, 165.
49 Marguerite de Navarre, *The Prisons*, II, 207ff.

> A rich award, the prize of victory.
> I heard the heralds call, the trumpets sound
> In celebration of those gallant deeds.[50]

Military music is mentioned by Joachim du Bellay, who found during his travels to Rome that all normal life had ceased due to battles. There he found,

> The music is silent and the dancing's stopped …
> Nothing to be heard but drums, and the noise of trumpets …[51]

And, in another sonnet,

> Like children they love trumpets and love guns,
> Bright flags and colored banners, fifes and drums …[52]

ENTERTAINMENT MUSIC

A specific description of entertainment music performed after a banquet is found in a poem by Marguerite de Navarre.

> Leaving the laden board to join the dance;
> Then followed mummery and masque, with farce
> And plays and noise of instruments and voice
> So great my ears were deafened by the sound,
> Such music as they never heard before.[53]

---

50 Ibid., II, 259ff.

51 Joachim du Bellay, *The Regrets*, Nr. 83.

52 Ibid., Nr. 114.

53 Marguerite de Navarre, *The Prisons*, II, 286ff.

11 SIXTEENTH-CENTURY FRENCH PROSE

THE GREAT FRENCH STORY TELLER, RABELAIS, was no doubt speaking for many Frenchmen when he had his character Panurge observe,

> And just see how the world has gone to seed: we put our souls in trust to the theologians, who for the most part are heretics; our bodies to the doctors, who all loathe medications and never take medicine; and our property to the lawyers, who never go to law with one another.'
> 'Spoken like a courtier,' said Pantagruel.[1]

This implied loss of confidence in these fundamental institutions had the effect of encouraging to some degree freer individual thought, resulting in some extraordinary prose.

ON THE PHYSIOLOGY OF AESTHETICS

One of the most curious, though interesting, philosophers of the sixteenth century was Jean Bodin, who advanced the notion that the basic nature of the earth's various peoples is formed primarily by climate. This is of interest to us because he includes the emotional development under this influence. In his book on *The Easy Comprehension of History*, Bodin discusses this theory at length.[2] Basically, he believed that people inhabiting northern regions excel in physical strength and stature (which, he says, is why England could never conquer Scotland!), while in warmer climates the people are more subtle of mind and exhibit nervous sensitivity. He found these characteristic to a lesser degree even within the same country and believed these considerations were reflected in both society and government. A typical passage reads,

> Let us therefore adopt this theory, that all who inhabit the area from the forty-fifth parallel to the seventy-fifth toward the north grow increasingly warmer within, while the southerners, since they have more warmth from the sun, have less from themselves. In winter the heat is collected within, but in summer it flows out. Whereby it happens that in winter we are more animated and robust, in summer more languid. The same reason usually makes us hungrier in winter so that we eat more in summer, especially when the north wind blows. The south wind has the

---

1 François Rabelais, *Pantagruel*, trans. Donald Frame (Berkeley: University of California Press, 1991), III, xxix.
2 Jean Bodin, *Method for the Easy Comprehension of History*, trans. Beatrice Reynolds (New York: Columbia University Press, 1945), 85ff. Boden (1530–1596) was educated in Paris and served as a counselor of Henry IV.

opposite effect, that is to say, living things are less hungry. So it comes to pass that when the Germans visit Italy, or the French, Spain, we observe that they eat more frugally.

As regards physical appearance, Bodin found,

The Mediterranean peoples, then, as far as concerns the form of the body, are cold, dry, hard, bald, weak, swarthy, small in body, crisp of hair, black-eyed, and clear-voiced. The Baltic peoples, on the other hand, are warm, wet, hairy, robust, white, large-bodied, soft-fleshed, with scanty beards, bluish gray eyes, and deep voices. Those who live between the two show moderation in all respects.

Similarly,

Since the body and the mind are swayed in opposite directions, the more strength the latter has, the less has the former; and the more effective a man is intellectually, the less strength of body he has, provided the senses are functioning.

Bodin extends these remarks to include the 'humors,' in particular the influence of blood and black bile. In this context he makes a specific reference to music therapy.

In Lower Germany there are almost none who are mad from black bile, but rather from blood; this type of lunacy the common man calls the disease of St. Vitus, which impels them to exultation and senseless dancing. Musicians imitate this on the lyre; afterwards they make use of more serious rhythms and modes, doing this gradually until by the gravity of the mode and the rhythm the madmen are clearly soothed.[3]

Later he provides a more extended discussion on the relationship of geography and musical preference.

A similar elegance of manner is found in the Persian posture and action. They also accomplish dulcet harmonies and use the Lydian mode on the lyre. The Scythians, however, dislike mellifluent speech and charming diction, as we understand from their language and their consonants striking together harshly without vowels. They cannot endure the Lydian mode, but the cultivate roughness of voice; as Tacitus wrote, with a battle cry they kindle their spirits, making a noise with their shields brought up to their lips so that the voice may swell to a fuller and heavier note. They listen gladly to trumpets and drums, but care nothing for the lyre …

The southerners seek the solitude and prefer to hide away in the woods rather than to move about in plain sight. Men of the middle region there is no need to describe, if one understands the extremes, since from these the means are easily understood. For instance, Scythians use the Phrygian mode more often; southerners, the Lydian; those in the intervening region become fiercer to the sound of the Dorian and stir up Mars with song, as [Virgil] says. The Lydian makes the southerners even more languorous. The Dorian, in harmony with nature, directs the striv-

---

3   Ibid., 103.

ings of souls toward valor and honor. This mode is therefore praised by Plato and vigorously approved by Aristotle in his books about the commonwealth. When the Christian religion was accepted by the Romans, the Dorian form was adopted with so much enthusiasm that a warning was issued lest anyone should use any other mode than the Dorian in the rites. On the other hand, the Spartans used the aulos, the Cretans the lute in warfare — not to restrain their wrath, as Thycydides and Plutarch wrote (for in the opinion of Plato and Aristotle it was given to men as helpful for purposes of revenge), but to suit their own nature, since in Europe there is no race more southerly than the Cretans and the Spartans.[4]

Bodin returns to this subject in another book, his *Six Books of the Commonwealth*. Here, in particular, he dwells on emotional character as it reflects geography.

> The southern peoples are cruel and vindictive in consequence of their melancholy, which engenders extreme violence in the passions and impels men to take vengeance for what they suffer.[5]

Later, however, he says of melancholy,

> This is the privilege of the melancholy temperament which is composed in spirit, and given to contemplation.[6]

Finally he also makes some curious broad generalizations, in this book, regarding the nature of society and climate.

> If one considers carefully the natures of the peoples of the northern, southern, and temperate zones, one finds that they can be compared to the three ages of man, youth, age and maturity, and the qualities characteristic of these ages ... Northerners rely on force, those in the middle regions on justice, and southerners on religion.[7]

It is our impression that Bodin was interested in a broader wisdom than he found as a student in Paris, where among other things he studied four languages. In a complaint we shall see again in Montaigne, he found formal education more interested in grammar than ideas.

> Clearly this grammatical pest begins to infest the approaches to all disciplines, so that instead of philosophers, orators, mathematicians, and theologians, we are forced to endure petty grammarians from the schools.[8]

The value in the study of history, in the view of Bodin, is that such study succeeds in inciting men to virtue and frightening them away from vice[9] and in the fact that history is the

---

4   Ibid., 129ff.

5   Jean Bodin, *Six Books of the Commonwealth*, trans. M. J. Tooley (New York: Macmillian, 1955), 150. By way of example, he mentions that the Persians stuff the skin of the victim and mount it on an ass.

6   Ibid., 153.

7   Ibid., 151.

8   Bodin, *Method for the Easy Comprehension of History*, 8.

9   Ibid., 9.

'preserver of all the arts.' In addition, of all branches of knowledge, he found history to excel in 'ease and pleasure,' which he regarded as a virtue.

> The ease, indeed, is such that without help of any special skill the subject is understood by all. In other arts, because all are linked together and bound by the same chains, the one cannot be grasped without knowledge of the other. But history is placed above all branches of knowledge in the highest rank of importance and needs the assistance of no tool, not even of letters, since by hearing alone, passed on from one to another, it may be given to posterity.[10]

He seems to overlook here, Music, which also requires no other knowledge on the part of the listener.

Bodin organizes history into four divisions: human, which is uncertain and confused; natural, which is definite, but can be inconsistent due to contact with an 'evil deity'; mathematical, which is more certain; and divine, which is most certain and changeless.[11] Writing history in the sixteenth century, Bodin implies, had its risks.

> Who seeks for truth from historians in a state where it is base to say what you do not think, but imprudent and dangerous to say what you do think?[12]

Nevertheless, his ideal was that history should 'be nothing else but the image of truth.'[13]

Finally, we have given numerous examples in these volumes of early literature which make reference to a preference to the right hand over the left. We understand this today by virtue of clinical research regarding the separate hemispheres of the brain, in particular in the fact that the speaking and writing left side, which is associated with the right hand, pretends that the mute right brain is nonexistent. As the ears also have a cross relationship with the separate hemispheres, like the hands, we find interesting this unusual comment by Bodin.

> But if a good man has turned to a wrong thought, suddenly he recognizes in the recesses of his soul a teacher and guide who leads him away from the base thought either by the gentlest twitching and humming in his right ear or by a prick, which [Plato] described in these words: 'Cynthius plucks my ear and advises me.' Socrates used to explain that this was done by a friendly demon or rather by an angel who pulled his right ear in assent and his left ear for dissent.[14]

Bodin mentions this again later in a passing remark,

> No one understands this twitching of the ear unless he has had experience.[15]

---

10 Ibid., 11.

11 Ibid., 19.

12 Ibid., 46. Later in this passage he observes that in the case of ancient history truth can only be assumed if several sources agree. By way of illustration he points to several accounts which mention that the senate in Rome had a festival repeated after it was brought to their attention that a public dancer had performed unskillfully. Would that our senate worried about the quality of a dancer's performance!

13 Ibid., 51.

14 Jean Bodin, *Colloquium of the Seven*, trans. Marion Kuntz (Princeton: Princeton University Press, 1975), 100ff.

15 Ibid., 180.

ON THE PSYCHOLOGY OF AESTHETICS

Emotions

Rabelais, in an intriguing passage in his *Gargantua*, begins to discuss the association of colors with emotions. Interestingly enough, he associates the color 'white' with 'joy, blitheness, solace, pleasure, and delectation.'[16]

Bodin regards all plans, words and deeds as having their origin in the will. The will, however, can be subject to the emotions.

> This applies whether the will is unpolluted and free from all passion, like that of a wise man, or diverted by emotions (for example, by lust or anger), as it is in many who are called intemperate, or even mad, and, as they say, do nothing wicked willingly, but, influenced by a certain weakness of character, will their act, nevertheless.[17]

He follows this thought with the curious statement that in the case of the insane their 'activities seem to be not so much human as divine,' by which he means the influence of the devil.

Boden mentions emotion again briefly in discussing the attributes needed to be a good historian, among which are integrity, learning and experience. If only, he adds, 'they could rid themselves of all emotion in writing history.'[18]

Pleasure and Pain

The philosopher, Bodin, who was greatly influenced by the Old Testament, discusses Pleasure in the manner of the medieval Church writers.

> Since there is no limit to our desire for pleasure, or because this is equally common to man and to beast, the more noble each man is, the further he disassociates himself from the level of the beasts.[19]

In another book, however, Bodin presents the following dialogue:

> CORONAEUS. If the appetites were not ruled by reason, man would be no different from the judgment of the beasts.
> TORALBA. What of this? Indeed we see that the beasts always follow the laws of nature.[20]

---

16   François Rabelais, *Gargantua*, trans. Donald Frame (Berkeley: University of California Press, 1991), I, x.
17   Bodin, *Method for the Easy Comprehension of History*, 29.
18   Ibid., 43.
19   Ibid., 29.
20   Bodin, *Colloquium of the Seven*, 404.

Nearly all writers of the Middle Ages and early Renaissance observed that the states of Pleasure and Pain always seemed to be inseparably connected. And so as well in Marguerite de Navarre's famous *The Heptameron*, one finds this comment in the discussion of the second day,

> You know, ladies, that a great joy is followed by tears, so bitter sorrow ends with gladness.[21]

In Bodin's *Colloquium of the Seven* a character asks, 'How does it happen that we see that salutary mean always confounded by some hindrance, as health with sickness, pleasure with pain, peace of mind with anxiety?'[22] The answer given is,

> That impediment is as useful as a drainage ditch is in a city. The poisonous toad in the garden or the spider in the house are as necessary for gathering poisons as the hangman in the state.

ON THE PHILOSOPHY OF AESTHETICS

Perhaps because of the general decay in culture in sixteenth-century France, suggested by Rabelais above and certainly symbolized in the person of Henry III, one finds little discussion of the philosophy of aesthetics in general among the prose writers. For philosopher Jean Bodin, universality is the essence of art.

> The arts and the disciplines, as you are well aware, are not concerned with particulars, but with universals.[23]

Rabelais, in the words of the queen of Quint Essence, advances an interesting theory on the nature of the impact of art on the observer.

> What gets human minds lost is not the perfection of the effects, of which they clearly perceive to arise from natural causes by virtue of the ingenuity of the astute artisans; it's the novelty of the experience entering the senses, which does not foresee the ease of the task when serene judgment is paired with diligent study.[24]

---

21 Marguerite de Navarre, *The Heptameron*, trans. Arthur Machen (New York: Knopf, 1925), 106. Marguerite (1496–1549) was a sister to the king, François I, and mother to an extraordinary woman, Jeanne d'Albret, mother to Henri IV. It is odd that this lengthy collection of tales of love, so clearly inspired by Boccaccio's *Decameron*, contains virtually no mention of music.
22 Bodin, *Colloquium of the Seven*, 147.
23 Bodin, *Method for the Easy Comprehension of History*, 2.
24 Rabelais, *Pantagruel*, V, xxi.

Even the traditional question of art imitating nature finds little comment. Bodin addresses this topic briefly in the fifth day of discussions of the *Colloquium of the Seven*. After the host has offered the guests a dish composed of both real and artificial apples, the following ensues.

> CURTIUS. Art in the making of this fruit seems to have surpassed nature or surely to have equaled it.
>
> SALOMON. Indeed, art is the ray of man, but nature is the ray of God; moreover, art is so far from conquering or equaling nature that it cannot even imitate it. Although art objects, statues, and paintings often deceive men's eyes, still, in this regard, it is remarkable that animals cannot ever be deceived. And so when the queen of Sheba tried to deceive king Solomon by placing a real and an artificial flower side by side and asked which was the real flower, the very wise ruler asked that bees be brought in; immediately they flew to the real flower and passed over the artificial one.[25]

ON THE AESTHETICS OF MUSIC

The philosopher Bodin, again following the dogma of the medieval Church philosophers, argues that it is not enough for man 'to progress no further than those disciplines whose subject matter is apprehended by the senses.' Rather, he contends, the goal must be for the knowledge acquired by the senses to carry man on to the higher knowledge of the mind and ultimately to divine understanding.[26] In this regard he divides man's occupations into three categories: the highest being those 'relating to the protection of men's lives,' including such things as medicine, cattle breeding and agriculture. The next category are occupations of mechanical arts, such as piloting and weaving. The lowest category is occupations which provide mere delight, among which is music. Here he adds a startling observation on the nature of music.

> Harmony weakened and overdone by excessive elaboration exerts an influence, for while one both simple and natural is wont to cure serious illness of the mind, on the contrary one contrived from a medley of sounds and rapid rhythms usually drives a mind insane. This happens to men too anxious to please their ears, who dislike the Doric mode and dignified measures. They affect the Ionian, so that it ought not to seem remarkable if many become insane.[27]

One finds much interesting commentary among the prose writers relative to the place of music in society. Bodin gave considerable thought to whether 'harmony' in society, so frequently mentioned by ancient writers, was merely a figure of speech or could be attributed

---

25 Bodin, *Colloquium of the Seven*, 234.
26 Bodin, *Method for the Easy Comprehension of History*, 30ff.
27 Ibid., 31.

to some natural mathematics ratio found in nature, and most clearly illustrated in music. In his *Method for the Easy Comprehension of History* he takes the position that this is nonsense.

> Let us see whether changes in empires can be calculated from the Pythagorean numbers. The fact that Plato measures the vicissitudes and the collapse of states by mathematical sequences alone seems to me clearly absurd ...
>
> The interpreters of Plato record that the fall of the state would occur at the point where the harmony of numbers fails. In that case, if the state were going to fall by an internal weakness or loss of equilibrium, it would not be that best form of government which Socrates had in mind. That this should have a mathematical origin would seem absurd, for even if numbers which fit together badly do create a disagreeable discord, because the sounds produced from these cannot mingle and, striking each other with some jangling, try to enter the ear, yet when the symphony of sounds is mingled harmoniously, that is, when they are arranged properly in numbers according to proportion, there can be no discord. A state thus tempered and blended in constantly pleasing concord, where there is no disagreement, no clashing of sounds, and from hypothesis cannot be—I do not see in what way it can totter.[28]

Later in this same book, however, he seems more comfortable with the idea of equating the internal organization of government with the ratios found in music.

> In this way, then, is royal power constituted, the most excellent of all, as indeed it seems to me, especially helpful for the citizen body and, like harmony, tempered by sweet concord. As for the fact that Plato wished his state to be governed according to geometric ratio, Aristotle decided subtly and cleverly said that this concerned rewards only. Arithmetic ratio he related to honoring pledges and to penalties ... Therefore if we should follow our investigation through a perpetual series it becomes plain that the division of authority among several is as abhorrent to nature as is harmony among many numbers. Moreover, that characteristic peculiar to a musical proportion—that is, that the interval is more important than the separate notes and if the ratio were reversed the notes would harmonize well among themselves—is fitted to a monarchy alone, in which authority is carried down gradually to the magistrates. As they govern the lower classes, so in turn they obey their superiors, until unity is achieved in the prince, from whom, like a fountain perennial, flows the majesty of the entire kingdom.[29]

Late in life, Bodin wrote his *Colloquium of the Seven* [*Colloquium heptaplomeres*], a dialogue among men of seven different faiths. In this work, which was not published until the nineteenth century, Bodin clearly has begun to question the exclusive authority of the Church. His vehicle for this was in large part music, in which he found the analogy of varying tones still producing harmony. Bodin sets the stage for the importance of his use of music as an analogy at the very beginning of this book, where he mentions that the home of Paulus Coronaeus, in which this fictional discussion took place, was 'a shrine of the Muses.' In describing the contents of the home, Bodin observes,

---

28 Ibid., 223.

29 Ibid., 286ff.

> Most important, however, was the fact that Coronaeus' home was filled not only with an infinite variety and supply of books and old records, but also instruments … for music.[30]

Further, at the end of most day's discussions there was music designed to bring the day to a close with a feeling of harmony. At the end of the first day, for example, we read,

> He called the boys who were accustomed to soothe everybody's spirits by sweetly singing divine praises with a harmony of lyres, flutes, and voices.[31]

At the beginning of the third day, before the discussions began, we find 'After dinner, they sang hymns.'[32]

It is in Book IV that Bodin presents his lengthy discussion of the harmony of music as an analogy for a modern society free from Church dogma. The Church itself was, in the sixteenth century, deep in debate over both polyphony and the expanding of the modes to include chromatic tones. This offered Bodin the opportunity to point out that in music no single system reigned supreme and that complex contrapuntal music could be appreciated by the enlightened [*auribus eruditis*] listener. In fact, he observes, when there is no blending of sounds [by which he means unison music, as in chant] the imbalance of individual tones tends to offend the delicate senses of wiser men.

This discussion began by singing hymns of praise 'to their soul's delight.' Then Coronaeus opens the discussion by observing,

> Often I have wondered why there is such sweetness in a tone that has the full octave, the fifth and the fourth blended at the same time; just now you have heard the sweetest harmony with the full system of the highest tone blended with the lowest, with the fourth and fifth interspersed; although the highest tone is opposite to the lowest, why is it that harmonies in unison, in which no tone is opposite, are not pleasing to the trained ear?
> FRIDERICUS. Many think that the harmony is more pleasing when the ratios of numbers correspond.
> CURTIUS. I am amazed that the most learned men approve of this, since no ratios seem to combine more aptly than geometric progressions; the last members accord with the first, the middle with each, all with all, and also positions and orders are related, as 2, 4, 8, 16. Still in these systems that most pleasing harmony fails. When the numbers are arranged in this manner, 2, 3, 4, 6, and the ratios have been separated, we delight in this harmony. Indeed, what is the reason that the interval of the pure fifth is most pleasing, but the apotome [9/8] is heavily offensive?
> OCTAVIUS. I think harmony is produced when many sounds can be blended; but when they cannot be blended, one conquers the other as the sound enters the ears, and the dissonance offends the delicate senses of wiser men.

---

30 Bodin, *Colloquium of the Seven*, 4.
31 Ibid., 15.
32 Ibid., 90.

> SENAMUS. I do not think a ratio of numbers or a blending of tones produce this sweetness, since a variety of colors presented to the eyes is more pleasing than if all are mingled simultaneously. Likewise, the flavor of fresh oil and vinegar is very pleasing, but it cannot be mingled by any force. Also the most dissimilar songs of birds, blended by no ratio, produce a most pleasing delight for the ears.[33]

The natural philosopher among this group, Toralba, expands the subject by contending that there is a basic form of harmony in each harmonic element.

> Indeed I think that pleasing delight of colors, tastes, odors, and harmonies depend on the harmony of the nature of each, a harmony which depends on the blended union of opposites. For example, something too hot or too cold offends the touch; likewise too much brightness or too much darkness offends the sight, and too much sweetness and too much bitterness offends the taste. But if these are blended by nature or art, they seem most pleasing.[34]

The point of this fictional discussion is that pleasing harmony can be based on multiplicity [*concordia discors*]. While the subject is music, they are really talking about the Church and suggesting that it can survive diversity of opinion. As the discussion continues, the participants begin to focus on diversity. Toralba observes that 'tones in unison would take away all sweetness of harmony.' Curtius agrees, adding,

> Even that keenest sweetness of harmony which we have heard most eagerly just now would not have been so pleasing unless the musician had contrived some dissonant or harsh note for our sensitive ears, since the pleasure is not perceived without a pain that precedes it and produces boredom when continued too long.[35]

This speaker then offers a poem in honor of God, making the same points,

> Creator of the world ...
> Who, moderating melody with different sounds and
> Voices yet most satisfying to sensitive ears ...

Rabelais raises another familiar question: is the performance of the musician the result of art or skill? He curiously includes organists among 'watchmakers, mirror makers, printers, dyers, and other such kinds of workmen.'[36] Later Rabelais introduces Messere Gaster, 'the first master of arts in the world.' Music is clearly not among his arts, as he was born without ears.[37] His 'arts' were in the area of mechanical invention, although Rabelais refers to the

---

33 Ibid., 144ff.
34 Ibid., 145.
35 Ibid., 147.
36 Rabelais, *Gargantua*, I, xxiv.
37 Rabelais, *Pantagruel*, IV, lvii. He also introduces here a lady named 'Want,' whom he calls the mother of the nine Muses!

ancient question of Art imitating Nature by observing 'Nature herself stood appalled and confessed she was vanquished by art.'[38]

One of the subjects often discussed since the time of the ancient Greek philosophers was the general subject of music therapy, the ability of music to cure real and specific forms of illness. Rabelais introduces this idea as well in the account of Pantagruel's visit to the kingdom of 'Quint Essence.' Here the visitors were told the queen cures all maladies just by playing an appropriate song. Rabelais is making fun of this whole idea, as is evident in the case of music curing the deaf, who of course could not hear it to begin with! In the demonstration given the visitors, first lepers were brought in.

> She played them a tune, but what one I don't know. Instantly they were perfectly cured. Then the poisoned were brought in; she played them another tune, and they were on their feet. Then the blind, the deaf, the mute, treating them similarly, which terrified us, not wrongly, and we fell to the ground, prostrating ourselves as people in ecstasy and rapt in contemplation of the powers we saw emanating from the Lady; and it was not in our power to say a single word.[39]

EDUCATIONAL MUSIC

Rabelais, in describing the education of Gargantua, includes music as one of the 'mathematical sciences,' in the tradition of the medieval and Renaissance universities. However, he also added 'practical music,' noting that Gargantua was taught to sing polyphonic works, and,

> he learned to play the lute, the spinet, the harp, the German flute and the one with nine holes, the viola [and] the sackbut.[40]

In describing Gargantua's visit to the people called Thélémites, Rabelais calls their education 'noble,' as they could all sing, play instruments, compose poetry and speak several languages.[41]

---

38 Ibid., IV, lxi.

39 Ibid., V, xix.

40 Rabelais, *Gargantua*, I, xxiii.

41 Ibid., I, lvii.

FUNCTIONAL MUSIC

Among the many curious countries invented by Rabelais is the Island of Clogs where is found the religious order of the Semiquaver Friars, whom he pictures singing in procession 'melodiously between their teeth some anthems or other.'[42]

Bodin argues for the importance of ceremony, including music, for attracting the faithful.

> I am persuaded that no religion can exist completely without rites and ceremonies. I believe the Roman religion has no greater secret for its so great duration than every imaginable variety of rites and ceremonies. Also the sweetness of songs with organ accompaniment and the splendor of vestments and sacred and costly furniture, hold the people in awe, as if in a wondrous spectacle.[43]
>
> ......
>
> If we were like heroes, we would need no rites nor ceremonies. However, it is hardly possible and even impossible for the common people and the untutored masses to be restrained by a simple assent of true religion without rites and ceremonies.[44]

Bodin also offers us some interesting sixteenth-century observations on the use of instruments in Church music. After the usual reference to instruments in the Old Testament, one character mentions the organ again.

> I think that the instruments of the Roman church which were invented at Constantinople about AD 700 and which use lead pipes by far surpass all ancient musical instruments, and I am amazed that those who have deserted the rites of the Roman church have completely abandoned that kind of instrument, since nothing could be more melodious.
>
> CURTIUS. I think this was done so that the people would not forget divine praises because of the enticements of the modulations. For this reason, Justin Martyr thought those musical instruments were for boys and ought to be taken out of the sanctuary, and Bishop Theodoret agreed ...
>
> I do not see what disadvantage can follow the use of David's most beautiful songs of praise in all languages. Still, if we must also use sacred musical instruments, as indeed we are ordered according to the divine prophecy of Nathan and Gadus, it would be better to use stringed instruments rather than lead pipes, for when voices are confounded with the sound from the pipes, they break forth with such force that no words are understood.[45]

The reference to military music among these writers is unremarkable. When Pantagruel visits the people called 'Chitterlings,' Rabelais describes their army marching 'to the sound

---

42 Rabelais, *Pantagruel*, V, xxvi. This book, which for years was translated and published almost as a children's fable, is, in the original, thoroughly obscene. Here, for example, the discussion of these friars and their singing introduces a new term to music theory, 'counterfart.'

43 Bodin, *Colloquium of the Seven*, 227.

44 Ibid., 462.

45 Ibid., 322ff.

of bagpipes and flageolets, sheeps' paunches and bladders, merry fifes and drums, trumpets and clarions.'[46] Or in another place, 'Run all, see that the warning bugle blows …'[47]

ENTERTAINMENT MUSIC

Rabelais, as part of his description of the kingdom of Quint Essence, presents a lengthy account of an allegorical tournament. The music was provided by two separate bands of musicians, playing 'sprightly' music, who controlled the movements of the participants.[48] The description here is in many ways similar to his description of the music for an actual tournament, found in a separate publication of 1549 called 'The Shadow Battle' [*La Sciomachie*]. Here, Rabelais describes an allegorical pageant which was given at the palace of Cardinal du Bellay on the occasion of the birthday of the Duke of Orléans. He mentions trumpeters serving as ambassadors and the,

> joyous harmony of bands of musicians, which had been set up on various stands over the square, such as oboes, cornetts, sackbuts, German flutes, trombones, little bagpipes, and the like, for the enjoyment of the spectators at each stage of the entertaining tourney.[49]

At the end of the day it was expected that a Comedy would be given, but as the hour was past midnight, 'music by cornetts, oboes, sackbuts, etc.,' was given instead.

Rabelais describes in detail in only one place the music for dancing, and then it is the music and dance of peasants.

> After dinner, they went pell-mell to the Willow Grove, and there, on the sturdy grass, they danced to the sound of joyous flutes [*flageolletz*] and sweet bagpipes [*doulces cornemuzes*], so gaily that it was heavenly fun to watch them sport.[50]

Rabelais, in his *Gargantua*, also describes a group of drinkers who call for a motet to sing.[51] In this scene one drinker observes, 'He drinks for nothing who gets no feeling from it.' We prefer to believe he meant that the same could be said of the motet singing.

---

46 Rabelais, *Pantagruel*, IV, xxxvi.
47 Rabelais, *Gargantua*, I, ii.
48 Rabelais, *Pantagruel*, V, xxiv.
49 Quoted in Donald Frame, *The Complete Works of François Rabelais*, (Berkeley: University of California Press, 1991), 796.
50 Rabelais, *Gargantua*, I, iv.
51 Ibid., I, v.

12 MICHEL DE MONTAIGNE

THE GREATEST FRENCH WRITER OF THE SIXTEENTH CENTURY was unquestionably Michel Montaigne (1533–1592). After an education in law at Toulouse, he became in turn a soldier, courtier, traveler and mayor of Bordeaux. He retired in 1585 to his Château de Montaigne where he spent his last years in reading, writing and publishing. Of his various experiences, it is clear that he found the least enthusiasm for the life of the courtier. One of Montaigne's chief objections to functioning as a courtier was that his very position of personal attachment to the court prevented him from free speech.

> A courtier can have neither the right to speak nor the desire to think other than favorably of a Master who from among so many thousands of his subjects has chosen to favor him with his own hand and to elevate him. Not unreasonably such favor and preferment will corrupt his freedom and dazzle him.[1]

In another place he observed, 'When serving princes it is not enough to keep a secret: you need to be a liar as well.'[2] In general, Montaigne associates with the courtiers: ambition, covetousness, irresolution, fear and desires.[3]

Taken altogether, the famous *Essays* of Montaigne, quite apart from the numerous subjects he treats, are particularly valuable as the most private, candid autobiography in Renaissance literature. He was clearly well read, as is evident from hundreds of quotations taken from ancient literature. There seemed to him a need to justify having used so many quotations, so he offers the following light-hearted explanation.

> Where my borrowings are concerned ... I get others to say what I cannot put so well myself, sometimes because of the weakness of my language and sometimes because of the weakness of my intellect ... I want [the reader] to flick Plutarch's nose in mistake for mine.[4]

While Montaigne was an extraordinarily free-thinker on many subjects, there was one subject upon which he remained very conservative. He had an almost medieval perspective

---

1 Michel de Montaigne, *Essays*, trans. M. A. Screech (London: Penguin, 1993), I, xxvi, 174.
2 Ibid., III, v, 954.
3 Ibid., I, xxxix, 268.
4 Ibid., II, x, 458. For the most part we have used only Montaigne's own ideas, as our intent is to reflect the sixteenth century.

on all matters touching on religion: we should not think of these things, we should merely accept the Church's answers. The alternative was a danger which he observed in man:

> Nothing is so firmly believed as whatever we know least about, thus our tendency to believe alchemists, astrologers, chiromancers, and those who offer their own explanations of religious questions.[5]

He returns to this again in his famous treatise, 'An apology for Raymond Sebond,' where he observes,

> Human reason goes astray everywhere, but especially when she concerns herself with matters divine. Who knows that better than we do? For we have supplied Reason with principles which are certain and infallible; we light her steps with the holy lamp of that Truth which God has been pleased to impart to us; yet we can see, every day, that as soon as she is allowed to deviate, however slightly, from the normal path, turning and straying from the beaten track traced for us by the Church, she immediately stumbles and becomes inextricably lost; she whirls aimlessly about, bobbing unchecked on the huge, troubled, surging sea of human opinion. As soon as she misses that great public highway she disintegrates and scatters in hundreds of different directions.[6]

In another essay he concludes,

> I do not believe, then, that purely human means have the capacity to [understand God]; if they had, many choice and excellent souls in ancient times—souls abundantly furnished with natural faculties—would not have failed to reach such knowledge by discursive reasoning. Only faith can embrace, with a lively certainty, the high mysteries of our religion …
>
> We must accompany our faith with all the reason that lies within us—but always with the reservation that we never reckon that faith depends upon ourselves or that our efforts and our conjectures can ever themselves attain to a knowledge so supernatural, so divine.[7]

ON THE PHYSIOLOGY OF AESTHETICS

When writing of the nature of Reason, Montaigne demonstrates a much broader understanding than we would expect from a man who so often reflects the official view of the Church. While earlier Church writers often simply referred to Reason as a kind of abstract, self-contained physical object, Montaigne saw it as a very broad subject.

---

5   Ibid., I, xxxii, 242.
6   Ibid., II, xii, 581.
7   Ibid., II, xii, 492. Later [II, xii, 594], he concludes,
    Man is indeed out of his mind. He cannot even create a flesh-worm, yet he creates gods by the dozen.

> Human reason is a dye spread more or less equally through all the opinions and all the manners of us humans, which are infinite in matter and infinite in diversity.[8]

He also departed from Church dogma by often commenting on the limitations of Reason.

> Human reason is a dangerous two-edged sword. Just see now, even in the hands of Socrates, its most familiar and intimate friend, it is a stick with a great many ends to it.[9]

In another place Montaigne seems to question the very nature of Reason and the general function of the mind.

> Man realizes that such truth as he does find out for himself is due to Fortune and to chance. Even when truth drops into his hands, Man has no means of seizing hold of it; his reason does not have power enough to establish any rights over it. Every single idea which results from our own reflections and our own faculties—whether it is true or false—is subject to dispute and uncertainty.
>
> ......
>
> Our minds are dangerous tools, rash and prone to go astray: it is hard to reconcile them with order and moderation. We have seen during my lifetime virtually all outstanding men, all men of abnormally lively perception, breaking out into licentiousness of opinion or behavior. It is a miracle if you find one who is settled and civilized. We are right to erect the strictest possible fences around the human mind. In the march of scholarship or anything else the mind must needs have its footsteps counted and regulated; you must supply artificial hedges and make it hunt only within them. We rein it in, neck and throat, with religions, laws, customs, precepts, rewards and punishments (both mortal and immortal), and we still find it escaping from all these bonds, with its garrulousness and laxity. It is an empty vessel: we can neither grasp it nor aim it; it is bizarre and misshapen and suffers no knot and no grapple.[10]

He takes care to ridicule the belief of some ancient philosophers that men achieve their greatest deeds when experiencing a kind of 'frenzy,' when 'the passions bring dislocation to our reason.'[11] Yet he placed great value on the validity of personal experience as a form of knowing. In a separate essay on this subject, he observes,

> No desire is more natural than the desire for knowledge. We try all the means that can lead us to it. When reason fails us we make use of experience ... Experience is a weaker and less dignified means: but truth is so great a matter that we must not disdain any method which leads us to it. Reason has so many forms that we do not know which to resort to: experience has no fewer.[12]

---

8   Ibid., I, xxiii, 126.
9   Ibid., II, xvii, 743.
10 Ibid., II, xii, 622, 629.
11 Ibid., II, xii, 640.
12 Ibid., III, xiii, 1207.

Later in this essay he adds, 'Were I a good pupil there is enough, I find, in my own experience to make me wise.'[13] He points out that of all disciplines, medicine should always 'have experience as the touchstone of its performance.'[14] He quotes Plato[15] as saying we should never submit ourselves to a doctor unless he himself had had the same illness and cured himself. This leads Montaigne to make the observation,

> If doctors want to know how to cure syphilis it is right that they should first catch it themselves!

Montaigne also objected to any form of intellectual conclusion which was opposed to Nature.[16]

> I do not doubt the power and fecundity of Nature nor her devotion to our needs. I can see that the pike and the swallows do well under her. What I am suspicious of are the things discovered by our own minds, our sciences and by that Art of theirs in favor of which we have abandoned Nature and her rules and on to which we do not know how to impose the limits of moderation.[17]

In another place he adds,

> You cannot extirpate the qualities we are originally born with: you can cover them over and you can hide them …
>
> Just take a little look at what our own experience shows. Provided that he listen to himself there is no one who does not discover in himself a form entirely his own, a master-form which struggles against his education as well as against the storm of emotions which would gainsay it.[18]

Montaigne begins his essay on Imagination with an old medieval axiom, 'A powerful imagination generates the event.'[19] Much of what he means by imagination is what we call today the power of suggestion. He gives an illustration from his youth when a doctor sent him to be with an older consumptive man, hoping that the latter might improve by being near the enthusiastic and healthy youth. Montaigne wryly adds that the doctor did not count on the possibility that it might work the other way around!

Montaigne also credits the power of suggestion as the explanation of all miracles, vision, etc., experienced by *common* people.[20] He also credits this as a primary tool of medicine:

---

13 Ibid., III, xiii, 1218.

14 Ibid., III, xiii, 1225.

15 Plato, *Republic*, III, 408 D-E.

16 In a nice phrase, Montaigne observes 'no man is poor by Nature's standards, but by opinion's standards, every man is.' [Ibid., III, x, 1141.]

17 Montaigne, *Essays*, II, xxxvii, 866.

18 Ibid., III, ii, 914. He adds here that because we are made by God as we are, the idea of repenting for our actions seems foreign to him.

19 Ibid., I, xxi, 109.

20 Ibid., 111ff.

Why do doctors first work on the confidence of their patient with so many fake promises of a cure if not to allow the action of the imagination to make up for the trickery of their potions?[21]

On the Senses

In spite of the support Montaigne often supplied to church dogma, he took a much more positive position on the importance of the senses than any of the earlier Church philosophers.

> Knowledge begins with them and can be reduced to them. After all, we would have no more knowledge than a stone if we did not know there exists sound, smell, light, taste, measure, weight, softness, hardness, roughness, color, sheen, breadth, depth. They form the foundations and principles on which our knowledge is built. Indeed, for some thinkers, knowledge is sensation. Anyone who can force me to contradict the evidence of the senses has got me by the throat: he cannot make me retreat any further. The senses are the beginning and the end of human knowledge.[22]

One of Montaigne's most revealing comments regarding his recognition of the power of the senses is in reference to religion.

> I shall leave aside other arguments marshaled on [the topic of the senses]; consider the sight of our crucifixes and the piteous chastisement which they portray; the ornaments and moving ceremonial in our churches; the voices [of singers] so aptly fitted to the reverent awe of our thoughts, and all the stirring of our emotions; you will have a hard time making me believe that such things do not set whole nations' souls ablaze with a passion for religion.[23]

In a long discussion on communication, which includes his interesting perception of animal communication, Montaigne offers a rather extraordinary list of non-verbal hand-signal communications, which we perceive by sight only. We find it interesting that his list includes *both* left and right hemisphere communication, as does normal language heard only by the ears.

> And what about our hands? With them we request, promise, summon, dismiss, menace, pray, supplicate, refuse, question, show astonishment, count, confess, repent, fear, show shame, doubt, teach, command, incite, encourage, make oaths, bear witness, make accusations, condemn, give absolution, insult, despise, defy, provoke, flatter, applaud, bless, humiliate, mock, reconcile,

---

21 Ibid., 116.
22 Ibid., II, xii, 663.
23 Ibid., II, xii, 573ff.

advise, exalt, welcome, rejoice, lament; show sadness, grieve, despair, astonish, cry out, keep silent and what not else, with a variety and multiplicity rivaling the tongue.[24]

Montaigne is the only early writer we know who raises the interesting question whether there exists the possibility for more senses than we are aware of.

> Now, on the subject of the senses, my first point is that I doubt that Man is provided with all the natural senses. I note that several creatures live full, complete lives without sight; others, without hearing. Who can tell whether we, also, lack one, two, three or more senses? If we do lack any, our reason cannot even discover that we do so. Our senses are privileged to be the ultimate frontiers of our perception: beyond them there is nothing which could serve to reveal the existence of the senses we lack …
>
> We need virtually all our senses merely to recognize an apple: we recognize redness in it, sheen, smell and sweetness. An apple may well have other qualities than that: for example powers of desiccation or astringency, for which we have no corresponding senses.
>
> Take what we call the occult properties of many objects (such as the magnet attracting iron). Is it not likely that there are certain senses known to Nature which furnish the faculties necessary for perceiving them and understanding them, and that the lack of such faculties entails our ignorance of their true essence?[25]

On Education

Montaigne had strong objections to formal education, which he saw as primarily an exercise in rote teaching by teachers who had memorized ancient principles but were, themselves, entirely lacking in practical wisdom needed for daily life. We should ask of our students, he says, not who knows more, but who is wiser—not who understands the most, but who understands the best. 'What use is it,' he asks, 'to have a belly full of meat if we do not digest it?'

> Whenever I ask a certain acquaintance of mine to tell me what he knows about anything, he wants to show me a book: he would not venture to tell me that he has scabs on his ass without studying his lexicon to find out the meanings of *scab* and *ass*.[26]

And in another place,

> I gladly come back to the theme of the absurdity of our education: its end has not been to make us good and wise but learned. And it has succeeded. It has not taught us to seek virtue and to

---

24 Ibid., II, xi, 507.
25 Ibid., II, xii, 664ff.
26 Ibid., I, xxv, 155.

embrace wisdom: it has impressed upon us their derivation and their etymology. We know how to decline the Latin word for virtue: we do not know how to love virtue.[27]

Even in the sciences he found this style of teaching produced students who never became more able, even though they knew more.[28]

This process of education had the second failing in leaving the professors themselves uninfluenced by their own lectures.

> It would seem that experience often shows us that doctors are the worst doctored, theologians the most unreformed and the learned the least able.
> In Ancient times Ariston of Chios was right to say that philosophers do harm to their hearers, since most souls are incapable of profiting from such teaching, which when it cannot do good turns to bad.[29]

He also wondered if there were natural limits to how much knowledge can be absorbed. He speaks of a man, who,

> by welcoming in as he did the brains of others, so powerful and so numerous, his own brain was forced to squeeze up close, crouch down and contract in order to make room for them all!
> I would like to suggest that our minds are swamped by too much study and by too much matter just as plants are swamped by too much water or lamps by too much oil; that our minds, held fast and encumbered by so many diverse preoccupations, may well lose the means of struggling free, remaining bowed and bend under the load ...[30]

One of the chief problems in education, in the view of Montaigne, was that 'since studies in France have virtually no other end than the making of money,' only persons of little financial means, hence people with lower souls, are left to be teachers.[31]

Montaigne did appreciate the importance of the education of children, calling it 'the most important difficulty known to human learning.'[32] A good teacher for children should be,

> an able man not an erudite one, I would wish you to be careful to select as guide for him a well-formed rather than a well-filled brain. Let both be looked for, but place character and intelligence before knowledge.[33]

---

27 Ibid., II, xvii, 750.
28 Ibid., I, xxv, 153.
29 Ibid., I, xxv, 161.
30 Ibid., I, xxv, 151.
31 Ibid., I, xxv, 159.
32 Ibid., I, xxvi, 167.
33 Ibid., I, xxvi, 168.

He objected to a teaching style of 'pouring knowledge through a funnel.' He wanted the student to have the opportunity to develop his own ideas, 'to trot in front of his tutor.' And again, 'we have been so subjected to leading-reins that we take no free steps on our own.' Montaigne's idea of education was to set a variety of ideas before the student and to let the student choose his own truths.

> Let this diversity of judgments be set before him; if he can, he will make a choice: if he cannot then he will remain in doubt … For if it is by his own reasoning that he adopts the opinions of Xenophon and Plato, they are no longer theirs: they are his.[34]

Interestingly enough, he saw no potential to the 'French practice' (also the modern practice) of teaching students in groups of dissimilar abilities. He also believed the student must learn to recognize Truth, virtue, sense of right and wrong 'and have no guide but Reason.' He must learn to keep his eyes open and that he can learn even from 'other people's stupidity and weakness.'

Montaigne wondered why philosophy, 'the art which teaches us how to live,' is not taught to children. 'They teach us to live when our life is over.' On the other hand, for him the Arts, represented in particular by poetry, were not essential. He mentions that Cicero said that even if he had two lives to live he would not bother with the lyric poets.

> Our boy is too busy for that: to school-learning he owes but the first fifteen or sixteen years of his life: the rest is owed to action. Let us employ a time so short on things which it is necessary to know.[35]

The student must learn that stubbornness and rancor are vulgar qualities. Sometimes one has a stubborn student, one who marches to his own beat. In such a case, Montaigne recommends,

> then I know no remedy except that his tutor should quickly strangle him when nobody is looking or apprentice him to make pastry cakes.[36]

Having said that, Montaigne returns to his thesis that too much education is bad.

> Despite all this I do not want to imprison the boy. I do not want him to be left to the melancholy humor of a furious schoolmaster. I do not want to corrupt his mind as others do by making his work a torture, slaving away for fourteen or fifteen hours a day like a porter. When you see him over-devoted to studying his books because of a solitary or melancholy complexion, it would not be good I find to encourage him in it: it unfits boys for mixing in polite society and distracts

---

34 Ibid., I, xxvi, 170.

35 Ibid., I, xxvi, 183.

36 Ibid., I, xxvi, 182.

them from better things to do. And how many men have I known in my time made as stupid as beasts by an indiscreet hunger for knowledge![37]

Montaigne strongly believed in the necessity of other kinds of learning than books and literature. The boy needs sports and social graces, among which he includes 'music-making.' After all, he observes, 'we are not bringing up a body: we are bringing up a man.' He mentions music in education again when addressing the general climate of the learning experience. His description of the teaching environment will strike the reader as quite remarkable.

> Go there during lesson time: you will hear nothing but the screaming of tortured children and of masters drunk with rage. What a way to awaken a taste for learning in those tender timorous souls, driving them to it with terrifying scowls and fists armed with canes! An iniquitous and pernicious system. And besides such imperious authority can lead to dreadful consequences—especially given our form of flogging.
>   How much more appropriate to strew their classrooms with leaf and flower than with blood-stained birch-rods. I would have portraits of Happiness there and Joy, with Flora and the Graces ...
>   When they have something to gain, make it enjoyable. Healthy-giving foods should be sweetened for a child: harmful ones made to taste nasty.
>   It is amazing how concerned Plato is in his Laws with the amusements and pastimes of the youths of his city and how he dwells on their races, sports, singing, capering and dancing ... He spends little time over book-learning; the only thing he seems specifically to recommend poetry for is the music.[38]

The cruel environment which Montaigne pictures here in the classroom is even exceeded by the treatment he observed of children in the home.

> How many times have I been tempted, among other things, to make a dramatic intervention so as to avenge some little boys whom I saw being bruised, knocked about and flayed alive by some frenzied father or mother besides themselves in anger. You can see fire and rage flashing from their eyes—(according to Hippocrates the most dangerous of distempers are those which contort the face)—as with shrill wounding voices, they scream at children who are often barely weaned. Children are crippled and knocked stupid by such batterings: yet our judicial system takes no note of it.[39]

In general, Montaigne seemed to subscribe to a belief that too much education had counterproductive effects on the 'normal' man. He even repeats the notion sometimes found in ancient literature that excessive study of the arts and sciences makes one effeminate.

> Both in that martial government and in all others like it examples show that studying the arts and sciences makes hearts soft and womanish rather than teaching them to be firm and ready for

---

[37] Ibid., I, xxvi, 184.
[38] Ibid., I, xxvi, 186.
[39] Ibid., II, xxxi, 810.

war. The strongest State to make an appearance in our time is that of the Turks; and the Turkish peoples are equally taught to respect arms and to despise learning. I find that Rome was more valiant in the days before she became learned … When the Goths sacked Greece, what saved their libraries from being burned was the idea spread by one of the marauders that such goods should be left intact for their enemies: they had the property of deflecting them from military exercises while making them spend time on occupations which were sedentary and idle.

When our own King Charles V found himself master of the kingdom of Naples and of a large part of Tuscany without even drawing his sword, he attributed such unhoped for ease of conquest to the fact that the Italian princes and nobility spent more time becoming clever and learned than vigorous and soldierly.[40]

For Montaigne, the personification of the man who had too much knowledge was the philosopher, whom he belittles time and time again.

> What good did their great erudition do for Varro and Aristotle? Did it free them from human ills? Did it relieve them of misfortunes such as befall a common porter? …
> I have seen in my time hundreds of craftsmen and ploughmen wiser and happier than University Rectors …
> There is a plague on Man: his opinion that he knows something. That is why ignorance is so strongly advocated by our religion as a quality appropriate to belief and obedience.[41]

In another example of the harm of excessive mental activity, Montaigne mentions an unnamed Italian poet, renowned for his judgment and genius.

> Yet his agile and lively mind has overthrown him; the light has made him blind; his reason's grasp was so precise and so intense that it has left him quite irrational; his quest for knowledge, eager and exacting, has led to his becoming like a dumb beast; his rare aptitude for the activities of the soul has left him with no activity … and with no soul. Ought he to be grateful to so murderous a mental agility?[42]

In the end, he wonders if whatever Truth can be known has been supplied by God, not to philosophers, but to the common man.

> Whatever share in the knowledge of Truth we may have obtained, it has not been acquired by our own powers. God has clearly shown us that: it was out of the common people that he chose simple and ignorant apostles to bear witness of his wondrous secrets.[43]

---

40   Ibid., I, xxv, 162.

41   Ibid., II, xii, 542ff. Later [II, xii, 567] he compiles a long list of ancient philosophers who questioned the validity of one or another of the liberal arts, although he lists none who question music.

42   Ibid., II, xii, 548.

43   Ibid., II, xii, 557.

He returns to this thought again in another place.

> It seems to me that the sorts of men who are simple enough to occupy the lowest rank are the least worthy of contempt and that they show us relationships which are better ordered. The morals and the speech of the peasants I find to be more in conformity with the principles of true philosophy than those of the philosophers.[44]

Even to believe that we are wiser than animals is, Montaigne contends, something we arrive at not 'by right of reason, but out of stubbornness and insane arrogance.' And unlike the animals, for our part we have been allotted,

> inconstancy, hesitation, doubt, pain, superstition, worries about what will happen (even after we are dead), ambition, greed, jealousy, envy, unruly, insane and untamable appetites, war, lies, disloyalty, backbiting and curiosity. We take pride in our fair, discursive reason and our capacity to judge and to know, but we have bought them at a price which is strangely excessive if it includes those passions without number which prey upon us.[45]

In the end, Montaigne laments on how little knowledge man has.

> Even if everything that has come down to us about the past by report were true and known to someone, that would be nothing compared with what we do not know. And against the idea of a universe which flows on while we are in it, how puny and stunted is the knowledge of the most inquisitive men.[46]

ON THE PSYCHOLOGY OF AESTHETICS

Emotions

Montaigne seemed to have accepted the Church's long tradition of minimizing the importance of the emotions in general and he offers many illustrations in support. An interesting example, runs,

> The natives of Brazil are said to die only of old age; they attribute that to the serenity and tranquility of the air. I would attribute it to the serenity and tranquility of their souls; they are not burdened with intense emotions and unpleasant tasks and thoughts: they pass their lives in striking simplicity and ignorance. They have no literature, no laws, no kings and no religion of any kind.
> Experience shows that gross, uncouth men make more desirable and vigorous sexual partners; lying with a mule-driver is often more welcome than lying with a gentleman. How can we explain

---

44 Ibid., II, xvii, 750.

45 Ibid., II, xii, 541.

46 Ibid., III, vi, 1028.

that except by assuming that emotions within the gentleman's soul undermine the strength of his body, break it down and exhaust it, just as they exhaust and harm the soul itself?[47]

No doubt reflecting, in part, his partiality to Church teachings, everywhere in his writings Montaigne attempts to leave the impression that he was very guarded in his emotions. A typical warning reads,

> With very little effort I stop the first movements of my emotions, giving up whatever begins to weigh on me before it bears me off. If you do not stop the start, you will never stop the race. If you cannot slam the door against your emotions you will never chase them out once they have got in.[48]

One of the principal reasons for the Church's long history of attacks on emotion was that it overpowers Reason. Montaigne mentions this first with respect to carnal pleasure, observing of Love that 'when its force is at its climax it overmasters us to such an extent that reason has no way to come into it.'[49] Interestingly enough for the modern reader, Montaigne places the adrenalin of hunting in the same category. He mentions that some men were so disturbed over their loss of Reason due to the emotions of love that they castrated themselves and that others applied compress of cold things such as snow on the offending member.[50] Regarding this conflict, he observes,

> It is a great thing to rein in our own appetites by reasoned argument or violently to compel our own members to keep to their duty: but to flog ourselves because of our concern for others, not merely ridding our own selves of that sweet passion which excites us and of the pleasure we feel when we find ourselves attractive to others and loved and courted by everyone, but to loathe and abhor our very qualities which provoke such things, damning our own beauty because it arouses somebody else: well, I do not find many examples of that.[51]

In this regard, Montaigne was particularly concerned with the emotion of anger.

> Why is it permissible for fathers and schoolmasters to punish and flog children in anger? ... While our pulse is beating and we can feel the emotion, let us put off the encounter: things will really and truly look different to us once we have cooled off a bit and quietened down. Until then passion is in command, passion does all the talking, not us.[52]

---

47   Ibid., II, xii, 547ff.
48   Ibid., III, x, 1150.
49   Ibid., II, xi, 481.
50   Ibid., II, xxxiii, 825.
51   Ibid., II, xxxiii, 830ff.
52   Ibid., II, xxxi, 810.

Later, he observes,

> Anger is a passion which delights in itself and fawns on itself. How often, if we are all worked up for some wrong reason and then offered some good defense or excuse, we are vexed against truth and innocence itself![53]

In another place, he suggests that it is excessive emotions which often lead to the downfall of philosophers.

> Philosophy has armed Man well against all the other ills which may befall him, teaching him either to bear them or else, if the cost of that is too high, to inflict certain defeat on them by escaping from all sensation. But such methods can only be of service to a vigorous soul in control of herself, a soul capable of reason and decision: they are of no use in a disaster such as this, where the soul of a philosopher becomes the soul of a madman, confused, lost and deranged. This can happen from several causes: by some excessive emotions which snatches the mind away; by some strong passion engendered by the soul herself ...[54]

In his essay, 'On Diversion,' Montaigne displays a very modern understanding that those who are sad must be allowed and encouraged to express their feelings.[55] Our ability to manage our emotions he finds to be supplied by Nature.

> God sends us cold according to our garment; he sends me emotions according to my means of sustaining them. Nature, having exposed me on one flank has covered in on the other.[56]

Two of Montaigne's contentions relative to the emotions are quite unusual. Philosophers had for a very long time observed that our emotions are communicated in large part by our face. In the course of a discussion on the importance of personal experience, Montaigne offers a rare contention that the face may not be an accurate form of emotional communication.

> I want to be enriched by me not by borrowings from others. Those outside us only see events and external appearances: anyone can put on a good outward show while inside he is full of fever and fright. They do not see my mind: they only see the looks on my face.[57]

---

[53] Ibid., II, xxxi, 813. In this same essay, Montaigne observes that his experience had been that in the case of big problems he could prepare himself against anger, but it was the little problems which caught him by surprise which produced the most dangerous anger.

[54] Ibid., II, xii, 620.

[55] Ibid., III, iv, 935. He criticizes here those who would hide their emotions, citing Polemon 'who did not even blench when a mad dog chewed off his calf!'

[56] Ibid., III, vi, 1019.

[57] Ibid., II, xvi, 710. In another place, however, he observes that in speaking, facial expressions and the voice 'lend value to things which in themselves are hardly worth more than chatter.' [Ibid., II, xvii, 726]

In another curious belief, Montaigne mistakenly believed that our separate body parts have their own emotions, uncontrolled by our mind. He points to facial expressions which give away thought we wish to keep secret, to our hands going where we do not tell them and our voices failing when *they* want to. His most amusing example is the penis, 'which thrusts itself forward so inopportunely when we do not want it to, and which so inopportunely lets us down when we most need it.' He recommends putting it on trial for rebelliousness.[58]

When it came to Love, where strong emotions are mixed with pleasure, Montaigne is particularly on his guard. He would have us believe he was successful in defending himself even against youthful love.

> We should not dash so madly after our emotions and selfish interests. When I was young I resisted the advances of love as soon as I realized that it was getting too much hold over me; I took care that it was not so delightful to me that it finally took me by storm and held me captive entirely at its mercy: on all the other occasions upon which my will seizes too avidly I do the same: I lean in the opposite direction when I see it leaping in and wallowing in its own wine; I avoid so far fueling the advance of its pleasure that I cannot retake it without loss and bloodshed.
>
> There are souls which, through insensitivity, see only half of anything; they enjoy the good fortune of being less bruised by harmful events.[59]

Montaigne shared the demeaning view of women which had long been voiced by the Church, as well as the Church's view of sex in marriage as a necessary evil. Consequently his view of Love places it below the noble love of true friendship among men. Love of women meant primarily passion, 'rash, fickle, fluctuating and variable; it is a feverish fire, subject to attacks and relapses … A mad craving for something which escapes us.'[60] Marriage is a bargain, fettered and constrained. Missing in marriage is friendship, because,

> women are in truth not normally capable of responding to such familiarity and mutual confidence as sustain that holy bond of friendship, nor do their souls seem firm enough to withstand the clasp of a knot so lasting and so tightly drawn.[61]

---

58 Ibid., I, xxi, 115.

59 Ibid., III, x, 1147.

60 Ibid., I, xxviii, 208ff.

61 Ibid., I, xxviii, 209ff. Montaigne found many objections to the institution of marriage, in particular that women failed to perform 'their matrimonial obligations' and that wives only prove their love after their husbands have died. [Ibid., II, xxxv, 842ff.] On the other hand, his essay, 'On Some Lines of Virgil,' which documents his wide knowledge of ancient texts on sex, is a brilliant argument for the equality of male and female in sexual practices. He concludes the discussion by observing,

> I say that male and female are cast in the same mold: save for education and custom the difference between them is not great.
> One is taken by the fact that so reasonable discussion was presented four centuries ago, yet we have made virtually no progress since the sixteenth century.

Reflecting on this subject as an older man, Montaigne crafts an ironic thought.

> In former days youth and pleasure never made me fail to recognize the face of vice within the sensuality: nor does the distaste which the years have brought me make me fail to recognize now the face of pleasure within the vice.[62]

Pleasure and Pain

Montaigne saw the search for and enjoyment of Pleasure as one of the fundamental drives of man, 'Even in virtue our ultimate aim—no matter what they say—is pleasure.'[63] We can once again see the Church's influence in his thinking, or at least his writing, when he suggests that only moderate pleasures can be fully appreciated, for the soul is overwhelmed by extreme pleasure.[64]

> Whether we are running our home or studying or hunting or following any other sport, we should go to the very boundaries of pleasure but take good care not to be involved beyond the point where it begins to be mingled with pain ... We must cling tooth and claw to the use of pleasures of this life which the advancing years, one after another, rip from our grasp.[65]

Pleasure, as he understood it, could only be associated with the lives of mortals on earth. He took curiously strong exception to those Christians who promised an after-life of Pleasure. This, he says, is what we should answer them on behalf of Reason:

> If the pleasures you offer me in the next life are related to ones I have experienced here on earth, that can have nothing to do with the Infinite. Even if my five natural senses were overwhelmed with joy; even if this soul of mine were seized of all the happiness she could ever hope for or desire, we know her limitations: that would amount to nothing. Where there remains anything of mine, there is nothing divine. If your promises merely relate to what can exist in our present condition, they cannot enter into the reckoning. All the pleasures of mortals are mortal ... We cannot condignly conceive those high, divine promises if we are able to conceive them at all. To imagine them condignly, we must imagine them unimaginable, unutterable, incomprehensible and entirely different from our own wretched experiences. 'Eyes cannot see,' says St Paul, 'nor can there rise up in the heart of man, what God has prepared for his own.'[66] And if we have to

---

62 Ibid., III, ii, 919.

63 Ibid., I, xx, 90.

64 Ibid., I, ii, 10. He points to several persons, including Leo X, who fell dead upon suddenly hearing joyous news, as well as the reason for occasional impotence in men.

65 Ibid., I, xxxix, 276.

66 I Corinthians II:9.

modify our being in order to render ourselves capable of celestial joy, that would mean a change so extreme and so total that (as we know from Physics) we could cease to be ourselves.[67]

Montaigne joined all early writers in commenting on the apparent close connection of Pleasure and Pain. He observes that 'the greatest of our pleasures has an air of groaning and lamentation.'[68]

> Pleasure and travail, so unlike in their natures, are yet fellows by some inexplicable natural relationship …
> Nature reveals this alloy to us; painters hold that the same wrinkling movements of our faces which serve to show weeping also show laughter. Indeed. Watch the picture in progress before either emotion has been finally delineated: you are in doubt towards which it is tending. And the extremes of laughter are mixed with tears.[69]
>
> ……
>
> The wise men teach us well to save ourselves from our treacherous appetites and to distinguish true wholesome pleasures from pleasures diluted and crisscrossed by pain. Most pleasures, tickle and embrace us only to throttle us, like those thieves whom the Egyptians call *Philistae*. If a hangover came before we got drunk we would see that we never drank to excess: but pleasure, to deceive us, walks in front and hides her train.[70]

Part of the explanation for the alternating effect on man of Pleasure and Pain he attributed to the various 'humors' of which he believed the body consists. A large part of our individuality lies in the strength and weakness of these humors, thus,

> although diverse emotions may shake them, there is one which must remain in possession of the field; nevertheless its victory is not so complete but that the weaker ones do not sometimes regain lost ground because of the pliancy and mutability of our soul and make a brief sally in their turn.[71]

This, for Montaigne, is sufficient explanation for the internal battle of emotions which he saw all around him.

> That is why we can see that not only children, who artlessly follow Nature, often weep and laugh at the same thing, but that not one of us either can boast that, no matter how much he may want to set out on a journey, he still does not feel his heart a-tremble when he says goodbye to family

---

67 Ibid., II, xii, 579. He also discusses here the idea of the after-life taking the form of another animal on earth, an idea which he attributes to Pythagoras, and for which he finds some credibility in the observation of the transformation of the butterfly. He also wonders what grounds the gods have for rewarding or punishing man after death, when they have created him.
68 Ibid., II, xx, 764ff.
69 Ibid., II, xx, 765.
70 Ibid., I, xxxix, 275.
71 Ibid., I, xxxviii, 263.

and friends ... And however noble the passion which inflames the heart of a well-born bride, she still has to have her arms pried from her mother's neck before being given to her husband.[72]

Another explanation he assumed must be found in Nature.

> Obstacles serve as a spur to that pleasure and as seasoning to its sweetness (on the grounds that in Nature contraries are enhanced by their contraries).[73]

He found this idea expressed in the Skeptic School of Philosophy, 'No reason but has it contrary.' He notes that we hold all the tighter that which we fear may be taken away from us and that the presence of cold helps fire burn brighter.[74] When he observes that we are equally troubled by desiring something and by possessing it, he is thinking of women. Here he finds many examples of the theory of contraries.

> Why do women now cover up those beauties—right down below their heels—which every woman wants to display and every man wants to see?

He concludes by observing that even the strongest of all pleasures only aims at the release of sensation and that if we want to eliminate pain, we must eliminate pleasure.

> Even that tickling excitement or that kind of shifting delight, active, inexplicably painful and sharp, which accompanies certain pleasures, eventually aims at a total freedom from sensation. The appetite which enraptures us when we lie with women merely aims at banishing the pain brought on by the frenzy of our inflamed desires; all it seeks is rest and repose, free from the fever of passion ...
> Truly, anyone who could uproot all knowledge of pain would equally eradicate all knowledge of pleasure and finally destroy Man: *That 'freedom from pain' has a high price: cruelty in the soul, insensate dullness in the body.* For Man, ill can be good at times; it is not always right to flee pain, not always right to chase after pleasure.[75]

Aside from the natures of Pleasure and Pain, it seemed clear to Montaigne that the real influence on man came more directly from how we perceive one or the other.

> There is an old Greek saying that men are tormented not by things themselves but by what they think about them. If that assertion could be proved to be always true everywhere it would be an important point gained for the comforting of our wretched human condition. For if ills can only enter us through our judgment it would seem to be in our power either to despise them or to deflect them towards the good: if the things actually do throw themselves on our mercy why do we not act as their masters and accommodate them to our advantage? If what we call evil or

---

72 Ibid.
73 Ibid., I, xx, 90.
74 Ibid., II, xv, 694ff.
75 Ibid., II, xii, 549ff.

torment are only evil or torment insofar as our mental apprehension endows them with those qualities then it lies within our power to change those qualities.[76]

In this same essay,[77] Montaigne gives the example of death which some call 'the dreadest of all dreadful things' while others look forward to as the only haven from life's torments. In another illustration of perspective, Montaigne quotes a line from an ancient Greek comedy [Philemon the Younger], 'No doctor derives any pleasure from the good health even of his friends.'[78]

Above all, Montaigne had no sympathy for those who dwell on pain.

> I loathe a morose and gloomy mind which glides over life's pleasures but holds on to its misfortunes and feeds on them—like flies which cannot get a hold on to anything highly polished and smooth and so cling to rough and rugged places and stay there.[79]

ON THE PHILOSOPHY OF AESTHETICS

Curiously, in all his essays Montaigne discusses Beauty only with respect to physical beauty.[80] He does this because he seemed to believe that the beautiful appearance of the face was a reflection of a special character, as if God rewards his special creations with Beauty. He claims, for example, that Aristotle 'says that the right to command belongs to the beautiful.' Perhaps he had this thought in mind when he observed,

> I am not at all sure whether I would not much rather have given birth to one perfectly formed son by commerce with the Muses than by commerce with my wife.[81]

Montaigne mentions Beauty again in a passage which we believe must represent one of his basic beliefs regarding the purpose of Art. In his essay in defense of Seneca and Plutarch, he makes an eloquent statement regarding how one can be lifted by the great minds of others. His discussion here, it seems to us, applies as well to Art in general and Music in particular.

---

76 Ibid., I, xiv, 52. In this regard he also quotes Cicero [*De finibus*, II, xx, 65–6]:
> Happiness is to be found not in gaiety, pleasure, laughing, nor in levity the comrade of jesting: those are happy, often in sadness, who are constant and steadfast.

77 'The taste of Good and evil Things Depends on our Opinion.'

78 Montaigne, *Essays*, I, xxii, 121.

79 Ibid., III, v, 953.

80 Ibid., III, xii, 1199ff. He correctly observes that the early Greek translation of the Bible uses 'beautiful' where the Latin translation uses 'good,' as for example in Matthew 13:48.

81 Ibid., II, viii, 451.

> It seems to each man that the master Form of Nature is in himself, as a touchstone by which he may compare all the other forms. Activities which do not take his form as their model are feigned and artificial. What brute-like stupidity! I consider some men, particularly among the Ancients, to be way above me and even though I clearly realize that I am powerless to follow them on my feet I do not give up following them with my eyes and judging the principles which raise them thus aloft, principles the seeds of which I can just perceive in myself, as I also can that ultimate baseness of minds which no longer amazes me and which I do not refuse to believe in either. I can clearly see the spiral by which those great souls wind themselves higher. I admire the greatness of those souls; those ecstasies which I find most beautiful I clasp unto me; though my powers do not reach as far, at least my judgment is most willingly applied to them.[82]

Such, apparently, is the power of our senses that even in the example of those who exhibit emotion professionally, they cannot avoid having their personal feelings stimulated.

> Is it right for the arts to serve our natural weakness and to let them profit from our inborn animal-stupidity? The orator (says Rhetoric) when acting out his case will be moved by the sound of his own voice and by his own feigned indignation; he will allow himself to be taken in by the emotions he is portraying. By acting out his part as in a play he will stamp on himself the essence of true grief and then transmit it to the judges (who are even less involved in the case than he is); it is like those mourners who are rented for funerals and who sell their tears and grief by weight and measure: for even though they only borrow their signs of grief, it is nevertheless certain that by habitually adopting the right countenance they often get carried away and find room inside themselves for real melancholy.[83]

In another place he writes of the other side of this coin, an observation which again seems to us particularly valid with respect to the exposure to inferior music.

> Just as our mind is strengthened by contact with vigorous and well-ordered minds, so too it is impossible to overstate how much it loses and deteriorates by the continuous commerce and contact we have with mean and ailing ones. No infection is as contagious as that is.[84]

Montaigne, always critical of abstract, academic education also raises the very interesting question why it is so difficult to *talk* about the really important things in Art.

> Take an arts don; converse with him. Why is he incapable of making us feel the excellence of his arts?[85]

The answer, of course, is in large part why we have Art—because you cannot *talk* about what we *feel* very well.

---

82 Ibid., II, xxxii, 822.
83 Ibid., III, iv, 944.
84 Ibid., III, viii, 1045.
85 Ibid., III, viii, 1050.

While always suspicious of 'knowledge,' Montaigne was able to see that there is something real about talent.

> A learned man is not learned in all fields: but a talented man *is* talented in all fields, even in ignorance.[86]

Since talent is by nature a personal attribute, does it follow that the artist creates only for himself? Perhaps, says Montaigne,

> Remember the man who was asked why he toiled so hard at an art which few could ever know about:
> 'For me a few are enough; one is enough; having none is enough.'[87]

Nevertheless, in another place he seems to suggest that comunication is the purpose of Art, quoting Cicero, 'No art is concerned with itself.'[88]

Another aesthetic principle which seemed important to Montaigne was that the value of an art work cannot be considered apart from its material substance.

> A craftsman gives sure proof of his stupidity when he has some rich substance in his hands and prepares it and mixes it contrary to the rules of his art ... and we are more offended by defects in a statue made of gold than in one made of plaster.[89]

As Montaigne discusses Art so little in his writings, it is no surprise that he says little of the most debated subject, whether Art should imitate Nature. In one place, however, he makes it clear that his position would have been that Art cannot imitate Nature.

> No art can achieve likeness. Neither Perrozet nor anyone else can so carefully blanch and polish the backs of his playing cards without at least some players being able to tell them apart simply by watching them pass through another player's hands. Likeness does not make things 'one' as much as unlikeness makes them 'other.' Nature has bound herself to make nothing 'other' which is not unlike.[90]

Perhaps the most interesting, and most unexpected, commentary on aesthetics in Art is found in Montaigne's views on the participation of Chance.

> I maintain that not only in medicine but in many of the surer arts Fortune plays a major part. Take those creative ecstasies which transport a poet and carry him outside himself in rapture,

---

86 Ibid., III, ii, 909.

87 Ibid., I, xxxix, 277.

88 Ibid., III, vi, 1022. The Cicero quotation is from *De finibus*, V, vi, 16.

89 Ibid., II, xvii, 749.

90 Ibid., III, xiii, 1208.

why do we not attribute them to good luck, since he himself confesses that they surpass his own strength and capacities, acknowledging that they come from without, being in no wise within his own power—no more than in the case of those adept at oratory, who claim that in their art, too, there are stirrings and perturbations, outside the natural order, which impel them well beyond what they had planned. The same applies to painting, which sometimes escapes free from the brush-strokes of the painter's hand, surpassing his own conceptions and artistry and bringing him to an ecstasy of astonishment which leaves him thunderstruck. Why, Fortune herself reveals to us even more clearly the part she plays in all such works as these by the evidence of that grace and beauty which are found in them not only without the artist's intention but without his knowledge. A competent reader can often find in another man's writings perfections other than those which the author knows that he put there, and can endow them with richer senses and meanings …

[As for military exploits] I think that the leaders engage in deliberation and reflection merely as a pure formality, surrendering the best part of their undertaking to Fortune, and, trusting in her aid, constantly going way beyond any bounds of rational decision. In the midst of their deliberations there comes upon them Fortune's joyful rapture and, from beyond them, inspired frenzies which as often as not push them towards the least likely of decisions and swell their hearts above the reach of reason.[91]

In another essay, in which he discusses his writing process, he implies that what he means by 'chance' is in part a reference to divine intervention or help.

My thought sketches out the matter for a while and dwells lightly on the first aspects of it: then I usually leave the principal thrust of the task to heaven …

I will go on to say that our very wisdom and mature reflections are for the most part led by chance. My will and my reasoning are stirred this way and that. And many of their movements govern themselves without me. My reason is daily subject to incitements and agitations which are due to chance.[92]

It is this non-rational aspect of an artist or writer's work which Montaigne felt made the work itself so difficult for others to judge.

For I normally find that men are as wrong in judging their own work as other people's, not simply because their emotions are involved but because they lack the ability to understand it and to analyze it. The work itself, by its own momentum and fortune, can favor the author beyond his own understanding and research; it can run ahead of him.[93]

---

91   Ibid., I, xxiv, 143ff. In another place [I, xxxiv, 248] he gives as an example of the role of Fortune in art in the case of a painter who, unable to achieve a certain effect, threw a paint-impregnated sponge at the canvas resulting in that which he could not consciously achieve. He was also intrigued by the fact that if one walks without thinking of the stride, one tends to make equal strides. But, if one tries to make equal strides he finds that 'he will never achieve so exactly by design what he had done naturally and by chance.' [Ibid., II, xvii, 739]

92   Ibid., III, viii, 1058.

93   Ibid., III, viiii, 1064.

On Poetry

The popular conception was that almost everyone was a poet, but Montaigne points out that these are only creators of rhyme. Real poets are recognized by rich description and 'delicate invention.'[94] He mentions this again in another essay, where he now continues in his most effective attempt to discuss aesthetics in poetry. He concludes with Plato's famous analogy of the magnet to explain the impact on the audience.

> Here is something of a marvel: we now have far more poets than judges and connoisseurs of poetry. It is far easier to write poetry than to appreciate it. At a rather low level you can judge it by the rules of art: but good, enrapturing, divine poetry is above reason and rules. Whoever can distinguish its beauties with a firm and settled gaze does not in fact see it all, no more than we can see the brilliance of a flash of lightning. It does not exercise our judgment, it ravishes it and enraptures it; the frenzy which sets its goads in him who knows how to discern it also strikes a third person who hears him relate and recite it, just as a magnet not only attracts a needle but also pours into it the faculty of attracting others. It can more easily be seen in the theater that the sacred inspiration of the Muses, having first seized the poet with anger, grief or hatred and driven him outside himself wither they will, then affects the actor through the poet and then, in succession, the entire audience.[95]

He mentions 'frenzy' again as a hallmark of great poetry.

> There are hundreds of poets who drag and droop prosaically, but the best of ancient [poetry] … sparkles throughout with poetic power and daring, and presents the characteristics of its frenzy …
> Scholars say that the ancient theology was poetry, as also the first philosophy. Poetry is the original language of the gods.[96]

Montaigne believed the discipline and restraints required in poetry resulted in greater emphasis in the communication of ideas. He wrote that it was 'just as the voice of the trumpet rings out clearer and stronger for being forced through a narrow tube.'[97] It was here that he found his own failings as a poet.

> My insight is clear and balanced but when I put it to work it becomes confused: I have most clearly found that in the case of poetry. I have a boundless love of it; I know my way well through

---

94 Ibid., I, xxvi, 192.
95 Ibid., I, xxxvii, 260.
96 Ibid., III, ix, 1125ff.
97 Ibid., I, xxvi, 164.

other men's works,[98] but when I set my own hand to it I am truly like a child: I find myself unbearable. You may play the fool anywhere else but not in poetry.[99]

For the talented poets, he was more forgiving.

> It is only appropriate for great poets freely to break the rules of poetry.[100]

A curious comment regarding poetry surfaces when Montaigne discusses women, toward whom he was nearly always demeaning.

> Should it nevertheless irk them to lag behind us in anything whatsoever, should they want a share in our books out of curiosity: then poetry is a pastime rightly suited to their needs: it is a frivolous, subtle art, all disguise and chatter and pleasure and show, like they are.[101]

Perhaps this explains, in part, one of his most frequently quoted observations,

> Poetry is never more gay than when treating a subject unruly and wanton.[102]

On Prose

Montaigne seems to have found the first aesthetic purpose of literature in general to be delight. Boccaccio and Rabelais quickly come to mind, but he tells us he is too old for Ovid, 'let alone Ariosto.'[103] In Terence he finds delight in the Latin language, as well as his depiction of the 'emotions of the soul.'

Montaigne placed on an even higher level literature which not only delights but educates.[104] In this regard he particularly appreciated Plutarch and Seneca. It was for this reason as well that Montaigne so appreciated reading the historians, again especially Plutarch. The best historians,

---

98 Montaigne believed the French poets of his day,

> have raised poetry as high as it ever will be and that in those qualities in which Ronsard and Du Bellay excel I find them close to the perfection of the Ancients. [Ibid., II, xvii, 751]

99 Ibid., II, xvii, 722.

100 Ibid., I, xxvi, 173.

101 Ibid., III, iii, 927.

102 Ibid., I, xxix, 221.

103 Ibid., II, x, 460ff.

104 Ibid., 463.

are those who write men's lives, since they linger more over motives than events, over what comes from inside more than what happens outside.¹⁰⁵

The most outstanding historians are those capable of 'choosing what is worth knowing.' He names Froissart as representative of the lesser historians, who merely report with diligence everything which comes to their attention.

Regarding the characteristics of important literature, Montaigne believed the fine writer achieves his effect through noble aims, not through 'display' or 'fantastic hyperbole,' etc.

> It is the same with our dancing: those men of low estate who teach it are unable to copy the deportment and propriety of our nobility and so try to gain favor by their daring footwork and other strange acrobatics.

In particular, Montaigne appreciated brevity and was bored and angered by authors who take too long to get to the point. One he criticized in this regard was Cicero.

> I want authors to begin with their conclusion: I know well enough what is meant by death or voluptuousness: let them not waste time dissecting them; from the outset I am looking for good solid reasons which teach me how to sustain their attacks. Neither grammatical subtleties nor ingenuity in weaving words or arguments help me in that. I want arguments which drive home their first attack right into the strongest point of doubt: Cicero's hover about the pot and languish.¹⁰⁶

Montaigne shared with many of the Renaissance educated class a disdain of the general public.

> Let us leave aside the ordinary people, they have no self-awareness; they never judge themselves and let most of their natural faculties stand idle.¹⁰⁷

He was also distrustful of the views of the public because the public no longer represents individual views. He observed, 'it is not enough to withdraw from the mob ... we have to withdraw from such attributes of the mob as are within us.'¹⁰⁸ In another place he reflects on the danger to the artist when his concern is the public.

> Whether it is art or nature which stamps on us that characteristic of living by what others say, it does us much more harm than good. We cheat ourselves of what is rightly useful to us in order

---

105 Ibid., 467.

106 Ibid., II, x, 464. He apologizes that he finds even Plato 'drags slowly.' He also takes the opportunity here to criticize the poetry of Cicero:

> It is no great crime to write bad verses but it was an error of judgment on his part not to have known how unworthy they were of the glory of his name.

107 Ibid., II, xii, 559.

108 Ibid., I, xxxix, 268ff.

to conform our appearances to the common opinion. We are not so much concerned with what the actual nature of our being is within us, as with how it is perceived by the public.[109]

ON THE AESTHETICS OF MUSIC

For a man who discussed such a broad range of topics, it is curious that he never treated music as a separate topic. Nearly all of his references to music are illustrations of some other idea. Nevertheless, we can gain from these some basic concepts regarding his aesthetic views of music.

In the course of his discussion of the senses, their relationship to Reason and whether there are additional senses of which we are unaware, Montaigne mentions several examples involving music. It seems safe to suggest that the nature of how we hear music appeared to Montaigne to be beyond the normal rational explanations. He points out how hearing can deceive us, as when 'a trumpet sounds a league behind us, but an echo in a valley may make it seem to come from in front.'[110]

His references to how the senses may deceive us, or to his belief that we may lack some senses, may have contributed to his mention of an idea which had long been abandoned by most philosophers—the Music of the Spheres.

> ... that those solid material circles rub and lightly play against each other and so cannot fail to produce a wondrous harmony (by the modulations and mutations of which are conducted the revolutions and variations of the dance of the stars) yet none of the creatures in the whole Universe can hear it, loud though it is, since our sense of hearing has been dulled by the continuity of the sound.[111]

This is comparable, he says, to how blacksmiths become able to tolerate the noise of their shops. He was also intrigued by the affect of music on the listener.

> No heart is so flabby that the sounds of our drums and trumpets do not set it ablaze, nor so hard that sweet music does not tickle it and enliven it; no soul is so sour that it does not feel touched by some feeling of reverence when it contemplates the somber vastness of our Churches, the great variety of their decorations and our ordered liturgy, or when it hears the enchantment of

---

109 Ibid., III, ix, 1081.

110 Ibid., II, xii, 669ff. Another example he gives is that even though we know the lady has false hair, false facial coloring, etc., we find her beautiful.

111 Ibid., I, xxiii, 123.

> the organ and the poised religious harmony of men's voices. Even those who come to scoff are brought to distrust their opinion by a shiver in their heart and a sense of dread.[112]

He adds, unfortunately without elaboration, that he knows some doctors who maintain that people with certain complexions can be driven mad by certain sounds or instruments.

Montaigne evidently considered music as an acquired skill and did not recognize a level of universality which enabled it to be understood by non-musicians. He mentions this in a discussion of the futility of men trying to understand the divine, where he quotes Plutarch as saying this makes no more sense than 'a man who knows nothing whatever about music to start criticizing singers.'[113] On the other hand, in another place he seems to argue for the universality of folk music.

> Popular and purely natural poetry has its naïf charms and graces by which it can stand comparison with that chief of beauties we find in artistically perfect poetry. That can be seen from our Gascony *villanelles* and from those songs which have been reported from nations which have no knowledge of any science nor even of writing.[114]

Having said that, he did not believe the ability to perform was something handed down genetically. Evidence suggests that from ancient times through the Baroque, music specialization, as well as in many other crafts, was passed down from father to son. Montaigne specifically objects to this tradition.

> It really should not be done as it was for the office-holders of the kings of Sparta—trumpeters, minstrels and cooks—who were succeeded in their charges by their sons, no matter how ignorant they might be, taking precedence over men best skilled at the craft.[115]

During Montaigne's discussion of his objections to the fact that professors are learned but not wise, he adds the additional observation that they can recognize bad qualities in literature but not in themselves. Here he adds a suggestion found from time to time in earlier literature that the quality of a musical performer cannot be separated from his quality as a person.

> Dionysius used to laugh ... at musicians whose flutes were harmonious but not their morals.[116]

---

112 Ibid., II, xii, 670. He mentions this subject again in another essay when he speaks of a soldier who, the day before the battle, displays little interest and states that he is merely serving his prince, but at the sound of drums is flushed with emotion. [Ibid., III, iv, 945]

113 Ibid., II, xii, 582.

114 Ibid., I, liv, 350.

115 Ibid., III, v, 960.

116 Ibid., I, xxv, 156. Interestingly enough, Montaigne exempts preachers from this standard. Observing that the personal sins of preachers was 'shaking the truth taught in our Church,' he suggests that 'we must consider the preaching and the preacher apart.' Writers, on the other hand, were held to the same standard as musicians: 'I never read an author ... without curiously inquiring what sort of man he was.' [Ibid., II, xxxi, 811ff]

Montaigne understood music education to be a matter of direct experience in performance, not in conceptional theory.

> Take Palvel and Pompeo, those excellent dancing masters when I was young: I would like to have seen them teaching us our steps just by watching them without budging from our seats, like those teachers who seek to give instruction to our understanding without making it dance—or to have seen other teach us how to manage a horse, a pike or a lute, or to sing without practice.[117]

Finally, we should mention some of the observations which Montaigne offers relative to music and animals, in case some reader is inclined to ponder Darwinian relationships. Leaving aside his quotation from Flavius Arrianus regarding an elephant which was said to simultaneously dance and play cymbals,[118] we find the following quite interesting.

> Even nightingales born free do not all sing one and the same song: each one sings according to its capacity to learn. They make jealous classmates, squabbling and vying with each other so heartily that the vanquished sometimes drops down dead, not from lack of song but lack of breath. The youngest birds ruminate thoughtfully and then begin to imitate snatches of song; the pupils listen to the lessons of their tutors and then give an account of themselves, taking it in turns to stop their singing. You can hear their faults being corrected; some of the criticism of their tutors are perceptible even to us …
>
> But strange indeed is the account of a female magpie vouched for by Plutarch, no less. It lived in a barber's shop in Rome and was wonderfully clever at imitating any sounds it heard. It happened one day that some musicians stopped quite a while in front of the shop, blasting away on their trumpets. Immediately the magpie fell pensive, mute and melancholic, remaining so all the following day. Everyone marveled, thinking that the blare of the trumpets had frightened and confused it, making it lose both hearing and song at the same time. But they eventually found that it had been deeply meditating and had withdrawn into itself; it had been inwardly practicing, preparing its voice to imitate the noise of those trumpeters. The first sound it did make was a perfect imitation of their changes, repetitions and stops; after this new apprenticeship it quit with disdain all that it was able to do before.[119]

---

117 Ibid., I, xxvi, 171.

118 Not to mention his discussion of the affinity of the tunny-fish for astrology, geometry and arithmetic! [Ibid., II, xii, 534]

119 Ibid., II, xii, 519ff.

FUNCTIONAL MUSIC

Montaigne finds the origin of Church music in the attempts by the ancients to create gods like men: therefore they must like music.[120] He mentions Church music again in a list of things which become boring by repetition, observing, 'nothing cloys and impedes like abundance':

> Do we believe that choirboys greatly enjoy the music or rather that, being glutted with it, they find it boring? Feasting and dancing, masquerades and tournaments give delight to those who do not often see them and who were yearning to see them; but for a man who attends them regularly they become tasteless and disagreeable.[121]

In Montaigne's travel diary we find some mention of Church music, but with few details. There is his praise of the organ in Trent, Italy—but praise of its appearance, not its sound,[122] and choirs of singers in procession in Rome.[123] The latter, the 'most magnificent thing I have seen anywhere' is not described with respect to the music itself.

The most detailed description of actual music is with regard to a Mass he heard in Lucca.

> In Lucca they take great delight in music, and they all join in the singing. It is apparent, however, that they have very few good voices. This Mass was sung with all possible effort, and yet it was not much.[124]

His comment nevertheless suggests he had an ear for music.

ENTERTAINMENT MUSIC

Montaigne does not think highly of entertainment in general. Even in common forms of entertainment he seemed to be more concerned with the ill effects on the rational man.

> Consider how even in vain and trivial pursuits such as chess or tennis matches, the keen and burning involvement of a rash desire at once throws your mind into a lack of discernment and your limbs into confusion: you daze yourself and tangle yourself up … The less passionate he is about the game, the more surely and successfully he plays it.[125]

---

120 Ibid., II, xii, 582.

121 Ibid., I, xlii, 295.

122 Donald Frame, *Montaigne's Travel Journal*, (San Francisco: North Point Press, 1983), 49.

123 Ibid., 95.

124 Ibid., 158.

125 Montaigne, *Essays*, III, x, 1140.

Consequently, Montaigne had little regard for any kind of large-scale public entertainment, such as civic festivals. He quotes Aristotle in this regard, although this observation is not found today in this philosopher's extant works.

> Such pleasures says Aristotle, have an effect only on the lowest of the low; they immediately vanish from their memory as soon as they have had enough of them; no serious man of judgment can hold them in esteem.[126]

In addition he objected to the waste represented by the spectators spending their money on such events.

Even in the case of banquet music, the most frequently mentioned form of entertainment music in early literature, Montaigne argues that music takes our attention away from the enjoyment of eating. There is, he says, a 'jealousy and rivalry among our pleasures: they clash and get in each other's way.'[127] He supports his argument by mentioning that Alcibiades banished music from his table so that it should not interfere with the conversation,

> justifying this with the reason which Plato[128] ascribes to him, that it is the practice of commonplace men to invite musicians and singers to their feasts since they lack that good talk and those pleasant discussions with which intelligent men understand how to delight each other.

In the diary of his travels across France in 1580, it is a disappointment to find that Montaigne almost never mentions the music which he must have heard at every stop. Only a few forms of entertainment music caught his ear, such as folksongs[129] in France and his observations on watching the dancing of the allemande[130] in Germany. He teases us by mentioning that he missed hearing a mechanical 'water music' device in Florence as he arrived there too late in the day.[131]

---

126 Ibid., III, vi, 1021.
127 Ibid., III, xiii, 1255.
128 *Protagoras*, 347.
129 Frame, *Montaigne's Travel Journal*, 6.
130 Ibid., 36.
131 Ibid., 68.

13 SIXTEENTH-CENTURY SPAIN

THE DEVELOPMENT OF SIXTEENTH-CENTURY MUSIC IN SPAIN was influenced in some degree by Italy, through the Spanish singers who participated in the Papal Choir[1] and returned, and by France through the intermarriage of the aristocracy. As a result, Spain is represented by those who reflect the conservatism caused by its geographical isolation and those who were introduced to more liberal ideas in other countries.

This mixture was evident at the important Spanish university at Salamanca. Known for its humanistic tendencies, it was in some ways very liberal. The statutes of 1538, for example, allow teaching of music in Spanish, rather than Latin, and specifies equal emphasis on speculative and practical music.[2] There seems to have been a close association between the music and medical faculties and students elected candidates to fill vacant chairs in music.

On the other hand, some of the sixteenth-century music treatises, such as one by Pedro Ciruelo, the most important mathematician of the century, remain in the old medieval tradition of consigning music to a branch of mathematics. The most dogmatic of these old style philosophers was Juan Espinosa, who in one treatise attacked a colleague for basing his conclusions on music on the basis of judgments of the ear!derhalb[3]

ON THE PHYSIOLOGY OF AESTHETICS

The most enlightened of sixteenth-century Spanish philosophers was Juan Vives (1492–1540). His experience as a student at the University of Paris turned him against Scholasticism and his attacks on this old Church view of philosophy brought him to the attention of Erasmus and Henry VIII, who invited him to England.

In his *Introduction to Wisdom*, an early treatise on education, Vives removes Wisdom from the mysteries of Scholasticism and presents a very factual definition, the ability 'to judge a thing correctly and to identify it for what it actually is.'[4] Those most likely to judge things

---

1 Among them, Antonio de Ribera, Morales and Bartolomé Escobedo, in addition to others who worked in Rome, such as Victoria and Bartolomé del Rey.
2 Nan Cooke Carpenter, *Music in the Medieval and Renaissance Universities* (Norman: University of Oklahoma Press, 1958), 210ff. Carpenter documents many examples of 'practical' music performed by the students.
3 Ibid., 219.
4 Juan Vives, *Introductio ad Sapientiam,* in *Introduction to Wisdom,* ed. Marian Tobriner (New York: Teachers College Press, 1968), 85ff.

incorrectly are those who are uneducated, thus he was particularly suspicious of anything 'a multitude approves with consensus.'

> There is nothing we ought more to strive for than to lift the student of wisdom above the emotions of the common crowd.

He was thinking of the 'common crowd' again when he bemoaned the quality of recreation.

> Regarding the recreation of the mind, consider what little time has been given for that in man's life, and that it ought not to be squandered in games, in revels, in childishness, or in trifles.[5]

Even guests invited to dinner should be chosen for the quality they bring to this form of recreation.

> Do not admit to the honor of your table such as are scoffers, parasites, evil babblers, buffoons, drunkards, filthy and shameless hangers-on, gluttons, and such other types, ready either by their words or deeds to arouse lewd laughter. Those cannot refresh you at your repast.[6]

He was one of few early philosophers who recognized the importance of early childhood in education, observing 'The rest of our life depends on our rearing in childhood.'[7] He was also a brilliant early psychologist, identifying as part of the mind characteristics which had rarely been associated with it in this way.

> Beauty is seen in those lineaments of the body which declare an inner splendor ... Pleasure—a pure, total, and continual delectation—arises only in those things which appertain to the mind.[8]

And he warns again, don't discuss such matters with the 'emotional mob.'

In this early treatise he also begins to formulate his ideas on education. Education is achieved through intelligence, memory and study.[9] Intelligence is refined by experience and practice; memory is enlarged by exercise. Of all our senses, he found hearing the most valuable for education.

He believed in some genetic knowledge, 'divine knowledge handed down from God.' As a good Catholic, he points out that it is unnecessary to study the works of 'philosophers contrary to our Religion.' And it was as a good Catholic that he concludes,

---

5   Ibid., 99.

6   Ibid., 105.

7   Ibid., 86.

8   Ibid., 88. He strongly disapproved of sexual gratification, however, as being low and bestial, bringing ignominy and shame and never coming without bitterness.

9   Ibid., 101ff.

> The highest subject in the liberal arts and learning is that moral philosophy which brings a remedy for the deadly diseases of the soul.[10]

In 1531 Vives published a more extended book on education, his *de Tradendis Disciplinis*, a work which he begins by observing that he finds 'nothing in life more beautiful or more excellent than the cultivation of the mind through what we call branches of learning.'[11] This work is clearly the most important philosophical work on education of its time and it is limited only by the fact that Vives remained a dedicated Catholic, which also explains his purpose.

> I have sought to free the sciences from impious doubts, and to bring them out of their heathen darkness into the light of our faith.[12]

Vives first recommends that the school should be located where fresh air is available, although not in so pleasant a place that the students are tempted to 'venture forth,' unless for the purpose of 'delightful studies, such as poetry, music, and history.'[13] Similarly, the school must not be located near workshops which produce loud noises, such as those of smiths and stone-cutters. Neither should it be situated too close to merchant areas, 'where idle people are accustomed to stroll about for pleasure,' nor near the borders where there might be battle.

Teachers must be selected for their good moral character and practical wisdom. The teacher should have a fatherly attitude toward his students and never be concerned about how much pay he will receive.

> Two faults are to be driven very far off from all learning and from learned men—avarice and ambition. These both spoil the arts, and bring literary men and letters into contempt.[14]

The teacher should be pleasant and demonstrate an upright life. It is incredible, Vives observes, 'what great influence the affections of the master and pupil exercise upon both good teaching and good learning.' Among the teachers with whom he was familiar, it is clear that Vives found grammar teachers to be the most likely to be drawn into ineffective educational methods.

> When grammar teachers spend their time in trifling amongst the boys who drag them into ineptitude and puerilities as if by contagion, they lose all seriousness and moderation. They are compelled to attend to the faults of the boys, which are innumerable, and repeated over and over again ..., so that they are almost driven to anger and ferocity; and, thrust down in that pounding-mill, as it were, the common sense of teachers becomes greatly diminished. Hence in their life and habits there exist moroseness and unpleasantness of manners ... Since nobody in

---

10 Ibid., 110.
11 Foster Watson, *Vives: On Education* (Cambridge: University Press, 1913), Preface.
12 Ibid.
13 Ibid., II, i.
14 Ibid.

the school contradicts the teacher, he puts on supercilious airs and arrogance, and particularly books no opposition, and perseveres pertinaciously in what he says lest he should lose any of his authority by giving way.[15]

In contrast to modern education practice, Vives discourages the spirit of competition, which he says leads to 'quarrels, wrangling and dissensions.'[16] He is also opposed to expecting all students to be given the same amount of time or to learn at the same speed. In this regard, he discusses at length the varying capacities of minds in students.[17] Some grasp things clearly, others do not. Some are 'exceedingly clever' in work done with the hands, others are 'devoted to the more sublime matters of judgment and reason.' He finds very few good at both.

Vives states that it is the teacher's job to sort out those capable of schooling, but here he is somewhat mystified. Why are there fewer minds capable of success in intellectual studies than in the crafts?

> Let the teacher see who are fit for learning; who are not. There are some minds which are stupid, very dull, rough and distorted. It is wonderful and pitiable to relate, that human minds produce good fruit more easily in the commoner and more worthless, than in the more liberal and distinguished arts. For in trade, in the practice of artificers, in weaving, finally in the manual and mechanical arts, we see fewer persons spending their labor in vain than in the pursuit of learning. What shall we say are the causes of this? Is it because in humbler pursuits the mind is not so greatly molested by the passions, whilst they join battle with it when it attempts the greater and more noble pursuits? Or is it because the mind is less strained in light and easy pursuits than in profound and lofty matters, so that in the former it seems to roll down a slope, and in the latter to have to climb up steep places?[18]

Consequently, Vives observes that the parent should not expect that every child is equally suitable for schooling. He is particularly sensitive toward the tendency of parents to assign their least capable child to a religious career.

> Some parents (and there is nothing more ridiculous) send to school those boys who are unfit for commerce or war, or other civil duties, and order them to be taught; and, what is a most impious deed, they devote to God the most contemptible and useless of their offspring, and think that he who has not judgment and intellect for the smallest and most trifling matters has quite enough for such great duties. When the boy is destined for study, as the father ought to conceive the highest hopes for his son, so should the teacher of his pupil. But there will be a difference, because a father's love is generally dim-sighted and even blind, while it is fitting that the kindness of the teacher should be combined with the keenest eyes.[19]

---

15 Ibid., III, ii.
16 Ibid., II, i.
17 Ibid., II, iii.
18 Ibid., II, iv.
19 Ibid., II, iv.

As for the student, he must listen intently and 'fix his look' on the teacher at all times, except when it is necessary to write or read. He must understand that everything which falls from the teacher's lips is 'as valuable as precious stones.'[20] Vives places much importance on the development of memory and offers two specific suggestions. Studying just before sleeping produces more effective memorization, as does writing down on paper that which is to be memorized.

As for the teaching process itself, we can see the long tradition of education in favoring the left hemisphere of the brain already firmly in place in Vives, when he singles out arithmetic as the chief means of distinguishing the best mind.

> Nothing displays the sharpness of the mind so much as a ready method of reckoning, and slowness of mind is proved by slowness in reckoning, as we have seen in the case of the feeble-minded.[21]

When Vives writes 'virtuous opinions must be instilled into the empty breast,' he is reflecting another ancient educational tradition still with us, the concept of the child as an 'empty slate' which the teacher fills.

It is interesting that Vives argues for the importance of developing a 'universal language of all nations,' as a means of facilitating education.[22] 'Such a language as the universal one should be sweet, learned and eloquent.' Vives' recommendation was Latin![23]

The teacher must not expect unreasonable progress and certainly must not get angry if the student cannot do what the teacher can.

> Although there is nothing more senseless, yet there are teachers who demand such tasks from little boys with cruel threats, blows and stripes. Such teachers themselves are more worthy of being beaten. Let the teacher observe moderation in his censure lest he should let anything slip himself, or lest he should arouse the fierceness of his pupils; do not let him crush their spirits by the harshness of his words, or confuse them by his severity.[24]

After making that humane plea, Vives suddenly admits that sometimes rather severe punishment is necessary. It is interesting that he introduces this circumstance by recalling the old Church dogma of Reason over the passions.

---

20 Ibid., III, iii.

21 Ibid., II, iv.

22 Ibid., III, i. He quotes St. Augustine as having said that he would prefer to converse with his dog than with a man of an unknown tongue.

23 Voltaire once observed that when such a universal language were created, it would be the one closest to Music. There was much interest in this subject in the nineteenth century, and Sudre actually created such a universal musical language.

24 *On Education*, III, iv.

> Since the mind of man is misled by passions, every thoughtless action must be checked and restrained by reproof and blame expressed in words, and if necessary in blows; so that as with animals pain may recall boys to the right, when reason is not strong enough. For all that, I should prefer this beating to be done as amongst free men, not harshly or as amongst slaves, unless the boy is of such disposition that he has to be incited to his duty by blows, like a slave ... If the boy will not comply with threats let the master beat him, but in such a way that while his still tender body suffers a sharp pain, it does not endure a permanent injury.[25]

After that, would the student believe him, as he suddenly changes his mood again, and writes,

> The teacher must also point out what delight there is in learning, what deep, lasting and permanent pleasure, to which nothing else can be at all compared.

Among the subjects taught in school, Vives is particularly concerned about poetry. He was clearly thinking of the long tradition of sung poetry, for of the poets, he says, 'the characteristic of their art is music.'

> From [poetry] the mind draws great refreshment on account of its harmony and character. But because of the subjects which the early poets have chosen to put into song, poetry is suspected by many of corrupting the morals and is openly hated by certain people.[26]

The words of this sung poetry he wants to be 'lofty, sublime, brilliant ... displaying human passions in a wonderful and vivid manner.'

> There breathes in them a certain great and lofty spirit so that the readers are themselves caught into it, and seem to rise above their own intellect, and even above their own nature.[27]

But, as he has said, there are dangers in poetry, and he is thinking of the love poetry of the ancient Greek lyric poets. Since he cannot bring himself to recommend the complete exclusion of such masters as Ovid and Catullus, the answer is to edit and he hopes, on behalf of education, that someone will publish these works in this form.

> Obscene passages should be wholly cut out from the text, as though they were dead, and would infect whatever they touched ... Whoever will undertake this expurgation will do a great service not only to his contemporaries and to posterity, but also to poetry itself and to poets. This would be, as in a garden; a gardener only leaves the healthy herbs, and weeds out all the poisonous plants. In this way poetry will be kept from ignominy and the readers from an evil poison.[28]

---

25 Ibid.
26 Ibid., III, v.
27 Ibid.
28 Ibid.

After all, he concludes, we must not ignore the fact, that

> poetry is to be relegated 'to the leisure hours of life.' It is not to be consumed as if it were nourishment, but is to be treated as a spice.[29]

He also encourages teachers to heavily edit the dramatic poetry of Terence and Plautus.

> I should like to see cut out of both these writers all those parts which could taint the minds of boys with vices, to which our natures approach by the encouragement, as it were, of a nod.[30]

Vives is also very concerned about the teaching of science in school, for fear it will present answers which are contrary to Scripture. For this reason he is even hesitant about the inclusion of 'heathen' writers such as Aristotle.

> We must not examine nature by the poor and bad light of heathen knowledge but by the brilliant torch, which Christ brought into the darkness of the world.[31]

Vives emphasizes the importance of play in yonger students, for this 'reveals the sharpness and their characters.'[32] For older students, more vigorous exercise is needed, such as playing ball and running—all conducted in Latin! Vives, in this regard, makes an important observation.

> The human mind is wonderfully inclined to freedom.. It allows itself to be set to work, but it will not suffer itself to be compelled. We may easily gain much by asking, but very little by extortion.[33]

In conclusion, Vives apparently felt the need to remark that man should not be ashamed to learn from another man. After all, he notes, the 'whole human race is not ashamed to learn many things from beasts.'[34] He ends his study of education by venturing to hope that 'having acquired our knowledge, we must turn it to usefulness, and employ it for the common good.'

In contrast to Vives, in St. John of the Cross we come to an old-style Church philosopher so severe the he seems to us to belong in the darkest of the Dark Ages. He begins his major treatise, 'The Ascent of Mount Carmel,' by declaring that in his writings he will not rely on his own experience or on science, 'for these can deceive us.' All answers will come from the

---

29 Ibid., III, vi.

30 Ibid.

31 Ibid., IV, ii.

32 Ibid., II, iv.

33 Ibid. He particularly recommends vigorous exercise for students studying philosophy!

34 Ibid., Appendix, i.

Scriptures.³⁵ This treatise, as all of his works, is intended to help the Christian prepare for 'union with God.' We are particularly interested in his discussion of the senses.

Even though most of the earlier Church philosophers, and even this St. John, admitted that human knowledge begins with information gained from the senses, the first step in St. John's preparation for union with God is the 'mortification of the appetites,' which includes all the senses.

> We are using the expression 'night' to signify a deprival of the gratification of man's appetite in all things. Just as night is nothing but the privation of light and, consequently, of all objects visible by means of the light—darkness and emptiness, then, for the faculty of sight—the mortification of the appetites can be called a night for the soul. To deprive oneself of the gratification of the appetites in all things is like living in darkness and in a void. The eye feeds upon its objects by means of light in such a way that when the light is extinguished the eye no longer sees them. Similarly does a man by means of his appetite feed and pasture on worldly things that gratify his faculties. When the appetites are extinguished—or mortified—he no longer feeds upon the pleasure of these things, but lives in a void and in darkness with respect to his appetites …
>
> By the mere fact, then, that a man loves something, his soul becomes incapable of pure union and transformation in God; for the baseness of a creature is far less capable of the sublimity of the Creator than is darkness of light.³⁶

To extend this meaning of 'darkness,' he now gives a number of examples of the total worthlessness of everything compared to God.³⁷

> A man attached to [any] creatures is nothing in the sight of God, and even less than nothing …
>
> ……
>
> All the beauty of creatures compared with the infinite beauty of God is supreme ugliness … So a person attached to the beauty of any creature is extremely ugly in God's sight.
>
> ……
>
> All the grace and elegance of creatures compared with God's grace is utter coarseness and crudity.
>
> ……
>
> All the world's wisdom and human ability contrasted with the infinite wisdom of God is pure and utter ignorance … Anyone, therefore, who values his knowledge and ability as a means of reaching union with the wisdom of God is highly ignorant in God's sight.

---

35 'The Ascent of Mount Carmel,' in Kieran Kavanaugh and Otilio Rodriguez, *The Collected Works of St. John of the Cross*, (Washington, D.C.: Institute of Carmelite Studies, 1979), 70. Juan de Yepes y Alverez (1542–1591), known as St. John of the Cross, was imprisoned for a time by the Inquisition for his liberal views, although the modern reader is hard pressed to find such views in his surviving works.

36 Ibid., 76ff.

37 Ibid., 78ff.

Among his 'Maxims and Counsels' we find another warning on the evils which follow man's appetites.

> Any appetite causes five kinds of harm in the soul: first, disquiet; second, turbidity; third, defilement; fourth, weakness; fifth, obscurity.[38]

He includes all the senses in contending that one must 'renounce and remain empty of any sensory satisfaction that is not purely for the honor and glory of God.'[39] The only positive benefit which can come to man from the senses is if they draw one's attention to God. Here for the first time he mentions music by name.

> I should like to offer a norm for discerning when this gratification of the senses is beneficial and when not. Whenever a person, upon hearing music or other things, seeing agreeable objects, smelling sweet fragrance, or feeling the delight of certain tastes and delicate touches, immediately at the first movement directs his thought and all the affection of his will to God, receiving more satisfaction in the thought of God than in the sensible object that caused it, and finds no gratification in the senses save for this motive, it is a sign that he is profiting by the senses.[40]

If he has not sufficiently diminished the very concept of the individual, he now commands,

> First, try to act with contempt for yourself and desire that all others do likewise. Second, endeavor to speak in contempt of yourself and desire all others to do so. Third, try to think lowly and contemptuously of yourself and desire that all others do the same.[41]

St. John divides knowledge into two general categories.[42] Natural knowledge includes everything which can be understood through the senses or through reflection. Supernatural knowledge is that which transcends all natural ability and capacity. Supernatural knowledge is divided into corporal and spiritual categories. Corporal knowledge is either knowledge originating from the exterior bodily senses or that received through 'interior senses.' Spiritual knowledge consists of both 'distinct' and 'particular' knowledge, the latter meaning visions, revelations, locutions, and spiritual feelings. One strengthens these capacities through discipline. For example,

> He first perfects the corporal senses, moving one to make use of natural exterior objects that are good, such as: hearing sermons and Masses, looking upon holy objects, mortifying the palate at meals, and disciplining the sense of touch through penance and holy rigor.[43]

---

38 'Maxims and Counsels,' in Ibid., 676.
39 'The Ascent of Mount Carmel,' in Ibid., 102.
40 Ibid., 255.
41 Ibid., 103.
42 Ibid., 131ff.
43 Ibid., 156.

In another treatise, 'The Spiritual Canticle,' he introduces a special form of knowledge, obtainable through meditation, and for this he coins the term 'silent music,' which is,

> tranquil and quiet knowledge, without the sound of voices. And thus there is in it the sweetness of music and the quietude of silence.[44]

ON THE PSYCHOLOGY OF AESTHETICS

Emotions

Vives, in his *On Education*, stresses the importance of using 'practical wisdom,' gained by reading, dialetic, rhetoric and experience, to control the emotions.

> Practical wisdom is the skill of accommodating all things of which we make use in life, to their proper places, times, persons, and functions. It is the moderator and rudder in the tempest of the feelings.[45]

Later in this book, he returns to this subject with more concern. Everyone, he says, should clearly agree that the body should obey the mind. Thus it follows that the 'unreasoning impulses' [emotions] must be subjected to Reason as mistress and empress. While one today might say that Nature works against this Church standard, for Vives it was because of ancient sin that,

> all things were inverted so that man's lower nature desires the higher position for itself; the passions contend for attention in place of Reason; Reason, conquered and overwhelmed is put to silence, and is made the slave to the temerity of the passions.[46]

Thus, for Vives, this is an eternal battle and it is Moral Philosophy which comes to the aid of Reason.

> All the precepts of Moral Philosophy have been prepared, like an army, to bring support to Reason. Wherefore the whole man must be understood, from within and without. Within the mind are the intellect and the emotions. We must know by what things the emotions are aroused and developed; by what things on the other hand they are restrained, calmed, removed …
> Our intellect is enveloped by too dense a darkness for it to see through, for the passions, aroused through sin, have spread a great and most obscuring mist before the eyes of Reason. Reason has need of being clear, and of being as little perturbed as possible.[47]

---

44 'The Spiritual Canticle,' in Ibid., 472ff.
45 Watson, *Vives On Education*, V, i.
46 Ibid., V, iii.
47 Ibid.

St. John of the Cross finds four basic emotions: joy, hope, sorrow and fear. He finds little that man should experience joy for, not riches, goods, titles or general prosperity.[48] 'Neither, indeed, is there any reason for joy in children … Indeed, it would also be vanity for a husband and wife to rejoice in their marriage, when they are uncertain whether God is being better served by it.'

According to St. John of the Cross, man suffers by even reflecting on the emotions. The solution he recommends is to erase from the mind all memory of pleasure deriving from appetites, for 'When all things are forgotten, nothing disturbs the peace or stirs the appetites.'[49]

> We have experience of this all the time. We observe that as often as a person begins to think about some matter, he is moved and aroused about it according to the kind of apprehension. If the apprehension is bothersome and annoying, he feels sadness or hatred, etc.; if agreeable, he will experience a desire and joy, etc.
>
> Accordingly, when the apprehension is changed, agitation necessarily results. Thus he will sometimes be joyful, at other times sad, now he will feel hatred, now love. And he is unable to preserve in equanimity, the effect of moral tranquility, unless he endeavors to forget all things.

Needless to say, he does not recommend any expression of the emotions.

> Never allow yourself to pour out your heart, even though it be but for the space of a creed.[50]

We wonder what he meant by enthusiasm, which he approved, if he did not categorize it as a form of emotional expression.

> Anyone who is lukewarm in his work is close to falling.[51]

Pleasure and Pain

Vives defines Pleasure in its relationship with knowledge.

> Knowledge arises out of the general whilst the particular affords us pleasure; the former is of the intellect, the latter of the senses.[52]

However, reflecting his Church perspective, he questions the very nature of Pleasure.

---

48 'The Ascent of Mount Carmel,' 241ff.
49 Ibid., 222.
50 'Maxims and Counsels,' in Ibid., 679.
51 Ibid., 682.
52 Watson, *Vives On Education*, IV, ii.

> What is the good of fatiguing oneself with [any] effort, if nothing is gained by desires except fresh desires; if the end of one longing is the beginning of another; if we work continually, and there is no end or rest? For what is more wretched than man, the most excellent of the animals, if, in this manner, he seeks after and desires the things which are exposed to his senses, and which are connected on all sides with his life, and then they bring him no rest or delight, and produce no pure, solid, or lasting joy?[53]

In one of his minor treatises, St. John of the Cross suggests that man cannot come to terms with Pleasure and Pain because he cannot understand them in their moral perspective.

> Man knows neither how to rejoice properly nor how to grieve properly, for he does not understand the distance between good and evil.[54]

ON THE PHILOSOPHY OF AESTHETICS

Vives, in examining the origins of education, found that the Arts evolved for the purpose of delight.

> When men had duly provided for the necessities of life, the human mind passed from necessities to conveniences, so that having acquired them, man might not only have something by which to protect himself from such great and constant danger, but something pleasant in which he might delight now that the sense of want had been driven away.[55]

Unfortunately, in his view, the birth of the arts for the purpose of delight only had the effect to making 'men become slaves of pleasure.' For him religious piety was the only appropriate goal of happiness. Thus, while he includes here as 'arts' the liberal arts as well, he concludes,

> Wherefore all arts and all learning, without religion, are childish play. For, just as the human mind has invented and occupies itself with what we call games, of small dice, or cards, or balls; or as with fiery energy it tries to be intent upon some pastime, but knows nothing better or has nothing better to do; or is slothful and lazy, and does not rouse itself to the labor of the good arts; or as it withdraws its attention from more difficult matters, so as to return to serious studies afterwards, refreshed by relaxation—so the mind of men has exercised itself in the arts and in the investigation of different kinds of subjects. Hence, partly through ignorance of religion and partly because it is fettered by the weight of studies, the mind cannot rise to religion or, through laziness, does not try; and thus neither bestows refreshment on the body to which it is attached, nor collects its renewed powers to efforts in the territory of religion. And just as among us, those who are not clever at games, but do possess experience of life and practical wisdom of life, are not

---

53 Ibid., I, ii.
54 'Sayings of Light and Love,' in *The Collected Works of St. John of the Cross*, 672.
55 Watson, *Vives On Education*, I, i.

blamed—but we hold him who plays games, but is untrained in practical wisdom, as disgraceful and blameworthy—so he who knows none of the arts but yet has a practical knowledge of virtue, and has formed and ordered his life by its rules, is so far from being blamed that he is deserving of praise. On the other hand, he is worthy of ignominy and dishonor who is learned and instructed in human arts, but is destitute of virtue.[56]

In this same chapter, Vives attempts to define Art a bit more. First, he observes that 'whatever is in the arts was in nature first.' Art itself is the exercise or application of this knowledge, as for example he quotes Manilius[57] as *singing*, 'Experience through various applications has made art.' In Vives words, again using the term broadly,

All our knowledge is a kind of close inspection which either consists in the contemplation of each particular object, e.g. when the eye observes closely the distinctions in a variety of colors, and again when the mind ponders over the memory of events, or considers closely and seeks after some end; if it collects general aspects or norms to a definite end, it is called an art.

Next he engages at length in stressing that 'experiences are casual and uncertain unless they are ruled by reason, which must preside over them like the rudder or the pilot in a ship.' Thus he believed that all the knowledge which comes from the senses must be guided by Reason. It is Reason, as well, which separates Art from random acts, as in the often cited story in Pliny[58] of a painter who, becoming frustrated, threw a paint-filled sponge at his canvas and thus achieved the desired effect. Therefore, he observes that art must have an end in view, towards which it aims everything 'like arrows to a target.'

In the following chapter, 'Arts and Sciences,' Vives finds all arts have two stages, reflection and then the production. He finds several kinds of arts, including music, among those whose end is action. Repeating an observation that worried some ancient Greek philosophers, he observes that when the music performance is ended, 'nothing is left.'[59]

In speaking of Art as we use the term today, Vives, again reflecting the ancient Church definition, finds Art more in the artist than the art object.

The practice of an art is nothing but the carrying out of its precepts; that indeed is the part of the pursuer of the art, and the precepts are his instruments rather than those of the art itself. The end of the artist is the carrying out of its precepts. The end of the art is always a very excellent work which will surely be the result of that action if nothing prevents …[60]

---

56 Ibid., I, ii.

57 *Astronomicon*, I, 1, lxi.

58 *Natural History*, XXXV, 104.

59 Watson, *Vives On Education*, I, iii.

60 Ibid.

Regarding the art observer, Vives concludes,

> There are some who seek the arts for the sake of pleasure and luxury. Others desire the cultivation and increase of piety: some desire some one of these things; other, many; others, very many. There are some who wish to acquire knowledge of arts for themselves; others who wish to share them when they are acquired; some, for themselves alone; others, for those who are dear to them—for instance, their children.[61]

Vives finds some arts injurious to man, in particular those which are 'harmful to piety.'[62] Among these he includes books written in the vulgar tongues (that is, not in Latin), much poetry and 'alluring popular songs.' If only man could live the perfect, angelic life, 'he would have no need of arts or any knowledge.'

Regarding the teaching of the arts, Vives recommends careful planning of the order in which ideas are presented and emphasizes the importance of first-hand observation.

> All the arts connected with doing, or making things, are best acquired from observing the actions and work of those who have been best instructed in them by nature, study and habit.[63]

Later he writes of the role of imitation in art education, a topic which he introduces with a curious observation.

> Although it is natural to talk, yet all discourse whatsoever belongs to an 'art' which was not bestowed upon us at birth, since nature has fashioned man, for the most part, strangely hostile to 'art.' Since she lets us be born ignorant and absolutely without skill in all arts, we require imitation. Imitation, furthermore, is the fashioning of a certain thing in accordance with a proposed model. Hence models which aid expression must be set forth, the best obtainable, not the best absolutely, but those which are best suited to the present state of progress of the pupil.[64]

ON THE AESTHETICS OF MUSIC

Vives, in his *On Education*, continues in the Church Scholastic tradition of classifying music as a branch of mathematics. However, whereas he finds geometry and arithmetic as vital instruments for the search of Truth, he assigns music a lesser value, 'for relaxation and recreation of the mind through the harmony of sounds.'[65] Interestingly enough, he then classifies all poetry under the heading of music.

---

61 Ibid.
62 Ibid., I, iv.
63 Ibid., II, iv.
64 Ibid., IV, iv.
65 Ibid., I, v.

When discussing the appropriate subject matter for schools, Vives again defines Music as 'arithmetic applied to sounds.' All the mathematical sciences, including music, have two aspects, the contemplative or theoretical and the practical.[66] Here, Vives makes his only detailed observations on the use of music in education.

> In music we have deteriorated much from the older masters, on account of the dullness of the ear which has utterly lost all discrimination of subtle sounds, so that now we no longer distinguish even the long and short sounds in common speech; and for this reason we have lost some kinds of meters, and that primitive harmony of tones, the effects of which the ancient writers testify were vast and marvelous. Young men should receive theoretical instruction in music, and should also have some practical ability. Only let the pupil practice pure and good music which, after the Pythagorean mode, soothes, recreates, and restores to itself the wearied mind of the student; then let it lead back to tranquility and tractability all the wild and fierce parts of the student's nature, as it is related in the ancient world, under the guise of stories, that rocks were moved and wild beasts allured by it.[67]

Francisco de Salinas (1513–1590) rejected the traditional medieval division of music into *mundana*, *humana*, and *instrumentalis* and instead divided music into that which moves only the sense, the intellect, or both. The music of birds, for example, pleases the senses, but (since he did not believe it corresponded to the ratios of music) it cannot properly be called music.[68]

Salinas was also uncomfortable with any theory which maintained music should be judged by the senses, or those which said it should be judged purely by reason, or by ratios, etc. Therefore he advanced the belief that both the senses and reason participate, but from different perspectives.

> In harmonics the judges are the sense and the reason, but not both the same way, because as Ptolemy asserted, the sense judges concerning the matter and affection, the reason, concerning the form and cause. From these words we can draw the conclusion that, just as matter is completed by form, so sensory judgment is completed by the rational.[69]

Finally, Salinas was one who had the courage to argue against the 'Music of the Spheres,' which was much discussed following the revival of interest in Greek philosophy. He sided with Aristotle, the only important early philosopher who also rejected this idea.

> We do not believe that celestial motions yield any sounds at all, whether as subject or as efficient cause, as it pleases the physicists. Now aside from the reasons of Aristotle, which we did not wish to translate here, lest we seem to want to teach physics rather than music, it appears certainly

---

66 Ibid., IV, v.

67 Ibid.

68 Quoted in Claude V. Palisca, *Humanism in Italian Renaissance Musical Thought* (New Haven: Yale University Press, 1985), 185.

69 'De musica,' I, 3, quoted in Ibid.

> probable that the creator of the universal framework would not have made anything superfluous any more than he would have failed to provide the necessities. For such would have been that celestial sound which could not be heard by anyone.[70]

Regarding the purpose of music, we have seen above that Vives mentions that it soothes, recreates and restores the wearied mind. In the preface to his 1581 *Book of Hymns*, Victoria gives the darker purpose.

> Many evil and depraved men abuse music as an excitant in order to plunge into earthy delights, instead of raising themselves by means of it to the contemplation of God and divine things.[71]

In his *Missaorum Libri Duo*, of the same year, Victoria cites a purpose never found in earlier periods, for posterity. It is a harbinger of modern aesthetics.

> What I originally had in mind was not to be satisfied with knowledge alone, and stop short at the point of bringing pleasure to ear and intellect only, but that I should go further—and to the best of my ability be of service to my contemporaries and to posterity.[72]

Finally we should mention a treatise by Tomás de Sancta Maria, published in 1565, which offers a few aesthetic rules for 'beautiful playing.' These include playing cleanly, in good time and with taste. He also suggests that choice of fingerings should reflect tempo.[73]

FUNCTIONAL MUSIC

Pietro Cerone, in his *El melopeo y maestro*,[74] written apparently to correct the faults which 'one hears sung today in churches,' offers some interesting commentary on the aesthetics of Church music. The Motet, he stresses, must have continual gravity and majesty and be slow, heavy and broad—characteristics he observes are 'disregarded in these times, particularly by those of my nation.'[75] He does not approve of basing the Motet on secular music, such as madrigals and chansons, which would result in the mixing of the spiritual with the profane, although, oddly enough, he finds this acceptable in the Mass.

---

70 'De musica libri septem,' I, 1, p. i, quoted in Ibid., 186.
71 Pedrell, *Opera Omnia*, I, 109.
72 Thomas Rive, 'An Investigation into Harmonic and Cadential Procedure in the Works of Victoria' (Dissertation, University of Auckland, 1963), 28.
73 *Libro llamado Arte de tañer fantasia assí para tecla como para vihuela*, quoted in Gustave Reese, *Music in the Renaissance* (New York: Norton, 1959), 630.
74 Cerone, born in Italy, spent his working life in Spain. Although his book was published in 1613, it represents views consistent with the late sixteenth century.
75 Pietro Cerone, *El melopeo y maestro*, quoted in Oliver Strunk, *Source Readings in Music History* (New York: Norton, 1950), 263.

In composing a Mass, Cerone suggests that for variety some internal parts may be composed for fewer voices, but 'these sections should be composed with greater art and greater learning and in a more lofty and more elegant style.'[76] The model which he offers for this, curiously, he takes from Comedy, wherein one sometimes finds a poem.

> These reduced parts are the flower of the whole work, so made in imitation of the perfect writer of comedy; assuming that in the course of a comedy he uses verses of great elegance, learning, and savor, all leading up to the detail that a character recites some sonnet or madrigal, who does not know that this sonnet or madrigal is woven with greater art, elegance, and grace than all the rest of the comedy?

In his discussion of Mass composition, he also reminds the reader that words such as 'Jesu Christe' or 'Crucifixus' must be composed only with harmonic intervals and with all voices singing the same slow rhythms. 'To use imitations and lively progressions here, with other graces, is a very great error and a sign of great ignorance.'[77] This is the same style he recommends for composing Psalms, for again the emphasis is on the words.

> The music should be such as does not obscure the words, which should be very distinct and clear, so that all the parts will seem to enunciate together, no more, no less ... without long or elegant passages or any novelty other than ordinary consonances, introducing from time to time some short and commonplace imitation.

While he says the use of polyphony in Psalms is rare in Spain, in Italy he finds some composers who write Psalms with 'more art than they use in writing Magnificats, which is, on due consideration, a great error.' Such compositions, while they may be considered good as music, are inappropriate as psalmody.

> Instead of being short, they are long; instead of using ordinary consonances, they use far-fetched and unauthorized passages; instead of setting the words clearly, they set them in a very obscure and cumbrous style; instead of making them plain, they make them solemn and more imitated.[78]

Cerone finds the Lamentations 'the most difficult to write judiciously and to make appropriate to the season and to the sense of the words.' The parts must proceed with the same rhythms, and with gravity and modesty.

> In this kind of composition, more than in any other, the composer makes use of dissonances, suspensions, and harsh passages to make his work more doleful and mournful, as the sense of the words and the significance of the season demand.[79]

---

76 Ibid., 267.
77 Ibid.
78 Ibid., 269ff.
79 Ibid., 273.

In general, Cerone stresses making Church music appropriate to its function. Nowhere is this more clear than in his objection to the elements of secular music which he finds forcing their way into Church music, in particular the syncopation.

> In all the varieties of composition thus far explained, the syncopated minim and quaver are out of place, equally so the semiminim rest, for these ... are opposed to the gravity, majesty, and devout character required by ecclesiastical music, for all that many do the opposite today, either because they lack the knowledge necessary to the finished composer and excellent musician, or because, having it, they use it only to delight the sensual and to attract with their *firinfinfin* the vulgar throng.[80]

It is interesting to find that religious dancing was still practiced in Spain, in particular in Seville by the boys of the choir known as the *seises*. They boys danced to percussion instruments and the dances were performed just before the Blessed Sacrament.[81]

There is abundant documentation for large numbers of instruments accompanying the singers in the major cathedrals of sixteenth-century Spain. An actual Seville cathedral document of 1586 specifies,

> At greater feasts there shall always be a verse played on recorders. At Salves, one of the three verses that are played shall be on shawms, one on cornetts and the other on recorders; because always hearing the same instrument annoys the listener.[82]

And, of course, Spain was responsible for the introduction of these instruments into the New World. Writing of Mexico, Geronimo de Mendieta's *Historia Eclesiastica Indiana* [ca. 1571–1596] observes that,

> nowhere in all of Christendom are there so many recorders, shawms, sackbuts, orlas, trumpets and drums as in the Kingdom of New Spain.[83]

Finally, in Spain, as in France, good Catholics joyously celebrated the infamous St. Bartholomew massacre of Protestants in Paris, as an eyewitness tells us.

> With anthems in Saint Gudule, with bonfires, festive illuminations, roaring artillery, with trumpets also, and with shawms, was the glorious holiday celebrated in court and camp, in honor of the vast murder committed by the Most Christian King upon his Christian subjects.[84]

---

80 Ibid.

81 Reese, *Music in the Renaissance*, 597.

82 Robert Stevenson, *Spanish Cathedral Music in the Golden Age* (Berkeley, 1961), 152ff. See also Walter Salmen, *Musikleben im 16. Jahrhundert* (Leipzig, 1976), 182, and Grove (1980) VII, 627, 789.

83 Quoted in J. A. Guzmán, 'Mexico, Home of the First Musical Instrument Workshops in America,' *Early Music* 6, no. 3 (1978): 355, doi: 10.1093/earlyj/6.3.350

84 John Motley, *The Rise of the Dutch Republic* (New York, 1864), II, 393.

From among the numerous extant contemporary descriptions of the musicians who welcomed the nobles of Spain when they traveled, we choose one which mentions the private musicians of Charles V as an example because there is also a brief phrase describing their playing. An eyewitness pictures his arrival in Valladolid in 1517.

> First were twenty timpani (of the princes and great men of Castile), mounted on mules, making a great noise. Afterward came twenty-eight Spanish trumpets, followed by the twelve trumpets of Charles, all dressed in sleeveless violet tunics covered with little silver and gold letter C's sown on. Later came twelve more timpani and twelve trumpets ...
>
> [When Charles presented himself in the field], first came thirty tambours on horse and two large tambours. Next came sixty more drums on foot as well as forty trumpets from Castile, Naples, and Aragon, making so much noise you could not have heard the thunder of God. Next came the twelve trumpets of Charles playing in 'bon art et mode.' Finally came ten German tambors on foot, and six fife players of German flutes.[85]

ENTERTAINMENT MUSIC

Philip I of Spain (1504–1506), son of the famous Maximilian I and husband of the tragic Juana, died at age twenty-six. Brief though his reign was, there is considerable documentation for his musical establishment. One of the most interesting of these accounts gives the musicians who accompanied him on a trip from France to Spain in 1506. These included twelve trumpets, a ten-member ensemble called 'Players of Instruments' and his church singers—who apparently had their own ship.[86] The instrumentalists were distributed on the other ships to provide entertainment, as one eyewitness remembered, 'it was fine to hear trumpets, drums, and other instruments all around on the ships.'[87]

---

85 Edmond Vander Straeten, *La Musique aux Pays-Bas* (Bruxelles, 1885), VII, 289ff. Vander Straeten writes that the expression, 'bon art et mode,' proves the royal trumpets were an organization based on rigorous principles of music. Charles V's reign was spent in his contests with François I and the popes, not to mention his role as the defender of the faith against Luther. Fluent in German, Spanish, Italian and French, at age fifteen he personally hired Erasmus. The private instrument collection he passed on to Philip II included eleven keyboard, forty-seven strings and some one hundred and fifty wind instruments.

86 Ibid., VII, 163ff, where the names of the musicians are given.

87 Van Doorslaer, *La Chapelle*, quoted in Louise Cuyler, *The Emperor Maximilian I and Music* (London, 1973), 69.

14 SIXTEENTH-CENTURY SPANISH PROSE

From the perspective of insight into aesthetics in music, some of the most interesting prose from the middle of the sixteenth century is the pastoral romance. This form became popular throughout Europe as a consequence of the humanists' interest in the ancient Greek lyric poets, but also as a kind of romantic escape from the formal life at court. While this literature is an escape to the innocence of Nature, youth and love, these writers remained at heart very much courtiers. Thus, we find a curious mixture of knights and aristocrats together with shepherds and nymphs.

The descriptions of music share this mixture, with the rural creatures of the forest playing on the sophisticated instruments of the city and palace. Therefore it is sometimes in the forest that we discover some insights to performance practice of the palace. One has to keep in mind that we are not reading of the performances of real shepherds or forest inhabitants. The forest served the same literary purpose that it did for the later Romantic Period. Here it offered an idealistic escape from the complexities of court life, whereas in the nineteenth century the poet was 'escaping' from urbanization.

> Didst thou ever in the magnificent and stately cities hear music that pleased the ear, and delighted the mind like this? Truly these pastoral and country songs, being full of simplicity and plainness, please me more, than the delicate voices set together with curious skill [polyphonic music], and full of new inventions and conceits [improvisation] in the brave palaces of kings and princes. And when I think this melody to be better than that, you must believe it, because I have been present at the best music that in any city of the world or kings court was ever heard.[1]

There are two major representatives of this genre appropriate to this chapter, the *Diana* (1559) by Jorge de Montemayor of Portugal (d. 1561) and the *Diana enamorada* (1564) by Gil Polo (d. 1591). These works are filled with music, especially numerous songs for which the lyrics are given in the form of poetry. Indeed, almost anything important which the characters of these romances have to say, is expressed in song. They are opera in prose.

The rural shepherds are always described as having musical skills far too sophisticated for real shepherds. The first ones we meet in *Diana* are described as 'tuning, and playing on their instruments with great grace and sweetness,' before they began to sing. At the conclusion of their song a shepherdess emerges from a thicket 'playing on a bagpipe, and singing with

---

[1] Gil Polo, *Diana enamorada*, trans. Bartholomew Yong (1598), in *George of Montemayor's Diana and Gil Polo's Enamoured Diana*, ed. Judith Kennedy, (Oxford: Clarendon Press, 1968), 321.

as sweet a grace and delicate voice.'² These are Art songs and at other times they are also accompanied by a fiddle³ or a rebec.⁴

The nymphs seem especially musical in these pastoral romances. At one point, three of them,

> with marvelous good consent so sweetly played on their instruments, to which they joined their angelic voices, that it seemed no less than celestial music.⁵

Later three nymphs perform on a harp, lute and a bass viol de gamba, 'with such sweetness and melody that they who were present were enchanted and ravished.'⁶ A similar Renaissance court ensemble, now with even keyboards in the forest, is found in *Diana enamorada*.

> The shepherds would have sung one verse or two more, when a goodly company of fair nymphs came to the fountain, and every one playing upon her several instruments, made strange and delightful harmony. One of them played on a lute; another on a harp; another made a marvelous sweet countertenor upon a recorder; another with a piece of fine quill made the silver stringed Cyterne sweetly to sound; others the strings of the bass Viol with rosined hairs; other with Virginals and Violins made delicate changes in the air, and filled it with so sweet music, that in a manner it astonished them that heard it, and made them to marvel no less at it ... The shepherds seeing this melodious choir of angels, left off the dance that they had begun, and sat down, giving attentive ear to the heavenly music, and the sundry sweet instruments that they played on, which joined sometimes with clear and delicate voices, moved strange and rare delight.⁷

In *The Trials of Persiles and Sigismunda*, Cervantes also describes a rural scene where one heard 'the sound of countless cheerful instruments,' including shepherds playing on percussion, flute, psaltery and reed-pipes.

> These sounds flowed together as though they were all one and lifted everyone's spirits with their harmony, the goal of music.⁸

---

2   Jorge de Montemayor, *Diana*, trans. Bartholomew Yong (1598), in *George of Montemayor's Diana and Gil Polo's Enamoured Diana*, ed. Judith Kennedy, (Oxford: Clarendon Press, 1968), 25ff.

3   Ibid., 43.

4   Ibid., 191.

5   Ibid., 58.

6   Ibid., 134.

7   Polo, *Diana enamorada*, 389.

8   Miguel de Cervantes, *The Trials of Persiles and Sigismunda*, trans. Celia Weller and Clark Colahan (Berkeley: University of California Press, 1989), III, viii. Cervantes (1547–1616), perhaps the greatest writer in Spanish history, lived a life as extraordinary as any of his fiction. He was wounded as a soldier, losing the use of his left hand; captured by pirates, sold in slavery in Algiers and held until ransomed five years later; and sent to prison for irregularities in his later profession as a tax collector.

In *Don Quijote*, Cervantes presents a survey of the instruments necessary to pastoral music.

> What soft flute sounds will come to our ears—what Zamoran bagpipes—what drums and tambourines—what timbrels—what lutes and violins! And just suppose, among all these other instruments, we hear the sound of cymbals [*albogues*]! Ah, then we'll have virtually everything that produces pastoral music.

Sancho asks,

> What are these symbols? I've never heard of them, in all my life, and I've never seen them, either.

Don Quijote replies,

> Cymbals are flat sheets of metal, and they're used like brass candlestick holders, banging one against the other, on the hollow parts, to produce a sound which, though it may not be terribly pleasing or harmonious, is nevertheless not displeasing, and goes well with the rustic quality of the bagpipes and tambourines. The name *albogues* comes from Arabic, like all the words in Spanish that start with *al*.[9]

ON THE PHYSIOLOGY OF AESTHETICS

Due to the generally light-hearted nature of this body of prose, there is little serious philosophic comment on the workings of the mind. In one specific reference, Cervantes seems to suggest that experience produces an ever more productive mind. He observes, in *Don Quijote*, 'you don't write with your gray hair but with your mind, which usually gets better as it gets older.'[10] However, in another place, Cervantes suggests that in the course of personal experience one often sees 'without paying attention [and] observes nothing,' while in reading books one 'reads with care [and] thinks over and over again about what he's reading.'[11] And reading is so important that Don Quijote tells Sancho,

> When a man doesn't know how to read, or when he's left-handed, it indicates one of two things: either he comes from a very low, a very humble family, or else he's such a wicked rogue that neither good models nor good teaching could have any effect on him.[12]

---

9 Miguel de Cervantes, *Don Quijote*, trans. Burton Raffel (New York: Norton, 1995), II, lxvii. In his *The Dialogue of the Dogs*, Cervantes writes that shepherds 'spend their days singing and playing bagpipes, flutes, rebecs, tabors, and other rare instruments.'

10 Ibid., II, Prologue.

11 Cervantes, *The Trials of Persiles and Sigismunda*, III, viii. In *Don Quijote* [II, Dedication] Cervantes says he wrote this book for the purpose of entertainment.

12 Cervantes, *Don Quijote*, II, xliii.

We notice here another illustration of the common association found in early literature of the left hand with something bad or evil. We understand today, through clinical research in left and right hemispheres of the brain, that this is a comment made by the left hemisphere—which pretends not to know of the existence of the right.

In contrast to the testimony of rather cruel treatment of students we found in France, in his *The Dialogue of the Dogs*, Cervantes paints a complimentary picture of sixteenth-century Jesuit education in Spain.

> I was much pleased to see the love, the kindliness, the concern and the devotion those blessed fathers and teachers brought to the teaching of those boys, inclining the tender twigs of their youth so they would not be bent and turned away from the path of virtue, a subject taught them along with their letters. I observed how they reproved them with gentleness, punished them with mercy, encouraged them by example, stimulated them with rewards, and handled them wisely; and, above all, how they painted the ugliness and horrors of vice and held before them the beauty of virtue so that, loathing the former and loving the latter, they might achieve the purpose for which they had been born.[13]

ON THE PSYCHOLOGY OF AESTHETICS

We have another illustration of our dissimilar left and right hemispheres of the brain in the common observation that our words do not always correspond with our feelings. Cervantes raises the question: is it our words or our feelings which communicate?

> Auristela finished her speech and began to weep tears that undid and erased everything she'd just said.[14]

A few lines later, he makes the observation that 'virtuous and highborn young women say one thing with their tongues but feel another in their hearts.' This last observation is probably a reference to the etiquette of the courtier not showing emotions, rather than one of young women in general, for in the pastoral romance, *Diana*, a young lady speaks of being overwhelmed on seeing a man at court and confesses,

> Truth it is, that I could not but shed some tears for joy and grief, which his sight did make me feel, but fearing to be noticed by the standers by I dried them up.[15]

---

13 Miguel de Cervantes, *The Dialogue of the Dogs*, trans. Harriet de Onís, in *Six Exemplary Novels* (Great Neck: Barron's Educational Series, 1961), 17.
14 Cervantes, *The Trials of Persiles and Sigismunda*, II, v.
15 Montemayer, *Diana*, 92.

The primary emotion described in these pastoral romances is, of course, Love. In *Diana*, we find a passionate testimonial to the power of Love.

> What [armor] is so impenetrable, and steel so well tempered, that may serve for a defense against the violence of this tyrant, whom so unjustly they call Love? And what heart (though it be harder than a diamond) which an amorous thought can not mollify and make tender?[16]

Because Love is experiential, and thus of the right hemisphere, Reason and language of the left hemisphere can block these feelings. Thus a singer in *Diana* sings, 'But there's no love, where Reason beareth sway.'[17] On the other hand, as Cervantes points out, strong feelings can block speech.

> When water is bottled up in a small-mouthed jar, the more it hurries to escape, the slower it pours out. The liquid at the mouth is pushed forward by the drops behind, which block each other's way and slow the forward motion of the current until at last it breaks through and the contents all empty out. The same thing happens with ideas conceived in the mind of a wounded lover; sometimes all of them rush together toward the tongue and block each other's way, and he doesn't know which one to express first to get his thoughts out. Thus, by keeping silent he often says more than he'd like.[18]

In this literature the strongest form of Pleasure is also Love. In a passage which equates sensuality with pleasure, a character in *The Trials of Persiles and Sigismunda* tells of sailing past a rock cliff and hearing the,

> very soft, mellow sound produced by various musical instruments which struck our ears and compelled us to listen closely.[19]

A siren-like allegorical figure called Sensuality leads a group of beautiful women out of the rock. They are carrying various kinds of instruments in their hands, 'making music that was alternately happy and sad.' Sensuality warns the teller of the story,

> It's going to cost you dearly to be my enemy, noble young man; if not your life, then at least your pleasure.

Whereupon the women carried off the sailors!

At the same time, the strongest form of Pain is also associated with Love. In *Diana*, Sylvanus details for a nymph a catalog of the woes of Love.

---

16 Ibid., 104.
17 Ibid., 124.
18 Cervantes, *The Trials of Persiles and Sigismunda*, IV, i.
19 Ibid., II, xv. Two other allegorical figures, Self-Control and Modesty, were apparently *not* musicians!

It is strange to see what a sorrowful heart (that is subject to the traunces of impatient love) doth suffer, because the least ill, that it causeth in us, is the deprivation of our judgment, the loss of our memory, and the surcharging of our imaginations with his only objects, making every one to alienate himself from himself, and to impropriate himself in the person of his beloved. What shall that woeful man then do, who sees himself so great an enemy to pleasure, such a friend to solitariness, so full of passions, filled with fears, troubled in his spirits, martyred in his wits, sustained by hope, wearied with thoughts, afflicted with grief, haunted with jealousies, and continually worn with sobs, sighs, sorrows, and woes, which he never wanted? And that which makes me more to marvel, is, that the mind doth not procure (this love being so intolerable and extreme in cruelty), nor hath any desire at all to part from it, but doth rather account it her enemy, that gives it any counsel to that effect.[20]

All early writers conclude that Pleasure and Pain seem always associated one with the other. Cervantes also draws this conclusion.

It seems good and bad fortune are separated from each other by so little space that they're like two convergent lines; even though they begin at different and distant points, they come together at the same one.[21]

And in another place, he observes,

So flimsy is the security with which man enjoys his pleasures that no one can promise himself even a minimal degree of certainty in them.[22]

ON THE PHILOSOPHY OF AESTHETICS

In *The Trials of Persiles and Sigismunda,* Cervantes makes an interesting observation on the similarity of the arts.

History, poetry, and painting resemble each other and indeed are so much alike that when you write history you're painting, and when you paint you're composing poetry. History doesn't always deal with weighty matters just as painting doesn't always portray great and magnificent things and poetry doesn't always have its head in the clouds. History accepts the trivial, painting allows weeds and brush in its pictures, and poetry sometimes does best when it sings about modest affairs.[23]

---

20 Montemayer, *Diana,* 158.

21 Cervantes, *The Trials of Persiles and Sigismunda,* IV, xii.

22 Ibid., IV, xiv.

23 Ibid., III, xiv.

Regarding the definition of Beauty, Cervantes offers, in *Don Quijote*, the most common definition of Beauty found in all early literature, that it is the 'harmony of one part with the whole, and the whole with all its parts.'[24] Many early writers also define Love as the desire to possess Beauty, but in this same work Cervantes questions this association.

> Some beauty is good to see, but does not give rise to affection; and if everything beautiful *did* inspire love, desire would become confused and lose its way, unable to understand where it was going, since an infinity of things beautiful makes for an infinity of desires.[25]

On Prose

In *Don Quijote*, Cervantes has a priest represent the Church view that it is proper to censure those who have,

> written without ever once stopping to think, paying no attention to either the art or the rules which one should obey.[26]

On Poetry

Of all the arts, Cervantes seems to hold poetry in the highest regard. In a passage in *The Trials of Persiles and Sigismunda*, he speaks of the value of poetry.

> Excellence in poetry is as clean as clear water, which improves everything unclean. It's like sunlight, which touches everything dirty without any dirt sticking to it; it's a skill as valuable as it is esteemed; it's a lightning bolt that leaps out from its hiding place, not to burn but to illuminate; it's a well-tuned instrument sweetly cheering the senses, bringing with it not only delight but purity and usefulness as well.[27]

A passage in *Don Quijote* defines poetry in this same high esteem, in addition to giving the author's views on the proper use of this form.

> Poetry is like a tender young maiden, marvelously lovely, who has been given over to the care of many other young maidens, so that they may enhance, refine, and adorn her, those other young maidens being all the other forms of knowledge, all of whom, deriving their authority

---

24 Cervantes, *Don Quijote*, I, xlvii.
25 Ibid., I, xiv.
26 Ibid., I, xlviii.
27 Cervantes, *The Trials of Persiles and Sigismunda*, III, ii.

from her, must serve and cherish her—yet this maiden does not care to be much handled, nor dragged through the streets, nor broadcast at every street corner or even in the nooks and crannies of palaces. She is framed by an alchemy so rare that whoever knows its secrets can turn her into the purest and most precious gold; but if you possess her, you need to keep her within her proper bounds and not let her run off into clumsy satires or icy-cold sonnets; she should only be marketed in the form of heroic poems, mournful tragedies, or happy and artful comedies; buffoons should be kept away from her, as well as the ignorant mob, all of whom are incapable of understanding or appreciating the treasures she can offer.[28]

And, similarly in the *Gypsy Maid*,

Poetry must be treated like the most valuable of jewels which its owner does not wear every day, nor show to everybody, on any occasion, but only when it is fitting and justified. Poetry is a beautiful maiden, chaste, modest, wise, understanding, retiring, who keeps within the limits of her greatest discretion. She is given to solitude; fountains beguile her; meadows console her; trees soothe her; flowers rejoice her; and, in a word, she delights and instructs all those who come in contact with her.[29]

In spite of centuries of stern denouncements by the Church, poets were still calling upon the Muses for inspiration. Cervantes refers to this in picturing Don Quijote trying to compose,

with a great deal of sighing and calling on the gods and fauns of those woods, and the nymphs in the rivers, and sad, damp Echo, and asking all of them to answer him, and console him, and hear his pleas.[30]

A student poet also appeals to the gods in *The Dialogue of the Dogs* and has similar difficulty in getting started.

At times he would be writing in a notebook, and every once in a while he would slap his forehead, bite his nails, and look up at the sky. At other times he would be so lost in thought that he did not move hand or foot, nor even his eyelashes.[31]

Can anyone be a poet? Many poets in early literature complain that in their time everyone is trying to be a poet. This subject is addressed in *The Trials of Persiles and Sigismunda* when a character named Rutilio, whom we are told had an extremely good voice, sings some Italian poetry. An older listener, Antonio, asks,

---

28 Cervantes, *Don Quijote*, II, xvi.
29 Cervantes, *The Gypsy Maid*, in *Six Exemplary Novels*, 117ff.
30 Cervantes, *Don Quijote*, I, xxvi.
31 Cervantes, *The Dialogue of the Dogs*, 52.

> Rutilio sings well and if by chance the sonnet he sang was his, then he isn't a bad poet. But how could someone with such a common occupation be a good poet? Still, I must be mistaken, for I remember having seen poets of all occupations in Spain, my homeland.

Mauricio answers,

> It's quite possible for a person with a common occupation to be a poet because poetry isn't in one's hands but in the mind, and the soul of a tailor is just as capable of poetry as that of a field marshall, for all souls are equal and have their origins in the same material, created and shaped by their Maker. Depending on the form and temperament of the body that encloses them, they seem more or less intelligent and show aptitude for and take pleasure in learning the sciences, arts, or skills toward which the stars most incline them. But more important and most correct is the saying, 'poets are born.' Thus, it isn't surprising that Rutilio should be a poet, even though he's been a dancing teacher.[32]

In Part II of his *Don Quijote*, Cervantes makes some specific observations on the nature of a good poet. First, he insists again that good poets are born and not made by either study or art. Then he qualifies this somewhat, noting,

> It must also be said, of course, that the natural poet who assists himself with art will be all the better for it, and will have the advantage over a poet who knows only what he has learned, since natural talent takes precedence over art: art can only perfect nature. Thus, blending art with nature, and nature with art, produces the best of all possible poets.[33]

He follows this with an observation made more frequently about musicians than poets in early literature, that 'a chaste poet will produce chaste poems, for the pen speaks for the soul.'

We have a more humorous view of poets in Cervantes' *Master Glass*, the story of a man who thinks he has been turned into glass and thereupon personifies the phrase frequently mentioned in the sixteenth century that 'Art should be the mirror of life.' When asked by a student if he were a poet, Master Glass responded that he was neither so foolish nor so fortunate—not so foolish as to become a bad poet, nor so fortunate as to have the merits of a good one.'[34]

Master Glass observes that he regards poetry very high, but poets very low, and that there are so few good ones that one can count them on one hand. He concludes,

> that he admired and reverenced the art of poetry, because it embraced all the other arts, making use of them all, adorning itself with all, refining and bringing out its own wonderful creations which fill the world with delight, benefit, and awe.

---

32 Cervantes, *The Trials of Persiles and Sigismunda*, I, xviii.
33 Cervantes, *Don Quijote*, II, xvi.
34 Cervantes, *Master Glass*, in *Six Exemplary Novels*, 75ff.

Finally, Cervantes makes an interesting observation about poetry contests.

> If it's for a poetry competition, you ought to aim at the second prize, your grace, because the first prize is always awarded as an act of patronage or in recognition of social standing, but second prize strictly on merit, so that third prize really amounts to second, and what's called first prize, if you calculate matters this way, has to be truly the third—much in the fashion that universities award advanced degrees.[35]

On the Theater

Cervantes, in *The Trials of Persiles and Sigismunda*, has a character advise Auristelia regarding how good it would be for her to become an actress.

> He told her that after a couple of stage appearances whole mines of gold coins would rain down on her, for the princes at that time acted as if money were made by alchemy and when they said gold, gold it was … and they often surrendered their hearts to the nymphs they saw in the theaters … He told her that if some royal festival should take place while she was there she could count on being covered with golden petticoats, for all or most of the gentlemen would send their liveried servants to her house to show their respects and to kiss her feet. He described to her how pleasant her tours would be, accompanied by two or three gentlemen in disguise who would act both as servants and lovers; and above all, he extolled and praised to the skies the eminence and honor that would be hers when she took on the major roles.[36]

However, Cervantes presents a less glamorous view of the actor in his *Master Glass*.

> They earn their bread by grueling work, memorizing all the time, knocking around from pillar to post like gypsies, studying how to please the public, for their well-being depends on others' pleasure. Besides, in their calling they deceive nobody, for their merchandise is always on display where all may see and judge it.[37]

In *The Dialogue of the Dogs*, Cervantes has a dog describe his master who represents the less talented playwright.

> The whole company had gathered there to hear the play of my master … and in the middle of the first act, one by one and two by two, they all left with the exception of the manager and myself, who acted as audience. The play was so bad that, even though I am a complete ass when it comes to poetry, it seemed to me that it had come from the pen of Satan himself, to the total ruin and confusion of the poet, who by this time was swallowing hard at seeing the solitude in which

---

35 Cervantes, *Don Quijote*, II, xviii.
36 Cervantes, *The Trials of Persiles and Sigismunda*, III, ii.
37 Cervantes, *Master Glass*, 83.

the audience had left him. And it would not be surprising if his prophetic soul had foretold the misfortune that was about to descend upon him, which was that the actors, more than twelve in number, returned and without saying a word, seized my poet ... I was speechless at what had taken place; the manager, disgusted, the actors, merry, and the poet crestfallen. With an air of resignation and great patience, though with a somewhat wry expression, he picked up his play and stuffing it in his bosom, said, half to himself: 'It is not good to cast pearls before swine.' And saying this he departed with great dignity.[38]

Regarding critics, Cervantes expressed his opinion, in *Don Quijote*, that they were unfair in condemning a work because of a few flaws.

They ought to stop and think how wide-awake [the author] had to be, most of the time, to make his book cast so much light and so little shade, for it may well be that what seems to them terribly serious defects are nothing more than beauty spots, which frequently heighten the loveliness of any face that bears them. Indeed, he who puts a book into print takes an enormous risk, for the most impossible of all impossibilities is that it can please and satisfy everyone who reads it.[39]

Cervantes had a similar lack of faith in the general public. In *Don Quijote*, he presents a priest who had contemplated writing prose, but then changed his mind.

I realized that there are many more fools than wise men; it's better to be praised by the smaller company of wise men than mocked by the larger crowd of idiots, nor do I have any interest in subjecting myself to the jumbled judgment of the haughty mob, which is exactly what most of the people who read such books are.[40]

A somewhat different view is found in the *Lazarillo de Tormes* (1554), the anonymous author observing,

Few would write for a single reader, for writing is a hard job; and writers who have done their work wish to be rewarded, not with money, but with the knowledge that their works are widely known and read, and—if they merit it—praised. In this regard Cicero tells us: 'The desire to be held in esteem creates all the arts.'
The same thing holds true for those who practice the Arts and Letters.[41]

---

38 Cervantes, *The Dialogue of the Dogs*, 54ff.
39 Cervantes, *Don Quijote*, II, iii.
40 Ibid., I, xlviii.
41 Anonymous, *Lazarillo de Tormes*, in *Masterpieces of he Spanish Golden Age*, ed. Angel Flores (New York: Holt, Reinhart, 1963), Prologue.

ON THE AESTHETICS OF MUSIC

Cervantes, in addition to the traditional pastoral scenes which include music, always seems to go out of his way to picture humble persons performing and enjoying music, thus commenting on the universality of music. In *Don Quijote*, for example, a goatherd is asked to sing 'and make us happy' and to let the guest 'know that even in the mountains and woods there are people who understand music.'[42]

Regarding the purpose of music, we have seen above the passage from *The Trials of Persiles and Sigismunda*, where Cervantes describes a performance which 'lifted everyone's spirits with their harmony, the goal of music.'[43] This, to soothe the listener, is the most frequently given purpose for music in all early literature. Cervantes refers to this again in *Don Quijote*.

> I had learned from experience that music settles a jangled soul and comforts all manner of spiritual troubles.[44]

Another interesting reference to the purpose of music is found in *Diana*, where the suggestion is made that one of its values is to strengthen emotions.

> For though music is no small means to increase his melancholy, that is ever sad and pensive, as the joy and mirth of he who lives a merry life …[45]

In *Diana enamorada* we find a reference to what we recognize today as the most important and universal purpose of music, to express what one cannot, or wishes not, to express in words.

> [He] resolved in song to tell Diana his mind, which shame would not permit him to acquaint her with in familiar talk.[46]

On Performance Practice

Because the performance of music is so closely tied to one's own feelings, one cannot sing when not in the mood. A character in *The Trials of Persiles and Sigismunda*, who says that 'it's the shared opinion of everyone who's heard me sing that I have the best voice in the world,' observes,

---

42 Cervantes, *Don Quijote*, I, xi.
43 Cervantes, *The Trials of Persiles and Sigismunda*, III, viii.
44 Cervantes, *Don Quijote*, I, xxviii.
45 Montemayer, *Diana*, 190.
46 Polo, *Diana enamorada*, 381.

'If this weren't more a time to be moaning than singing, I'd easily prove the truth of this to you. But if things improve and my tears have a chance to dry, I'll sing, and while they may not be happy songs, at least they can be sad dirges that will cast their spell as they're sung and make you happy as you cry over them.' Feliciana's words made everyone want to hear her sing as soon as possible, but they didn't dare plead with her to do it because, as she herself had said, the time wasn't right.[47]

We also note the reference here to catharsis, the purging of emotions, when she says they will be happy as they cry over her song. The emotion with which some singers sang in the sixteenth century is perhaps documented in *Diana enamorada* by a shepherd singing to his bagpipe 'with swelled tears standing in his eyes.'[48]

In the pastoral romance, *Diana enamorada*, we find what must actually be a reference to improvisation customarily heard at court.

The delicate voice and excellent graces of Diana, surmounted far the praises of the fairest and most skillful shepherdesses of her time. And the quavers and fine conceits wherewith so sweetly she broke her voice, and adorned her songs, made her to be the more admired: for they were so rare and singular, that they rather seemed to be taken from some majestical court, then known in her home country.[49]

Finally, in one place Cervantes refers to a man as 'a great joker, as most drummers are.'[50]

ART MUSIC

The prose of sixteenth-century Spain is filled with characters who sing art songs, often with the lyrics provided. We will cite only a few examples. One interesting singer of art songs described by Cervantes was a gypsy, which was rare for he says they are mostly thieves.

Preciosa proved to be a treasure house of carols, ballads, *seguidillas*, sarabands,[51] and other types of poetry ... which she sang with singular charm ... She sought out and secured these materials in every way she could. There were even poets who gave them to her; for there are poets who make deals with gypsies and sell them their works, just as there are those whose customers are blind street singers for whom they invent miracles and receive a share of their

---

47 Cervantes, *The Trials of Persiles and Sigismunda*, III, iv.
48 Polo, *Diana enamorada*, 336.
49 Ibid., 290.
50 Cervantes, *The Dialogue of the Dogs*, 32.
51 The sarabande is usually thought of as an instrumental dance, but in *The Jealous Hidalgo*, in *Six Exemplary Novels*, 212, Cervantes mentions the singing of 'sarabandes in the sacred mode, which leave the Portuguese themselves amazed.'

earnings. Everything is to be found in the world, and this business of hunger drives wits to turn out extraordinary things.[52]

This girl danced while she sang and her song 'filled all who heard her with admiration.'

Cervantes has given us a humorous account of Don Quijote, after hearing a lovestruck young girl sing a song of love, being so 'wrapped in all his thoughts' that he could not sleep. His thoughts are described as 'fleas, they would allow him neither sleep nor rest.' To relieve himself, he decides to sing a love song himself and a lute is brought to him.

> Don Quijote found that a guitar had in fact been brought to his room, so he tuned it, adjusted the frets as well as he was able, then opened the window and, seeing people walking in the garden, spat[53] and cleared his throat and promptly began, his voice hoarse, but his pitch true, to sing the following ballad, which he had composed that very same day:
>
> > Love leans his mighty weight
> > on hearts, and bends them out of shape,
> > whenever hands have nothing to do,
> > and minds are full.
> >
> > The only protection against this venom
> > is womanly work, washing and sewing
> > and all the bustle of busy lives
> > and no time for lingering …[54]

In the *Diana enamorada* we find one of the art song singing contests which are so familiar in the works of the ancient Greek lyric poets. Here the second singer appears to play a kind of overture before singing.

> Arsileus, after Syrenus had ended his song, began to tune his bagpipe, and after he had played a little while upon it, answered every staff of his competitor in order, as he sung …[55]

Here, as was also often the case in the repertoire of the lyric poets, a tie was declared.

What is of most interest to us in these many accounts of art singers is the constant emphasis on the listener, for it is the contemplative listener which is a necessary component of art music. In *The Trials of Persiles and Sigismunda*, for example, the company is passing an island when they hear someone singing a love song, 'a voice was heard coming from one of the other two boats, a voice so soft and sweet that it made them listen with rapt attention.'[56] They invited

---

52 Cervantes, *The Gypsy Maid*, 91ff.
53 Another singer who spits (twice) before he sings is found in Cervantes, *The Illustrious Kitchen Maid*, in *Six Exemplary Novels*, 264.
54 Cervantes, *Don Quijote*, II, xlvi.
55 Polo, *Diana enamorada*, 369.
56 Cervantes, *The Trials of Persiles and Sigismunda*, I, ix.

the singer to come aboard, 'to find out what had befallen him, since anyone singing at such a time either felt deeply or was beyond feeling.' It turned out to be a soldier, from a wealthy family, who told of his expected wedding, describing the sanctuary as overflowing with the music of voices and instruments.[57]

Later, Auristela is ill in bed, but the doctors recognized it was an illness of the soul (jealousy) and not of the body and ordered that her friends 'try to entertain and amuse her with music.' When a singer begins, Cervantes describes the company as 'listening closely.'[58]

This phrase occurs again in *Don Quijote*, as when Don Quijote and Sancho hear a well-trained singer. 'It filled them with wonder,' and they are described as 'listening carefully' as they heard a second song.[59] In another passage, Dorotea 'listened carefully' to a 'delicate, loving song.'[60]

In one of his shorter novels, *The Illustrious Kitchen Maid*, Cervantes describes a singer who,

> sang in tone so melodious and captivating that it filled them with wonder and they could not choose but listen until the end.[61]

And in his *The Jealous Hidalgo*, Cervantes describes a group of women listening to a guitar player as 'lost in admiration. And how shall I describe their feelings when they heard him play.' Later he played some *seguidillas*, 'which raised the pleasure of his listeners to its peak.'[62]

The listener is also often emphasized in the pastoral romances. In the first book of *Diana* Sylvanus takes his bagpipe, plays on it a while and then sings 'with great sorrow and grief.' The listener, Syrenus,

> was not idle when Sylvanus was singing these verses, for with his sighs he answered the last accents of his words, and with his tears did solemnize that which he conceived [in the verses].[63]

Another listener hears a singer's voice and 'awaked as it were out of a slumber, he gave attentive ear to the verses that she sang.'[64] Yet another singer, Arsileus, sang 'with so marvelous sweet grace and delectable voice, that he held all his listeners in a great suspense.'[65] Even Orpheus makes an appearance in this pastoral tale. First he sings while playing a harp and

---

57 Ibid., I, x. At the last moment the bride-to-be became a nun.
58 Ibid., II, iii.
59 Cervantes, *Don Quijote*, I, xxvii.
60 Ibid., I, xliii.
61 Cervantes, *The Illustrious Kitchen Maid*, 268.
62 Cervantes, *The Jealous Hidalgo*, 218.
63 Montemayer, *Diana*, 15ff.
64 Ibid., 54.
65 Ibid., 120ff.

the listeners were so ravished they forgot everything.⁶⁶ Then he begins another song, 'such heavenly music that he suspended their amazed senses.'

> But I will sing with pure and sweetest voice
> Of those perfections, and that grace display,
> That wisdom, wit and beauty of such choice,
> Of those who do illustrate Spain this day.

Yet another reference to listeners' 'giving attentive ear to his song,' is particularly interesting because it indicates it was the music, and not the text which captured the listeners, the text in this case being in Arabic which they did not understand.⁶⁷

There are also some interesting descriptions of evening serenades in this literature. In *The Illustrious Kitchen Maid*, Cervantes describes a singer being escorted to and from the performance site by a group of shawm players, although the serenade was sung to the accompaniment of a harp.⁶⁸ This same novel includes another street singer who was not so successful.

> The final verses and two brickbats which came flying through the air were all one. If instead of landing at his feet they had found their mark on the musician's head, they would easily have driven out of his mind once and for all both music and poetry. The poor fellow was amazed, and he started up the slope with such speed that a greyhound could not have overtaken him. Unhappy state that of musicians, bats, and owls, always exposed to downpours and abuse of this sort!⁶⁹

In *Diana* we read of a much higher level of serenade. The narrator takes a room in an inn and just after midnight he hears below his window three cornetts and a sackbut playing 'with such skill and sweetness, that it seemed celestial music.'⁷⁰ Later these musicians accompany a song on a lute and a 'silver sounding harp,' then on four lutes and finally (in the street!) on two harpsichords 'with such heavenly melody, that the whole world could not afford sweeter music to the ear, nor delight to any mind.' This serenade ended, we are told, at dawn.

FUNCTIONAL MUSIC

In *The Trials of Persiles and Sigismunda* one finds several references to music aboard ship, perhaps recollections by Cervantes from the time when he was captured by pirates. First we find the usual festivities of a ship leaving port, 'the air was split by the sounds of recorders

---

66 Ibid., 143ff.
67 Ibid., 162.
68 Cervantes, *The Illustrious Kitchen Maid*, 252ff.
69 Ibid., 270.
70 Montemayer, *Diana*, 88ff.

and other festive musical instruments.'⁷¹ More interesting are those references which describe the actual music.

> The tranquil sea, and the clear sky, together with the sound of the [fifes] and other instruments as military as they were cheerful, were breathtaking.⁷²
>
> ......
>
> Arnaldo signaled the ship to shoot off the artillery while the barbarian gave a sign for his men to play their instruments, and so the artillery and the music of the barbarians thundered into the sky at the same instant, filling the air with confused and discordant sounds.⁷³

An unusual reference to military music describes 'various other musical instruments making a cheerful though warlike sound.'⁷⁴ In *Don Quijote*, there is a description of the military music of the Moors, 'which was so jumbled together, so rapid and unrelenting, that anyone in his right mind would have lost it in the confused blaring.'⁷⁵

In *The Trials of Persiles and Sigismunda* there is an unusual reference to a trumpet giving the signal to begin a foot race.⁷⁶

A common form of Functional Music was that used to announce the arrival of important persons. In sixteenth-century literature the choice of instrument is carefully matched to the social standing of the person, thus always a trumpet for a king and often a cornett for a duke. In *Don Quijote*, we find in this regard a humorous example of a blast on a reed whistle which announces the arrival of a pig-gelder.⁷⁷ In this same work, there is a curious mixture of drums and a flute to announce the return of a lady.⁷⁸

Wedding music is another frequently mentioned form of functional music in early literature. In *Diana enamorada* we find a typical description of the music played as part of a wedding celebration.

> When Arsileus had made an end to his song, there was such a general rejoicing, that it would have cheered up the most sorrowful hearts that ever were. Sweet and delightful songs resounded in every part of the garden, the tuned instruments made more than earthly Harmony.⁷⁹

---

71 Cervantes, *The Trials of Persiles and Sigismunda*, I, xviii.

72 Ibid., I, ii.

73 Ibid., I, iii.

74 Ibid., III, xi.

75 Cervantes, *Don Quijote*, II, xxxiv.

76 Cervantes, *The Trials of Persiles and Sigismunda*, I, xxii.

77 Cervantes, *Don Quijote*, I, ii.

78 Ibid., II, xxxviii.

79 Polo, *Diana enamorada*, 379.

ENTERTAINMENT MUSIC

Interestingly enough, in this literature there is little reference to true entertainment music. We may suppose that this reflects to some degree the climate arising from the struggle between religious forces. Indeed, Cervantes refers to 'this age of ours—so deficient in cheerful amusement.'[80]

In *Diana enamorada* there is one reference to actual dinner music, 'the fair maid's song, and our supper ended all at one time.'[81]

---

80 Cervantes, *Don Quijote*, I, xxviii.
81 Polo, *Diana enamorada*, 334.

15 SIXTEENTH-CENTURY SPANISH POETRY

FRAY LUIS DE LEÓN, in the preface to the publication of his poems, records for us a glimpse of the intellectual climate of sixteenth-century Spain, a turbulent atmosphere of passions fueled by the Reformation and the Counter-Reformation in which nearly everyone was under attack. Four centuries later, it still sounds familiar, differing perhaps only in degree.

> Amid the years of study in my young manhood, almost in my childhood, these small works came upon me, falling into my hands. I devoted myself to them by inclination of my star more than out of judgment and will. Not because Poetry, when used principally in given arguments, is not worthy of anybody, whatever his name (the proof of which that God used it in many of his sacred books, as is well known); but rather because I knew the mistaken judgments of our people, and their slight inclination toward everything which has some light of genius and courage; and I understood the art and manner of ambition and of the pursuit of personal gain, and of ignorant suspicion, which are plants that are born and grow together and which instruct us now about our days. And so I decided out of excusable vanity and at the cost of my own work to make myself a target for the blows of a thousand raving opinions, and to provide material for gossip to those who live for no other thing.[1]

One should also notice here Luis de León's reference to his poetry as 'falling into my hands,' rather than being the result of 'judgment and will.' In Poetry, as in music, it was felt that the power of the performance could not quite be explained in the usual rational terms. Often the extra element is called the 'divine furor,' or in the case of medieval music one sometimes finds the phrase 'the science and *mystery* of minstrelsy.' Luis de Camões, at the beginning of his historical epic, *The Lusiads*, makes a similar distinction, between knowledge and art, in predicting the fame of his work.

> My Song shall spread where ever there are Men,
> If Wit and Art will so much guide my Pen.[2]

---

1 Quoted in Willis Barnstone, *The Unknown Light, the Poems of Fray Luis de León* (Albany: State University of New York Press, 1979), 37. Luis de León (born in 1527) was educated at the University of Salamanca, one of the most important centers for humanism in Spain. After he became a professor at the same university, he soon came under attack by the competing professors of the Dominican order because he had dared to make his own translations of Scripture from the Hebrew, rather than accepting the Latin Vulgate. Thus, he was called a Jew and when out of town accused to the Inquisition. Luis de León spent nearly five years in prison before being restored to his university chair. When this occurred, amidst great celebration by the students, he made no reference to the lost five years and simply began his lecture, 'As we were saying yesterday …'

2 Luis de Camões, *The Lusiads*, trans. Richard Fanshawe [1655], ed. Geoffrey Bullough (Carbondale: Southern Illinois University Press, 1963), I, ii. We have modernized some spelling.

For help in acquiring this inspiration necessary to art, the poets were still addressing pleas to the Muses—sixteen centuries of Church edicts being to no avail. Thus Camões prays,

> Give me a mighty Fury, Not rude Reed's
> Or rustic Bag-pipes sound, But such as War's
> Loud Instrument (the noble Trumpet) breeds,
> Which fires the Breast, and stirs the blood
> Give me a Poem equal to the deeds.[3]

At the end of this very lengthy epic poem, Camões once again addresses his Muse complaining that he is exhausted and discouraged from singing to an audience which pays no attention.

> No more, my Muse, no more; my Harp's ill strung,
> Heavy, and out of tune, and my Voice hoarse:
> And, not with singing, but to see I've sung
> To a deaf people and without remorse.[4]

We find another bias of the Catholic Counter Reformation, in a poem by Andrés Fernández de Andrada, written ca. 1600, which renews the Church's ancient objection to the theater.

> May God forbid that I copy these pale,
> Lean men that haunt our squares, infamous actors
> That bring disgrace on the fair name of virtue;
>
> Unclean tragedians seeking for applause
> Of men, whose hearts accursed are within,
> Sad monuments of darkness and of gloom.[5]

ON THE PHYSIOLOGY OF AESTHETICS

In the poetry of the priest, San Juan de la Cruz, we find another representative of the Counter Reformation trying once again, on behalf of the Church, to offer the old dogma that only Faith is needed, not Reason, knowledge or the senses.

> I came into the unknown
> and stayed there unknowing,
> rising beyond all science.

---

[3] Ibid., I, v.

[4] Ibid., X, cxlv.

[5] Andrés Fernández de Andrada (fl. ca. 1600), 'Epístola Moral,' in Eleanor Turnbull, *Ten Centuries of Spanish Poetry* (Baltimore: The Johns Hopkins Press, 1955), 263.

I did not know the door
but when I found the way,
unknowing where I was,
I learned enormous things,
but what I felt I cannot say,
for I remained unknowing,
rising beyond all science.

It was the perfect realm
of holiness and peace.
In deepest solitude
I found the narrow way:
a secret giving such release
that I was stunned and stammering,
rising beyond all science.

I was so far inside,
so dazed and far away
my senses were released
from feelings of my own.
My mind had found a surer way:
a knowledge by unknowing,
rising beyond all science.[6]

ON THE PSYCHOLOGY OF AESTHETICS

These sixteenth century Spanish poets always speak of Love in strong sensory language, as, for example, Lope de Vega,

> Verses of my love, conceits set free,
> Engendered in the soul my cares to frame,
> The offspring of my senses set aflame …[7]

As he clarifies in another poem, Love is something completely apart from Reason.

> For very love inflames and torments me,
> And does my reason and my freedom steal.
> Why frown you when a soul must love recite?

---

6 San Juan de la Cruz, 'I Came into the Unknown,' in Barnstone, *The Poems of Saint John of the Cross*, 59.

7 Carl Cobb, *Anthology of Lope de Vega's Lyric Poetry* (York, South Carolina: Spanish Literature Publications, 1991), 113. Lope de Vega (1562–1635) was the greatest playwright of the 'Golden Age.'

> That I not write, you say, not live (for me)?
> Then you see to it I my love don't feel,
> And I'll see to it that my pen not write.[8]

He mentions the conflict of Love and Reason again in a Moorish ballad, where the poor Moor finds himself tongue-tied by his emotions.

> I think this Moor long-reasoning
> Might thus be talking yet,
> If his poor tongue had not failed him,
> It being half-upset.[9]

Regarding the traditional topics of Pleasure and Pain, we find the poet, Pedro de Padilla, objecting to the pain which Love carries with it.

> Love does whatever he likes, 'tis true,
> But never what he ought to do …
> There is no grief, there is no pain,
> Which he inflicts not …
>
> It would become him well to give,
> For sorrows deep, and sufferings long,
> One gleam of joy, one short reprieve,
> One thought of bliss 'midst misery's throng.
> But no! he flies the alternative,
> And throws again the bolts he threw:—
> He does not what he ought to do.[10]

One might as well learn to find pleasure in the pain of love, advises Lope de Vega in his play, *La Dorotea*, where Fernando reads a poem.

> Amaryllis, in reflecting
> how divine your beauty is,
> I'd forfeit every blessing
> for pleasuring in pain.[11]

In one of his poems, he uses a musical instrument as a symbol of the pain and uselessness felt by one who has been exiled.

---

8   Ibid.,131.

9   Ibid., 53.

10 Pedro de Padilla (fl. first half, sixteenth century), 'Hace el amor lo que quiere,' in John Crow, *An Anthology of Spanish Poetry* (Baton Rouge: Louisiana State University Press, 1979), 57.

11 Lope de Vega, *La Dorotea*, trans. Alan Trueblood and Edwin Honig (Cambridge: Harvard University Press, 1985), IV, i.

A thousand years I have not sung
Since I've a thousand cried
The troubles of exile from which
Some others would have died.

My instrument bereft of strings
And madly out of tune,
Without four of its tuning pegs,
With dust both filled and strewn;

The mice have made a nest among
Its golden tracery,
From where soft, sharp, or raucous, grave,
The air escape did see.

Now many wrongly think, since I
Am mute I just rocks throw …[12]

ON THE PHILOSOPHY OF AESTHETICS

The original Spanish editor of Luis de Camões', *The Lusiads*, in his foreword discusses the ideals of lofty poetry, which are the usual aesthetic principles of dramatic poetry: observance of the Unities, an heroic action by high born people with the language appropriate to these people. He adds, however, something new, an emphasis on Beauty.

> It must include episodes, figures, imitation, and other adornments to beautify it. The style must be elegant and sublime, yet in its sublimity must not lose ease, suavity and sweetness.[13]

San Juan de la Cruz states the Church position, warning man of anything related to the senses, even Beauty. His message is found in the closing,

On earth you never must rely
on what the senses understand
or all the knowledge you command
although it rises very high.

His poem begins,

For all the beauty there may be
I'll never throw away my soul;

---

12 Cobb, *Anthology of Lope de Vega's Lyric Poetry*, 93ff.
13 Manuel de Faria y Sousa (1639), quoted in Luis de Camões, *The Lusiads*, 13.

only for something I don't know
that one may come on randomly.[14]

There remains always a need for the ancient type of epic poetry which praises the deeds of the great, as Luis de Góngora promises the count of Niebla.

Taste today favors now one Music, now another,
and if my own Muse can send forth such resounding
tones, not second, in fame, to others, then
the ends of the earth shall hear your name.[15]

ON THE AESTHETICS OF MUSIC

Regarding the purpose of music, for any good sixteenth-century Catholic, who also had at least an intellectual interest in humanism, music represented a comforting middle ground. Reaching back to the ancient Greek concept of understanding the organization of the world through the analogy of music, which had such apparent order and proportion, one could think of music as an important vehicle for restoring the harmony of the soul and retracing one's steps to the divine. Fray Luis de León makes a beautiful presentation of this idea in his 'Ode to Francisco Salinas,' the latter being a blind professor of music at the University of Salamanca.

The air becomes serene
and robed in beauty and an unknown light,
Salinas, when the unseen
deep music soars in flight,
governed by your hand that is wise and right.

Before that holy song
my soul, submerged in its oblivion,
recovers sense and long
forgotten memory in
its dazzling and primordial origin.

And having knowledge of
itself, it comes alive in thought and fate,
and has contempt, above
all, for mere gold, the bait
of blind mobs, or beauty in its false state.

---

14   San Juan de la Cruz, 'For all the Beauty there may be,' in Barnstone, *The Poems of Saint John of the Cross*, 85ff.
15   Luis de Góngora (1561–1627), 'Fábula de Polifemo y Galatea,' Dedication,' in Crow, *An Anthology of Spanish Poetry*, 100

Piercing the air, the soul
reaches into the very highest sphere
and there it hears a
wholly different mode;
imperishable music, first and without peer.

It sees the way the grand
master works the immense zither, and the way
he shapes the holy strand
of sound with dexterous play,
by which that deathless temple is sustained.

It is composed, then, by
concordant numbers that accompany
a consonant reply,
and both work stubbornly
to mingle lost in sweetest harmony.

Here the soul sails around
inside a sea of sweetness, and finally wheels
about and then is drowned
so that it hears or feels
nothing that foreign accident reveals.

O happy deep collapse!
O death conferring life! O sweet oblivion!
Now let me never lapse
into the low, vile run
of senses! Let my rest in you be won!

I call you to this good
joy, you the glory of Apollo's holy
choir, friends whom I could
love beyond all wholly
vain wealth, for all the visible is sad folly.

O Salinas, let me hear
the music of your fingers as it rings
constantly in my ear,
my senses wakening
to holy grace and dulled to earthly things![16]

The most frequently mentioned purpose of music in early literature is to bring solace, as Garcilaso de la Vega mentions in a line of one of his sonnets, 'In heavenly notes sing solace to my woe!'[17] For this reason, Luis de León also turns to music.

---

16 Barnstone, *The Unknown Light*, 45ff.
17 Garcilaso de la Vega (1503–1536), 'Sonnet,' in Turnbull, *Ten Centuries of Spanish Poetry*, 163.

How peaceful is the life
of one who breaks away from worldly sound
and follows, free of strife,
the hidden path: the ground
of those few wise men who were in the world!

      ......

And while the others are
miserably and with an insatiable thirst
reaching for futile power,
conspiring to be first,
let me lie down singing, in shade immersed,

lie down in shade, a pleat
of ivy and eternal laurel on my head,
my ear turned to those sweet
concordant notes, and led
to hear plectrum and strings artfully wed.[18]

One of the most beautiful Spanish poems of the late sixteenth century, a 'Roundelay,' by Luis de Góngora, has the hope of solace as its theme. Not all music, he says, is like the sad songs of the nightingale.

> They are not only nightingales,
> They who sing in flowery dales,
> But little silver bells that play
>   To welcome day,
> And little golden horns that blow
>   A greeting gay
>   To eyes aglow.
>
> Not every song upon the breeze
> Comes from feathered songster's throat,
> Sung by siren birds who float
> Atop the spray of crested seas,
> Green foliage of poplar trees,
> Should you hearken to their tales.
> They are not only nightingales,
> They who sing in flowery dales,
> But little silver bells that play
>   To welcome day,
> And little golden horns that blow
>   A greeting gay
>   To eyes aglow.

---

18 Barnstone, *The Unknown Light*, 53ff.

This artful charm, this dulcet choir
Of soft melodious decrial
Against despair; no winged viol
Plays this, nor any restless lyre.
but other melodies inspire
And stir one's heart, so good prevails.
They are not only nightingales,
They who sing in flowery dales,
But little silver bells that play
    To welcome day,
And little golden horns that blow
    A greeting gay
    To eyes aglow.[19]

Another traditional purpose of music was to express grief. In an Eclogue, Garcilaso de la Vega tells of a young man, who 'Poured forth in melancholy song his soul of sorrow,' over the death of his lover. He compares his song with that of the nightingale, which is usually associated with sad music in early literature.

Dying with passion and desire, she flings
A thousand concords from her various bill,
Till the whole melancholy woodland rings
With gurglings sweet, or with philippics shrill.
Throughout the silent night she not refrains
Her piercing note, and her pathetic cry,
But calls as witness to her wrongs and pains,
The listening stars and the responding sky.
So I in mournful song pour forth my pain;
So I lament,—lament, alas, in vain …[20]

Lope de Vega also mentions, in a poem, his use of music to express grief.

If with long sadness what I sang as song
Has weighed on me, and would me weeping bring …[21]

---

19 Luis de Góngora (1561–1627), 'Sonnet,' in Turnbull, *Ten Centuries of Spanish Poetry*, 283.
20 Garcilaso de la Vega (1503–1536), 'Eclogue I,' in Ibid., 157. Garcilaso de la Vega entered the service of Charles V as a young man and died in the French campaign of 1536.
21 Cobb, *Anthology of Lope de Vega's Lyric Poetry*, 183.

ART MUSIC

Most of the art songs were songs of love, but one poet complains that even his song has no effect.

> Celinda, by what potent art
> Or unresisted charm,
> Dost thou thine ear and frozen heart
> Against my passion arm?
>
> Or by what hidden influence
> Of powers in one combined,
> Dost thou rob love of either sense,
> Made deaf as well as blind?[22]

There are numerous art songs which make reference to the singing of birds, especially the melancholy character of the nightingale's music. An unusual humorous example concerns a fly criticizing the song of the frog.

> Out of the Wine-Pot cry'd the Fly,
> Whilst the Grave Frog sat croaking by,
> Than live a Watery Life like thine,
> I'd rather choose to die in Wine.
> ......
> In Gardens I delight to stray,
> And round the Plants do sing and play:
> Thy Tune no Mortal does avail,
> Thou are the Dutchman's Nightingale:
> Wouldst thou with Wine but wet thy Throat,
> Sure thou would'st leave that Dismal Note;
> Lewd Water spoils thy Organs quite,
> And Wine alone can set them right.[23]

Camões in *The Lusiad* speaks of the musicians on board ship, in a reverse reference to the ancient concept of the 'Music of the Spheres.'

> Others on lofty Cornetts played:
> And These with Music did the Spheres invade.[24]

---

22 Lope de Vega, 'Doriano a los zarcillos de Lucinda,' in Crow, *An Anthology of Spanish Poetry*, 104ff.
23 Francisco de Quevedo (1580–1645), 'Letrilla burlesca,' in Ibid., 113.
24 Luis de Camões, *The Lusiads*, II, xc.

This in contrast to the native music heard when the ship reached an island.

> Grating the Ear with a harsh noise. The whole
> Consort, was only crooked Horns, wreath'd round
> Which keep no time, but make a dismal sound.[25]

The music of other natives, those of Sofala, was much more sophisticated. Aside from the rare reference to shepherds singing part-songs, we notice that the faces of these performers were filled with emotion.

> Sweet madrigals (in rhyme or prose complete
> In their own Tongue) to rustic reeds applied,
> They sing in Parts, as gentle Shepherds use,
> That imitate Tytirus the Muse.
>
> These (and no less was written in their Faces)
> Love and Humanity to us afford …[26]

Another special form of Art Music is heard when, to reward these Portuguese sailors, Venus prepares a floating island stocked with amorous Nereids. These ladies were string players.

> Some touch the grave Theorba in shades dark,
> Some the sweet Lute, the gentle Violeen …[27]

After the love making a great feast is given for the sailors, with special music.

> Musical Instruments not wanting (such
> As to the damned spirits once gave ease
> In the dark Vaults of the Infernal Hall)
> Joined with a Siren's Voice, angelical:
>
> The fair Muse sang, and with her shrill Accents
> (Which from the lofty Battlement rebound)
> In equal harmony the Instruments,
> Keeping just time, their softer Notes confound.[28]

---

25   Ibid., II, xcvi.
26   Ibid., V, lxiiiff.
27   Ibid., IX, lxiv.
28   Ibid., X, vi.

FUNCTIONAL MUSIC

Camões describes the signal trumpets on board ship playing for joy, rather than in their military role of inspiring courage.

> The rattling Trumpets, now, their joy augment
> As, other times, they had their courage done.[29]

Later, in Canto III, xlviii, the author mentions other unspecified military instruments,

> The Trumpets sound;
> Loud Instruments of war go bellowing round,

which in Canto IV, xxvii, are identified.

> The vocal Trumpets challenge, and accept:
> The Drums, and whistling Fifes in consort join.

This passage continues with a more typical reference to the military trumpet, mentioning that for the listener it always brought a sense of fear for it symbolized battle.

> Castilian Trumpets did the on-set sound,
> Loud, furious, dismal, terrible, and hoarse …
> And Mothers (who that baleful noise did hear)
> Clasped to their Breasts their tender Babes for fear.

Another interesting reference to the trumpet is given in retelling the visit to the king of Melinde. The ship trumpets play a fanfare for the king and the accompanying Moors do likewise with cornetts. In sixteenth-century literature the cornett, being a kind of lesser trumpet, is often used to symbolize a lesser person, in this case the Moor. Camões also mentions the native king's awe on hearing the European trumpet for the first time.

> With which the Guns salute him from the Fleet.
> The Trumpets play unto him in shrill notes:
> The Moors with Cornetts answer from the Boats.
> But when the generous King had ceased to note
> All that he would, nor heard with little wonder
> The unusual Instrument with the wide Throat
> That speaks so big, and tears the clouds asunder …[30]

---

29 Ibid., II, c.
30 Ibid., II, cviff.

Camões also mentions an unusual form of occupational song, the songs of love sung by makers of instruments of war!

> Some whetting arrow-heads on bloody hone,
> Others the shafts of arrows shaving small.
> Working they sing, and sing of love alone,
> And then that Love it is Seraphical:
> In Parts; and in the burthen all do join;
> The Ditty excellent, the Tune Divine.[31]

---

31   Ibid., IX, xxx.

16 SIXTEENTH-CENTURY SPANISH DRAMA

CERVANTES, IN THE 'PROLOGUE TO THE READER' of his 1615 publication of eight one-act plays, called *Entremés*, or Interludes, provides a brief history of modern theater in Spain. He tells us that in the earliest plays the musicians were hidden from view, being placed behind the stage in the actors' dressing room. It was the playwright, Navarro, who first brought the musicians onto the stage.

By the sixteenth century, as we can see in the plays of Lope de Vega, Spanish plays nearly always have musicians, both instrumentalists and singers, who often have speaking parts as well. In his *Acting is Believing*, when the characters are planning a play within a play, the question is raised, 'Do you have music?' The answer is, 'Excellent; and we'll use it if you're interested.'[1] Later, as the actors are ready to begin the play, however, the playwright, Genesius, observes, 'A fine state of affairs, upon my life! We're always short a musician.'[2]

When one considers the strong belief of the humanists in Italy and France that in sung poetry the emotions are found in the words and not the music, the following observation by Lope de Vega that, on the contrary, in drama the emotions are supplied by music, is quite remarkable.

> The instruments occupied the front part of the theater, without being seen, and to their harmony the actors sang the verses; all the effects, such as surprise, lamentation, love, anger, being expressed in the composition of the music itself.[3]

In another place, Lope de Vega speaks of the emotion of Love in its relationship with music.

> CÉSAR. Don't put down your instrument, Fernando, I beg you.
> FERNANDO. The words have by now given the strings permission to rest.
> CÉSAR. It's no less well sung than written.
> FERNANDO. One's taste is no judge of the skills of friends.

---

1 Lope de Vega, *Lo fingido verdadero*, trans. Michael McGaha (San Antonio: Trinity University Press, 1986), 54. Lope de Vega (1562–1635), the greatest playwright of sixteenth-century Spain, is thought to have written between twelve and twenty-five hundred plays. As Gustave Reese, *Music in the Renaissance* (New York: Norton, 1959), 630ff, adds, instrumental music is frequently found in the plays of Cervantes as well. In particular he finds the Moorish music interesting in Los Baños de Argel and La Gran Sultana.

2 Lope de Vega, *Lo fingido verdadero*, 71.

3 Reese, *Music in the Renaissance*, 631, where he gives the original Spanish source as Emilio Cotarelo y Mori, *Historia de la Zarzuela* (1934), 36. We know from clinical research today that Lope de Vega was right and the humanists wrong: words (left hemisphere of the brain) do not have feelings.

CÉSAR. Assume I'm not one, in your case.
FERNANDO. Music is a divine art.
CÉSAR. Some say it was invented by Mercury; others, by Aristogenes. The truth is that love invented it. Because harmony is concord, and concord, the agreement between low and high notes, and such agreement was established by love; because from that mutual attraction there follows the effect of music, which is pleasure. This union in love Marsilio Ficino called the lord and master of music; thus beautiful Lamia drove the great Demetrius mad with love.[4]

Various passages in the works of Lope de Vega reveal his extensive knowledge of music, musicians, their techniques and their instruments. For example, the following dialogue from *La Dorotea*, intended as a humorous comment on women, reveals his knowledge of the construction of instrumental strings.

FERNANDO. Whoever said it would be convenient to buy ready-made letters and trimmed beards should have added [ready-made] tuned instruments.
JULIO. That would be impossible. The substance strings are made of, you see, causes them to slacken with moisture and tauten with excessive heat. In other words, like some women, strings always need tuning.
FERNANDO. Which is why they are worked on so much—to bring them up to the pitch of the tuner.
JULIO. Many break.
FERNANDO. Look only for the genuine and discard the false. That's what musicians do.
JULIO. Which brings up something curiously à propos.
FERNANDO. Namely?
JULIO. That as they undo the skein, they flip it with one finger, holding the end of the string between the teeth, and if the string casts two shadows, they discard it as faulty and go on to the next. The same applies to trying out a woman; if she casts shadows in two directions, change her for another.[5]

He also reveals a thorough knowledge of musical styles. In one passage, much like Arbeau in France, he criticizes the modern dance music and bemoans the disappearance of the older styles.

May God forgive Vicente Espinel, who brought us this novelty and the fifth string on the guitar, so that now people are neglecting the nobler instruments and ancient dances for the wild gesticulations and lewd movements of the chaconnes, so offensive to the virtue of chastity and to a lady's decorous reserve. Alas and alack, oh *allemande* and *pie de gibao*, who for so many years dignified our soirées.[6]

---

4 Lope de Vega, *La Dorotea*, trans. Alan Trueblood and Edwin Honig (Cambridge: Harvard University Press, 1985), V, iii.
5 Ibid., I, iv. Later [III, viii] a character says, 'he has replaced a broken treble string and is starting up again.'
6 Ibid., I, vii.

The references to music in the stage directions follow their usage in ordinary life. Thus in *Peribáñez*, when 'Drums are heard,' it is to announce a military personage.[7]

While, of course, the actual music used in these plays is not always extant, Reese does mention that the music of Blas de Castro, a friend of Lope de Vega, gives the impression of being intended for use in plays.[8] At least two of Lope de Vega's plays, *Peribáñez* and *El Caballero de Olmedo*, found the inspiration for their plots in popular songs of the day which he heard.[9]

Finally, we see in these plays descriptions of the sixteenth-century courtier. In one place, in *The Duchess of Amalfi's Steward*, Lope de Vega presents the ideal courtier. Here a discussion ensues which lists the qualities needed by a courtier. They include the ability to recite Latin poetry, be a skillful swordsman, fine manners, impeccable dress, and 'how well he sings!'[10]

In general, however, Lope de Vega is critical of the courtier, beginning perhaps as a matter of simple honesty. He presents a courtier in *Justice Without Revenge*, for example, who observes,

> For though I show an outward pleasure, as courtesy demands, my soul is full of deep displeasure.[11]

In the *La Dorotea*, Lope de Vega makes another complaint regarding the courtier—that he appears to be more educated than he really is.

> CELIA. There's always more to know than one man can know.
> LAURENCIO. Right you are, and take my word for it: as there's an infinite amount to learn, and life is short, the most learned man knows next to nothing.
> CELIA. Has this master of yours ever studied anything?
> LAURENCIO. Enough to show off what he knows, like the bachelor of arts—the worst breed of courtier to deal with.[12]

ON THE PHYSIOLOGY OF AESTHETICS

There is little conjecture in these plays on the nature of Reason and intellect, although Lope de Vega refers to the subject in a musical analogy:

---

7   Lope de Vega, *Peribáñez*, trans. Jill Booty, in *Lope de Vega, Five Plays* (New York: HIll and Wang, 1961), 39.
8   Reese, *Music in the Renaissance*, 617.
9   See Booty, *Five Plays*, 34, fn., and 222, fn.
10 Lope de Vega, *El mayordomo de la duquesa de Amalfi*, trans., Cynthia Rodriguez-Badendyck (Ottawa: Dovehouse, 1985), I, 249.
11 See Booty, *Five Plays*, 235.
12 Lope de Vega, *La Dorotea*, II, v.

> Minds are like instruments, you know; they must be played on to display the harmonies they possess.[13]

In his *Justice Without Revenge*, he contends that imagination 'soars beyond the bounds of Reason,' as is evident in dreams. A character agrees and then, in what was comedy for the sixteenth-century observer but is an alarming insight to sixteenth-century manners for the modern reader, offers illustrations of his imagination.

> Yes, sir, you are right. Why, sometimes, when I am with a group of gentlemen, suddenly I have a great urge to hit one of them, or bite him in the throat. Or, if I am on a balcony, sometimes I feel I might throw myself off and kill myself. Or in church, during the sermon, I imagine myself shouting out and telling the priest: 'I've already read that!' Often I want to burst out laughing at a funeral. Or when I see two men earnestly gaming together and oblivious to all else, I long to pick up a candlestick and throw it at them. If I hear anyone singing, I want to sing myself.[14]

As one might expect in this repertoire, consisting mostly of comedies, the philosopher is a familiar target. In Lope de Vega's, *The Lady Simpleton*, for example, the character, Nise, says,

> Since he does it in the Greek way
> You don't know what he has to say
> Until book number five is read,
> And then you'll understand and get
> What went on in the other four.[15]

In his *Fuente Ovejuna*, we find the common sixteenth-century observation that the most educated man knows the least.

> What I can't stand is those astrologers,
> who claim to know the future, though they don't,
> and lecture us, in lengthy disquisitions
> on mysteries that are known to God alone.
> It's so absurd, they talk like theologians,
> and when it comes to pressing, present matters,
> the wisest man amongst them knows the least.[16]

And later in the same work we find,

> BARRILDO. You see so many printed books these days
>   that everybody thinks they know it all.

---

13 Ibid., II, iv.

14 Lope de Vega, *Justice Without Revenge*, in Booty, *Five Plays*, 247.

15 Lope de Vega, *La Dama Boba*, trans. Max Oppenheimer (Lawrence: Coronado Press, 1976), I, v.

16 Lope de Vega, *Fuente Ovejuna*, trans. Victor Dixon (Warminster: Aris & Phillips, 1989), [II], 113.

LEONELO. For that same reason, I think they know less,
    now learning's not condensed in summaries;
    so much is printed that it breeds confusion,
    knowledge is mixed with airy-fairy nonsense,
    and those who spend most time in reading find
    so many titles just bemuse the mind.[17]

ON THE PSYCHOLOGY OF AESTHETICS

One of the most interesting references we have found to any of the emotions in general is found in *La Dorotea*, where Dorotea makes a curious association of anger with poetry.

> Anger and love are the principal human passions. So tell me, Celia, if the ancients held that anger created poetry, why should it not be more accessible to love, which laments its sufferings in the sweetest of harmonies?[18]

Love is clearly the most common subject in this repertoire of comedy. We find a number of original and interesting definitions of love in the plays of Lope de Vega. In the first line of *The Knight from Olmedo*, he reminds us that Love is something understood only by experience.

> Let no man speak Love's name that has not felt his power.[19]

Another definition of Love is as a desire for personal pleasure—forget what the scholars say, he warns in *Fuente Ovejuna*,

> MENGO. Tell me, what's love?
> LAURENCIA. It's a desire for beauty.
> MENGO. And why does love want beauty?
> LAURENCIA. Why, to enjoy it.
> MENGO. Yes, I agree; but when it seeks that pleasure,
>   isn't that for itself?
> LAURENCIA. Well, yes.
> MENGO. And therefore
>   it wants the thing that gives it satisfaction
>   because it loves itself?
> LAURENCIA. That's true.
> MENGO. That proves it.

---

17 Ibid., [II], 115. The author also mentions here that some persons had 'rubbish' published under the name of a man they hated.
18 Lope de Vega, *La Dorotea*, V, x. We do not believe such a statement among the ancients exists.
19 Lope de Vega, *The Knight from Olmedo*, in Booty, *Five Plays*, 179.

> There is no love, except the sort I say,
> that I pursue to indulge my private whim
> and wholly to give pleasure to myself.
> BARRILDO. One day the village priest said in his sermon
> some man called Plato taught us how to love,
> and said we should love nothing but the soul
> and virtue of the person whom we loved.
> PASCUALA. This is the sort of thing that academics
> in colleges and schools must boil their brains with.
> LAURENCIA. She's right, you're wrong to tie yourselves in knots
> by copying their contentious arguments.[20]

Another reference to an ancient definition of Love, as a kind of harmony in man, is found in Lope de Vega's, in *Fuente Ovejuna*.

> BARRILDO. There's no such thing as love.
> LAURENCIA. In general? That's too sweeping.
> BARRILDO. Yes, and stupid.
> The world itself could never last without it.
> MENGO. I can't philosophize—wish I could read!
> But if the elements from which our bodies
> draw sustenance—phlegm, melancholy, blood,
> and choler too—are in perpetual conflict,
> it stands to reason.
> BARRILDO. Mengo, all the world,
> here and up there, is perfect harmony,
> and harmony is love, for love is concord.[21]

A particularly interesting discussion of Love credits it with educational virtues. Found in Lope de Vega's *Lady Simpleton*, he gives us a review of what Love has taught man. First, he believes, Love was the origin of science,

> Love has been that great genius
> As the world's spirit known to us;
> It also held the science chair,
> For just through love man everywhere
> Will learn much more accurately
> What divine traits in him might be.
>
> ......
>
> Contemplating one starts to wonder,
> Then to philosophize and ponder,

---

20 Lope de Vega, *Fuente Ovejuna*, [I], 81ff.
21 Ibid., [I], 79.

This in turn does the light provide
With which ingenious science might
Be founded. And to love we owe
Man's natural desire to know.[22]

Love, 'gently but firmly gave man feeling,' then laws, then the arts,

Love taught the coarsest men to dress
And master elegance no less.
Music, painting and poetry,
Without love they would never be.

Lope de Vega found Love to be an inconsistent, ever changing thing, as he observes in *The Duchess of Amalfi's Steward*, where Antonio says:

For love's delight, my lord,
Is a kite upon the wind.[23]

In another play this idea, expressed in stronger imagery and from the point of view of the woman, involves music.

DIANA. One who loves can, if he will, turn his love to hatred and hate as truly as he loved. So will I do.
ANARDA. Is that possible?
DIANA. I will do it. I loved because I wanted to. Now I wish it no more, I will love no longer. *[Music is heard off-stage]* Who is that singing?
ANARDA. Fabio and Clara.
DIANA. I would their music could solace me.
ANARDA. Music and love agree well together. Listen.
SINGERS *[off-stage]*. Oh, for the power to turn love's darts at will:
  Turn love to hate,
  And Hate to love.
  Oh, for the power to turn love's darts at will.
ANARDA. Do you hear the song, madam? Does it not contradict what you were saying?
DIANA. I hear it, but I best know my mind, and will change to hatred a love which so ill suits my state.[24]

In *Acting is Believing*, a character observes,

Love lasts as long as the fear of losing what one loves; for as soon as it's possessed, love wanes.[25]

---
22 Lope de Vega, *La Dama Boba*, II, i.
23 Lope de Vega, *El mayordomo de la duquesa de Amalfi*, I, 110.
24 Lope de Vega, *The Dog in the Manger*, in Booty, *Five Plays*, 140.
25 Lope de Vega, *Lo fingido verdadero*, 86.

In the same play, a character notices that 'being upset is always the best sign that someone's in love.'[26]

Lope de Vega gives us a somewhat more positive view of Love in *Peribáñez*, with a description of falling in love which employs musical analogies.

> No music that ever set my feet tapping can thrill me as much as you do, however hard the drummer beat his stick or blew on his pipe. Myrtle and vervain were never so sweet, nor are the horses whinnying on Midsummer morning as exciting to me as the sound of your voice. What gay, tinkling tambourine or psalm in church can equal you?[27]

Regarding the universal experience of the pain of loss of love, Lope de Vega wonders, in *La Dorotea*, whether even music can ease the pain.

> LUDOVICO. This illness, which doctors call *erotes*, is melancholia arising from amorous proclivities or from losing possession of a beloved whom one has enjoyed. The cure is baths, music, wine and theater.
> JULIO. Wine Fernando does not drink; as for music, singing makes him all the sadder.[28]

In another place, Fernando implies that a song might at least temporarily displace his suffering.

> I know perfectly well that, except for a few mournful ditties I might sing, this jealous passion will leave room for nothing else.[29]

Another interesting musical analogy, in this regard, is found in Fernando de Rojas' *Celestina*.

> CALISTO. The sweetness of her voice hath ravished me! Dear lady and glory of my life, if thou lovest me, give not over thy singing!
> MELIBEA. My desire of thee was that which made me air my notes; now that thou art come, that desire disappears.
> CALISTO. O interrupted melody, short-timed pleasure![30]

Regarding Pleasure, Lope de Vega, in *The Dog in the Manger*, offers a noble definition.

> Pleasure is not in greatness, but rather in the fitness of what is desired by the loving soul.[31]

Like all early writers, however, he cannot help but observe that Pleasure and Pain always seem to come together.

---

26 Ibid., 76.
27 Lope de Vega, *Peribáñez*, 4.
28 Lope de Vega, *La Dorotea*, III, iv.
29 Ibid.
30 Fernando de Rojas, *Celestina*, trans., James Mabbe (New York: Applause Publishers, 1986), 89.
31 Lope de Vega, *The Dog in the Manger*, 174.

There is no pleasure which does not give way in the end to displeasure; even day, beautiful and pleasant as it is, must finally yield to night.[32]

Fernando de Rojas advises that one should keep one's grief to one's self.

Uncover not your grief unto strangers since the drum is in their hands who know best how to beat it.[33]

ON THE PHILOSOPHY OF AESTHETICS

In *La Dorotea*, Lope de Vega provides the most frequently found classical definition of Beauty.

> FERNANDO. And where can beauty be found outside of Dorotea?
> JULIO. In everything possessing proportion, for beauty is exactly that. As Leo Hebraeus says in his *Philography*: that form which best informs matter makes the parts of the body, one with another, more proportionate to the whole, and unifies the parts with the whole.[34]

The most interesting discussions of aesthetics in general in these plays are relative to theories of writing plays. Since plays were considered a branch of poetry, the first requisite in Lope de Vega's mind was that the playwright must be a good poet. In *Acting is Believing*, a character observes of Genesius, another character who is being considered to write a play, 'If he's a bad poet, he should forget about it and not get involved in writing plays.'[35]

Genesius presents some obstacles, so another playwright, Aristeles, is suggested. Genesius, in a comment meant to be belittling, says, 'He will obey the rules.' This results in some dialogue in which we see the purpose of the playwright is not to follow the rules, even if the critics object, but to achieve delight.

> CARINUS. Enough! Find Aristeles, and he'll do it quickly.
> GENESIUS. He'll observe the rules.
> CARINUS. No, do it just like always. I don't like to be limited by art and the precepts.
> GENESIUS. The intellectuals will be annoyed.
> CARINUS. Well, let them be. Delight the ears, and that's enough, as long as there's no absurdity that can be seen.[36]

---

32 Lope de Vega, *La Dorotea*, III, ii.
33 Fernando de Rojas, *Celestina*, 68.
34 Lope de Vega, *La Dorotea*, III, i.
35 Lope de Vega, *Lo fingido verdadero*, 53.
36 Ibid., 55.

The implication here, in having Genesius speak in contempt of a playwright who strictly observes all the rules, carries the suggestion, of course, that Lope de Vega himself had priorities higher than following the rules. In his foreword to the *La Dorotea* we see a concrete example, where he explains why the presentation of Truth is more important than observing the traditional 'Unities.'

> If there is any flaw in the craftsmanship—especially from the inclusion of the interval of an absence—may truth be its justification, for the poet preferred to follow truth and not be bound by the irrelevant laws governing time and place in dramatic fictions.[37]

The classical definition of the purpose of comedy is given in Lope de Vega's *Justice Without Revenge*, when the duke says,

> Do you not know, Ricardo, that a play is a mirror in which the fool, the sage, young men and old, the warrior, the courtier, king, governor, maiden, wife, may all learn by example, concerning life and honor? Our customs are portrayed for what they are, fickle, or severe. Truth is mingled with the mockery, and censure is in the wit and the tragedy that entertain us.[38]

The most important question of purpose involved in any performing art regards the distinction between higher art versus entertainment. Lope de Vega, in his treatise, *The New Art of Writing Plays in this Age*, seems to take the view that Comedy must be entertainment. He admits that he has written his plays 'without art,' but not because he was ignorant of the rules, which he had studied in school,

> But because, in fine, I found that comedies were not at that time, in Spain, as their first devisers in the world [the ancient Greeks] thought that they should be written;[39] but rather as many rude fellows managed them, who confirmed the crowd in its crudeness; and so they were introduced in such wise that he who now writes them artistically dies without fame or money.
>
> True it is that I have sometimes written in accordance with the art which few know; but, no sooner do I see coming from some other source the monstrosities full of painted scenes where the crowd congregates and the women who canonize this sad business, than I return to that same barbarous habit, and when I have to write a comedy I lock in the precepts with six keys, I banish Terence and Plautus from my study, that they may not cry out at me; for truth, even in dumb books, is wont to call aloud; and I write in accordance with that art which they devised who aspired to the applause of the crowd; for, since the crowd pays for the comedies, it is fitting to talk foolishly to it to satisfy its taste.[40]

---

37   Lope de Vega, *La Dorotea*, Foreword.
38   Lope de Vega, *Justice Without Revenge*, 235.
39   Later he contends that whatever is written in Spain, is written 'in defiance of art.'
40   Quoted in Barrett Clark, *European Theories of the Drama* (New York: Crown, 1959), 89.

Cervantes, on the other hand, takes a higher view of art and refuses to accept that plays must be mere entertainment. In *Don Quixote* he discusses the theater at length, noting, in particular,

> If these dramas we see—both those with invented plots and those based on historical events—are all, or for the most part, famous nonsense, monstrosities with neither heads nor feet and, nevertheless, the crowd listens to them with great pleasure, and considers and speaks of them as good, though they're immensely far from being anything of the sort, and the authors who write them as well as the actors who appear in them say that's how they have to be, because these plays and nothing else are what the crowd wants, while those who work out a careful plan and trace out an artful plot won't be appreciated except by a few wise men who understand what they're up to, and all the rest are blind to such artful cleverness, and they're better off earning their living from the vulgar many rather than from this precious few …
>
> And although I've sometimes tried to persuade the actors that they're wrong, and that more people will come to see, and much greater fame will be won by, artful rather than ridiculous plays, they're so set and settled in their opinions that they can't be shaken by reason or evidence.[41]

Later he speaks of the adverse effect of works written 'merely to please the people.'

> They even stick miracles into secular plays, without paying the slightest attention to whether such wondrous stage-business happens to belong there, but just so ignorant people will be astonished and come to see the play—all of which seriously compromises truth and discredits history, as well as disgracing the Spanish mind, since the people in other countries, who are strictly punctilious about dramatic laws, see the absurdities and foolishness we put into our plays and think us ignorant barbarians. And it's not a good enough excuse to say that, in tolerating the existence of a public stage, well-ordered governments chiefly intend to provide their people with some seemly recreation, giving them a chance to dissipate the nasty moods idleness can generate.[42]

Good drama, written with higher purpose, Cervantes says, has the effect of improving the character of the observer. It is interesting that the excuse which he says playwrights give him for doing otherwise is the same excuse composers of educational music give today for their music.

> But I would counter by pointing out that the same goal can be a great deal better accomplished, and with no compromises whatever, by good rather than bad plays, because once having heard artful, well-structured theater, an audience will be pleased with its jokes, educated by its truths, caught up in its plot, made more alert by its arguments, put on their guard by its deceptions, made wiser by its examples, angered by its vices, and charmed by its virtues, for a good play produces all these feelings in the souls of those who hear it, no matter how rough and slow-witted they may be: the most impossible of all impossibles is a play that has all these qualities failing to amuse,

---

41 Miguel de Cervantes, *The History of that Ingenious Gentleman Don Quijote de La Mancha*, trans. Burton Raffel (New York: Norton, 1995), 320.

42 Ibid., 321.

entertain, satisfy, and generally please better than a play that doesn't have them—and most of the plays put on, these days, don't have them. Nor are the poets who write these plays basically to blame, because some of them are very well aware of their mistakes, and have a very precise knowledge of what they ought to be doing, but since plays have become a salable commodity, they say, and they say truly, that producers won't buy them if they're not the kind they want, so the poets try to please the hand that feeds them by giving it what it wants.[43]

The solution Cervantes envisioned was to establish a kind of court censor to approve plays before they were allowed to be performed. Subsequently, he contends, the playwrights would work 'far more carefully and thoughtfully, because [they] would be worried about their work having to undergo a rigorous, informed inspection—and thus we'd have good plays.'[44]

Regarding the frequently discussed aesthetic question of Imitation, Lope de Vega, in his general definition of comedy in his *The New Art of Writing Plays in this Age*, includes music as one of the three forms of imitation in plays.

> Yet the comedy has its end established like every kind of poem or poetic art, and that has always been to imitate the actions of men and to paint the customs of their age. Furthermore, all poetic imitation whatsoever is composed of three things, which are discourse, agreeable verse, harmony, that is to say music, which so far was common also to tragedy.[45]

With regard to imitation, in this same treatise Lope de Vega stresses that speech and dress should be consistent with the character.[46]

Lope de Vega, in *Acting is Believing*, provides one of the earliest references to 'method acting,' by which an actor recreates emotion drawing from his own experience. Genesius, the playwright within this play, observes,

> Acting is just imitation. However, just as a poet can't write convincingly and with feeling about love unless he's in love, since it's love that teaches him the verses he writes, it's the same way with actors. If an actor doesn't feel love's passion, he can't perform it. If he feels the pain of absence, jealousy, insult, the rigor of disdain and other tender feelings of love, he'll play them tenderly, but if he doesn't feel them, he won't know how to play them.[47]

Soon, indeed, we see Genesius preparing in this manner for his role.

---

43 Ibid., 321ff. He follows with a direct criticism of Lope de Vega for his failure in this regard.

44 Ibid., 322.

45 Quoted in Ibid., 90. De Vega distinguishes tragedy from comedy primarily in the social status of the characters. Later [Ibid., 91] he observes that tragedy can be mixed with comedy, for this variety causes much delight. 'Nature gives us good example, for through such variety it is beautiful.' However, he warns, one cannot 'mingle tragic style with the humbleness of mean comedy.'

46 Ibid., 92ff.

47 Lope de Vega, *Lo fingido verdadero*, 69.

Love, your burning flame will increase my fame in proportion to your rigor. Your fire, your deep feeling reaches up even to the great emperor, who is already longing to see me imitate what I feel. But it hardly seems proper to use the word imitation for what is truth itself. My will is the play, my intellect the poet of the story I'm inventing, wherein with worthy verse it paints the inevitable stages my thought has gone through. All my mad senses with similar figures have become the actors of my enslaved emotions.[48]

Lope de Vega adds some additional definitions of the good actor in *Acting is Believing*, where we are told he must study his lines, not skip rehearsals and enjoy acting.[49] Fernando de Rojas contributes the thought, 'Experience makes men artists in their profession.'[50]

Regarding critics, in the *La Dorotea*, Lope de Vega particularly objected to those who always assumed that what they saw on the stage was an imitation of the playwright's own behavior.[51] In general, however, he seems to have believed there was little which the artist could do to answer criticism. In *The Dog in the Manger*, the character, Tristán, observes,

Take a great artist, for example, he will spend months chasing, engraving, and polishing a work of art until it reaches perfection, and then, if fools should say it is only worth melting down, what can he do about it? Nothing.[52]

Lope de Vega's only answer was the one he gave, anticipating critics in the Foreword of his *La Dorotea*, saying, in effect, 'See if you can do as well!'

Let anyone who thinks me mistaken take up his pen and use the time he would spend upon reprehension in proving that he can produce his own more perfect imitation, a truth of his own better appareled in witticisms and colors of rhetoric, with learning more suited to its context, humor more entertaining, sententiousness more serious, and with so many components of natural and moral philosophy that one is amazed the author could treat them so clearly in dealing with such a subject.[53]

Although, as we have seen above, Lope de Vega admitted he wrote for the public, his comments regarding the general public are often derogatory. In *Acting is Believing*, we also find a reference to the size of the audience.

---

48 Ibid., 70.
49 Ibid., 71.
50 Fernando de Rojas, *Celestina*, 37.
51 Lope de Vega, *La Dorotea*, I, v.
52 Lope de Vega, *The Dog in the Manger*, 123.
53 Lope de Vega, *La Dorotea*, Foreword. He also comments here on the fact that his reputation was such that others were publishing their own plays with his name on the cover. Such men, he says, are 'men detested by all, the scum of the earth, envious of all virtue, gnawed inwardly by the glory others achieve through study.'

> [Regarding a play with lots of stage machinery] But they usually amaze the ignorant mob and bring in more money than good plays, because they talk nonsense; and even if a couple of people take offense, there are still over five hundred who like it.[54]

Lope de Vega is critical of the general public again in *Justice Without Revenge* and in this passage we find the rather aristocratic definition of the 'common herd' as those who have no access to the palace.

> The common herd is no judge of truth, and they are fools that base their good name on what crude minds believe. Common opinion is inconstant and variable, not ruled by Reason, but by the personal jealousies of those that will tell any lie to satisfy their thirst for news and gossip. And those that are so base that they have no entry into palaces and great houses to know the truth, murmur against that which they may not know.[55]

In the end, Lope de Vega seems resigned to a predestined reaction by the general public.

> A friendly audience applauds and it is called a good play. Enemies will hiss and report it a bad play.

Finally, Debussy once observed the the highest form of praise is the praise which comes from those most expert in your art. However, he observed, 'fame' is a gift of the masses who know nothing. He was right of course, although we would speak of Universality, rather than the masses who know nothing. It is in this perspective that we notice a passage in Lope de Vega's *Justice Without Revenge*, which contends the reverse. While this passage therefore suggests he did not understand Universality, probably he was thinking along different lines—of the distinction between Entertainment and Art.

> I admit that I should like to be famous among wise men, men of science and letters, for fame among the ignorant herd is not true fame, but a harvest where those who sow senseless acts reap worthless praise.[56]

ON THE AESTHETICS OF MUSIC

Lope de Vega's comments about musicians in general are often less than complimentary. In his *The Lady Simpleton*, Otavio seems to include poets and musicians in a category with 'effeminate fops, the madmen, the idle with smelly make-ups.'[57] And in the *Fuente Ovejuna* a group of musicians are brought in to sing a song during a wedding celebration. One char-

---

54 Lope de Vega, *Lo fingido verdadero*, 69.
55 Lope de Vega, *Justice Without Revenge*, 233ff.
56 Ibid., 239.
57 Lope de Vega, *La Dama Boba*, II, ix.

acter responds, 'Call that a song? You didn't strain yourselves!' and another asks, 'You think you could compose a better one?'[58] Perhaps Lope de Vega was accustomed to hearing such musicians' apologize for their performances, for he has Dorotea, in *La Dorotea*, comment before playing on a harp, 'The one thing about being a musician I shall not do is ask indulgence for all my deficiencies.'[59]

Music itself he respected highly, as we see in the opening lines of the Foreword addressed to the audience of his *La Dorotea*, where he provides a moving tribute to the ability of music to affect manners.

> Music and song arouse such soft delight in our soul that some have called the soul itself harmony. Hence the ancient poets invented the mode of meters and feet for prosodic measures, so that they might thus more sweetly incline men's spirits to virtue and good conduct. Thus one sees how boorish and barbaric he must be who fails to esteem this art, which includes all the others, an art respected by the ancient theologians who used it, unenlightened though they were, to laud and glorify their false gods; and now by our own, who use it to laud with sacred hymns the one true God.[60]

The most frequently given purpose of music, in early literature, is to soothe. We find this in Lope de Vega's *Peribáñez* as well, when the Commander says to his musicians,

> Tune your instruments. Perhaps their music may resolve the discord in my heart.[61]

In *La Dorotea*, Fernando says he will express his pain through music and even if Dorotea does not hear him, he will feel better anyway.

> JULIO. For goodness sake, master, stop your ranting. Pick up your instrument and sing, if only to lift yourself out of such a black mood …
> FERNANDO. Try as you will, you cannot lift my spirits. Whether or not she knows I am here, I intend to make these strings tell Dorotea how unstrung I feel. And if she does not listen, it won't matter, because the soul delights in music naturally.[62]

In these comedies of Love, however, there are always some characters who protest that even music cannot provide solace. Earlier in *La Dorotea*, Fernando, cries, 'But neither composing

---

58 Lope de Vega, *Fuente Ovejuna*, [II], 151. The musicians, no doubt, felt they did not receive the credit they deserved. In *La Dorotea* [IV, iii], Lope de Vega quotes an anecdote regarding Michelangelo, who apparently felt that *he* did not receive the credit he deserved. Lope de Vega reports that Michelangelo, tired of being called inferior to the Greeks, broke a foot off a statue he had made and buried it in order that when it was found and praised he could prove that he had made it.

59 Lope de Vega, *La Dorotea*, II, v.

60 Ibid., 'To the Audience.' Although Lope de Vega has signed the name, 'Don Francisco López de Aguilar,' to this Foreword, autograph manuscripts prove it is his own work.

61 Lope de Vega, *Peribáñez*, 47.

62 Lope de Vega, *La Dorotea*, III, vii.

verse nor singing it will calm the stormy oceans of my thoughts.'⁶³ Another character, in *The Knight from Olmedo*, says music cannot even express his love.

> It is my love that is belied in the song, for no verses could ever convey such depths of meaning as lie in my love for you.⁶⁴

One purpose of music often mentioned by the Renaissance humanists was that of prophesy. In Lope de Vega's *The Knight from Olmedo* a musician is heard, and we first note here the reference to the state of the listener with respect to the affect of music,

> There is someone singing. Who can it be? It sounds far off. A peasant going early to the fields and singing as he goes. It is nearer now. That is no rustic accent—he has an instrument, and the song is sweet and sonorous. How melancholy music sounds when one's own thoughts are sad!

The musician is identified as a peasant and he sings a song of warning, prophetizing the death of Alonso. When the singer is questioned further about the meaning of his song, he replies,

> I cannot tell you more about the song or its history than that I learned it from one Fabia. If it concerns you, I can do no more for you; you have heard me sing it. Go back. Do not pass this stream.⁶⁵

Finally, Lope de Vega occasionally provides comments which reflect on the aesthetic value of various musical instruments in sixteenth-century Spain. In *Lady Simpleton* we find disrespect for the drum,

> FINEA. Tomorrow bring me a small drum.
> MASTER. An instrument gay, but loathsome.⁶⁶

and in *Fuente Ovejuna* a high value placed on the string instrument.

> I'll give the pair of you my boxwood fiddle.
> It's worth a granary full of corn or more.⁶⁷

---

63 Ibid., III, i.
64 Lope de Vega, *The Knight from Olmedo*, 199.
65 Ibid., 221ff,
66 Lope de Vega, *La Dama Boba*, II, vii.
67 Lope de Vega, *Fuente Ovejuna*, [I], 73.

ART MUSIC

The plays of Lope de Vega frequently have solo Art Songs, such as the following rural example. Here Dorotea, while accompanying herself on a spinet, sings,

> To the murmur of the rills
> from flower to flower birds sing
> of love, most heavenly thing,
> and jealousy, hell's worst ill.
>
> In these delightful groves,
> to the waters' melodies,
> birds chant antiphonies
> of jealousy and love.
> As veins of ice relent,
> their sweet crystal flow
> makes music as they go,
> on Nature's instrument.[68]

Some references to singing also give evidence of the contemplative listener. After Dorotea sings another song, Bela, a listener, comments that she 'has abstracted me from myself' during the song. Another character adds,

> Don Bela, do beg her to sing something else. If you had anything to oblige her with, you would already have repaid her for the pleasure she has bestowed upon you.[69]

Later a lady expresses delight in hearing Fernando sing.[70]
After several more songs, it is revealed that Dorotea is also a composer.

> BELA. What a delightful refrain! Who wrote the melody?
> GERARDA. The person singing it. Is that a question to ask?
> BELA. Oh, how wrong of me to ask! One whom heaven has endowed with so many talents could not be lacking in any skill.
> GERARDA. Why, should you ever see her set hands to a spinet, you'd think a crystal spider was running over the keys.[71]

The description of another song in this play reveals Lope de Vega's familiarity with vocal technique.

---

68   Lope de Vega, *La Dorotea*, II, iii.
69   Ibid., II, v.
70   Ibid., III, viii.
71   Ibid., II, v.

FERNANDO. I believe I sang poorly because my voice was unsteady.
JULIO. On the contrary, never in my life have I heard you produce such excellent trills and chromatics. And when your voice shifted to falsetto an octave or two higher, it sounded superb.
FERNANDO. You are still trying to lift my spirits, I see. A trembling heart rarely makes for a steady voice.[72]

Many of the songs for which the lyrics are given in sixteenth-century plays are, of course, love songs. In what must mirror a frequent occurrence, Cervantes, in *The Biscayan Imposter*, has a character command, 'Gentlemen musicians, strike up the ballad I gave you and that you have learned.'[73] While the sixteenth-century humanists generally maintained that the emotions must be in the words, and not the music, we find some Spaniards who recognize that the reverse is actually true, words in themselves having no emotions. This seems to be suggested as well in the line by Fernando de Rojas, 'These words are of another tune than those we heard at our first [meeting].'[74]

When instrumental playing is introduced, Lope de Vega often makes some reference to tuning—something he no doubt frequently heard musicians discuss. In this example he again reveals his knowledge of music practice.

DOROTEA. Forgive the tuning—governing this commonwealth of strings is such a task.
BELA. Two sets of strings make the chromatics easier.
DOROTEA. You must know music.
BELA. I *am* fond of it.[75]

An especially interesting passage dealing with tuning makes use of an analogy, frequently found in early literature, of the person being 'out of tune.' Early writers often used the word 'distemper' for a person 'out of tune,' a term we employ today only to describe mad dogs!

DOROTEA. I go there, Celia? May God fail me if I ever …!
CELIA. Don't go flailing about and swearing if you expect me to believe you. You've been torturing those poor pegs for an hour, not tuning the harp strings so much as your own unstrung thoughts.
DOROTEA. I removed a few because they did not ring true on the flat notes.
CELIA. Those must have been your thoughts of Don Fernando.
DOROTEA. You're quite right, Celia, for the genius of music, as my master Enrique used to tell me, lies not in skilled fingers nor in a voice well trained, but in the soul itself—so the theory of music teaches.[76]

---

72 Ibid., III, vii.
73 Cervantes, *El Vizcayo Fingido*, in Randall Listerman, trans., *Miguel de Cervantes' Interludes* (Lewiston: Edwin Mellen Press, 1991), 86.
74 Fernando de Rojas, *Celestina*, 39.
75 Lope de Vega, *La Dorotea*, II, v.
76 Ibid., V, ix.

A similar reference to a person being 'out of tune' is found in Fernando de Rojas.

> CALISTO. Sempronio!
> SEMPRONIO. Sir!
> CALISTO. Reach me that lute.
> SEMPRONIO. Sir, here it is.
> CALISTO [singing].
>   Tell me what grief so great can be
>   As to equal my misery?
> SEMPRONIO. This lute, sir, is out of tune.
> CALISTO. How can he tune it, who himself is out of tune? Take this lute and sing me the most doleful song thou canst devise.[77]

In the *La Dorotea* we also are given a charming description of Dorotea playing the harp.

> If you could only see her now, the siren at her harp, her nimble fingers gliding over the strings, which seem to be laughing as if she were tickling them; her tresses loosely falling over the harp, which sometimes enviously wish they were strings she might play on. And, indeed, I think the strings were resonantly telling her tresses not to meddle in their affairs, since as strings they didn't try to interfere when Dorotea was dressing her hair.[78]

FUNCTIONAL MUSIC

According to the information given by Cervantes, the musicians who supplied functional music, such as weddings, as well as much entertainment music, were often part-time musicians, who otherwise worked as barbers. In *Trampagos*, for example, a musician says to another musician who is leaving,

> And on the way tell my wife that if a customer comes into the barber shop, to wait for me a little. I'll have a few more drinks, sing a couple of songs and be right there.[79]

As sixteenth-century playwrights often called the theater a 'mirror' of life, so we find in these plays all the functional uses of music which the observer would have found familiar. A common type of functional music was for welcoming ceremonies and in Lope de Vega's

---

77 Fernando de Rojas, *Celestina*, 4ff.

78 Lope de Vega, *La Dorotea*, V, ii.

79 Cervantes, *El Rufian Viudo, Llamado Trampagos*, in Randall Listerman, trans., *Miguel de Cervantes' Interludes* (Lewiston: Edwin Mellen Press, 1991), 43. Another reference to barber-musicians can be found in the Interlude, *La Guarda Cuydodosa*.

Fuente Ovejuna a group of musicians sing a song of welcome to the Commander, who acknowledges it as a proper greeting.[80]

There is frequent use of trumpets and drums to participate in announcements, as in Lope de Vega's *Fuente Ovejuna*, where a call is given to 'sound the trumpets in the square.'[81] Related to this is the ancient tradition that musicians, trumpeters in particular, served as ambassadors. For this reason they were always guaranteed safe passage behind enemy lines. It is in context of this background that we understand, in the play within a play in Lope de Vega's *Acting is Believing*, two members of the enemy disguised as musicians are allowed in the presence of Caesar and kill him.[82]

Of course there are frequent references to music for weddings and in one rather unusual example, in Lope de Vega's *Peribáñez*, we read of 'musicians playing the psalms as if their lives depended on it.'[83]

Finally, in Cervantes' *La Guarda Cuydadosa* there is a housewife who sings as she 'sweeps and scrubs' and in Lope de Vega's *Peribáñez*, a song is sung for the purpose of putting the (adults) to sleep.[84]

ENTERTAINMENT MUSIC

We may assume there was much music heard in the streets of sixteenth-century Spain, in the form of casual serenades. In *The Jealous Old Man*, Cervantes mentions an ill-tempered old man who made the practice of throwing stones at the street musicians![85]

Musicians are always present for dancing, of course, but we find it interesting in Lope de Vega's *The Lady Simpleton*, that musicians are called on stage to *sing*, rather than play instruments, while two sister's dance.[86] Musicians sing for the dance again in his *Peribáñez*.[87] Cervantes, in *Trampagos*, lists a number of folk dances popular at the time, including *el canario, las gambetas, al villano se lo dain, zarabanda, zambapalo, el pesame dello* and *el rey don Alonso el Bueno*.

---

80 Lope de Vega, *Fuente Ovejuna*, [I], 91.

81 Ibid., [II], 131.

82 Lope de Vega, *Lo fingido verdadero*, 57.

83 Lope de Vega, *Peribáñez*, 45.

84 Ibid., 26ff.

85 Cervantes, *El Viejo Zeloso*, in Randall Listerman, trans., *Miguel de Cervantes' Interludes* (Lewiston: Edwin Mellen Press, 1991), 117.

86 Lope de Vega, *La Dama Boba*, III, vi.

87 Lope de Vega, *Peribáñez*, 5.

BIBLIOGRAPHY

Ample Discours de l'Arrivee de la Royne catholique soeur du Roy à sainct Jehan de Lus: de son entrée à Bayonne.... Paris: Jean Dallier Labraire, 1565.

Anthon, Carl. 'Some Aspects of the Social Status of Italian Musicians during the Sixteenth Century.' In *Journal of Renaissance and Baroque Music* (New Haven, 1946), II.

Arbeau, Thoinot. *Orchesography*. Translated by Mary Evans. New York: Kamin Dance Publishers, 1948.

Aretino, Pietro. *Dialogues*. Translated by Raymond Rosenthal. New York: Marsilio, 1971.

———. *Il Marescalo*. Translated by Leonard Sbrocchi. Ottawa: Dovehouse, 1986.

———. *The Works of Aretino*. Translated by Samuel Putnam. New York: Covici, 1926.

Ariosto, Ludovico. *Orlando Furioso*. Translated by Guido Waldman. London: Oxford University Press, 1974.

———. *The Comedies of Ariosto*. Translated by Edmond Beame. Chicago: The University of Chicago Press, 1975.

———. *The Satires of Ludovico Ariosto*. Translated by Peter Wiggins. Athens: Ohio University Press, 1976.

Armenini, Giovan Battista. *De' veri precetti della pittura*. Ravenna, 1586.

Arnold, Denis. 'Brass Instruments in the Italian Church Music of the Sixteenth and Early Seventeenth Centuries.' *Brass Quarterly* (1957).

———. 'Music at the Scuola di San Rocco.' *Music and Letters* 40, no. 3 (July, 1959): 229–241, http://www.jstor.org/stable/729389.

Baines, Anthony. *Woodwind Instruments and their History*. New York: Norton, 1962.

Bandello, Matteo. *Tragical Tales*. Translated by Geoffrey Fenton (1567). London: Routledge, [n.d.].

Bardi, Giovani, 'Discourse on Ancient Music and Good Singing,' in Oliver Strunk, *Source Readings in Music History*. New York: Norton, 1950.

Barnstone, Willis. *The Poems of Saint John of the Cross*. Bloomington: Indiana University Press, 1968.

———. *The Unknown Light, the Poems of Fray Luis de León*. Albany: State University of New York Press, 1979.

Bartholomew, L. E. *Alessandro Raueriji's Collection of Canzoni per Sonare* (1608). Fort Hayes, KS: Kansas State College, 1965.

Bellay, Joachim du. *The Regrets*. Translated by C. H. Sisson. Manchester: Carcanet Press, 1984.

Bernstein, Jane. *French Chansons of the Sixteenth Century*. University Park: Pennsylvania State University Press, 1985.

Bertolotti, A., 'Speserie segrete e pubbliche di Paolo III.' *Atti e Memorie delle RR. Deputazioni di Storia Patria, per le provincie dell'Emilia* (Nuova serie, III).

Blunt, Anthony. *Artistic Theory in Italy, 1450–1600*. Oxford: Clarendon Press, 1959.

Bodin, Jean. *Colloquium of the Seven*. Translated by Marion Kuntz. Princeton: Princeton University Press, 1975.

———. *Method for the Easy Comprehension of History*. Translated by Beatrice Reynolds. New York: Columbia University Press, 1945.

Bodin, Jean. *Six Books of the Commnwealth*. Translated by M. J. Tooley. New York: Macmillian, 1955.

Booty, Jill. *Lope de Vega, Five Plays*. New York: Hill and Wang, 1961.

Bottrigari, Hercole. *Il Desiderio*. Translated by Carol MacClintock. [Rome.]: American Institute of Musicology, 1962.

Bref et sommaire rcueil de ce qui a esté faict, et de l'ordre tenüe à la joyeuse et triumphantes Entrée de Prince Charles IX de ce nom Roy de France, en sa bonne ville et cité de Paris... Paris, 1572.

Bruno, Giordano. *Cause, Principle and Unity.* Translated by Jack Lindsay. New York: International Publishers, 1962.

———. *The Expulsion of the Triumphant Beast.* Translated by Arthur Imerti. New Brunswick: Rutgers University Press, 1964.

Burton, Elizabeth. *The Pageant of Elisabethan England.* New York: Scribner's, 1959.

Calvin, Jean. Geneva Psalter. Quoted in Oliver Strunk. *Source Readings in Music History.* New York: Norton, 1950.

Camões, Luis de. *The Lusiads.* Translated by Richard Fanshawe edited by Geoffrey Bullough. Carbondale: Southern Illinois University Press, 1963.

Cardano, Girolamo. *Hieronymi Cardani Mediolensis opera omnia.*

———. *The Book on Games of Chance.* Translated by Sydney Gould. New York: Dover, 1953.

Carpenter, Nan Cooke. *Music in the Medieval and Renaissance Universities.* Norman: University of Oklahoma Press, 1958.

Castiglione, Baldassare. *The Courtier.* Translated by Charles Bull. New York: Penguin Books, 1967.

Cellini, Benvenuto, 'La Vita.' Translated by David Whitwell. *Opere.* Milano: Rizzoli, 1968.

———. *The Life of Benvenuto Cellini.* Translated by John Addington Symonds. New York: Scribner's, 1914.

Cerone, Pietro. *El melopeo y maestro.* Quoted in Oliver Strunk. *Source Readings in Music History.* New York: Norton, 1950.

Cervantes, Miguel de. *The History of that Ingenious Gentleman Don Quijote de La Mancha.* Translated by Burton Raffel. New York: Norton, 1995.

———. *Don Quijote.* Translated by Burton Raffel. New York: Norton, 1995.

———. *The Trials of Persiles and Sigismunda.* Translated by Celia Weller and Clark Colahan. Berkeley: University of California Press, 1989.

Chamberlin, E. R. *Marguerite of Navarre.* New York: Dial Press, 1974.

Chambers, Frank. *The History of Taste.* New York: Columbia University Press, 1932.

Chantelou, M., de. *Journal du voyage du Chavalier Bernin.* Paris, 1885.

Charlotte, Catherine. *The Court of France.* Boston: Grolier Society, 1900.

———. *The Last of the Valois.* Paris: Grolier Society, 1900.

Chubb, Thomas. *The Letters of Pietro Aretino.* New Haven: Shore String Press, 1967.

Cinthio, Giraldi. *Discorso intorno al comporre dei romanzi.* Translated by Henry Snuggs as *Giraldi Cinthio on Romances.* Lexington: University of Kentucky Press, 1968.

Cinzio, Giraldi. *Hecatommithi, overo Cento novella.* Venice: 1608.

Clark, Barrett. *European Theories of the Drama.* New York: Crown, 1959.

Clements, Robert J. *Michelangelo: A Self-Portrait.* New York: New York University Press, 1968.

Cobb, Carl. *Anthology of Lope de Vega's Lyric Poetry.* York, SC: Spanish literature Publications, 1991.

Crow, John. *An Anthology of Spanish Poetry.* Baton Rouge: Louisiana State University Press, 1979.

Cunningham, Caroline. 'Estienne du Tertre, 'Scavant Musicien,' Jean d'Estrée, 'Joueur de Hautbois du Roy' and the Mid-Sixteenth Century Franco-Flemish Chanson and Ensemble Dance.' Dissertation, Bryn Mawr College, 1969.

Cuyler, Louise. *The Emperor Maximilian I and Music.* London: Oxford University Press, 1973.

D'Amico, John. *Renaissance Humanism in Papal Rome.* Baltimore: Johns Hopkins University Press, 1983.

De Tolnay, Charles. *The Medici Chapel*. Princeton: Princeton University Press, 1848.
Doni, Anton Francesco. *Disegno*. Venice, 1549.
Fernando de Rojas. *Celestina*. Translated by James Mabbe. New York: Applause Publishers, 1986.
Flores, Angel. *Masterpieces of the Spanish Golden Age*. New York: Holt, Reinhart, 1963.
Frame, Donald. *Montaigne's Travel Journal*. San Francisco: North Point Press, 1983.
———. *The Complete Works of François Rabelais*. Berkeley: University of California Press, 1991.
Freedman, Richard, 'Paris and the French Court under François I.' *The Renaissance*. Englewood Cliffs: Prentice Hall, 1989.
Frey, H. 'Regesten zur päpstlichen Kapelle unter Leo X und zu seiner Privatkapelle,' in Dietrich Kämper. *Studien zur Instrumental Ensemblemusik des 16. Jahrhunderts in Italien*. Köln, 1970.
Fyvie, John. *The Story of the Borgias*. New York: G. P. Putnam's Son, 1913.
Galilei, Vincenzo. 'Dialogo della musica antica e della moderna,' in Oliver Strunk. *Source Readings in Music History*. New York: Norton, 1950.
———. *Fronimo*. Translated by Carol MacClintock. Neuhasen-Stuttgart: Hänssler, 1985.
Gilbert, Creighton. *Complete Poems of Michelangelo*. Princeton: Princeton University Press, 1963.
Giustiniani, Vicenzo. *Discorso sopra la Musica*. Translated by Carol MacClintock. [Rome.]: American Institute of Musicology, 1962.
Glixon, Jonathan, 'Music at the Venetian Scuole Grandi, 1440–1450.' In *Music in Medieval and Early Modern Europe*. Edited by Iain Fenlon. Cambridge: Cambridge University Press, 1981.
Gregorovius, Ferdinand. *Lucretia Borgia*. New York: D. Appleton, 1904.
Grove, George. *The New Grove Dictionary of Music and Musicians*. Edited by Stanley Sadie. London: Macmillan, 1980.
Guarini, Giambattista. *The Faithful Shepherd*, in *Five Italian Renaissance Comedies*. New York: Penguin Books, 1978.
Guicciardini, Francesco. *Maxims and Reflections*. Translated by Mario Dornandi. New York: Harper Torchbooks, 1965.
Guizot, M. *History of France*. London, 1872.
Guzmán, J. A., 'Mexico, Home of the First Musical Instrument Workshops in America.' *Early Music* 6, no. 3 (1978): 350–355, doi: 10.1093/early/6.3.350.
Hall, Edward. *The Triumphant Reigne of Kyng Henry VIII*. London, 1542.
Harriet de Onis. *Six Exemplary Novels*. Great Neck: Barron's Educational Series, 1961.
Heartz, Daniel. 'The 'Chanson in the Humanist Era.' In *Current thought in Musicology*. Austin: University of Texas Press, 1976.
———. *Pierre Attaingnant Royal Printer of Music*. Berkeley: University of California, 1969
Hibbert, Christopher. *The House of Medici*. New York: Morrow, 1975.
Hollanda, Francisco. *Four Dialogues of Painting*. London: Oxford University Press, 1928.
Jacquot, Jean. *Les Fêtes de la Renaissance*. Paris: Centre national de la recherche scientifique, 1973.
Jouan, Abel. *Recueil et Discours de Voyage du Roy Charles IX*. Paris, 1566.
Judith Kennedy. *George of Montemayor's Diana and Gil Polo's Enamoured Diana*. Oxford: Clarendon Press, 1968.
Kade, Otto, 'Zwei archivalische Schriftstücke aus dem 16. Jahrhundert.' *Monatschefte für Musikgeschichte* (1872), IV.
Kämper, Dietrich. *Studien zur Instrumentalen Ensemblemusik des 16. Jahrhunderts in Italien*. Köln, 1970.

Kavanaugh, Kieran and Otilio Rodriguez. *The Collected Works of St. John of the Cross*. Washington, DC: Institute of Carmelite Studies, 1979.
Keating, L. Clark. *Joachim du Bellay*. New York: Twayne, 1971.
Kilmer, Nicholas. *Poems of Pierre Ronsard*. Berkeley: University of California Press, 1979.
Le recueil des Triumphes et Magnificences qui ont estez faictes au Logis de Monseigneur le Duc D'orleans, frere du Roy. Troyes: Trumeau.
Lesure, François. *Musicians and Poets of the French Renaissance*. Translated by Elio Gianturco. New York: Merlin Press, 1955.
———. *Musique et Musiciens Français du XVIe Siècle*. Geneva, 1976.
Lewis, Mary, 'Antonio Gardane's Early Connections with the Willaert Circle.' In *Music in Medieval and Early Modern Europe*. Edited by Iain Fenlon. Cambridge: Cambridge University Press, 1981.
Listerman, Randall. *Miguel de Cervantes' Interludes*. Lewiston: Edwin Mellen Press, 1991.
Lockwood, Lewis, 'Vincenzo Ruffo and Musical Reform after the Council of Trent.' *The Musical Quarterly* 43, no. 3 (July, 1957): 342–371, http://www.jstor.org/stable/740279.
Lomazzo, Giovan Paolo. *Trattato della pittura, scultura ed architettura*. Roma, 1844.
Lope de Vega. *La Dama Boba*. Translated by Max Oppenheimer. Lawrence: Coronado Press, 1976.
———. *El mayordomo de la duquesa de Amalfi*. Translated by Cynthia Rodiguez-Babdendyck. Ottawa: Dovehouse, 1985.
———. *Fuente Ovejuna*. Translated by Victor Dixon. Warminster: Aris & Phillips, 1989.
———. *La Dorotea*. Translated by Alan Trueblood and Edwin Honig. Cambridge: Harvard University Press, 1985.
———. *Lo fingido verdadero*. Translated by Michael McGaha. San Antonio: Trinity University Press, 1986.
Machiavelli, Niccolò. *Machiavelli, the Chief Works*. Translated by Allan Gilbert. Durham: Duke University Press, 1965.
Marguerite de Navarre. *The Heptameron*. Translated by Arthur Machen. New York: Knopf, 1925.
———. *The Prisons*. Translated by Hilda Dale. Reading: Whiteknight's Press, 1989.
Mariejol, Jean. *A Daughter of the Medicis*. New York: Harper & Bros., 1929.
Marot, Clément, 'Le Second Chant d'amour fugtif,' in *Oeuvres satriques*. Edited by Claude Mayer. London: Athlone Press, 1962.
Mei, Girolamo. *Letters on Ancient and Modern Music*. Translated by Claude Palisca. [S.l.]: American Institute of Musicology, 1960.
Mellini, Domenico. *Descrizione Dell' Aparato Della Comedia Et Intermedii D'essa Recitata in Firenze il giorno di S. Stefano l'anno 1565....* Florence, 1565.
Messisburgo, Christoforo. *Banchetti, compositioni di vivande, et apparecchio generale*. Ferrara: Per Giovanni de Buglhat et Antonio Hucher Compagni, 1549.
Michel de Montaigne. *Essays*. Translated by M. A. Screech. London: Penguin, 1993.
Miller, Clement. *Hieronymus Cardanus, Writings on Music*. [Rome]: American Institute of Musicology, 1973.
Motley, John. *The Rise of the Dutch Republic*. New York: Harper & Bros., 1864.
Newcomb, Anthony, 'Secular Polyphony in the 16th Century.' In *Performance Practice in Music before 1600*. Edited by Howard Brown. New York: Norton, 1989.
Ore, Oystein. *Cardano the Gambling Scholar*. New York: Dover, 1953.
Page, Curtis. *Songs and Sonnets of Pierre de Ronsard*. Westport: Hyperion Press, 1924.

Palisca, Claude V. *Humanism in Italian Renaissance Musical Thought*. New Haven: Yale University Press, 1985.
Pearson, Hesketh. *Henry of Navarre*. New York: Harper & Row, 1963.
Pico della Mirandola, Giovanni. *Commentary on a Canzone of Benivieni*. Translated by Sears Jayne. New York: Peter Lang, 1984.
———. *On the Imagination*. Translated by Harry Caplan. Westport: Greenwood Press, 1957.
Pirrotta, Nino and Elena Povoledo. *Music and Theatre from Poliziano to Monteverdi*. Cambridge: Cambridge University Press, 1982.
Pirrotta, Nino. 'Ars Nova and Stil Novo, ' in *Music and Culture in Italy from the Middle Ages to the Baroque*. Cambridge: Harvard University Press, 1984.
———. *Music and Culture in Italy from the Middle Ages to the Baroque*. Cambridge: Harvard University Press, 1984.
Polk, Keith. 'Civic Patronage and Instrumental Ensembles in Renaissance Florence.' Unpublished AD, ca. 1982.
Pontus de Tyard. *Solitaire second* (1555). Genève : Droz, 1980.
Prunières, Henri. 'La musique de la Chambre et de L'Écurie sous le Regne de François 1er.' *L'Année Musicale* (Paris, 1911).
———. 'La musique de la Chambre et de L'Écurie sous le regne de François 1er.' *L'Année Musicale* (Paris, 1911).
Rabelais, François. *Gargantua*. Translated by Donald Frame. Berkeley: University of California Press, 1991.
———. *Pantagruel*. Translated by Donald Frame. Berkeley: University of California Press. 1991.
Ramsden, E. H. *The Letters of Michelangelo*. Stanford: Stanford University Press, 1963.
Recueil des Choses Notables qui ont esté faites à Bayonne.... Paris, 1566.
Reese, Gustave. *Music in the Renaissance*. New York: Norton, 1959.
Rive, Thomas. 'An Investigation into Harmonic and Cadential Procedure in the Works of Victoria.' Dissertation, the University of Auckland, 1963.
Rodocanachi, E. *Château S. Ange*. Paris, 1909.
Russell, Joycelyne. *The Field of Cloth of Gold*. New York: Barnes & Noble [1969].
Sandberger, A. *Beiträge zur Geschichte der bayerischen Hofkapelle unter Orlando di Lasso*. Leipzig: Breitkopf & Härtel, 1895.
Sannazaro, Jacopo. *Arcadia & Piscatorial Eclogues*. Translated by Ralph Nash. Detroit: Wayne State University Press, 1966.
Shearman, John, 'Leo X and the Sistine Chapel.' London: BBC Radio 3 (August 20, 1971).
Sichel, Edith. *Women and Men of the French Renaissance*. Port Washington: Kennikat Press, 1970.
Smithers, Don. *The Music and History of the Baroque Trumpet*. London: Dent, 1973.
Stevenson, Robert. *Spanish Cathedral Music in the Golden Age*. Berkeley: University of California Press, 1961.
Stinger, Charles. *The Renaissance in Rome*. Bloomington: Indiana University Press, 1985.
Strunk, Oliver. *Source Readings in Music History*. New York: Norton, 1950.
Symonds, John Addington. *Renaissance in Italy*. New York: Capricorn Books, 1964.
Tasso, Torquato. 'Discourse on the Art of the Dialogue,' in *Tasso's Dialogues*. Translated by Carnes Lord. Berkeley: University of California Press, 1982.
———. 'Minturno, or On Beauty,' in *Tasso's Dialogues*. Translated by Carnes Lord. Berkeley: University of California Press, 1982.

Tasso, Torquato. 'The Father of the Family,' in *Tasso's Dialogues*. Translated by Carnes Lord. Berkeley: University of California Press, 1982.

———. *Creation of the World*. Translated by Joseph Tusiani. Binghamton: Center for Medieval & Early Renaissance Studies, 1982.

———. *Discourses on the Heroic Poem*. Translated by Mariella Calvalchini. Oxford: Clarendon Press, 1973.

———. *Jerusalem Delivered*. Translated by Ralph Nash. Detroit: Wayne State University Press, 1987.

———. *The Aminta*. Translated by Louis Lord. Oxford: Oxford University Press, 1931.

———. *Tasso's Dialogues*. Translated by Carnes Lord. Berkeley: University of California Press, 1982.

Turnbull, Eleanor. *Ten Centuries of Spanish Poetry*. Baltimore: The Johns Hopkins Press, 1955.

Vale, G., 'La Capella Musicale di Duomo di undine dal Secolo XIII al XIX.' *Note d'Archivio* (1930), VII.

Van Dyke, Paul. *Catherine de Medicis*. New York: C. Scribner's sons, 1922.

Vander Straeten, Edmond. *La Musique aux Pays-Bas avant le XIXe Siècle*. New York, 1969.

Vasari, Giogorio. *Le Vite de' piu excellenti pittori, scultori, ed architettori*. Florence, 1878.

Vessella, Alessando. *La Banda*. Milan, 1935.

Vida, Marco Girolamo. *The Art of Poetry*. Translated by Albert Cook. In *The Poetical Treatises of Horace, Vida, and Boileau*. Boston: Ginn, 1892.

———. *The Christiad*. Translated by Gertrude Drake. Carbondale: Southern Illinois University Press, 1978.

Vives, Juan. Introductio ad Sapientiam, in *Introduction to Wisdom*. Edited by Marian Tobriner. New York: Teachers College Press, 1968.

Watkins, Glenn. *Gesualdo, The Man and His Music*. Chapel Hill: University of North Carolina Press, 1973.

Watson, Foster. *Vives on Education*. Cambridge: University Press, 1913.

Wright, Craig, 'Performance Practices at the Cathedral of Cambrai 1475–1550.' *The Musical Quarterly* 64, no. 3 (July 1978): 295–328, http://www.jstor.org/stable/741504.

Wykes Alan. *Doctor Cardano*. London: Muller, 1969.

Yates, Frances. *The French Academies of the Sixteenth Century*. London: University of London, 1947.

Zarlino, Gioseffo. *On the Modes*. Translated by Vered Cohen. New Haven: Yale University Press, 1983.

———. *The Art of Counterpoint*. Translated by Guy Marco and Claude Palisca. New Haven: Yale University Press, 1968.

INDEX

A

Aesop, 142
Albert de Rippe, 16th century French lutenist, 210
Alfonso II, 1533–1597, Duke of Ferrara, 78
Alphonso dalla Vivola, 16th century Italian composer, 77
d'Ambra, Francesco, 16th century dramatist, 81
Anerio, Felice, 1560–1614, Italian composer, 67
Anthoine de Bertrand, ca. 1530–1581, French composer, 193, 198ff
Antoniano, Silvio, 16th century Italian singer, 116
Arbeau, Thoinot, 1519–1595, French canon and author, 206ff
Arcadelt, Jacques, 1507–1568, Franco-Flemish composer, 65
Archilei, Vittoria, 1582–1620, Italian singer, 67
Arcimboldo, Antonello, 16th century composer, 38
Aretino, Pietro, 1492–1556, Italian writer, 1 fn. 1, 3, 11 17, 18ff, 20ff, 33ff, 40ff, 92ff, 94, 96, 123, 127, 132, 133
Ariosto, Ludovico, 1474–1533, Italian poet, 94, 106, 114ff, 119ff, 121, 126, 127, 132, 133, 135
Aristotle, 384–322 BC, Greek philosopher, 8, 26, 93, 105, 114, 128, 130,, 166ff, 230, 252, 254, 260, 279, 287, 317
Attaingnant, Pierre, 16th century publisher in Paris, 195

B

Bach, J. S., 71
Baïf, Jean Antoine de, 1532–1589, French poet, 197ff, 203, 205
Bandello, Matteo, 1480–1562, Italian writer of secular tales, 13, 33ff
Bardi, Giovanni, 1534–1612, Italian critic, composer, 44, 60, 71
Bargagli, Elfinspell, 1540–1612, Italian poet, 85
Bellay, Joachim de, b. 1525, French poet, 200, 215ff, 220ff, 222ff, 226, 228
Bembo, Pietro, 1470–1547, Italian cardinal, scholar, 17, 136ff
Benelli, Alemanno, character in Bottrigari, 68ff
Benivienti, Girolamo, 1453–1542, Florentine poet, 88
Bernardino de Padova, first cornett in the Lucca civic band, 83
Berni, Francesco, subject of a poem by Michelangelo, 187
Blas de Castro, 16th century Spanish composer, 327
Boccaccio, Giovanni, 1313–1375, Italian writer, 142ff, 265
Bodin Jean, 1530–1596, French philosopher, 229ff, 235ff
Bombasi, Gabriele, 1531–1571, Italian philosopher, 27
Borromeo, Cardinal, 16th century, 38
Bottrigari, Hercole, 1531–1612, Italian scholar, 48ff, 56, 59ff, 68ff, 78ff, 83ff
Brancaccio, Giulio, 65
Bruno, Giordano, 1548–1600, Italian friar, philosopher, 8ff, 12, 14, 24, 27, 30, 34, 40

C

Caccini, Giulio, 1551–1618, Italian composer, 85
Calvin, Jean, 1509–1564, French cleric, 212ff
Camões, Luis de, 1524–1580, Spanish poet, 311ff, 322
Canossa, Lodovico, 1476–1532, Veronese noble, 146ff
Capone, Neri, 16th century noble, 77
Cardano, Girolamo, 1501–1576, physician, mathematician, writer, 43, 148, 159 Castelvetro, Ludovico, 1505–1571, Italian drama critic, 131
Castiglione, Baldassare, 1478–1529, Italian writer, 1, 61ff, 135ff, 178
Catherine de Medici, 1519–1589, 212ff
Cavalieri, Emilio, 1550–1602, Italian composer, 35
Cavalieri, Tommaso, recipient of sonnet by Michelangelo, 180, 183
Cecchi, Giovan, 1518–1587, Italian playwright, 127
Cellini, Benvenuti, 1500–1571, goldsmith, writer, 14, 28, 33, 39, 75

Cerone, Pietro, 1566–1625, Italian music theorist living in Spain, 288ff
Cervantes, Miguel de, 1547–1616, Spanish prose writer, 294ff, 325, 335, 342ff
Charles IX, 1560–1574, 194, 202ff, 209ff, 214
Charles V, 1500–1558, Emperor, Holy Roman Empire, 211, 252, 291
Cicero, 106–43 BC, Roman orator, 250, 262, 266
Cini, Giovanbattista, 1525–1586, Italian playwright, 30
Cinthio, Giraldi, 1504–1573, Italian novelist and poet, 106ff
Ciruelo, Pedro, 1470–1548, Spanish music theorist, 273
Clemens, Jacobus ('Clemens non Papa'), 1510–1556, Flemish composer, 75
Clement VII, 1523–1534, pope, 75, 96, 135
Colonia, Johannes, 15th century Italian composer, 64
Comanini, 16th century writer, 23
Courville, 16th century French poet and singer, 204
Cristoforo, Giovanni, Italian musician and sculptor, 145

D

Dalla Casa, Girolamo, d. 1601, leader of the civic wind band in Venice, 84
Daniello, Bernardino, d. 1565, Italian drama critic, 128
de' Medici, Francesco, 81
Demetrius, 326
Desiderio, Gratioso, noble in Bottrigari, 68ff
Donatello, 1386–1466, Italian artist, 178
Doni, Antonfrancesco, 16th century writer, 77

Dorat, Jean, 1508–1588, French poet, philosopher, 199
Dorati, Nicolao, 16th century leader of civic band in Lucca, 83
Duc de Joyeuse, 16th century French noble, 209
Dürer, Albrecht, 1471–1528, 178

E

Erasmus, Desiderius, 1466–1536, Dutch humanist philosopher, 167, 273
Ercole d'Este of Ferrara, 16th century duke, 77
Espinosa, Juan, 16th century Spanish music theorist, 273

F

Federico, Duke of Urbino, 152
Fessta, Constanzo, 16th century composer, 190
Ficino, Marsilio, 1433–1499, Italian humanist philosopher, 31ff, 326
Finé, Oronce, 16th century French professor, 193
Fogliano, Lodovico, 16th century Italian theorist, 60
Fontanelli, 16th century Cardinal, 76
Fra Angelico, 1395–1455, Italian painter, 184
Fra Sebastiano del Piombo, receipient of poetry by Michaelangelo, 190
Francesco da Milano, 1497–1543, lutanist, 85
François I, 1515–1547, 76, 193ff, 199ff, 211 214
François II, 1559–1560, 194, 210

G

Gabrieli, Giovanni, 87
Gafurius, 1451–1522, Italian music theorist, 44, 54, 60

Galilei, Vincenzo, 1533–1591, composer, theorist, 43ff, 50ff, 54ff, 62, 73ff
Garcilaso de la Vega, 1503–1536, Spanish poet, 317ff
Gaspare, Pallavicino, 1488–1511, 139ff
Genesius, 16th century Spanish playwright, 336
Gesualdo, Carlo, 1566–1613, Prince di Venosa, composer, 67, 76ff
Ghiberti, Lorenzo, 1378–1455, Italian artist, 178
Giovanni da Udine, 16th century painter, 23
Giuliano de Medici, 1479–1516, brother to Leo X, 148
Giulio Cesare of Oriveto, flutist, 85
Giulio del Bene, 16th century Italian philosopher, 36
Giustiniani, Vincenzo, 1516–1582, Italian critic, 49ff, 53, 55ff, 61, 65, 84ff, 89
Glaren, Heinrich, 1488–1563, theorist, poet, 44
Góngora, Luis de, 1561–1627, Spanish poet, 316
Guarini, Giambattista, 1538–1612, Italian poet, 122ff, 124ff, 126ff, 132, 134
Guicciardini, Francesco, 1483–1540, 1, 5, 10, 13, 40

H

Henry II of France, 1547–1559, 194, 214
Henry III, 1574–1559, 194, 205
Henry VIII, 1491–1547, King of England, 211, 214, 273
Hollanda, Francisco, 16th century sculptor, 179, 191
Homer, 108

I

Isaac, Heinrich, 75

J

Janequin, Clément, 1485–1558, French composer, 195, 198, 219
Jean d'Estrée, 16th century, oboist of the king, 195
Jean de la Taille, b. 1540, French poet, 224ff
Johanna of Austria, 81
Josquin des Près, 155
Juana, la loca, 291
Julius II, , 1443–1513, pope, 177, 182

L

Lassus, Orlando, 1532–1594, Franco-Flemish composer, 65
Le Jeune, Claude, 1528–1600, French composer, 205
Leibniz, Gottfried, 1646–1716, German mathematician, 161
Leo X, 1475–1521, pope, 75, 89, 96, 135
León, Luis de Fray, b. 1527, Spanish professor, poet, 311ff, 317
Leonardo da Vinci, 1452–1519, 91, 112
Lomazzo, Giovanni, 16th century Italian philosopher, 23
Lope de Vega, 1562–1635, Spanish playwright, 313ff, 325ff
Louis XII, 1498–1515, 193
Louis XIV, 194
Lucrezia Borgia, 1480–1519, daughter to Alexander VI, pope, 88
Luigi del Cornetto of Ancona, cornett virtuoso, 84
Luther, 4
Lycurgus, Ancient Greek leader, 820–730 BC, 148

M

Machiavelli, Niccolò, 1469–1527, Italian writer, politician, 2, 11, 13, 37ff, 39ff, 39ff, 125ff, 130, 132ff
Maffei, 70
Maffei, Raffaello, 1451–1522, Italian humanist, 4, 70
Malvezzi, 16th century composer, 82
Marguerite de Navarre, 1496–1649, French poet, mother to Henri IV, 217ff, 220, 222, 227ff, 234
Marot, Clément, 16th century French poet, 215
Maximilain I, 5, 291
Mei, Girolamo, 1519–1594, Italian historian, 24ff, 67, 91
Mendieta, Geronimo, 16th century in Mexico, 290
Merlo, Alessandro, 16th century Italian singer in Sistine Chapel, 65
Mersenne, Marin, 1588–1648, French philosopher, 203
Michelangelo, 1475–1564, artist, 4, 18, 21 91, 177ff, 339 fn. 58
Milanuzzi, Carlo, 16th century organist of Venezia, 86
Minturno (Antonio Sebastiano Antonio), d. 1574, Italian bishop and drama critic, 129
Montaigne, Michel, 1533–1592, French essayist, 243ff
Montalto, Alessandro, 1571–1623, Italian cardinal and musician, 66
Monte, Filippo, di, 1521–1608, Flemish composer, 65
Montemayor, Jorge de, d. 1561, Portugese prose writer, 293
Monteverdi, Claudio, 1567–1643, Italian composer, 67

N

Nanino, 67
Nanino, Giovanni Maria, 1543–1607, Italian composer, 65
Nardo, Matteo, 16th century Italian philosopher, 31
Navarro, Spanish playwright, 325
Neuschel, Hans, 16th century instrument maker in Nürnberg, 75

O

Ockeghem, Johannes, 164
Oglonus, Leo, 16th century music teacher to Cardano, 159
Orlando de Lassus, 226
Orpheus, 7
Ovid, 43 BC – 18 AD, Roman poet, 265

P

Palestrina, Giovanni, 1525–1594, Italian composer, 96
Pasquino Bastini, Vincenzo, second cornet in the Lucca civic band, 83
Patrizi, Francesco, 1529–1597, anti-humanist Italian writer, 96
Paul III, 1468–1549, pope, 76, 194
Pedro de Padilla, 16th century Spanish poet, 314
Peri, Jacopo, 1561–1637, Italian composer, 85
Petrarch, 142
Philemon the Younger, ancient playwright, 260
Philip I of Spain, 1504–1506, 291
Philip of Hessen, 15th century German noble, 76
Pico della Mirandola, Gianfrancesco, 1470–1533, Italian philosopher, 5ff, 15, 17
Plato, 114, 142, 230, 236, 246, 271
Plautus, 279, 334
Plutarch, 46–120 AD, Greek biographer, 230, 260, 265, 266, 268, 269
Polo, Gil, d. 1591, Spanish writer, 293ff

Praetorius, Michael, 16th century German composer, 71, 208
Protogenes, ancient painter, 150
Puligo, Domenico, 1492–1527, Italian painter, 18
Pythagoras, 154, 236

R

Rabelais, François, 1494–1553, French fiction writer, 229ff, 239ff, 265
Raphael, 184, 188
Raphel (Sanzio, Raffaello), 1483–1520, Italian painter, 18
Rojas, Fernando de, 1470–1541, Spanish playwright, 332, 337
Ronsard, Pierre de, 1524–1585, leading French poet, 198ff, 219, 221, 223ff, 226
Rore, Cipriano de, 1516–1565, Franco-Flemish composer, 65
Rossi, Bastiano, 16th century court official, 82

S

Salinas, Francisco de, 1513–1590, Spanish music theorist, 287
Salinas, Francisco, 16th century professor of music at the Univ. of Salamanca, 316
Sannazaro, Jacopo, 16th century Italian poet, 114ff, 118
Sappho, lyric poet, 223
Savonarola, Girolamo, 1452–1498, friar, 88
Scaliger, Julius Caesar, 1484–1558, Italian drama critic, 128
Sebastiano, 16th century painter, 20
Sebillet, Thomas, 1512–1589, French poetry critic, 224
Segni, Agnolo, 1522–1576, Italian scholar, 17

Seneca, 260, 265
Shakespeare, William, 1564–1616, 160, 210
Socrates, 114, 142, 154, 245
Soriano, Francesco, 1548–1621, Italian composer, 65
Spataro, Giovanni, 16th century Italian theorist, 60
St. John of the Cross (Juan de Yepes y Alverez), 1542–1591, philosopher, 279ff, 312ff
Striggio, Alessandro, 1531–1593, Italian composer, 65, 85

T

Tasso, Torquato, 1544–1595, Italian poet, 1, 10, 17, 19, 91ff, 96, 103ff, 113, 115, 117ff, 125, 200
Terrence, 190–158 BC, Roman playwright, 265, 279, 334
Thibault, Joachim, 16th century French poet, 203
Thycydides, 230
Tintore, Jacopo, 16th century painter, 20
Titian, 1488–1576, Italian painter, 18, 22, 178
Tomás de Sancta Maria, 16th century Spanish music theorist, 287
Tyard, Pontus de, 1522–1605, French poet and philosopher, 32, 195ff, 200

V

Valgulio, Carlo, Italian papal 1481–1485 treasurer, 27
Varchi, Benedetto, 16th century Italian poet, 84, 188
Varro, ancient Roman writer, 252
Vasari, Giorgio, 1511–1574, Italian biographer of artists, 14, 18, 22
Venneo, Stephano, 16th century Italian music theorist, 43

Victoria, Luis de, 1548–1611, Spanish composer, 288
Vida, Marco, 1485–1566, Italian humanist, bishop, 96ff, 115
Vincentino, Nocola, 16th century Italian composer, 198
Virgil, 108
Vitellozzi, Cardinal, 16th century, associated with the Council of Trent, 38
Vives, Juan, 1492–1540, Spanish philosopher, 273ff, 283ff

W

Waelrant, Hubert of Antwerp, 227

Z

Zarlino, Gioseffo, 1517–1590, Italian music theorist, 26, 44, 47ff, 50ff, 56ff, 60, 62, 70ff

ABOUT THE AUTHOR

Dr. David Whitwell is a graduate ('with distinction') of the University of Michigan and the Catholic University of America, Washington DC (PhD, Musicology, Distinguished Alumni Award, 2000) and has studied conducting with Eugene Ormandy and at the Akademie für Musik, Vienna. Prior to coming to Northridge, Dr. Whitwell participated in concerts throughout the United States and Asia as Associate First Horn in the USAF Band and Orchestra in Washington DC, and in recitals throughout South America in cooperation with the United States State Department.

At the California State University, Northridge, which is in Los Angeles, Dr. Whitwell developed the CSUN Wind Ensemble into an ensemble of international reputation, with international tours to Europe in 1981 and 1989 and to Japan in 1984. The CSUN Wind Ensemble has made professional studio recordings for BBC (London), the Köln Westdeutscher Rundfunk (Germany), NOS National Radio (The Netherlands), Zürich Radio (Switzerland), the Television Broadcasting System (Japan) as well as for the United States State Department for broadcast on its 'Voice of America' program. The CSUN Wind Ensemble's recording with the Mirecourt Trio in 1982 was named the 'Record of the Year' by The Village Voice. Composers who have guest conducted Whitwell's ensembles include Aaron Copland, Ernest Krenek, Alan Hovhaness, Morton Gould, Karel Husa, Frank Erickson and Vaclav Nelhybel.

Dr. Whitwell has been a guest professor in 100 different universities and conservatories throughout the United States and in 23 foreign countries (most recently in China, in an elite school housed in the Forbidden City). Guest conducting experiences have included the Philadelphia Orchestra, Seattle Symphony Orchestra, the Czech Radio Orchestras of Brno and Bratislava, The National Youth Orchestra of Israel, as well as resident wind ensembles in Russia, Israel, Austria, Switzerland, Germany, England, Wales, The Netherlands, Portugal, Peru, Korea, Japan, Taiwan, Canada and the United States.

He is a past president of the College Band Directors National Association, a member of the Prasidium of the International Society for the Promotion of Band Music, and was a member of the founding board of directors of the World Association for Symphonic Bands and Ensembles (WASBE). In 1964 he was made an honorary life member of Kappa Kappa Psi, a national professional music fraternity. In September, 2001, he was a delegate to the UNESCO Conference on Global Music in Tokyo. He has been knighted by sovereign organizations in France, Portugal and Scotland and has been awarded the gold medal of Kerkrade, The Netherlands, and the silver medal of Wangen, Germany, the highest honor given wind conductors in the United States, the medal of the Academy of Wind and Percussion Arts (National Band Association) and the highest honor given wind conductors in Austria, the gold medal of the Austrian Band Association. He is a member of the Hall of Fame of the California Music Educators Association.

Dr. Whitwell's publications include more than 127 articles on wind literature including publications in Music and Letters (London), the London Musical Times, the Mozart-Jahrbuch (Salzburg), and 39 books, among which is his 13-volume *History and Literature of the Wind Band and Wind Ensemble* and an 8-volume series on *Aesthetics in Music*. In addition to numerous modern editions of early wind band music his original compositions include 5 symphonies.

David Whitwell was named as one of six men who have determined the course of American bands during the second half of the 20th century, in the definitive history, *The Twentieth Century American Wind Band* (Meredith Music).

A doctoral dissertation by German Gonzales (2007, Arizona State University) is dedicated to the life and conducting career of David Whitwell through the year 1977. David Whitwell is one of nine men described by Paula A. Crider in *The Conductor's Legacy* (Chicago: GIA, 2010) as 'the legendary conductors' of the 20th century.

> 'I can't imagine the 2nd half of the 20th century—without David Whitwell and what he has given to all of the rest of us.' Frederick Fennell (1993)

www.ingramcontent.com/pod-product-compliance
Lightning Source LLC
Chambersburg PA
CBHW080724300426
44114CB00019B/2488